OXFORD IB STUDY GUIDES

Alexey Popov

Psychology

FOR THE IB DIPLOMA

2nd edition

OXFORD
UNIVERSITY PRESS

OXFORD
UNIVERSITY PRESS

Great Clarendon Street, Oxford, OX2 6DP, United Kingdom

Oxford University Press is a department of the University of Oxford. It furthers the University's objective of excellence in research, scholarship, and education by publishing worldwide. Oxford is a registered trade mark of Oxford University Press in the UK and in certain other countries

British Library Cataloguing in Publication Data
Data available

978-0-19-839817-2

9 10 8

The manufacturing process conforms to the environmental regulations of the country of origin.

Printed in Great Britain by Bell and Bain Ltd., Glasgow.

Acknowledgements

The publishers would like to thank the following for permission to use copyright material:

Darley, J. M. and Latané, B.: Table 1 from 'Bystander intervention in emergency: diffusion of responsibility', Journal of Personality and Social Psychology, Vol. 8, No. 4, 1968, pp. 377-383, published by APA and reprinted with permission.

Batson, C.D., Duncan, B.D., Ackerman, P., Buckley, T., and Birch, K.: Table 2 from 'Is empathic emotion a source of altruistic motivation?' Journal of Personality and Social Psychology, Vol. 40, No. 2, 1981, pp. 290-302, published by APA and reprinted with permission.

MIX
Paper | Supporting
responsible forestry
FSC® C007785
www.fsc.org

The publisher and author would like to thank the following for permission to use photographs and other copyright material:

Cover: Pasieka/Getty Images; **p2:** Rice University/CC BY 4.0/http://cnx.org/contents/14fb4ad7-39a1-4eee-ab6e-3ef2482e3e22@8.81; **p4:** Reprinted from Merzenich, M. M., Nelson, R. J., Stryker, M. P., Cynader, M. S., Schoppmann, A. and Zook, J. M. (1984), Somatosensory cortical map changes following digit amputation in adult monkeys. J. Comp. Neurol., 224: 591–605. doi: 10.1002/cne.902240408; **p9:** Eye Ubiquitous/Shutterstock; **p10:** Marina Pousheva/Shutterstock; **p15:** Robin M. Hare, Sophie Schlatter, Gillian Rhodes, Leigh W. Simmons, R. Soc. open sci. 2017 4 160831; DOI: 10.1098/rsos.160831. Published 8 March 2017/CC BY 4.0; **p22:** Nature Photographers Ltd/Alamy Stock Photo; **p24:** Reprinted from Curtis, Val, Robert Aunger, and Tamer Rabie. "Evidence That Disgust Evolved to Protect from Risk of Disease." Proceedings of the Royal Society B: Biological Sciences 271.Suppl 4 (2004): S131–S133.; **p34:** Reprinted from Journal of Verbal Learning and Verbal Behaviour, 11, John D. Bransford and Marcia K. Johnson, Contextual Prerequisites for Understanding: Some Investigations of Comprehension and Recall, 717-726, 1972, with permission from Elsevier.; **p45:** zmeel/iStockphoto; **p106:** Incomible/Shutterstock; **p110:** OAK RIDGE NATIONAL LABORATORY/US DEPARTMENT OF ENERGY/SCIENCE PHOTO LIBRARY ; **p112:** Reused from Angelo DelParigi, Kewei Chen, Arline D. Salbe, Eric M. Reiman, P. Antonio Tataranni, Sensory experience of food and obesity: a positron emission tomography study of the brain regions affected by tasting a liquid meal after a prolonged fast, NeuroImage, Volume 24, Issue 2, 2005, Pages 436-443, ISSN 1053-8119, https://doi.org/10.1016/j.neuroimage.2004.08.035; **p122:** Proejct Eat/University of Minnesota; **p126:** WHO/West Pacific Region; **p133:** Reprinted from Benedict C Jones, Lisa M DeBruine, Anthony C Little, Robert P Burriss, David R Feinberg, Proc. R. Soc. B 2007 274 899-903; DOI: 10.1098/rspb.2006.0205. Published 22 March 2007/Copyright © 2007 The Royal Society; **p134:** © Getty Images/Stockbyte; **p154:** The Public Library of Science (PLOS) Creative Commons Attribution (CC BY) license.; **p164:** Reprinted from Trends in Cognitive Sciences, Volume 12 , Issue 5, Call, Josep et al., Does the chimpanzee have a theory of mind? 30 years later / 187 - 192, Copyright 2008, with permission from Elsevier.; **p165:** 2017 The Author(s). Published with license by Taylor & Francis© Fumihiro Kano, Christopher Krupenye, Satoshi Hirata, and Josep (Creative Commons Attribution-NonCommercial-NoDerivatives License); **p166:** OUP; **p171:** The nature of love. Harlow, Harry F. American Psychologist, Vol 13(12), Dec 1958, 673-685/Public Domain.

Artwork by Thomson Digital.

Although we have made every effort to trace and contact all copyright holders before publication this has not been possible in all cases. If notified, the publisher will rectify any errors or omissions at the earliest opportunity.

Links to third party websites are provided by Oxford in good faith and for information only. Oxford disclaims any responsibility for the materials contained in any third party website referenced in this work.

Introduction

How to use this book

"Essential understanding"

At the start of each topic you will find a shaded "Essential understanding" box. It provides a summary of the topic with the main arguments and links to the other boxes within that topic. As you read, it might be a good idea to refer to this "Essential understanding" box frequently. This will allow you to see the key flow of arguments behind the specifics of separate studies and theories.

In addition, to make it easier for you to keep track of the main flow of arguments, individual boxes throughout the text start with a short paragraph labelled "Essential understanding". This paragraph links back to the shaded "Essential understanding" box at the start of the topic.

Types of boxes and icons

Throughout the text you will find several types of boxes and icons.

- Dotted line boxes contain theoretical material, whereas solid line boxes contain details of research studies or other factual information.
- Boxes labelled "Theory" contain a specific theory that has a name and belongs to particular authors.
- Boxes labelled "Research" contain details of a specific research study. Where relevant, studies are described using such elements as Aim, Participants, Method, Procedure, Results and Conclusion.
- Boxes labelled "Exam tip" are self-explanatory.
- Finally, the star icon is used to highlight key information.

The Course Companion

This book is intended as a tool for revision and reading with a focus on assessment. To build up the necessary skills throughout the course and develop a deep understanding, you are encouraged to read the *IB Psychology Course Companion*—the main textbook for the course. Using the Course Companion in conjunction with this book will enhance both the depth and the structure of your responses.

How much to study

IB is not about rote learning. IB is about understanding the material and applying critical thinking to it. A question that students frequently ask is "How many research studies do I need to learn for this topic?"— but it is not the number of research studies you have used that matters. Even one research study may be enough to get high marks for an extended response question. What matters is how well you have answered the question on the theoretical level and how well you have supported your theoretical arguments with research. So the value of using one research study that supports multiple arguments is much higher than the value of using two or three research studies that all support the same argument. This is why the "Essential understanding" boxes in this book clearly bring out the arguments that are central to every theory and research study.

The structure of assessment

The Subject Guide

Please see the "IB Psychology Subject Guide" to learn about the structure of test papers and the assessment requirements. The Subject Guide is the official IB document regulating the syllabus of IB psychology (please do not confuse it with the Study Guide—the book you are reading now). Your teacher will explain all the necessary details to you. However, below is a very brief overview of assessment in IB psychology.

Paper 1

Paper 1 covers the core approaches to behaviour—biological, cognitive and sociocultural (**Units 1–3** of this book). The paper consists of two parts. In part A you will be asked three mandatory SAQs (short answer questions), one from each approach to behaviour. In part B you will be given three ERQs (extended response questions), again, one from each approach to behaviour. You will need to choose one of these questions.

There are two overarching topics: research and ethics. This means that you can always be asked questions concerning the application of research methods or ethical considerations to a particular topic.

Paper 2

Paper 2 covers the options—Abnormal psychology, Health psychology, Psychology of human relationships and Developmental psychology (**Units 4–7** of this book). HL students study two of these options and SL students study only one. For each option you will be given three ERQs, and you will need to choose one. There are no SAQs in paper 2.

The overarching topics (research and ethics) are applicable to this paper too.

Paper 3

Paper 3 is for HL students only. In this paper you will be given a description of a research study and asked a series of questions regarding it. The study may be qualitative, quantitative or a combination of both. The questions are taken from a list of static questions and require the application of your knowledge of research methodology and ethics to the concrete research study. Material relevant for paper 3 is directly covered in **Units 8 and 9** of this book.

Contents

The bibliography can be found at:
www.oxfordsecondary.com/9780198398172

Topics

1.1 Brain and behaviour

1.1.1 Localization

DEFINITIONS

- **Localization of function**—the theory that certain areas of the brain are responsible for certain psychological functions

- **Strict localization**—the idea that there is a clear correspondence between psychological functions and brain areas, and that all functions can be clearly mapped onto the brain

- **Weak localization**—the idea that one brain area may be responsible for a function, but not exclusively, and other areas may also take over the function

- **Widely distributed functions**—functions that cannot be localized anywhere in the brain

ESSENTIAL UNDERSTANDING

Strict localization

Research into localization of function has not been entirely conclusive. We do believe now that functions are localized, but the idea of strict localization has been gradually replaced by the belief that localization is relative.

The first research studies to support the idea of strict localization were based on patients with specific brain damage. The earliest localization phenomena that were thoroughly documented are Broca's aphasia and Wernicke's aphasia. See **"Broca's aphasia and Wernicke's aphasia"**.

This research inspired attempts to create comprehensive "brain maps". One such attempt belonged to Wilder Penfield (1891–1976), who used the method of neural stimulation to create his cortical homunculus (Penfield, Boldrey 1937). See **Wilder Penfield**.

Contrary to strict localization

There has, however, been research that opposed the idea of strict localization and even rejected the belief that some

psychological functions may be localized anywhere in the brain. One such example is research by Karl Lashley (1929) who claimed that memory of a maze in rats was distributed rather than localized. See **Karl Lashley (1929)**.

Relative localization

Today's approach recognizes the concept of weak localization—the idea that several brain areas are responsible for the same function (and can potentially take over), but only one of these areas is dominant. An example of research supporting the idea that language (both production and comprehension) is weakly localized in the left hemisphere is split brain research conducted by Sperry (1968) and Gazzaniga (1967). See **Sperry (1968) and Gazzaniga (1967)**.

Looking at a larger variety of psychological functions, it can be claimed that psychological functions are relatively localized. See **"Relative localization of function"**.

BROCA'S APHASIA AND WERNICKE'S APHASIA

Essential understanding

✪ *The first case studies used post-mortem examination of the brains of patients with unique speech disorders. Results of these studies inspired the idea of strict localization. It appeared that the production of articulate speech is localized in Broca's area, and speech comprehension in Wernicke's area.*

Paul Broca (1861) documented the case study of "Tan", a patient who lost the ability to speak or write but retained all other functions such as intelligence and speech

comprehension. He understood everything said to him and tried to communicate back, but the only sound he could make was the syllable "tan". This condition, the loss of articulated speech, became known as Broca's aphasia. When Tan died, an autopsy was performed and it was discovered that his brain had a very specific lesion in the left hemisphere, in the posterior inferior frontal gyrus. This brain region is now known as Broca's area.

Shorty after that **Carl Wernicke (1874)** in similar case studies discovered the brain area responsible for comprehension of written and spoken language. Wernicke's area is located in the temporal lobe of the dominant hemisphere (usually the left). People with Wernicke's aphasia have an impairment of speech comprehension, but their articulate speech is intact.

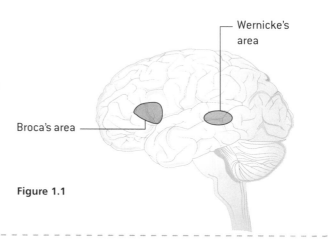

Figure 1.1

WILDER PENFIELD—MAPPING SENSORY AND MOTOR CORTEX

Essential understanding

✪ *Attempts to establish strict localization of function have culminated in the creation of cortical maps.*

Wilder Penfield used the method of neural stimulation—he stimulated various parts of the cortex with electrodes while the patient was awake and observed the effects this stimulation had on sensations and behaviour. Little by little he covered the whole cortex and created the cortical homunculus, a map that shows the relative representation of various parts of the body in the cortex (Penfield, Boldrey 1937).

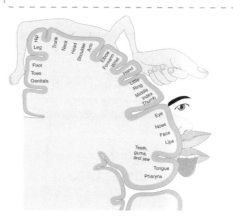

Figure 1.2 Cortical homunculus

RESEARCH   Karl Lashley—some psychological functions are distributed rather than localized

Essential understanding

✪ *Experiments with induced brain damage in rats showed that memory is widely distributed rather than localized anywhere in the cortex.* **Karl Lashley (1929)** *used carefully controlled induced brain damage in the cortex of rats that were trained to run through a maze.*

Procedure

In a typical study, he trained a rat to go through a maze without mistakes in search of food, then removed a part of its cortex and observed what effect this would have on its memory of the maze. He removed 10–50% of the cortex on different trials.

Results

Results of these experiments did not support Lashley's original hypotheses and led him to formulate the following ideas.
- **The principle of mass action.** Memory of the maze depended on the percentage of cortex destroyed, but not on the location of the lesion.
- **Equipotentiality.** The idea that one part of the cortex can take over the functions of another part of the cortex when necessary.

Conclusion

Based on these observations Lashley concluded that memory is not localized; it is widely distributed across the cortex as a whole. Even if one part of the cortex is lost, other parts may take over the functions of the missing part.

RESEARCH   Sperry (1968) and Gazzaniga (1967)—research with split-brain patients

Essential understanding
✪ *As demonstrated by split brain research, both production and comprehension of language are weakly localized (lateralized) in the left hemisphere.*

Aim
To investigate how the two hemispheres function independently when the connection between them is severed.

Participants
Four patients who underwent novel treatment for epilepsy that involved surgically cutting the corpus callosum.

Method
This was an in-depth case study of four unique individuals.

Procedure
A technique was used that allowed researchers to project stimuli to either the left or the right eye of the participant. They used a table with a board on it. Participants sat in front of the board, fixing their eyes on the dot in the centre. Stimuli were then flashed on the far right or the far left of the board for one-tenth of a second.

The idea was that since optic nerves from the right eye are connected in our brain to the left hemisphere and vice versa, the researchers could present stimuli to one of the hemispheres only.

For some trials the table also had a curtain with some objects behind it. Participants could reach behind the curtain and feel the objects with their hands.

Results
Multiple results were obtained in these studies; we will only mention some examples that illustrate the idea of relative localization of function.

– When a picture of a spoon was shown to the left visual field (connected to the right hemisphere) and participants were asked to describe the object, they said nothing. However, when asked to pick an object behind the curtain, they could feel around and pick a spoon but only with their left hand (because it is connected to the right hemisphere). Participants could not explain why they picked the spoon. This result supports the idea that language is localized in the left hemisphere—the right

hemisphere saw the object and was able to tell the left hand what to do, but since language is localized in the left hemisphere, participants were not able to explain what they did and why.

– When a simple word (such as "pencil") was flashed to the right hemisphere, participants were able to reach behind the curtain and pick a pencil. This goes contrary to the previous finding and shows that the right hemisphere is able to process some simple speech. Perhaps while language production may be confined to the left hemisphere, language comprehension may be a function of both. This shows weak localization of language comprehension.

– When researchers placed four plastic letters in a pile behind the curtain and asked participants to "spell a word", one participant was able to spell "love" with his left hand. He was not able to name the word he just spelled. This shows that even language production, in some rudimentary form, may be present in the right hemisphere in some but not all people.

Figure 1.3 Visual test for split brain patients

Conclusion
These results support the idea that localization of language is not strict. Both language production and language comprehension are mostly localized in the left hemisphere, but the right hemisphere can also perform some simple tasks.

Note: Split brain studies are studies of lateralization—the division of functions between the left and the right hemisphere. Lateralization is a special case of localization, and if you explicitly acknowledge this, you can use Sperry's and Gazzaniga's research in answers to exam questions.

RELATIVE LOCALIZATION OF FUNCTION

Essential understanding
✪ *Localization of function is relative.*

The accumulated body of evidence suggests that localization of function in the human brain is relative. This idea of relative localization includes the following aspects.

– Some functions are indeed strictly localized. Examples include Broca's aphasia and Wernicke's aphasia.
– Some functions such as memory are widely distributed. Refer to Karl Lashley's research for an example.
– Some functions are weakly localized rather than strictly— several brain areas are responsible for the same function,

but one of these areas is dominant. This is illustrated by split brain research, for example.
– Some components of a function may be localized while other components of the same function may be distributed. For example, speech production seems to be more localized than speech comprehension.
– Localization is not static: brain areas can respecialize due to neuroplasticity.

1.1.2 Neuroplasticity

- **Cortical remapping**—neuroplasticity on the level of the cortex
- **Hippocampus**—a part of the limbic system, known to be implicated in emotional regulation and long-term memory

- **Neuroplasticity**—the ability of the brain to change itself in response to environmental demands
- **Synaptic plasticity**—neuroplasticity occurring on the level of a separate neuron, construction of new synaptic connections and elimination of the ones that are not used

ESSENTIAL UNDERSTANDING

Neuroplasticity is the ability of the brain to change through the making and breaking of synaptic connections between neurons. It occurs on different scales, from synaptic plasticity to cortical remapping.

The ability of the brain to remap its functions has been demonstrated in a study by Merzenich *et al* (1984). The study showed that cortical remapping of the fingers occurs in adult owl monkeys around two months after amputation. See **Merzenich *et al* (1984)**.

Apart from the function of adapting to damage or injury, neuroplasticity is the biological mechanism of learning. Draganski *et al* (2004) showed that there was a structural change in the brain in response to a simple learning routine such as practising juggling periodically. See **Draganski *et al* (2004)**.

Maguire *et al* (2000) looked at human neuroplasticity in a natural setting and demonstrated that London taxi drivers experience significant changes in the relative distribution of grey matter in the hippocampus in response to the demands of the job. See **Maguire *et al* (2000)**.

RESEARCH   **Merzenich *et al* (1984)—cortical remapping of digits in owl monkeys**

Essential understanding

✪ *The sensory cortex has the ability to remap its functions following an injury.*

Aim

To investigate how the sensory cortex responsible for the hand will respond to injury.

Participants

Eight adult owl monkeys.

Method

Experiment; repeated measures design.

Procedure

Sensory inputs from all the hand digits (fingers) were mapped in the cortex. To do this, electrodes were attached to the part of the cortex known to be responsible for sensations from the hand, then different fingers were stimulated. It was noted which of the electrodes respond to the stimulation.

One or several digits on the monkey's hand were amputated. A remapping was done 62 days after the amputation to see how the cortex adapted to the injury.

Results

The first mapping showed that there were five distinct areas in the cortex, each responsible for one digit. Adjacent fingers were represented by adjacent areas in the cortex.

Post amputation, the now unused area of the sensory cortex was occupied by adjacent intact fingers. For example, if digit 3 had been amputated, the cortical areas for digits 2

and 4 spread and "consumed" the cortical area previously responsible for digit 3.

Conclusion

The sensory cortex of adult owl monkeys adapts to injury by cortical remapping.

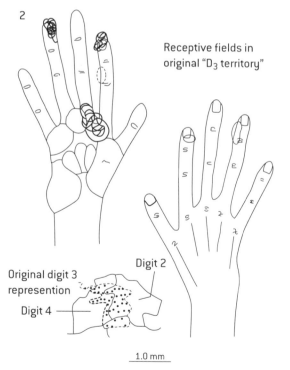

Figure 1.4 Cortical remapping after digit amputation

RESEARCH   Draganski *et al* (2004)—structural changes in the brain in response to juggling

Essential understanding
✪ *Neuroplasticity occurs in response to regular learning practices, which suggests that neuroplasticity is the neural basis of learning.*

Aim
To investigate whether structural changes in the brain would occur in response to practising a simple juggling routine.

Participants
A self-selected sample of volunteers with no prior experience of juggling.

Method
Experiment; mixed design.

Procedure
The sample was randomly divided into two groups: jugglers and non-jugglers. Jugglers spent three months learning a classic juggling routine with three balls followed by three months in which they were instructed to stop practising. Participants in the control group never practised juggling.

Three brain scans (MRI) were performed in both groups: one before the start of the experiment, one after three months, one after six months.

Results
There were no differences in brain structure between jugglers and non-jugglers before the experiment.

After three months of practice, the jugglers had significantly more grey matter in the mid-temporal area of the cortex in both hemispheres. These areas are known to be responsible for coordination of movement.

After six months (that is, three months of non-practice) the differences decreased. However, the jugglers still had more grey matter in these areas than at the first brain scan.

Conclusion
Grey matter grows in the brain in response to environmental demands (learning) and shrinks in the absence of stimulation (lack of practice). This shows that there is cause-and-effect relationship between learning and brain structure.

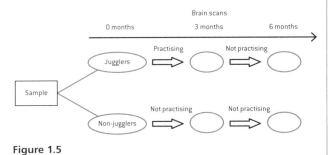

Figure 1.5

RESEARCH   Maguire *et al* (2000)—neuroplasticity in London taxi drivers

Essential understanding
✪ *Neuroplasticity occurs in natural settings. Redistribution of grey matter in the hippocampus is observed in taxi drivers as a function of their driving experience.*

Aim
To investigate how the brain structure of London taxi drivers is different from the average brain.

Participants
16 right-handed male taxi drivers. The average experience as a taxi driver was 14.3 years.

A control group: 50 healthy right-handed male subjects who did not drive a taxi.

Method
Quasi-experiment (comparison of two pre-existing groups); correlational study in the part where driving experience was correlated with grey matter volume. MRI was used to measure the variables.

Procedure
MRI scans were compared between drivers and non-drivers.

Researchers also correlated the number of years of taxi driving experience with results of the MRI scans.

Results
Taxi drivers had increased grey matter volume in the posterior hippocampus, compared to the control group subjects. On the other hand, control subjects had increased grey matter volume in the anterior hippocampus.

A correlation was observed between the number of years of taxi driving experience and grey matter volume in the hippocampus: the longer they drove a taxi, the larger the volume of their posterior hippocampus. The opposite was true for anterior hippocampus.

This means that redistribution of grey matter occurred in the hippocampus of taxi drivers, from the anterior to the posterior.

Conclusion

Redistribution of grey matter in the hippocampus occurs in taxi drivers in response to gaining navigational experience.

The posterior hippocampus is known to be involved in using previously learned spatial information, while the anterior hippocampus is known to be responsible for learning new spatial information.

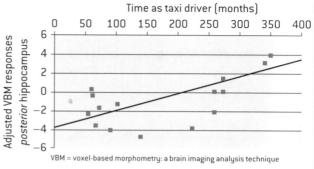

VBM = voxel-based morphometry: a brain imaging analysis technique

Figure 1.6 Hippocampal volume and amount of time as a taxi driver

1.1.3 Neurotransmitters and behaviour

DEFINITIONS

- **Agonist**—a chemical that enhances the action of a neurotransmitter
- **Antagonist**—a chemical that inhibits the action of a neurotransmitter
- **Neurotransmitter**—a chemical messenger stored in the axon and released into the synaptic gap

- **Selective serotonin reuptake inhibitors (SSRIs)**—a class of chemicals that act by preventing reuptake of excess serotonin in the synapse, hence increasing its concentration in the synaptic gap

ESSENTIAL UNDERSTANDING

The nature of information transmission in the nervous system is both electrical and chemical. The chemical part of the process is enabled by neurotransmitters. See **"Nervous system processes"**.

Neurotransmission affects a wide range of behaviours.

Crockett *et al* (2010) demonstrated the effect of serotonin on prosocial behaviour. They found that increased levels of serotonin cause people to be more opposed to the idea of inflicting harm on someone, promoting prosocial behaviour and making it less likely for participants to justify aggression. See **Crockett *et al* (2010)**.

Freed *et al* (2001) investigated the role of dopamine in Parkinson's disease. They showed that transplantation of dopamine-producing cells into the putamen of patients with severe symptoms of Parkinson's could lead to a 28% reduction in symptoms. See **Freed *et al* (2001)**.

Fisher, Aron and Brown (2005) demonstrated that dopamine may be implicated in feelings of romantic love. See **Fisher, Aron and Brown (2005)**.

We need to be aware that research which attempts to isolate the effect of one neurotransmitter is inevitably oversimplified. See **"Limitations in neurotransmitter research"**.

NERVOUS SYSTEM PROCESSES

Essential understanding

✪ *The nature of information transmission in the nervous system is both chemical and electrical. Neurotransmitters are chemical messengers that are released in the synaptic gap. They are affected by a variety of chemicals: agonists and antagonists.*

Neurons

The nervous system is a system of neurons. A neuron consists of three parts: the body, dendrites and the axon. Where the axon of one neuron approaches another neuron, a synapse is formed.

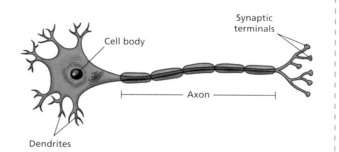

Figure 1.7 A neuron

Information transmission

The nature of information transmission in the nervous system is partly electrical and partly chemical. An electrical impulse builds up at the synapse and travels across the neuron and its axon, passing the excitation on to the next synapse.

At the synapse the mechanism becomes chemical. When the electrical impulse reaches the end of the axon, a neurotransmitter is released into the synaptic gap. This neurotransmitter can then:

- be pulled back into the axon that released it (this process is called reuptake)
- reach the end of the synaptic gap and bind itself to one of the receptors on the surface of the next neuron.

When the neurotransmitter binds to a receptor, this changes the next neuron's electric potential and contributes to building up the impulse.

Agonists and antagonists

Neurotransmitters themselves are affected by certain chemicals: agonists and antagonists. Agonists act by enhancing the action of neurotransmitters and antagonists counteract neurotransmitters. For example, some of the widely used antidepressants are SSRIs (selective serotonin reuptake inhibitors). They act as agonists for the neurotransmitter serotonin; they inhibit its reuptake thus increasing its concentration in the synapse.

RESEARCH   Crockett *et al* (2010)—the effect of serotonin on prosocial behaviour

Essential understanding

✪ *Neurotransmitters affect not only behaviours that are obviously biologically based (such as mood or fatigue), but also behaviours that seem to be the result of free will, such as prosocial acts.*

Aim

To investigate the effect of serotonin on prosocial behaviour.

Participants

30 healthy volunteers.

Method

Experiment; repeated measures design. The design was counterbalanced. The study was double-blind.

Procedure

In condition 1 participants were given a dose of citalopram (an SSRI). In condition 2 they were given a placebo.

Participants were given moral dilemmas based on the classic "trolley problem": there is a runaway trolley moving along the tracks and you see that it is about to hit and kill five people; you have a choice between doing nothing and interfering.

- **In impersonal scenarios** interfering implied pulling a lever that diverts the trolley onto another track where it kills one person.
- **In personal scenarios** interfering implied pushing a man on the tracks, so that the man's body will slow down the trolley and prevent it from hitting the five workers.

In both these scenarios the choice is between killing one person or letting five people die, but in the personal scenario killing is a more direct and emotionally aversive act.

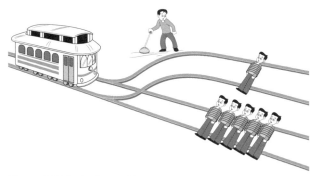

Figure 1.8 The trolley problem

Results

In the impersonal scenario participants' responses were unaffected by citalopram. In the personal scenario citalopram made participants less likely to interfere (that is, less likely to push the man off the bridge).

Conclusion

Citalopram reduces the acceptability of personal harm and in this sense promotes prosocial behaviour. Increased levels of serotonin in the brain may cause people to be more opposed to the idea of inflicting harm on someone.

RESEARCH   Freed *et al* (2001)—the role of dopamine in Parkinson's disease

Essential understanding
✪ *Dopamine at least partially affects symptoms of Parkinson's disease, especially in younger patients.*

Aim
To investigate the effects of dopamine on the behavioural symptoms of Parkinson's disease.

Participants
40 patients with severe Parkinson's disease. The mean duration of the disease was 14 years and ages ranged from 34 to 75 years.

Method
Experiment; independent measures design.

Procedure
In the experimental group nerve cells containing dopamine-producing neurons were taken from aborted embryos and transplanted into the patient's putamen. Four holes were drilled through the skull and the tissue was transplanted through long needles.

The control group underwent sham surgery: holes were drilled in the skull but the tissue was not transplanted.

All patients were followed for one year. PET scans were made to estimate changes in the brain; clinical observations and interviews were used to register changes in symptoms.

Results
PET scans revealed significant growth of dopamine-producing cells in the putamen of participants in the transplant group. Patients in the transplant group demonstrated a reduction of Parkinson's symptoms by 28%, but only in the relatively younger group (below 60).

Conclusion
Transplantation of dopamine-producing neurons in the putamen of patients with severe symptoms of Parkinson's disease leads to an improvement in younger but not older patients. This shows the influence of dopamine on behaviour.

RESEARCH   Fisher, Aron and Brown (2005)—dopamine and romantic love

Essential understanding
✪ *Dopaminergic activity may be the biological basis of romantic love.*

Aim
To investigate neural mechanisms of romantic love.

Participants
17 participants who were "intensely in love" with someone, mean age 21 and mean duration of being in love 7 months.

Method
Experiment; repeated measures design. Variables were measured in fMRI scans.

Procedure
Participants were placed in a fMRI scanner and went through the following four steps, which were repeated six times:

- viewing a photograph of the person they love—30 seconds
- filler activity—40 seconds
- viewing a photograph of an emotionally neutral acquaintance—30 seconds
- filler activity—20 seconds.

Brain responses to the picture of a loved one and to the picture of a neutral acquaintance were compared.

Results
There was a specific pattern of activation in the brain in response to the photographs of the loved ones. Activation was especially prominent in dopamine-rich brain areas.

Conclusion
Dopaminergic activity plays a role in feelings of romantic love.

LIMITATIONS OF NEUROTRANSMITTER RESEARCH

Essential understanding
✪ *Research that attempts to isolate the effect of one neurotransmitter is inevitably oversimplified. However, it leads to important insights.*

Neurotransmission is a complex process. There are more than 100 known neurotransmitters, and each of them has multiple effects on behaviour. Neurotransmitters in the synaptic gap affect each other and, on top of that, are affected by agonists and antagonists.

When it comes to research, however, we typically increase the level of one isolated neurotransmitter (X) and observe the changes in behaviour (Z). Can we say that X influences Z? Yes, but with the following limitations.

- The effect may be indirect. For example, X acts as an agonist for neurotransmitter Y, and it is Y that influences Z.
- The effect may be postponed. For example, X triggers a long-lasting process of change in interconnected variables, ultimately resulting in Z.
- X may not be the only factor affecting Z.
- X is never the only factor that changes: when we increase the level of X, this results in various side effects.

1.1.4 Techniques used to study the brain in relation to behaviour

- **BOLD (blood-oxygen-level dependent) signal**— pulses of energy emitted by oxygenated blood when placed in an external magnetic field, used in fMRI
- **Spatial resolution**—the ability of a scanner to discriminate between nearby locations, a unit of space that is discernable in a brain scan
- **Temporal resolution**—the smallest time period in which a brain scan can register changes in the brain

ESSENTIAL UNDERSTANDING

For a long time, brain research was limited to conducting post-mortem autopsies on patients with unusual behavioural deviations (such as Broca's and Wernicke's patients). After the invention of brain imaging techniques it was possible to study the human brain non-invasively.

The most commonly used brain imaging techniques are:
- computerized axial tomography (CAT)
- positron emission tomography (PET)
- magnetic resonance imaging (MRI)
- functional magnetic resonance imaging (fMRI)
- electroencephalography (EEG).

The choice of brain imaging techniques is full of trade-offs, such as structure versus process, spatial resolution versus temporal resolution, amount of detail and time of the scanning procedure, and so on. See **"Comparison of brain imaging techniques"**.

Examples of research studies that used brain imaging technology can be found in other sections and other units. A few examples from this unit are: Draganski *et al* (2004), Maguire *et al* (2000), Freed *et al* (2001), Fisher, Aron and Brown (2005). See **"Examples of research using brain imaging techniques"**.

COMPUTERIZED AXIAL TOMOGRAPHY (CAT)

Principle of work
When an X-ray passes through the head, it is picked up by a detector on the opposite side and analysed. Since bone and hard tissue absorb X-rays better than soft tissue (such as nervous cells), analysis of the residual rays can reveal information about brain structure.

Procedure
The subject lies on a table that slides into a large cylindrical apparatus. The apparatus produces a moving source of X-rays that pass through the subject's head.

Strengths
This is a quick and non-invasive method of studying brain structure. Since it does not use magnetic fields, CAT can be used with people who have medical implants.

Limitations
There is some level of radiation exposure.

MAGNETIC RESONANCE IMAGING (MRI)

Principle of work
When placed in an external magnetic field, some atomic nuclei (for example, those of hydrogen) can emit energy. These pulses of energy can be detected. Since we know that the concentration of hydrogen differs in different types of tissue, we can use this information to produce a three-dimensional picture of brain structure.

Procedure
Similar to CAT, the subject is placed on a table that slides inside a cylindrical apparatus.

Strengths
There is no radiation exposure. MRI has a better spatial resolution than CAT.

Limitations
Due to its high resolution, the scanner sometimes picks up slight abnormalities in the brain that are not related to the original complaint. This may create anxiety and cause people to pursue unnecessary treatment. Due to the strong magnetic fields, people with metal in their body cannot undergo the procedure. Being placed in a narrow tube for a long time may be an issue for people suffering from claustrophobia. This may be difficult for young children. Furthermore, MRI scans are expensive.

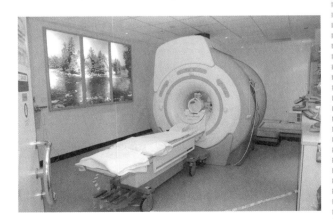

Figure 1.9 MRI machine

FUNCTIONAL MAGNETIC RESONANCE IMAGING (FMRI)

Principle of work
This method uses the BOLD (blood-oxygen-level dependent) signal. When a brain region is active during the performance of a task, the organism supplies it with oxygenated blood. When oxygenated blood is placed in an external magnetic field, it emits pulses of energy, but this response depends on the blood flow and level of oxygenation. Since we know that the most active brain areas are supplied with the most blood, this also allows us to see which brain areas are most active during the performance of a particular task.

Procedure
Similar to MRI, but subjects are also required to carry out a task while their brain is being scanned.

Strengths
Unlike MRI and CAT that can only be used to map brain structure, fMRI also shows ongoing brain processes. It produces excellent spatial resolution.

Limitations
It is necessary to discriminate between systematic patterns of activation and random noise. Some sources of noise include head movements, fidgeting and random thoughts. Eliminating noise requires a lengthy experimental procedure with many trials.

Temporal resolution is around 1 second, which means that only relatively long-lasting processes can be studied.

POSITRON EMISSION TOMOGRAPHY (PET)

Principle of work
A radioactive tracer is injected in the subject's bloodstream. This tracer binds to molecules such as glucose. It decays quickly and emits energy. The more active a brain area, the more blood supply it needs, hence the higher the energy level emitted by the tracer.

Procedure
After the injection the subject is placed in a scanner that picks up the energy emissions.

Strengths
Like fMRI, this shows both the structure and the processes in the brain. It provides good spatial resolution, and the scanner can be small and even portable.

Limitations
There is exposure to radioactivity and it provides poor temporal resolution (as compared to fMRI), so only relatively slow processes can be registered.

ELECTROENCEPHALOGRAPHY (EEG)

Principle of work
When large groups of neurons are activated simultaneously, electric potentials generated by these impulses become detectable on the skull surface. Electrodes can be attached to the scalp to detect this electrical activity.

Procedure
Electrodes are attached to the scalp at predetermined points. The subject is required to lie still for several minutes while the electroencephalogram is generated.

Strengths
This provides perfect temporal resolution—changes in the electric potentials are detected within milliseconds. It is useful in diagnosing such conditions as epilepsy or sleep disorders, and is cheap, mobile, silent and non-invasive.

Limitations
It provides poor spatial resolution—the origin of the signal cannot be established. It is only good for detecting changes in the overall patterns of brain activity. It is useful for detecting electrical activity in the cortex, but the signal from subcortical areas is too weak to be registered on the surface of the scalp.

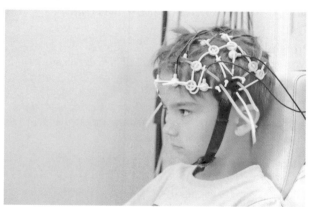

Figure 1.10 EEG machine in use

Essential understanding

✪ *Choosing between the techniques is not easy. It is determined by a number of trade-offs and criteria such as structure versus process, spatial and temporal resolution, and artificiality and cost of the procedure.*

The first important distinction is between structure and process. Some techniques are used to produce a three-dimensional image of brain structure. Other techniques are used to detect patterns of brain activity. They can be used to study brain response to performing task A in comparison to performing task B.

Once this is decided, you need to choose your desirable spatial and temporal resolution. There is a certain trade-off involved. Higher spatial resolution means a longer scanning time. It can be problematic in some cases. Every imaging technique has a threshold of spatial and temporal resolution above which it cannot go. Excellent temporal resolution comes at the cost of low spatial resolution.

Finally, there is the scanning procedure. One needs to take into account the cost and influence on the participant.

All brain imaging techniques, however, have a major advantage over post-mortem examination: they allow us to study the living brain in a non-invasive way.

Criteria	MRI	CAT	fMRI	PET	EEG
Structure or process?	Structure	Structure	Process	Process	Process
Spatial resolution	Up to 1–2 mm	Up to 1–2 mm	Up to 1–2 mm	4 mm	Very poor
Temporal resolution	Not applicable	Not applicable	1 second	30–40 seconds	Milliseconds
Major advantage for research	Gives a detailed three-dimensional image of the brain	Lower cost; used more and more rarely as MRIs become cheaper	Shows patterns of brain activation while performing a task	Portable; less artifacts associated with the scanning procedure	Detects very quick changes in the patterns of cortical activity ("brain waves")

Table 1.1 Summary of brain imaging techniques

EXAMPLES OF RESEARCH USING BRAIN IMAGING TECHNIQUES

Examples of such research studies can be found throughout the course in various units. Here are a few examples from this unit.

Study	Brain imaging technique	Aim
Draganski *et al* (2004)	MRI	To investigate changes in grey matter volume as a result of practising a simple juggling routine
Maguire *et al* (2000)	MRI	To compare brain structure in people with extensive navigational skills (London taxi drivers) and controls
Freed *et al* (2001)	PET	To investigate if dopamine has any role on behavioural symptoms of Parkinson's disease, by transplanting dopamine-producing tissue to the putamen of patients with severe Parkinson's disease
Fisher, Aron and Brown (2005)	fMRI	To investigate which areas of the brain are activated when participants look at pictures of people they love, and to study the role of dopamine in feelings of romantic love

Table 1.2

1.2 Hormones and pheromones and behaviour

1.2.1 The influence of hormones on behaviour

- **Endocrine system**—a chemical messenger system of the organism; the system of glands that secrete hormones
- **Gene knockout (KO)**—a genetic technique in which one of the genes of an organism is "switched off"; the term can also be used to describe the organism that carries this inoperative gene
- **Oxytocin**—a hormone produced by the hypothalamus and released by the pituitary gland; it is known for its role in social interaction and sexual reproduction

ESSENTIAL UNDERSTANDING

Like neurotransmitters, hormones are chemical messengers. However, their mechanism of action is different. They are released into the bloodstream and regulate relatively slower processes. See "**Comparison of hormones and neurotransmitters**".

There are many different hormones, but we will focus on the role of oxytocin, a hormone known as "the love hormone". See "**Oxytocin**".

Ferguson *et al* (2000) observed that when the oxytocin gene in mice is switched off, it prevents them from recognizing familiar social stimuli. This may be potentially helpful in understanding what causes autism in humans. See **Ferguson et al (2000)**.

Scheele *et al* (2012) tested if oxytocin would have an effect on a man's willingness to approach an attractive woman if the man is in a stable relationship. They found that this approach behaviour is inhibited in men who are in a stable relationship (but not single men) when they are given a dose of oxytocin (but not placebo). This suggests that oxytocin plays a role in human fidelity. See **Scheele et al (2012)**.

COMPARISON OF HORMONES AND NEUROTRANSMITTERS

Essential understanding

✪ *Unlike neurotransmitters, hormones are released into the bloodstream and regulate relatively slower processes.*

The function of hormones differs from the function of neurotransmitters in several ways.

	Neurotransmitters	Hormones
What means of communication are used?	The nervous system	The system of blood vessels (hormones are released into the bloodstream)
What processes are regulated?	Relatively rapid processes such as emotions, decisions, attention and so on	Relatively slow processes such as growth, metabolism, digestion or reproduction

Table 1.3

Hormones are released by endocrine glands such as adrenal glands, the hypothalamus or pancreas. Together all these glands are known as the endocrine system.

There is a large variety of hormones produced in the body. Examples include adrenaline, noradrenaline, cortisol, oxytocin, insulin, testosterone and oestrogen.

OXYTOCIN

Oxytocin is released by the pituitary gland. It plays a role in sexual reproduction, childbirth and social bonding, which is why it has been given such labels as "the love hormone" and "the cuddle chemical". It is also released during breastfeeding, which plays a role in establishing the bond between the mother and the child.

RESEARCH   Ferguson *et al* (2000)—social amnesia in mice lacking the oxytocin gene

Essential understanding

✪ *When the oxytocin gene in mice is switched off, it prevents them from recognizing familiar social stimuli. This may be potentially helpful in understanding what causes autism in humans.*

Background

Social familiarity in rodents is based on olfactory cues. If a rodent repeatedly meets another member of the same species, the olfactory investigation time (time spent sniffing the other animal on meeting it) decreases.

Aim

To investigate the role of oxytocin in social memory in rodents.

Participants

42 oxytocin gene knockout mice and 42 mice with normal genotype. All mice were male.

Method

Experiment; mixed design (independent measures and repeated measures).

Procedure

A female mouse was introduced into the home cage of the "participant" for a one-minute confrontation. This was repeated four times with ten-minute intervals between trials. These were called "habituation trials". The same mouse was used on all four trials. On the fifth trial (dishabituation) a new female mouse was introduced.

Behaviour was recorded and scored by trained raters. Olfactory investigation was operationalized as the amount of time spent in nasal contact with the female mouse.

Results

Mice with normal genotype showed considerable habituation from the first trial to the fourth. The amount of time they spent in olfactory contact with the female mouse decreased on each subsequent trial. On the fifth trial (when the new female mouse was introduced) dishabituation occurred and the amount of time in olfactory contact returned to the original level.

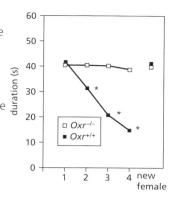

Figure 1.11 Results of Ferguson *et al* (2000)

Oxytocin gene knockout mice showed no habituation. They spent equal time in olfactory contact with the female mouse each time she was placed in the cage.

Conclusion

Oxytocin is necessary for the development of social memory in mice. It plays a role in recognizing familiar members of the same species.

Notes: In terms of its application to humans, results of this research could be useful for the development of new treatments for autism. Although not directly about autism, this study suggests that oxytocin levels may be responsible for reacting to social cues, which is one of the deficits in people suffering from disorders of the autistic spectrum (Modi, Young 2012).

RESEARCH   Scheele *et al* (2012)—the role of oxytocin in human fidelity

Essential understanding

✪ *Oxytocin modulates social distance between men and women.*

Aim

To investigate the role of oxytocin in promoting fidelity in humans.

Participants

86 heterosexual men, some single and some in a stable relationship.

Method

Experiment; independent measures design; double blind study.

Procedure

Either oxytocin or placebo was administered to the participants intranasally. After this, participants were required to engage in two tasks.

1. Stop-distance paradigm—the participant stood at one end of the room; an attractive female confederate stood at the other end. Participants were instructed to slowly approach the female confederate and stop at a distance that made them feel slightly uncomfortable.

2. Approach/avoidance task—participants were positioned in front of a screen. They also had a joystick. They were then shown a series of pictures of four types, in random order:

- positive social pictures (such as attractive women)
- positive non-social pictures (such as beautiful landscapes)
- negative social pictures (such as mutilations)
- negative non-social pictures (such as dirt).

If the participant liked the picture, he had to pull the joystick, increasing the size of the picture. If he did not like the picture, he had to push the joystick, making the picture smaller.

Results

Results of the first task showed that oxytocin caused men to keep a greater distance from the attractive female confederate, but only if the man was in a stable relationship.

Results of the second task showed that the only group of pictures affected by oxytocin and relationship status was the positive social group (pictures of attractive women). Men in a relationship (but not single men) pulled the joystick more slowly in the oxytocin condition but not in the placebo condition.

Conclusion

Oxytocin causes men in a relationship to keep a greater distance from attractive women who are not their partner. Researchers explained that this promotes fidelity.

The second task makes it evident that this effect of oxytocin is highly specific and selective to a certain group of stimuli: attractive women.

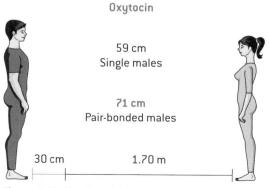
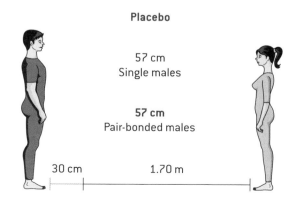

Figure 1.12 The stop-distance paradigm

1.2.2 The influence of pheromones on behaviour

ESSENTIAL UNDERSTANDING

Pheromones are chemical messengers that communicate information from one member of a species to another. They are processed in the accessory olfactory bulb in animals, but whether or not there exists a biological mechanism to process pheromones in humans is unclear. See "Biology of pheromones".

The search for human pheromones has taken the form of both laboratory and field experiments.

For example, Lundstrom and Olsson (2005) in an experimental procedure showed that androstadienone (AND) increased the mood of female participants if the study was carried out by a male, but not a female experimenter. This seems to suggest that androstadienone can modulate women's emotional reaction to men, indicating its possible function as a human pheromone. See **Lundstrom and Olsson (2005)**.

On the other hand, Hare *et al* (2017) in a carefully designed experimental procedure demonstrated that neither AND (androstadienone) nor EST (estratetraenol) could signal gender or attractiveness. Since these are the basic functions a human pheromone must be able to perform, these results bring into question the status of these chemicals as putative human pheromones. See **Hare *et al* (2017)**.

In a field experiment, Cutler, Friedman and McCoy (1998) showed that a synthetic human pheromone applied to aftershave cream increased the attractiveness of men to women, which resulted in a higher incidence of sexual behaviours. See **Cutler, Friedman and McCoy (1998)**.

These research studies, however, only serve as examples of laboratory and field experiments in this area. Summarizing all available research, it must be concluded for the time being that research has been contradictory and inconclusive, and the human pheromone has not been found. See "Criticism of human pheromone research".

BIOLOGY OF PHEROMONES

Essential understanding

✪ *Pheromones are chemicals that signal information (such as fertility or sexual attractiveness) from one member of a species to another. While pheromones are important for communication in various species, including mammals, their role in humans is debatable.*

Pheromones are chemical messengers

Pheromones are chemicals that provide chemical communication between members of the same species. In this way, just like neurotransmitters and hormones, they are chemical messengers. However, unlike the other chemical messengers, pheromones communicate information from one species member to another.

An example of information that is communicated by pheromones is female fertility. Such pheromones have been shown to play an important role in the sexual behaviour of a number of species including many mammals.

Where in the brain are pheromones processed?

Mammals have a structure called the **vomeronasal organ (VNO)** located in their nasal cavity. This structure is connected through nerves to the brain region called the **accessory olfactory bulb**. This region is adjacent to, but separate from, the brain area responsible for processing regular smells, the **main olfactory bulb**.

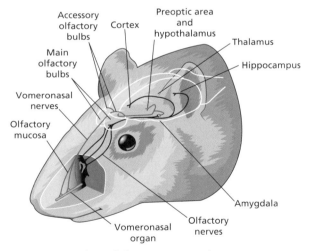

Figure 1.13 Biology of pheromone processing

Processing pheromonal information in the human brain

Human fetuses have the accessory olfactory bulb, but it regresses and disappears after birth. As for the VNO, some people have it and some don't. Even in those people who do have it, it appears to be disconnected from the nervous system. However, there is still a possibility that pheromonal information in humans is processed elsewhere.

Two chemicals that have been extensively studied as putative human pheromones are androstadienone (AND) and estratetraenol (EST).

RESEARCH   Lundstrom and Olsson (2005)—effects of androstadienone on women's attraction to men

Essential understanding
✪ *Being exposed to androstadienone increases the mood of women in the presence of a male experimenter, which suggests that this chemical may trigger attraction.*

Aim
To investigate the effect of androstadienone on the mood of women in the presence of men.

Participants
37 heterosexual women, mean age 25 years, with a normal menstrual cycle.

Method
Experiment; 2 x 2 experimental design (two independent variables with two levels each).

Procedure
Female participants' mood was studied in a 2 x 2 experimental design. They were assessed after being exposed to either androstadienone or a control solution, and in the presence of either a male or a female experimenter.

The experimenter carried out a number of measurements including several questionnaires. One of the questionnaires measured participants' mood.

The experimenter was either female (age 28) or male (age 30).

Results
Androstadienone increased women's mood in the presence of a male experimenter, but not a female experimenter.

Conclusion
Androstadienone may serve the function of signaling sexual attractiveness, which supports its role as a pheromone.

RESEARCH   Hare *et al* (2017)—the ability of androstadienone and estratetraenol to signal gender and attractiveness

Essential understanding
✪ *Any chemical that is hypothesized to be a human pheromone signaling sexual attractiveness must be able to perform two functions: 1) signal gender and 2) affect perceived attractiveness of the faces of the opposite sex. Hare et al's research showed that neither AND nor EST perform either of these functions, which brings into question their status as human pheromones.*

Aim
To investigate if androstadienone (AND) and estratetraenol (EST) signal gender and affect mate perception.

Participants
140 heterosexual adults.

Method
Experiment; repeated measures design.

Procedure
Participants completed two computer-based tasks on two consecutive days. On one of the days they were exposed to the putative pheromone (AND or EST) masked with clove oil; on the other day they were exposed to the control scent (clove oil alone). The order of conditions was counterbalanced.

In the first task, participants were shown five "gender-neutral facial morphs" and had to indicate the gender (male or female).

In the second task they were shown photographs of individuals of the opposite sex and asked to rate their attractiveness on a scale from 1 to 10.

Figure 1.14 Gender-neutral facial morphs

Results
There was no difference in gender assigned to the morphed faces in the pheromone versus control condition. There was no difference in the average attractiveness ratings of the photographs of the opposite sex.

Conclusion
The two chemicals (AND and EST) do not act as signals of gender or of attractiveness. Based on this result, researchers concluded that these chemicals do not qualify as human pheromones.

RESEARCH   Cutler, Friedman and McCoy (1998)—a field experiment with a synthetic human pheromone

Essential understanding
✪ *In a field experiment, researchers showed that a synthetic human pheromone applied to a man's aftershave lotion increased the incidence of behaviours that seemed to suggest sexual contact initiated by women. From this, researchers concluded that pheromones may increase sexual attractiveness of men to women.*

Aim
To investigate if a synthesized human pheromone can increase sociosexual behaviour of men.

Participants
Male volunteers, all heterosexual, 25–42 years old, in good health and with regular appearance.

Method
Field experiment; independent measures design.

Procedure
Each participant was asked to use his regular aftershave lotion after every shave for the duration of the study. Participants were also given a behavioural calendar that they had to fill out on a daily basis, indicating the incidence of the following six behaviours on that day:
– petting, affection and/or kissing
– sleeping next to a romantic partner
– sexual intercourse
– informal dates
– formal dates
– masturbation.

There was a baseline period of two weeks. After the baseline, a technician added either ethanol or a synthesized pheromone with ethanol to their aftershave lotion (depending on the condition). Ethanol was used as a masking agent to compensate for the possible smell of the pheromone.

This was followed by six more weeks of using the aftershave regularly and filling out the behavioural calendar.

Results
Compared to the control group, a larger number of participants in the pheromone group showed an increase over the baseline in the first four behaviours (petting, sleeping next to a partner, sexual intercourse and informal dates). Differences were not observed in the last two behaviours (formal dates and masturbation).

Conclusion
Researchers took this result as evidence that the synthetic human pheromone applied to the aftershave lotion increased sexual attractiveness of men to women.

An alternative explanation would be to say that it was the men's own libido that increased (so that they initiated contact with women more often). However, the fact that there was no change in formal dates and masturbation contradicts this explanation.

On the other hand, spontaneous sexual encounters were affected, indicating that the contact might have been initiated by women.

CRITICISM OF HUMAN PHEROMONE RESEARCH

Essential understanding
⭐ *Research in the area of human pheromones has produced contradictory findings. Much of this research is flawed by the fact that authors are commercially interested in the results. There are also a number of methodological limitations compromising the quality of a typical study.*

Research is inconclusive
It must be admitted that research is inconclusive and the existence of human pheromones is not a scientifically established fact.

Contradictory findings
First of all, for every laboratory experiment that supports the existence of human pheromones, we can probably find a study that doesn't—this is the case with Lundstrom and Olsson (2005) versus Hare *et al* (2017).

Commercial interest

Secondly, field experiments in this area are rarely conducted due to the effort and funding that is required. When they are conducted, it is done by companies who are financially interested in the results. This was the case with Cutler, Friedman and McCoy (1998)—the first author of the study was the founder of a company that produced and marketed a synthetic human pheromone. That is why they do not reveal the formula of the chemical in their research paper. But this also means that an independent researcher cannot try and replicate the results of the study!

Inherent methodological limitations
Thirdly, there are major methodological limitations inherent in any research study in this field (Verhaeghe, Gheysen, Enzlin 2013).

Typical limitation	Explanation
Demand characteristics	It may be easy for participants to guess the true aim of the study because: – they are aware of the exclusion criteria, for example, women taking contraceptive pills are not allowed to participate in the study – the study includes surveys with questions about the participants' sexual orientation and sexual behaviours.
Ecological validity	Even in field experiments the concentration of pheromones used in the solution is much higher than that found naturally in human sweat. Some participants can even identify the unusual smell in the substance they are exposed to. If they use an aftershave lotion that smells unusual, this in itself can change their behaviour, making it less natural.
Internal validity	We are exposed to a large variety of smells in our daily lives, and these act as confounding variables. Effort is made to keep participants "odourless" for the duration of the experiment, but this is practically impossible to achieve.

Table 1.4

1.3 Genetics and behaviour

1.3.1 Genes and behaviour, genetic similarities

- **DNA methylation**—the process by which certain chemicals (methyl groups) are added to the DNA molecule, affecting gene transcription

- **Epigenetic changes**—deviations of the phenotype from the genotype occurring as a result of changes in gene expression

- **Gene**—a part of DNA responsible for a specific trait or behaviour

- **Gene expression**—the process of synthesizing organic molecules based on the DNA blueprint; the manifestation of the genotype in phenotypical traits

- **Gene transcription**—part of gene expression; replicating the DNA sequence in a freshly synthesized RNA molecule

- **Gene translation**—part of gene expression; decoding the RNA molecule into a sequence of amino acids in a protein

- **Genotype**—the set of traits as it is coded in an individual's DNA

- **Phenotype**—a set of traits that actually manifest in an individual's body, appearance or behaviour

ESSENTIAL UNDERSTANDING

Debate and methods

The nature-nurture debate in its classic form asks whether it is biological or environmental factors that primarily affect behaviour. In the modern version of the question, the focus is on quantifying the relative contributions of the two factors and studying their dynamic interaction with each other. See **"The nature-nurture debate"**.

A variety of methods can be used to investigate genetic influences on behaviour. Some of these methods (twin studies, adoption studies and family studies) are based on the principle of genetic similarity. Other methods (molecular genetics) can be used to establish the role of specific genes in specific behaviours. See **"Methods of research"**.

The Falconer model

One of the ways to estimate heritability of a trait from results of a twin study is the Falconer model. This model assumes that the phenotypical variation of a trait is explained by the contribution of three independent factors: genetic inheritance, shared environment and individual environment. See **"The Falconer model"**.

Interaction of genes and environment

The Falconer model, however, does not take into account the possibility that these factors may themselves influence each other. For example, genetic factors can influence environmental factors by causing a growing individual to choose those bits ("niches") of the environment that are more in line with their genetic predisposition. See **"The influence of genetics on environment: niche-picking"**.

Conversely, environmental factors can influence gene expression—this is known as epigenetic changes. See **"The influence of environment on genetics: epigenetics"**.

Twin studies: example

Bouchard and McGue (1981) conducted a meta-analysis of 111 twin studies looking at heritability of intelligence. Applying the Falconer model to their data shows that 54% of variation in intelligence is due to genetic inheritance. While this is a large estimate, it also means that genetic inheritance is not the only factor influencing intelligence. See **Bouchard and McGue (1981)**.

Adoption studies: example

Scarr and Weinberg (1983) obtained two seemingly controversial findings.

- There is a considerable increase in IQ points when children with a poor socio-economic status are adopted by wealthier and more educated families.

- The IQ of adopted children correlates more strongly with the IQ of their biological, but not adoptive, parents.

This controversy is resolved by the idea of additive influence of genetic and environmental factors. See **Scarr and Weinberg (1983)**.

Studies employing methods of molecular genetics: examples

An example of a research study that used the methods of molecular genetics is **Caspi et al (2003)**. It was demonstrated that people with one or two short alleles of the 5-HTT gene are more vulnerable to stress and as a result more prone to depression. See **Caspi et al (2003)**.

Epigenetic studies also use modern technology to establish molecular mechanisms in the regulation of gene expression. **Weaver et al (2004)** explored how environmental factors (nurturing behaviour of rat mothers) can influence behaviour (stress reactivity) through the regulation of gene expression (methylation of certain gene sequences) without changing the gene itself. They found that less nurturing from the rat mother results in higher methylation of the glucocorticoid receptor gene, which in turn leads to fewer glucocorticoid receptors in the brain and higher vulnerability to stress. They were also able to reverse this effect with a drug. See **Weaver et al (2004)**.

EXAM TIP

There are two overlapping topics: "Genes and behaviour" and "Genetic similarities". It is important to understand which arguments and research studies are relevant to each topic.

This is best explained with reference to research methods. The four main methods used to study the influence of genetic versus environmental factors on behaviour are:

1. twin studies
2. adoption studies
3. family studies
4. molecular genetics (and epigenetics).

The first three methods are based on the principle of genetic similarity. Arguments and research studies based on these methods are relevant for the topic "Genetic similarities".

Methods of molecular genetics are used to establish specific genes responsible for a particular behaviour.

There are two possible ways in which questions on the topic "Genes and behaviour" may be asked.

1. If the question implies the influence of specific genes on behaviour, you should use arguments and research studies based on the methods of molecular genetics (and epigenetics).
2. If the question implies the influence of genetics in general, you can use any arguments and studies including those based on the principle of genetic similarities.

THE NATURE-NURTURE DEBATE

Essential understanding

✪ *The nature-nurture debate in its classic form asks if it is primarily biological or environmental factors that influence behaviour. Modern reformulation of the debate is concerned with quantifying the relative contributions of both factors and investigating their dynamic interaction with each other.*

The nature-nurture debate is one of the longest debates in psychology and philosophy. In its original form the question was whether human behaviour is primarily determined by biological factors (nature) or environmental influences (nurture).

This original form is outdated. There is little doubt that human behaviour is determined by both these factors to

some extent. But once we acknowledge that, there are follow-up questions that need to be investigated.

– How can we quantify the relative contributions of nature and nurture to behaviour?

– Are nature and nurture really independent factors or is there some sort of interaction between nature and nurture themselves? For example, can biological factors influence the environment? Can environmental factors influence genetics?

An attempt to answer these questions would require sophisticated research methods.

METHODS OF RESEARCH

Essential understanding

✪ *Research into the role of genetics in human behaviour is conducted using methods like twin studies, adoption studies, family studies and molecular genetics. The first* *three are based on the principle of genetic similarity between various groups of individuals. The last one is aimed at identifying specific genes responsible for specific behaviours.*

Method	Explanation
Twin studies	Twin studies are based on comparing the similarity between monozygotic (MZ) twins to the similarity between dizygotic (DZ) twins for a particular trait or behaviour. MZ twins share 100% of their genotype and DZ twins share 50% on average. If a behaviour is genetically inherited, one might expect that MZ twins will be more similar to each other in terms of this behaviour than DZ twins.
Adoption studies	Adoption studies compare behavioural similarities in such groups of people as: – adopted children and their adoptive parents – adopted children and their biological parents – adopted children and their biological siblings.
Family studies	Family studies are based on collecting data about families on a broader scale, spanning several generations. The level of genetic relatedness is then compared to the observed similarities in a certain trait or behaviour. For example, assuming heritability of a trait, we might expect children to be more similar to their parents than to grandparents, more similar to siblings than cousins, equally similar to grandparents and aunts, and so on.
Molecular genetics	These methods use modern genetic mapping technology to investigate how behaviour is influenced by specific genes. Genetic mapping can reveal particular alleles of every gene in a given individual, and behaviour is then compared across groups of individuals who have different variants (alleles) of the same gene. Methods of molecular genetics are also used in epigenetics, the study of gene expression.

Table 1.5 Methods commonly used to study the effect of genotype on behaviour

THE FALCONER MODEL

Essential understanding

✪ *The Falconer model is a way to estimate heritability of a trait from the observed similarities between MZ twins and DZ twins (rMZ and rDZ).*

The Falconer model is used with twin research data to quantify the relative contribution of heredity to a trait or behaviour. It makes the following assumption:

A + C + E = 1

(100% of observed variation in phenotype is explained by contributions from heredity A, shared environment C and individual environment E)

As applied to twins, shared environment is the part of the environment that two twins have in common, and individual environment refers to those bits of the environment that are unique to each twin.

To estimate A (heritability) in this model, you also need to take into consideration that:

rMZ = A + C

(there are two sources of similarity between monozygotic twins: 100% of shared genotype and the common environment)

rDZ = 1/2A + C

(the sources of similarity between dizygotic twins are the same, except that they only share 50% of their genotype, so the contribution from A is half as much)

Both rMZ and rDZ are measured directly in research. Plugging these values into the formulas above, it is easy to estimate A:

A = 2(rMZ − rDZ)

THE INFLUENCE OF GENETICS ON ENVIRONMENT: NICHE-PICKING

Essential understanding

✪ *Niche-picking is one of the ways in which genetic and environmental factors can dynamically interact. In niche-picking, genetic predisposition causes the individual to select certain aspects of the environment.*

Niche-picking is an example of how genetic factors can influence the environment. It is the phenomenon in which genetic predisposition causes individuals to select certain environments (or "niches" in the environment) which in turn influence their behaviour.

For example, a child who is genetically predisposed to depression may intentionally seek out environments where it is hard to succeed. This reinforces the child's low self-esteem and in turn contributes to depression. On the surface (for example, based on results of a twin study and the Falconer model) it may look like the main factor of depression is the demanding environment, but the environment itself was caused by genetics in the first place.

THE INFLUENCE OF ENVIRONMENT ON GENETICS: EPIGENETICS

Essential understanding

✪ *Environmental factors can play a role in the regulation of gene expression. Genotype as such is not changed, but the processes of synthesizing proteins based on the DNA may be affected.*

Gene expression is the biological process of manifesting the genotype as the phenotype. The DNA contains instructions for the synthesis of proteins, but constructing the protein based on these instructions is itself not simple. It includes two steps: transcription and translation. In **transcription**, the DNA sequence gets replicated in a freshly synthesized RNA molecule. In **translation**, this RNA molecule is decoded into a sequence of amino acids in a protein. Once the protein is synthesized, it is transported to its destination in the body.

A wide range of factors can play a role in regulating gene expression at any stage, from transcription to transportation. Some genes may be suppressed completely.

In the process known as **methylation**, certain chemicals (methyl groups) are added to the DNA molecule which represses gene transcription.

Methylation may be caused by environmental factors. This is how nurture can affect nature (not the genotype itself, but the expression of it).

Regulation of gene expression results in deviations of the phenotype from the genetic code. These deviations are known as **epigenetic changes**, and the area of research that investigates them is known as epigenetics.

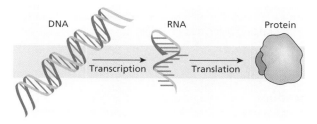

Figure 1.15 Gene expression

RESEARCH   Bouchard and McGue (1981)—twin studies on heritability of intelligence

Essential understanding
✪ *Correlations of IQ scores tend to be higher for MZ twins than for DZ twins, which shows that intelligence is inherited to a considerable extent.*

Aim
To estimate heritability of IQ.

Method
Meta-analysis.

Participants
The meta-analysis included 111 twin studies that looked into heritability of intelligence. Participants in these studies included MZ and DZ twins (reared together and apart), siblings (reared together and apart), parents and their offspring.

Procedure
Researchers selected the studies based on a number of criteria, cleaned the data and calculated median correlations between IQ scores of individuals of interest (for example, MZ and DZ twins).

Results
There were numerous results obtained in the study, but we will only focus on a subset.

IQ correlation between:	% of shared genes	Median IQ correlation
MZ twins reared together	100	0.85
MZ twins reared apart	100	0.67
DZ twins reared together	50	0.58
Siblings reared together	50	0.45

Table 1.6

One way to process this data is to estimate heritability coefficients from the Falconer model. If you use the values of rMZ and rDZ (reared together) and plug them into the formula, you will obtain the heritability coefficient of 54%.

Conclusion
The study demonstrates that intelligence is inherited to a considerable extent (54% according to the Falconer estimate).

At the same time, it is not completely inherited. Even for MZ twins reared together, the correlation between their IQ scores is not perfect, which shows that the environment plays a certain role in the development of IQ.

RESEARCH   Scarr and Weinberg (1983)—the Transracial Adoption Study

Essential understanding
✪ *This study shows a somewhat contradictory pattern of results—adopted children demonstrate a considerable improvement of IQ scores, but the correlation of their IQ is higher with the biological parents, not with the adoptive parents. This controversy is resolved in the idea of additive influence of genetic and environmental factors.*

Aim
To investigate environmental malleability of intelligence.

Participants
This study looked at 101 adoptive families who had both biological and adopted children. Some of the adopted children were black and some white. Some children were adopted in the first 12 months of life and some were adopted later. The study took place in Minnesota.

It needs to be understood that back at the time when the study was conducted, in Minnesota being black meant, on average, coming from a poorer socio-economic status background and being less educated.

Method
Adoption study.

Procedure
All children were assessed on IQ and school achievement tests. Correlations were calculated between the IQ of children and their parents (both adoptive and biological).

Results
The table shows the results of comparing IQ in various subgroups.

No	Group	Average IQ
1	Black children reared in their own homes	90
2	Adopted black children	106
3	Black children adopted in the first 12 months	110
4	Adopted white children	111
5	Natural children of the adoptive parents	119
6	Adoptive parents	120

Table 1.7

As can be seen from the table, black children placed in white families saw a substantial increase in their IQ. If they were adopted in the first year of life, they achieved the same level as adopted white children (although they had experienced a year of deprivation in the orphanage).

The table below shows the results of correlational research.

Correlation between	Value
Adopted children and their adoptive parents	0.29
Adopted children and their biological parents	0.43

Table 1.8

Conclusion
Results of the study may seem somewhat contradictory at first. On the one hand, there was a considerable

improvement in the IQ of adopted children. On the other hand, the correlation was higher with the IQ of biological parents, not adoptive parents.

These results demonstrate the idea of **additive influence** of genetics and environment in the development of IQ. The additive influence suggests that IQ can be influenced by environmental factors, but the extent to which an individual will be responsive to these favourable influences depends on genetic factors.

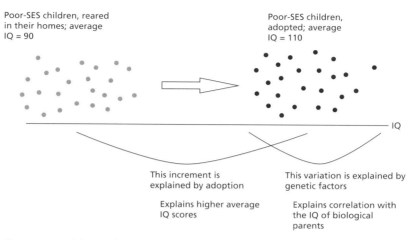

Figure 1.16 Additive influence of genetic and environmental factors

---

RESEARCH   **Caspi *et al* (2003)—the 5-HTT gene and its role in depression**

Essential understanding
✪ *Methods used in molecular genetics help identify specific genes responsible for specific behaviours. One such example is the 5-HTT gene which is responsible for modulating the reaction to stressful life events. Individuals with short alleles of this gene reacted to stressful life events with more depressive symptoms.*

Aim
To investigate the role of the 5-HTT gene in developing depression in response to stressful life events.

Participants
1,037 children from New Zealand.

Method
A longitudinal study. Genetic mapping was used to divide participants into three groups:
– both short alleles of 5-HTT (s/s)
– one short allele and one long allele (s/l)
– both long alleles (l/l).

Procedure
Participants were assessed longitudinally between ages 3 and 26. Two measures were used: a "life history calendar" to assess stressful life events and an interview to assess symptoms of depression.

Results
Participants who had one or two short alleles of 5-HTT (s/l and especially s/s) reacted to stressful life events with more depressive symptoms. For example, participants who had a major stressful life event at age 21 tended to develop depression by age 26, but only if they carried a short allele of 5-HTT.

Conclusion
It was concluded that the 5-HTT gene is responsible for modulating an individual's vulnerability to stress.

Weaver *et al* (2004)—the epigenetics of vulnerability to stress in rats

Essential understanding
✪ *The less nurturing young rats receive from their mothers, the more transcription of the glucocorticoid receptor gene is inhibited. This results in fewer glucocorticoid receptors in the brain. Psychologically this means being more vulnerable to stress.*

Aim
To investigate the epigenetic mechanism in the influence of nurturing on vulnerability to stress.

Background
There exist stable, naturally occurring individual differences in nurturing behaviours of mother rats in the first week of lactation, for example licking and grooming (LG) and arched-back nursing (ABN).

Figure 1.17 Arched-back nursing

Participants
Laboratory-bred rats.

Method
A combination of methods:
– comparison of pre-existing groups (quasi-experiment)
– a rat adoption study
– an experiment, independent measures design

Measuring variables:
– genetic mapping technology, used to determine patterns of methylation of the gene sequence
– to measure response to stress, rats were placed in a Plexiglass restrainer for 20 minutes. Blood samples were taken before and after this procedure. Corticosterone (stress hormone) was measured in the blood.

Procedure and results

Method	Procedure/trial	Results	Notes
Comparison of pre-existing groups	Hippocampal tissue was obtained from adult offspring of high-LG-ABN and low-LG-ABN mothers. Mapping was carried out to investigate methylation of specific genes, most notably, the glucocorticoid receptor (GR) gene.	Significantly higher levels of methylation were registered in the offspring of low-LG-ABN mothers. These rats also showed more acute responses to stress.	**Glucocorticoids** (**gluco**se + **cor**tex + ste**roid**) are a class of steroid hormones. They regulate a variety of functions, including the organism's response to stress. Glucocorticoids affect a cell by binding to **glucocorticoid receptors (GR)** in that cell.
Rat adoption study	Biological offspring of high-LG-ABN mothers were cross-fostered to low-LG-ABN dams, and vice versa.	Results showed that GR gene methylation depended purely on the behaviour of the nurturing (adoptive) mother. For example, rats of low-LG-ABN mothers cross-fostered to high-LG-ABN dams showed the same patterns of GR methylation as biological children of high-LG-ABN rats.	These receptors, just like anything else in the organism, are synthesized based on a genetic plan, **the GR gene**.
Experiment	A group of rats was given treatment with TSA (trichostatin A), a drug that counteracts the process of methylation in the GR gene.	Excessive methylation of the GR gene in the offspring of low-LG-ABN mothers was reversed. Responses to acute stress became normal (same as in the high-LG-ABN group).	**Corticosterone** is a steroid hormone produced in the adrenal glands. In many animals it is the main glucocorticoid involved in the regulation of stress responses. In humans, the same function is performed by **cortisol**.

Table 1.9

Conclusion
– Vulnerability to stress may be determined by epigenetic factors—methylation of a gene responsible for the production of stress hormone receptors.
– Such methylation may be the result of environmental factors (such as mother nurturing).
– Effects of methylation in the first week of life (in rats) may be sustained throughout life and keep affecting their behaviour in adulthood.
– Such effects are reversible. Using drug treatment to stop methylation results in reducing vulnerability to stress.

1.3.2 Evolutionary explanations for behaviour

- **Adaptation**—the process of changing to better suit demands of the environment
- **Disgust**—one of the basic human emotions; a feeling of revulsion caused by something unpleasant
- **Evolution**—the process by which organisms change from generation to generation due to the transmission of heritable characteristics
- **Massive modularity**—the assumption that the mind has evolved to serve different survival-related functions

and hence must consist of "modules", each responsible for one of these functions
- **Natural selection**—the key mechanism of evolution; differential survival of individuals based on the extent to which they are adapted to the environment
- **Post-hoc reasoning**—explaining something after it has already happened

ESSENTIAL UNDERSTANDING

Evolutionary psychology attempts to apply the modern theory of evolution to explaining the observed variations in human behaviour. See **"The theory of evolution"**.

It has been applied to a wide range of behaviours, but we will focus on one example to illustrate the typical reasoning behind evolutionary explanations in psychology: the emotion of disgust.

The study of Curtis, Aunger and Rabie (2004) is an example of how evolutionary explanations in psychology are put to the test. Usually a phenomenon universal for all humans is selected (in this case the basic emotion of disgust). The evolutionary explanation for this phenomenon serves as a model upon which several predictions are made (if A is true, then B, C, D, E and F must also be true). The predictions are tested in an empirical study and if all observations fit the

model well, the model is accepted. In this particular study, researchers demonstrated that several predictions about participants' ratings of disgust in response to disease-salient stimuli were in line with the evolutionary explanation: disgust is a response to disease-salient stimuli that allows the organism to avoid disease. See **Curtis, Aunger and Rabie (2004)**.

Although evolutionary psychology has a very high explanatory power and provides neat explanations for a wide range of phenomena, there are inherent and often unavoidable limitations that must be kept in mind: the assumption of mass modularity, lack of knowledge about ancestral environments, lack of testability and the existence of cross-cultural differences. See **"Criticism of evolutionary explanations in psychology"**.

THEORY

THE THEORY OF EVOLUTION

Essential understanding
❂ *The theory of evolution is based on the ideas of differential fitness, survival of the fittest and natural selection. Evolutionary explanations have been applied to a wide range of behaviours.*

The theory of evolution was first formulated by Charles Darwin in 1859 and was later expanded, accumulating the modern discoveries in genetics. Today's theory of evolution is based on the following main principles.
- Organisms are driven by the need to survive and reproduce.
- Organisms having different traits are adapted to their environment to varying degrees (differential fitness).

- Better-adapted organisms have higher chances of surviving and producing offspring (survival of the fittest).
- Less-adapted organisms produce less offspring, so their genes gradually disappear from the population. Genes of better-adapted organisms survive and are passed on to further generations (natural selection).

The theory provides some powerful explanations for the observed variation of species in the natural world. By analogy, evolutionary psychology attempts to apply this theory to explain the observed variation in human behaviour. Evolutionary explanations have been suggested for a wide range of behaviours.

RESEARCH   Curtis, Aunger and Rabie (2004)—evolutionary explanation for disgust

Essential understanding
❂ *Findings of the study suggest that the emotion of disgust evolved as protection from risk of disease.*

Aim
Hypothetically, if disgust really is a product of evolution, the following must be true.
- Disgust should be stronger in response to stimuli that are associated with disease.

- Disgust responses should be similar cross-culturally.
- Disgust should be more pronounced in females since they have to protect the immune system of their babies as well as their own.
- Disgust should become weaker as the individual becomes older (because reproductive potential declines).

The aim of the study was to test these predictions.

Participants

Volunteers who completed a survey online. The total sample was over 77,000 people from 165 countries.

Method

Correlational study.

Procedure

Data was gathered in a survey placed on the BBC Science website. First, participants were asked a series of demographic questions, such as age and country of origin. Then they were asked to rate 20 photographs for disgust on a scale from 1 to 5. These photographs were similar pairs of digitally manipulated stimuli—one of the photographs in the pair was disease-salient and the other one less salient.

Results

All four predictions formulated by the researchers found support.

– Ratings of disgust in response to disease-salient stimuli were higher than ratings of disgust towards similar stimuli that were digitally manipulated to be less disease-salient. For example, a plate of organic-looking fluid was rated as more disgusting than a plate of blue fluid that looked chemical.

– Results were consistent across cultures.

– Results were more pronounced in the sub-sample of females.

– Ratings of disgust in response to disease-salient stimuli declined with age.

Figure 1.18 Examples of photographs used in the study by Curtis, Aunger and Rabie (2004)

Conclusion

Results of the study supported the evolutionary explanation: disgust is a biologically based response to disease-salient stimuli that reduces the risk of disease.

An evolutionary explanation is a model. The model is fit into observational data, and if it fits well, our confidence in the correctness of this model increases. Since in this study all four predictions formulated on the basis of the model were supported, one can say that the evolutionary explanation of disgust stood the test.

CRITICISM OF EVOLUTIONARY EXPLANATIONS IN PSYCHOLOGY

Essential understanding

✪ *Evolutionary explanations in psychology have a number of inherent limitations, most notably, the assumptions of mass modularity and linearity of development, lack of knowledge about ancestral environments, lack of testability and the existence of cross-cultural differences.*

Evolutionary psychology has a great explanatory power, but there are limitations inherent in all evolutionary explanations in psychology. These limitations are by and large unavoidable, so one needs to take them into account to avoid unjustified generalizations.

Limitation	Explanation
Massive modularity versus neuroplasticity	Massive modularity is the idea that the mind consists of certain "modules", each of which serves a particular survival-related function. For example, one such module may be responsible for feelings of disgust, another one may be responsible for quick detection of potential enemies, and so on. If we accept that the mind on the whole is a product of evolution, we must also accept the idea of massive modularity. The brain evolved and its different parts evolved to serve different survival-related functions. However, we also know that the brain demonstrates remarkable neuroplasticity, and this contradicts the idea of massive modularity.
Speculations about the environment	Adaptation is always adaptation to some environment, so in order to explain a change in behaviour using the theory of evolution, one must have knowledge about the environment in which such a change occurred. However, our knowledge of the environments in which our human ancestors existed is very limited. Much of this knowledge is speculative.
Testability	Evolutionary explanations are very difficult and often impossible to test. Critics claim that evolutionary psychology uses post-hoc reasoning—taking an already existing phenomenon and designing a believable explanation for it.
Cultural variation	Observed cultural variations weaken evolutionary explanations of behaviour. One can claim that different cultures evolved in different environments so such variation is perfectly plausible, but if cross-cultural differences are observed for basic phenomena that are thought to be universal (such as the basic emotion of disgust), then evolutionary explanations become questionable.

Table 1.10 Limitations of evolutionary explanations

1.4 The role of animal research in understanding human behaviour (HL only)

- **Animal model**—a living organism whose behaviour resembles some aspects of human behaviour, which enables researchers to study this organism with the intention of generalizing results of the study to humans

ESSENTIAL UNDERSTANDING

Value of animal models

A fully identified animal model includes the species that is being used, the human behaviour that is being modelled and the type of experimental manipulation used in research. See "Animal models: definition".

To what extent are animals biologically similar to humans? Structurally many parts of the human brain resemble the brain of other species. Some researchers believe that many parts of the human brain are equivalent to the brain of animal species. However, some have claimed that it is how the brain structure is connected to other parts of the brain that is of primary importance, and that although some parts of human and animal brain are similar structurally, their function may be very different. See **"To what extent are animals biologically similar to humans?"**

The major advantage of working with animal models is the possibility to carry out multiple experiments in highly controlled environments, often across generations. The major disadvantages are generalizability to humans, ecological validity and ethical issues. See **"Advantages and disadvantages of working with animal models"**.

Ethical considerations

Ethical considerations in animal research are regulated by professional bodies such as the APA. Most ethical considerations revolve around making justified research choices, carefully monitoring potential pain inflicted on the animals, and getting approval from independent review teams. See **"Ethical considerations in animal research"**.

Examples of research studies

Examples of research using animal models that have already been discussed in this unit are Lashley (1929), Merzenich *et al* (1984), Ferguson *et al* (2000), and Weaver *et al* (2004). These studies can be used to illustrate both the value of animal models in psychology and ethical considerations in animal research. These studies also cover all parts of the biological approach to behaviour (brain and behaviour, hormones and pheromones and behaviour, genetics and behaviour).

EXAM TIP

This HL extension includes three topics that can be applied to any of the three parts of the biological approach to behaviour. Combining these gives you nine potential areas from which exam questions may be asked.

Parts of biological approach to behaviour	a. Brain and behaviour	b. Hormones and pheromones and behaviour	c. Genetics and behaviour
1. The value of animal models in psychology	1a	1b	1c
2. Whether animal research can provide insight into human behaviour	2a	2b	2c
3. Ethical considerations in animal research	3a	3b	3c

Table 1.11

However, there is considerable overlap in these areas. Areas 1 and 2 are very similar because the value of animal models in psychology is determined mostly by the extent to which findings from research using such models can be applied to humans.

There is a lot of overlap also between a, b and c. Ethical considerations in animal research will be similar regardless of what we are investigating, brain structure, hormones or genetics. The same concerns the value of animal models in psychology. Specifics may differ, but the major arguments will be the same.

With this in mind, we will:
- consider common arguments related to the value of animal models in psychology (in general)
- consider the main ethical considerations in animal research (in general)
- discuss examples of animal research in psychology that will allow you to apply these general arguments to concrete research studies.

ANIMAL MODELS: DEFINITION

Essential understanding
✪ *A fully identified animal model includes the species that is being used, the human behaviour that is being modelled and the causal factor that is tested in research.*

An animal model is a concept that refers to using animal research to test a certain cause-effect hypothesis about a certain human behaviour. This term is often used somewhat loosely, for example, you can see mentions of "mouse models" to denote the general idea that mice can be used to model human behaviour. However, to fully identify an animal model, it is important to include the following information:

– what animal species is being used

– what behaviour is being modelled

– what causal factor is being investigated (or what hypothesis is being tested).

For example:

– a mouse stress model of depression (read: using mice to investigate the idea that exposure to stress increases the risk of developing depression in humans)

– a rhesus monkey separation model of cognitive delay (read: using rhesus monkeys to investigate if separation from attachment figures will cause delays in cognitive development, and generalizing these findings to humans).

TO WHAT EXTENT ARE ANIMALS BIOLOGICALLY SIMILAR TO HUMANS?

Essential understanding
✪ *It has been suggested that since some parts of our brain are very similar to the brain structures of animals, on some level our psychological functions should be equivalent. However, some researchers claim that the similarity can be deceitful, and the new additions have changed our psychological functions fundamentally. An example is the use of chunking in short-term memory. Although some separate brain structures in animals and humans may be similar, it is the way these structures are connected to the rest of the brain that makes a difference.*

Some theories have suggested that the human brain is a reflection of the evolution of the species and that genuinely "human" brain structures were added in the process of evolution on top of the more primitive structures that can be found in lower animals. This suggests that the human brain is very similar to that of animals.

However, evolution of the brain may have been more complex than simply building newer structures on top of the older ones.

Premack (2007) suggested that researchers should compare psychological functions as well as brain structure. He also claimed that we should focus on finding dissimilarities between animals and humans so that we better understand the limitations of generalizing from animal studies.

An example of comparing psychological functions in animals and humans (Premack 2007) is short-term memory in humans and chimpanzees. A chimpanzee has the same limit for the number of units it can remember without rehearsing (about seven units). However, unlike primates, humans are able to "chunk". You can train a chimpanzee to recognize letters such as B, M, W, X, B, O and X. However, although the capacity of short-term memory is the same, the sequence BMW XBOX will represent seven units of information for a chimpanzee and only two units for a human being. Arguably, chunking makes a qualitative difference to how memory works. Hence, short-term memory in humans and chimpanzees may be similar, but it is not equivalent.

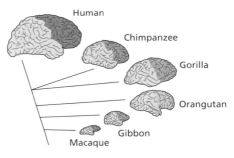

Figure 1.19 Human brain and animal brain

ADVANTAGES AND DISADVANTAGES OF WORKING WITH ANIMAL MODELS

Essential understanding
✪ *The major advantage of working with animal models is the possibility to carry out multiple experiments in highly controlled environments, often across generations. The major disadvantages are generalizability to humans, ecological validity and ethical issues.*

Some of the **advantages** of working with animal models include the following.

– In some ways humans and animals are biologically and genetically identical. This means that some

aspects of animal behaviour may be generalizable to humans.

– Studies with animal models have produced useful results. For example, many drugs were first discovered in animal studies and tested on humans later.

– Some animals (such as mice) have a short lifespan, which allows researchers to see how behaviour changes from generation to generation. This is especially helpful in genetic research.

- In animal research it is possible to control confounding variables more strictly than in research with humans. For example, the "knockout" technique allows researchers to selectively switch off one of the genes in the DNA sequence.
- Animal subjects are easily accessible, easy to handle and manage.

Some of the **disadvantages** include the following.
- As discussed (Premack 2007), even if animals and humans are similar biologically, they can still be different psychologically.
- Successful trials from animal research still need to be replicated with humans to be sure that results are generalizable. As a matter of fact, in biomedical research

(when developing new drugs) tests are often conducted in a hierarchy: first mice, then mammals, then great apes, then humans.
- Many studies that are successful in animals fail to achieve the same results with humans. The reasons are usually unclear. Such was the case with potential HIV treatments: 85 different vaccines worked well for primates, but none of them worked for humans (Bailey 2008).
- Animal studies tend to be strictly controlled laboratory experiments, which creates issues with ecological validity. There is a possibility that animals would behave differently in their natural habitat.
- There are ethical considerations related to experimentation with animals.

ETHICAL CONSIDERATIONS IN ANIMAL RESEARCH

Essential understanding
✪ *Ethical considerations in animal research are regulated by professional bodies such as the APA. Most ethical considerations revolve around making justified research choices, carefully monitoring potential pain inflicted on the animals, and getting approval from independent review teams.*

APA guidelines
The American Psychological Association (APA) has published guidelines on conducting research with animals that regulate every step of the research process. Some of the major guidelines are summarized below (American Psychological Association 2012).

Justified choices
- Any animal study should be clearly justified with a scientific purpose. It should either increase our knowledge or benefit humans or other animals.
- The chosen species must be the best choice for the research purpose.
- The minimum required number of animals must be used.

Inflicting pain
- It has to be assumed that whatever procedures cause pain in humans would cause pain in animals too.
- Researchers conducting the study must be familiar with the species-specific characteristics of normal behaviour so that they will be able to tell when the animal is stressed or unhealthy.

- Whenever possible, laboratory procedures must be designed in a way that minimizes animal discomfort.
- Whenever reasonable, researchers must first test the painful stimuli to be used with animals on themselves.
- If a research animal is observed to be in distress or chronic pain and this is not necessary for the purposes of the study, it should be euthanized.
- Animals reared in the laboratory must not be released into the wild.

Obtaining approval
- All animal research proposals must be submitted to the Ethics Committee prior to conducting the study.

BPS guidelines
The British Psychological Society (BPS) published a policy (British Psychological Society 2012) on the use of animals in psychology which is based on three principles (three Rs):
- replacement (animals should only be used when no alternative exists)
- reduction (the minimal necessary number of animals must be used)
- refinement (it must be ensured that experimental procedures cause minimal necessary distress in the animals).

EXAMPLES OF RESEARCH USING ANIMAL MODELS

Essential understanding
✪ *Examples of research using animal models that have already been discussed in this unit are Lashley (1929), Merzenich et al (1984), Weaver et al (2004) and Ferguson et al (2000). These studies can be used to illustrate both the value of animal models in psychology and ethical considerations in animal research. These studies also cover all parts of the biological approach to behaviour (brain and behaviour, hormones and pheromones and behaviour, genetics and behaviour).*

Examples from this unit
In this unit you have come across several research studies using animal models. These studies can be used to support all arguments in this topic—the value of animal models in psychology, whether animal research can provide insight into human behaviour, and ethical considerations in animal research.

Research study	Description
Lashley (1929)	Removing various portions of the cortex to investigate where the memory of the maze is localized. See "**1.1.1 Localization**".
Merzenich et al (1984)	Investigating cortical representations of the hand in adult owl monkeys (amputation of fingers). See "**1.1.1 Localization**".
Weaver et al (2004)	Investigating the epigenetic mechanism of how nurturing received by rats from their mothers affects the way their brain responds to stress later in life. See "**1.3.1 Genes and behaviour, genetic similarities**".
Ferguson et al (2000)	Investigating the role of oxytocin in social memory by studying oxytocin gene knockout mice models. See "**1.2.1 The influence of hormones on behaviour**".

Table 1.12

Coverage of topics

	Brain and behaviour	Hormones and pheromones and behaviour	Genetics and behaviour
Lashley (1929)	X		
Merzenich et al (1984)	X		
Weaver et al (2004)		X	X
Ferguson et al (2000)		X	X

Table 1.13

Insight into human behaviour and ethical considerations

	To what extent can the study provide an insight into human behaviour?	Ethical considerations
Lashley (1929)	Lashley's experiments with rats cannot be replicated with human participants for ethical reasons. However, the study was insightful because it suggested that some functions can be widely distributed in the brain. This idea can be used to explain findings from human studies (for example, Sperry and Gazzaniga).	Rats in the study were harmed because invasive surgery was performed on their brain. Such studies must ensure that this degree of suffering is absolutely necessary for the purposes of research, that potential benefits of research results justify the experimental procedure, that the minimum necessary number of animals is used, and that approval is obtained from the Ethics Committee.
Merzenich et al (1984)	Neuroplasticity in response to structural damage is observed in the human brain as well, but a direct experiment would not be possible for ethical reasons (that would require producing physical impairment in human subjects). So human research in this area is limited to case studies of people with injury. Cause-and-effect inferences cannot be made from case studies. Research with animal models helps test cause-effect hypotheses and in this sense provides further insight into human behaviour.	This research used a very invasive experimental manipulation which had a damaging and irreversible effect on the animals' lives (amputation of fingers). The technique used to measure the cortical response also involved inserting electrodes into the brain. Such research proposals must be carefully scrutinized by the Ethics Committee and only approved if potential gains outweigh the costs. Experimenters must make sure that animals are properly anaesthetized during the procedure and taken care of after the end of the study for the duration of their lives.
Weaver et al (2004)	This research is insightful because it gives birth to many interesting hypotheses about human behaviour. Potentially it is also very useful. It suggests that effects of bad parenting may be epigenetic. By analogy, one can suggest that effects of poverty on cognitive development, for example, may also be epigenetic. If this is so, potentially we can invent drugs that will reverse these effects (imagine an "anti-bad-mother pill"). This has led researchers to construct many ingenious research studies to test similar hypotheses with human subjects.	Animals in this study were laboratory-bred in a special way to obtain the necessary genotype. Epigenetic tests were invasive—they required obtaining a sample of cells from the brain. Stress tests where animals were placed in a narrow tube that restrained their movements were also harmful for the rats, as were the increased levels of stress hormones. Such studies must be carefully justified and approved by the Ethics Committee. If approval is obtained, researchers must be accountable for humane handling of the animal subjects.
Ferguson et al (2000)	As a knockout study, it provides a very direct test to the role of oxytocin in behaviour. In humans we can only temporarily increase the level of oxytocin, so research is limited to short-term effects. With animal models these effects can be studied over the lifespan of the animal.	Mice were specially bred in this study. They were also cross-fostered. In fact, female oxytocin gene knockout mice do not lactate, so they cannot foster offspring. Ethical considerations that apply in this study are similar to Weaver et al (2004).

Table 1.14

Topics

2.1 Cognitive processing
2.1.1 Models of memory

DEFINITIONS

- **Articulatory suppression**—a research technique where participants are required to repeat a sequence of sounds while at the same time performing the experimental task

- **Capacity**—the number of units of information that can be held in a memory store

- **Dual task technique**—a research technique where participants are exposed simultaneously to two sets of stimuli, either of the same or different modalities

- **Duration**—the amount of time for which information can be held in a memory store

- **Heuristic model (theory)**—a model or theory that inspires new hypotheses in a certain area

- **Memory**—a cognitive process of encoding, storing and retrieving information

- **Parsimonious model**—a model that can explain a lot of observations with only a limited number of components

- **Phonological similarity effect**—a memory phenomenon where stimuli that have a similar pattern of articulation are more likely to be confused in memory, even when they are presented visually

- **Primacy effect**—a memory phenomenon where the first several words on the list are remembered better than words from the middle of the list

- **Recency effect**—a memory phenomenon where the last several words on the list are remembered better than words from the middle of the list

- **Word length effect**—a memory phenomenon where the estimated capacity of short-term memory depends on the length of the words on the list presented to the participants

ESSENTIAL UNDERSTANDING

The multi-store memory model: theory

Memory is a basic cognitive process used to encode, store and retrieve information. There exist many models in psychology to describe human memory. A well-known classic is the multi-store model of memory by Atkinson and Shiffrin (1968), that states the following.

- Memory consists of three separate components: sensory memory store, short-term memory (STM) store and long-term memory (LTM) store.
- Information flows from sensory memory to long-term memory if certain conditions are met: attention and rote rehearsal. See **Atkinson and Shiffrin (1968)**.

Research

Although the model is quite simple, there are many aspects that require testing, such as the idea that the three stores are in fact separate or the idea that rehearsal is necessary and sufficient for the transfer of information from STM to LTM. As a result, no single study can test the model in its entirety: a collective effort by researchers is needed for the task.

An example is the study of Glanzer and Cunitz (1966) that supported the notion that STM and LTM are two separate memory stores. This conclusion is based on the disappearance of the latency effect (but not the primacy effect) after an interference task. See **Glanzer and Cunitz (1966)**.

Evaluation

The model has been criticized for reasons of oversimplification and failing to explain some memory phenomena. At the same time, it needs to be understood that there is a trade-off between simplicity of the model and its explanatory power. The multi-store model of memory was parsimonious and heuristic, and it prompted many insightful research studies. It is widely accepted today, but other models are used to elaborate on certain components. See "Evaluation of the multi-store model of memory".

The working memory model: theory

The working memory model was proposed by Baddeley and Hitch (1974). It was built to further elaborate on the structure of STM. The model includes four components in the structure of working memory (the visuospatial sketchpad, the phonological loop, the central executive and the episodic buffer). See **Baddeley and Hitch (1974)**.

Research

The working memory model explained some findings that the multi-store model did not. Examples are:

- the phonological similarity effect (discovered by Conrad and Hull in 1964)
- the word length effect (Baddeley, Thomson, Buchanan 1975).

Both these effects could be explained by the introduction of the articulatory rehearsal component. It was further demonstrated that both effects disappear when articulatory suppression is used and material is presented visually (Murray 1968; Baddeley, Lewis, Vallar 1984; Baddeley, Thomson, Buchanan 1975). This evidence supports the idea that visual and auditory information is processed in separate stores within working memory. See "**Support for the working memory model**".

Evaluation

The working memory model has greater explanatory power, but it is more complicated than the multi-store model of memory. This increased complexity means that it is more difficult to conduct empirical tests of the model. See "**Evaluation of the working memory model**".

THEORY: ATKINSON AND SHIFFRIN (1968)—THE MULTI-STORE MODEL OF MEMORY

Essential understanding

✪ *The multi-store model presents the structure of memory as consisting of three separate stores and the process as a unidirectional flow of information from one store to another.*

Components

In this model human memory consists of three components ("stores"):

- sensory memory store
- short-term memory (STM) store
- long-term memory (LTM) store.

Characteristics

Each of these components is characterized by:

- duration (how long information can be kept in this store)
- capacity (how much information can be kept there)
- conditions necessary for information to move from this store to the next one.

Component	Duration	Capacity	Conditions required to move to the next store
Sensory memory	This depends on the modality, but is very short: 1 second for visual stimuli, 2–5 seconds for auditory stimuli.	Everything in the perceptual field	Attention (if a unit of information is attended to, it does not decay but moves to short-term memory).
Short-term memory (STM)	This depends on the modality, but generally is no longer than 30 seconds; rehearsal increases the duration of STM.	7±2 chunks of information (Miller 1956). A chunk is a meaningful combination of units, for example, the letters C, A, N, D, L and E can be combined into one word and this way six information units may be turned into one chunk.	Rehearsal (it makes information stay in the short-term memory longer and eventually the memory trace gets consolidated and the information enters long-term memory).
Long-term memory (LTM)	The limit has not been established; potentially longer than the duration of a human life.	The limit has not been established; potentially it is virtually unlimited.	N/A

Table 2.1 The multi-store model

Process

According to the multi-store model, information travels from sensory memory through STM to LTM. Rehearsal (that is, mental repetition of the stimulus) is the main means of transferring information into LTM, where it can be stored indefinitely. However, not all information that is stored in LTM is easily retrievable.

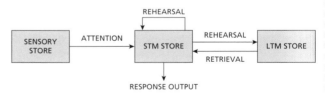

Figure 2.1 Multi-store memory model

Source: https://ceirepsych.wordpress.com/2012/09/23/multi-store-model-atkinson-and-shiffrin-1968/

Essential understanding
✪ *Although the model is simple, there are many aspects that require testing. The whole model in its entirety cannot be tested in a single study—it is a task for a research programme. Just like any other model of a complex mental process, the multi-store model of memory includes many aspects that generate many different predictions. All these predictions must be tested separately in a series of research studies, and information from all this research must be combined to inform further development of the model.*

Some of the aspects of the multi-store model of memory that require testing are:
- the number of memory stores
- the memory stores being separate from each other
- rehearsal being necessary and sufficient for the transfer of information from STM to LTM
- direction of information flow: the model suggests that it flows in one direction from sensory memory to LTM, but can there be a reverse process?

One example of a research study that (partially) supported the model is the study of **Glanzer and Cunitz (1966)**.

RESEARCH   **Glanzer and Cunitz (1966, experiment 2)—primacy and recency effect**

Essential understanding
✪ *The fact that inclusion of a filler task results in disappearance of recency effect but not primacy effect supports the idea that STM and LTM are two separate memory stores.*

Aim
To investigate the serial position effect with and without interference from a filler activity. Serial position effect is the tendency to recall the first and the last items on a list better than items in the middle.

Method
Experiment; repeated measures design.

Participants
46 army-enlisted men.

Procedure
A series of 15-word lists was read out to participants. After hearing all the words on the list participants were required to do a free-recall task. There were three conditions:
- a free-recall task immediately after hearing the words on the list
- a filler activity (counting out loud backwards from a random number for 10 seconds), then free recall
- the same filler activity, but for 30 seconds.

Each participant was given 15 lists, 5 for each of the 3 conditions. The order of the conditions was random. The dependent variable (DV) was the proportion of words correctly recalled, separately for each of the 15 positions of the word on the list (so you can say that there were 15 DVs).

Results
- In the condition without a filler task, both the aspects of the serial position effect could be observed: primacy effect (participants were better at remembering words at the start of the list) and recency effect (participants were also better at remembering words at the end of the list).
- In the condition with the filler task the primacy effect stayed, but the recency effect disappeared—more so in the 30-second condition than in the 10-second condition.

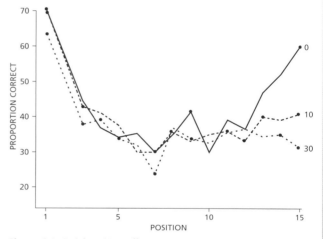

Figure 2.2 Serial position effect

Source: Glanzer and Cunitz (1966: 358)

Conclusion
The results fit well into the multi-store model of memory, in particular the following ideas.
- STM and LTM are two separate memory stores.
- Information moves from STM to LTM if it is rehearsed, but gradually decays if it is not.
- The duration of STM is around 30 seconds.

As participants hear words on the list one by one, they may start rehearsing them subvocally. As they are getting closer to the middle of the list it becomes impossible to repeat all the words, so the first words on the list are repeated more often, and they enter LTM. That is why primacy effect does not disappear even after the interference task.

When participants recall words immediately after the presentation of the list, the last several words on the list may be easy to remember because they have just entered STM. With the presence of the interference task when rehearsal is suppressed, these traces decay. That is why recency effect disappears in the condition with the interference task.

EVALUATION OF THE MULTI-STORE MODEL OF MEMORY

Essential understanding
✪ *The model is parsimonious and heuristic, but it has been criticized for its simplicity and inability to explain some memory phenomena.*

Criticism
- The model emphasizes structure over process. It does not pay enough attention to how information flows between the three components.
- The only mechanism that enables transfer of information from STM to LTM in this model is rote rehearsal. This is an oversimplification. It was shown in further research that apart from rote rehearsal people can use more elaborate structures such as semantic encoding (Craik, Lockhart 1972).

- The model only explains the flow of information in one direction, from sensory memory to LTM. Arguably, though, information can also flow in the opposite direction.
- It has been argued that both STM and LTM are not unitary stores and should be further subdivided. Some of the observed memory phenomena do not fit into the idea of unitary stores.

Strengths
It has been one of the most influential models of memory that proved capable of explaining multiple observed phenomena. The model is parsimonious—it can explain a lot of observed data with only a few components. The model is also highly heuristic—it inspired numerous research studies.

THEORY

BADDELEY AND HITCH (1974)—THE WORKING MEMORY MODEL

Essential understanding
✪ *This model is a zoom-in on the structure of STM. It includes four components that interact with each other.*

Background
Essentially, this model is a zoom-in on the structure of STM. The researchers felt this model was needed because there were some findings that were not entirely consistent with the multi-store model of memory, where it is assumed that STM is a unitary store.

The model: working memory in this model consists of four components each having a different function.
- **The visuospatial sketchpad ("the inner eye")**: its function is to hold visual and spatial information.
- **The phonological loop**: its function is to hold auditory information. It is further subdivided into two parts.
  - **"The inner ear"**: this holds sound in a passive manner.
  - **Articulatory rehearsal component ("the inner voice")**, which is rewords thus increasing their duration in memory. The inner voice can also turn visual speech information into sounds (for example, we subvocally pronounce words as we read them).

This way the inner voice can change the modality of perceived speech material (from visual to auditory).
- **The central executive** is responsible for the allocation of resources between the visuospatial sketchpad and the phonological loop.
- **The episodic buffer** (added in a later version of the model) integrates information from the visuospatial sketchpad and the phonological loop and links it to LTM.

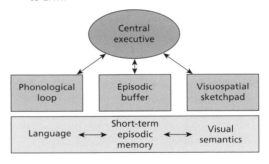

Figure 2.3 Working memory model

Source: https://jonokowal.wordpress.com/2012/10/01/the-working-memory-model/

RESEARCH   Support for the working memory model

Essential understanding
✪ *The working memory model provided an explanation for some phenomena that the multi-store model could not explain, for example, the phonological similarity effect, the word length effect, and the effects of articulatory suppression.*

Findings that could not be explained by the multi-store model of memory
- **The phonological similarity effect**: this was first discovered by **Conrad and Hull in 1964**. They showed that lists of phonologically similar letters (such as B, D, P) are more difficult to remember than lists of letters that

do not sound similar (such as P, R, X). Presumably, this is because acoustically encoded traces of rhyming letters are easier to confuse with each other. However, the effect also appeared when the stimulus was presented in writing.
- **The word length effect—Baddeley, Thompson and Buchanan (1975)**: this showed that the capacity of STM is greater for short words than for long ones. There is nothing in the multi-store model of memory to explain why STM capacity should change from the standard 7 ± 2 units depending on the length of the words.

Explanation of these findings

Introducing the articulatory rehearsal component (the inner voice) in the working memory model explained these effects.

- The phonological similarity effect may be explained by assuming that all speech material (even when in writing) is subvocally pronounced and encoded as an articulation pattern. Letters with similar articulation patterns are more easily confused with each other.
- The word length effect is explained because articulation patterns of longer words are also longer. In a given amount of time you can subvocally pronounce fewer long words than short words.

Further testing was done by suppressing the inner voice. If the explanation is correct, suppressing the inner voice (so that speech information is processed visually, for example) should result in disappearance of both the phonological similarity effect and the word length effect. This was observed in a number of experiments that used **articulatory suppression**.

Further research: effects of articulatory suppression

Articulatory suppression is a technique that requires participants to repeat a sequence of sounds while at the same time performing the experimental task. This is used to block the "inner voice" and see how human memory performs without it.

- It was shown that the phonological similarity effect disappears under articulatory suppression when material is presented visually (Murray 1968; Baddeley, Lewis, Vallar 1984). In terms of the working memory model, information cannot enter the phonological loop, so it goes to the visuospatial sketchpad instead, where it is stored visually. It makes no difference for the visuospatial sketchpad whether or not letters sound similar.
- It was also shown that when articulation is suppressed, the word length effect disappears with visual presentation (Baddeley, Thomson, Buchanan 1975). By the same logic, information cannot enter the phonological loop through the inner voice, so it enters the visuospatial sketchpad instead. When it is processed visually, it does not matter anymore how long the word is.

This evidence supports the idea that visual and auditory information is processed in separate stores within working memory.

EVALUATION OF THE WORKING MEMORY MODEL

Essential understanding

✪ *The working memory model has large explanatory power, but this comes at the cost of complexity.*

Strengths

The strength of the working memory model is its explanatory power. It allows us to explain a range of observed memory phenomena that cannot be explained by the multi-store model, for example, the phonological similarity effect, the word length effect and the disappearance of both under articulatory suppression.

Limitations

The major limitation of the model is its complexity as this makes it more difficult to test the model empirically in its entirety. Also the model only involves STM and does not include other memory structures such as sensory memory or LTM.

2.1.2 Schema theory

- **Encoding**—a process of memory; transferring information from sensory organs to internal mental structures (such as LTM)
- **Mental representation**—a reflection of an object or an event in the mind

- **Retrieval**—a process of memory; extracting information from the long-term store when it is needed
- **Schema**—a stable, deeply rooted mental representation that can influence our knowledge, beliefs and expectations
- **Scripts**—schemas about sequences of actions or events

ESSENTIAL UNDERSTANDING

What is a schema?

Cognitive schemas (or schemata) are mental representations that organize our knowledge, beliefs and expectations. A "mental representation" is a very broad concept that can be applied to practically everything in the mind, but only the most stable and deeply rooted mental representations can influence our knowledge, beliefs and expectations.

How do schemas influence memory?

- Schemas can influence memory at all its stages, both encoding and retrieval.

- That schemas can influence the encoding of information in memory has been demonstrated in the study of Bransford and Johnson (1972). They showed that a visual context provided prior to reading a text passage doubles the rate of recall of ideas from that passage. See **Bransford and Johnson (1972)**.
- That schemas can also influence retrieval of information from memory (once it is already there) has been demonstrated in the study by Anderson and Pichert (1978). They showed that a change in perspective when

recalling a text passage results in recalling more units of information relevant to this new perspective. See **Anderson and Pichert (1978)**.

Types of schemas

Schemas are distinguished based on what aspect of reality they represent. Below are examples of types of schema.

- **Social schemas** (mental representations about groups of people) create the foundation for stereotypes—see "**3.1.3 Stereotypes**" in "**Unit 3 Sociocultural approach to behaviour**". Darley and Gross (1983) demonstrated that schemas about someone's socio-economic status (SES) influence how that person's behaviour will be interpreted. See **Darley and Gross (1983)**.

- **Scripts** (mental representations about sequences of events) enable us to make sense of sequential data. Bower, Black and Turner (1979) demonstrated that scripts can be used to fill in the gaps in memory of sequential events. See **Bower, Black and Turner (1979)**.

- **Self-schemas** (mental representations about ourselves) are generalized representations of ourselves. Aaron Beck, in his cognitive theory of depression, suggested that negative self-schemas were the driving factors behind development of depression. See "**4.2.3 Explanations for disorders: Cognitive explanations for depression**" in "**Unit 4 Abnormal psychology**".

RESEARCH   Bransford and Johnson (1972)—schemas influence encoding

Essential understanding

✪ *Providing a full context prior to an unfamiliar text passage leads to better recall of the idea units contained in this passage. Arguably, this happens because a mental representation (schema) is created and the new ideas are then linked to this schema, making encoding more effective.*

Aim

To investigate the effect of context on comprehension and memory of text passages.

Method

Experiment; independent measures design.

Participants

50 male and female high school students who volunteered to participate in the experiment.

Procedure

Participants heard a tape-recorded passage and were required to recall it as accurately as they could, writing down as many ideas as possible. The passage was as follows.

If the balloons popped, the sound wouldn't be able to carry since everything would be too far away from the correct

floor. A closed window would also prevent the sound from carrying, since most buildings tend to be well insulated. Since the whole operation depends on a steady flow of electricity, a break in the middle of the wire would also cause problems. Of course, the fellow could shout, but the human voice is not loud enough to carry that far. An additional problem is that a string could break on the instrument. Then there could be no accompaniment to the message. It is clear that the best situation would involve less distance. Then there would be fewer potential problems. With face to face contact, the least number of things could go wrong". (Bransford, Johnson 1972)

There were five conditions (groups of participants).

- No context (1): participants heard the passage once.
- No context (2): participants heard the passage twice.
- Context before: prior to hearing the passage participants were given a context picture.
- Context after: the context picture was given after participants already heard the passage.
- Partial context: participants were given a context picture prior to hearing the passage, but the picture only contained the elements mentioned in the passage without showing how they operate together.

Figure 2.4
Source: Bransford and Johnson (1972)

Results

The passage contained 14 idea units in total. Table 2.2 shows average ideas recall in the five groups.

Group	Average ideas recalled
No context (1)	3.6
No context (2)	3.8
Context before	8.0
Context after	3.6
Partial context	4.0

Table 2.2 Results from Bransford and Johnson (1972)

Conclusion

The "context before" condition was the only one that clearly made a difference in terms of participants' ability to comprehend the passage and recall it correctly. This can be explained by schema theory: the full context picture creates a mental representation which then influences the way information is encoded in memory. Idea units encountered in the passage are linked with the schema and in this way encoding is enhanced.

RESEARCH   Anderson and Pichert (1978)—schemas influence retrieval

Essential understanding

✪ *A change of perspective when recalling a text passage results in an additional 7.1% of information being recalled, which supports the idea that schema influences retrieval of information from memory.*

Aim

To investigate the influence of schema on the retrieval of information from long-term memory.

Method

Experiment; mixed design.

Participants

Introductory psychology students who were participating in order to fulfill a course requirement.

Procedure

1. Participants were assigned either a homebuyer or a burglar perspective.

2. They were then asked to read a text passage about a house where two boys were staying to skip school. The passage contained a total of 73 ideas, some of them being potentially interesting to a burglar and some to a real estate agent.

3. Participants were given a filler task, then asked to reproduce the story in writing as accurately as possible.

4. Participants were given another filler task, then some were required to change the initial perspective (from a homebuyer to a burglar or vice versa). Other participants kept the initial perspective.

5. Participants had to reproduce the story one more time, without reading it again.

Results

- For the first recall, participants who had the burglar perspective recalled more burglar-relevant information and participants who had the homebuyer perspective recalled more homebuyer-relevant information.

- Participants who changed perspective recalled more information (an additional 7.1%) important to the second perspective but unimportant to the first. Note that they did not read the passage for the second time, so before the change of perspective this additional information had been encoded, but had not been retrieved. Change of perspective influenced retrieval, not encoding.

Conclusion

Perspective in this situation is a type of schema. The study supports the idea that schemas influence the process of retrieval of already stored information from memory.

RESEARCH   Darley and Gross (1983)—effects of social schemas

Essential understanding

✪ *Social schemas influence interpretation of ambiguous social information.*

Procedure

Two groups of participants watched the same video of a child (a girl) taking an academic test. One group of participants was led to believe that the girl came from a low SES background, while the other group believed that the girl had a high SES background (that is, came from a rich family). Participants were required to rate the academic performance of the girl in the video.

Results

Results showed that the ratings were significantly higher in the group of participants who believed that the child came from a high SES background.

Conclusion

It was concluded that SES-associated schemas influenced the way participants perceived and interpreted an ambiguous social situation.

RESEARCH   Bower, Black and Turner (1979)—effects of scripts

Essential understanding

✪ *Generalized mental representations (scripts) underlie our interpretation and memory of sequential events.*

Procedure

The researchers used short texts describing sequences of actions, for example, visiting the dentist (having a toothache, making an appointment, checking in with the receptionist, and so on). Some of the steps in these descriptions were missing.

Results

It was demonstrated that when recalling the texts, participants would fill in the gaps and "remember" actions that were not actually in the text. For example, they would recall checking in with the receptionist even if this was skipped in the text.

Conclusion

This shows that participants encoded the text based on an underlying script.

2.1.3 Thinking and decision-making

- **Decision-making strategy**—a specific algorithm that enables one to solve a multi-attribute choice problem
- **Descriptive models**—models of thinking and decision-making that describe how people actually think and make decisions, taking into account irrational factors
- **Macro-scale models**—models that focus on observable actions and their predictors

- **Micro-scale models**—models that focus on the transient process of making a decision (what goes on in a person's mind when he or she is making a decision)
- **Multi-attribute problem**—a choice problem involving choosing between several alternatives (options) each characterized by several attributes (parameters)
- **Normative models**—models of thinking and decision-making that describe the rules of rational thinking and decision-making

---

ESSENTIAL UNDERSTANDING

Thinking and decision-making

- Thinking is the cognitive process responsible for modifying previously encoded information. Unlike other cognitive processes, thinking results in obtaining new information from existing information.
- Decision-making is the cognitive process of choosing between given alternatives. It always involves a choice.
- Thinking and decision-making are closely connected because in order to make a choice you need to use thinking (for example, breaking alternatives down into smaller parts or aspects). So thinking is a prerequisite of decision-making.

Models of thinking and decision-making: two types

In the variety of models of thinking and decision-making we can broadly distinguish two categories—normative models and descriptive models. Normative models describe thinking the way it should be, while descriptive models describe thinking as it is. See "**Normative models and descriptive models**".

The theory of planned behaviour (TPB)

- The TPB sees decision-making as actions that result from behavioural intentions which, in turn, are determined by: attitudes, perceived social norms and perceived behavioural control. It is a macro-level theory: it looks at actions as visible results of decision-making processes. See "**Ajzen (1985)—The theory of planned behaviour (TPB)**".

- One of the ways to test the TPB is to establish its predictive validity: the extent to which the combination of variables postulated in the theory actually predicts real-life behaviour.
- Albarracin *et al* (2001) investigated predictive validity of the TPB in the domain of condom use. They found a 0.51 correlation between intention and behaviour in their meta-analysis. **See Albarracin *et al* (2001)**.

The adaptive decision-maker framework

The adaptive decision-maker framework (Payne, Bettman, Johnson 1993) is a micro-level cognitive model—it zooms in on the transient internal process of making a decision. The theory states the following.

- People possess a toolbox of strategies they can use to make decisions.
- The choice of strategy is dictated by four meta-goals: maximizing decision accuracy; minimizing cognitive effort; minimizing the experience of negative emotion; maximizing the ease of justification. In this way the theory claims that factors other than accuracy must be integrated directly into a model of decision-making. See **Payne, Bettman and Johnson (1993)**.
- Luce, Bettman and Payne (1997) provided support to the model by demonstrating that in a situation that is emotionally pressing, people tend to process information more extensively, but at the same time avoid emotionally difficult trade-offs. See **Luce, Bettman and Payne (1997)**.

- **Normative models** describe "ideal" thinking and decision-making that result in "correct" choices. These are models of what thinking and decision-making should be. Examples of normative models are formal logic, statistical theory of probability, normative utility theory. Formal logic describes correct thinking patterns. Statistical theory of probability may be used as a normative model in formulating predictions. Normative utility theory tells us what is right and wrong in choosing between economically attractive alternatives. It uses monetary value to define utility.
- **Descriptive models** describe the processes of thinking and decision-making as they are. It is impossible for people to use normative models to make every decision because normative models require too many resources and also assume that we are fully informed, while decisions in real life are usually made under uncertainty (incomplete information) and limited time.

Psychology focuses on descriptive models because what interests us is a prediction of people's decisions, with all their biases and fallacies. However, normative models are used as a background for this research, because we look at how people deviate from normative models and try to determine whether or not the deviations are predictable.

AJZEN (1985)—THE THEORY OF PLANNED BEHAVIOUR (TPB)

Essential understanding
✪ *Actions are determined by behavioural intentions which, in their turn, are determined by a number of subjective beliefs.*

Macro-level
The theory of planned behaviour is a macro-level cognitive model: it looks at behaviour at a large scale, on the visible level of whether an action is performed or not.

The theory
Behavioural intention determines effort: the stronger it is, the harder we try to implement the behaviour. Behavioural intention is determined by three factors:

- attitudes—individual perceptions of the behaviour (positive or negative)
- subjective norms—perceived social pressure regarding this behaviour (acceptable or unacceptable)
- perceived behavioural control—the perception of one's ability to perform the action.

In other words, the theory holds that if your attitude to a particular behaviour is positive, you believe this behaviour to be socially acceptable, and you believe you are able to perform the action, this will create a behavioural intention. If the intention is strong enough, the action will be performed.

Research
- The theory of planned behaviour requires the researcher to have self-report measures of four predictor variables (attitudes, norms, behavioural control, intention) and one target variable (future behaviour itself).
- The theory predicts that there should be a correlation between: attitudes and intention; behavioural control and intention; subjective norms and intention; intention and behaviour. However, behaviour should not be significantly correlated directly with attitudes, subjective norms or perceived control.
- If the theory provides a good fit to empirical data, it should have high **predictive validity**: the four predictor variables collectively should be able to predict the target variable (future behaviour) with high probability.

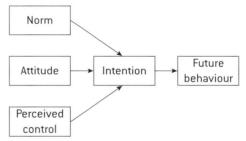

Figure 2.5 The model for the TPB

RESEARCH   Albarracin *et al* (2001)—a meta-analysis of TPB as a model of condom use

Essential understanding
✪ *The TPB fits well into observed behaviour in the domain of condom use.*

Aim
To investigate predictive validity of the theory of planned behaviour for people's decisions to use or not to use condoms (this is essential to enhance prevention of sexually transmitted diseases).

Method
A meta-analysis.

Participants
42 published and unpublished research papers with a total of 96 data sets.

Procedure
All data sets from published research were combined in a single large data matrix, which was then used to analyse the fit of the model of planned behaviour.

Results
- TPB turned out to be a successful predictor of condom use. The correlation between intention and behaviour in this model was 0.51.

- There were significant correlations between behavioural intentions (on the one hand) and norms, attitudes and perceived control (on the other hand).

Conclusion
It was concluded that people are more likely to use condoms when they have formed an intention to do so. In their turn, these intentions are based on attitudes, subjective norms and perceived behavioural control. On a broader scale, the study also confirms predictive validity of the TPB in the specific domain of condom use.

PAYNE, BETTMAN AND JOHNSON (1993)—THE ADAPTIVE DECISION-MAKER FRAMEWORK

Essential understanding
✪ *People possess a toolbox of decision-making strategies, and the choice is guided by emotion-related goals (such as minimizing negative emotion in the process of making a decision) as well as an attempt to achieve accuracy.*

Micro-level
The adaptive decision-maker framework is a micro-level cognitive model. It zooms in on the process of making a decision and looks at what is happening in a person's mind when he or she is making the decision.

A typical decision-making scenario
This model suggests that people have a toolbox of strategies that they use in various decision-making situations involving making a choice between several alternatives compared against several attributes.

Alternatives	Attributes		
	Quality of food	Quality of service	Location
Restaurant 1	…	…	…
Restaurant 2	…	…	…
Restaurant 3	…	…	…

Table 2.3 Examples of alternatives and attributes

The strategies in the toolbox are summarized in Table 2.4.

Strategy	Alternative-based or attribute-based?	Process
Weighted additive strategy (WADD)	Alternative-based	Calculate the weighted sum (utility) of attributes for each alternative, choose the alternative with the highest weighted sum.
Lexicographic strategy (LEX)	Attribute-based	Choose the most important attribute and then the option that has the best value on this attribute.
Satisficing strategy (SAT)	Alternative-based	Determine a cut-off point for every attribute (no less than…). Find the option that exceeds the cut-off points on all attributes.
Elimination by aspects (EBA)	Attribute-based	Choose the most important attribute and eliminate all the options that do not satisfy your requirements for this attribute. Choose the second most important attribute and eliminate more options. Continue until only one option is left.

Table 2.4 Strategies in the toolbox

All strategies may be divided into alternative-based and attribute-based.
- In **alternative-based strategies** (WADD and SAT) you select an alternative and compare attributes within it.
- In **attribute-based strategies** (LEX and EBA) you select an attribute and compare alternatives against it.

It is important to know that alternative-based strategies are emotionally tougher, because they involve more trade-offs (an alternative often combines some attractive attributes with unattractive ones).

Meta-goals
According to the adaptive decision-maker framework, what strategy a person selects from the toolbox is guided by four meta-goals.

Meta-goal	Which strategy to choose
Maximizing decision accuracy	WADD
Minimizing cognitive effort	LEX
Minimizing the experience of negative emotion	Choose any attribute-based strategy (and avoid alternative-based strategies): LEX, EBA
Maximizing the ease of justification	This depends on the context, but most often SAT and EBA are chosen.

Table 2.5 The four meta-goals

Essential understanding

✪ *Emotional variables should be directly incorporated into the model of decision-making because it can be demonstrated that decision-making adapts to emotion.*

Aim

The researchers predicted that, if decision-making really adapts to emotion, people who make choices involving emotionally difficult trade-offs will:

- process information more extensively (because they want to make an accurate decision), and at the same time
- choose strategies that allow them to avoid emotionally difficult trade-offs.

Method

Experiment; independent measures design.

Participants

27 undergraduate students.

Procedure

Subjects assumed the role of members of a charity and were required to decide which of five candidate children would get financial support. Each of the five children was described in terms of five attributes (such as living conditions and family size). All attributes were relevant to the decision-maker.

Participants were split into two groups.

- Higher-emotion group, in which participants were told that the other four children were not likely to receive help from anywhere else.
- Lower-emotion group, in which participants were told that the four remaining children were likely to receive help elsewhere at a later time.

Measurement of DVs was done with "Mouselab", a software in which information was presented in the form of a table (children × attributes), but information in the cells was hidden and participants had to click the mouse on a particular cell to reveal that information. The software recorded the order in which participants opened cells. Occurrence of two types of transitions was counted. The types were:

- alternative-based transitions (after opening cell A, open a cell for a different attribute but the same alternative)
- attribute-based transitions (after opening cell A, open a cell for the same attribute but a different alternative).

Results

- Participants in the higher-emotion group spent more time on the task and opened a larger number of cells in total, which shows that they were considering the decision more carefully.
- Participants in the higher-emotion group engaged more frequently in attribute-based transitions. As you know, attribute-based strategies involve less emotionally difficult trade-offs. This shows that participants were avoiding experiencing negative emotion in the process of making the decision.

Conclusion

Predictions of the adaptive decision-maker framework were confirmed so it may be concluded that emotional variables need to be incorporated directly into a model of decision-making because the strategies of decision-making are not only influenced by, but directly adapt to, task-related emotion.

2.2 Reliability of cognitive processes

2.2.1 Reconstructive memory

DEFINITIONS

- **Misleading question**—one of the forms that post-event information can take; misleading questions suggest information that is not entirely consistent with what actually happened

- **Post-event information**—information about an event provided (directly or indirectly) after the event already occurred

- **Recall**—a form of retrieval, retrieval of required information from memory in the absence of any prompts

- **Recognition**—a form of retrieval that involves identifying an object as previously seen

- **Reconstructive memory**—the theory that views memory to be an active process of recreation of past events as opposed to a passive process of retrieval

ESSENTIAL UNDERSTANDING

The theory of reconstructive memory

- There are cases of memory unreliability, such as memory distortions, when you remember things that did not actually happen (or not exactly the way they happened).
- These phenomena can be explained by the **theory of reconstructive memory** which suggests that memory is not passive retrieval of information from a long-term store, but rather an active recreation of the event in the mind every time it is remembered. The theory recognizes two kinds of information: information obtained during

the perception of the event and external post-event information. Over time, information from these two sources can get integrated to the extent that we are unable to tell them apart.

Supporting research

- A classic study supporting this theory is Loftus and Palmer (1974), where the researchers demonstrated that in an eyewitness situation people's accounts of an event can be influenced by slight differences in the way the question is formulated. See **Loftus and Palmer (1974)**.

- The researchers also discussed and tested two potential explanations: genuine memory change or simple response bias (when the memory is unchanged, but participants tweak their responses based on what they think is expected of them).
- The phenomenon of reconstructive memory was found both for recall tasks and recognition tasks, both for verbal information and visual information. For example, Loftus, Miller and Burns (1978) in an experiment involving a recognition task found that misleading verbal post-event information can integrate with visual memory and distort it. See **Loftus, Miller and Burns (1978)**.

- One criticism of research in this area is lack of ecological validity. Yuille and Cutshall (1986) conducted a study in naturalistic settings (a real-life gun store robbery) and found that misleading questions had very little effect on how eyewitnesses recalled the events, thus contradicting the theory of reconstructive memory. See **Yuille and Cutshall (1986)**.
- However, results of Yuille and Cutshall's study may be a reflection of a completely different memory mechanism—flashbulb memory.

RESEARCH   Loftus and Palmer (1974)—the eyewitness study

Essential understanding

✪ *In an eyewitness situation misleading post-event information can integrate with memory of the event and alter it.*

Aim

To investigate if memory can be altered by misleading post-event information (in an eyewitness situation).

Method

Experiment; independent measures design.

Participants

University students, convenience samples. Experiment 1—45 students, 5 groups; experiment 2—150 students, 3 groups.

Procedure

Experiment 1: participants were shown recordings of traffic accidents, then they were given a questionnaire with a number of questions about the accident they had just witnessed. Only one of these questions was critical for the research: "About how fast were the cars going when they hit each other?"

The five groups in experiment 1 only differed in the emotional intensity of the verb used in that sentence. The verbs used were: group 1 "smashed"; group 2 "collided"; group 3 "bumped"; group 4 "hit"; group 5 "contacted". The independent variable (IV) was therefore the misleading post-event information, operationalized as the emotional intensity of the verb in the question. The dependent variable (DV) was the speed estimate.

Experiment 2: participants were shown a film of a car accident. After the film they filled out a questionnaire. Three groups of participants got three different versions of the critical question: group 1 "smashed into each other"; group 2 "hit each other"; group 3: no critical question (control group).

A week later, participants were given another questionnaire that consisted of 10 questions and included one critical yes/no question: "Did you see any broken glass?" The IV in experiment 2 was therefore the emotional intensity of the verb in the leading question and the DV was whether or not participants reported having seen broken glass. In reality there was no broken glass.

Results

Experiment 1: the mean speed estimates varied significantly for the five groups (see Table 2.6).

Verb	Speed estimate (mph)
Smashed	40.5
Collided	39.3
Bumped	38.1
Hit	34.0
Contacted	31.8

Table 2.6 Findings from Loftus and Palmer (1974)—speed estimates

Experiment 2: emotional intensity of the verb in the leading question influenced the probability that participants would report seeing broken glass in the video (see Table 2.7).

Verb	% of participants saying "yes" to the question about broken glass
Smashed	32%
Hit	14%
No critical question	12%

Table 2.7 Findings from Loftus and Palmer (1974)—broken glass

Conclusion

Experiment 1 clearly demonstrated that misleading post-event information influences eyewitness accounts of an event. However, there could be two potential explanations for this finding.

- There could be genuine memory change (the question causes a change in the participant's representation of the event).
- There could be response bias (memory of the event does not change, but verbs of a higher emotional intensity causes participants to give higher estimates when they are uncertain).

Experiment 2 was conducted to rule out the second explanation. Since it demonstrated that verbs of a higher emotional intensity may cause participants to recall events that never occurred, researchers concluded that we should reject the response bias explanation and accept genuine memory change.

Essential understanding
✪ *Effects of misleading verbal post-event information can also be seen in visual recognition tasks.*

Aim
To investigate whether verbal post-event information can be integrated with visual information obtained originally.

Method
Experiment, independent measures, 2 × 2 experimental design.

Participants
195 university students.

Procedure
Participants were shown a series of slides depicting a car (a red Datsun) that was approaching an intersection with a sign, then turned right and knocked down a pedestrian. The critical slide was the one showing the sign at the intersection.
- For half the participants, the slide showed a stop sign.
- For the other half, it was a yield sign.

After seeing the slides, participants were asked a series of questions, with the critical one as follows.
- Half the participants were asked: "Did another car pass the red Datsun while it was stopped at the stop sign?"
- The other half were asked: "Did another car pass the red Datsun while it was stopped at the yield sign?"

This resulted in a 2 × 2 experimental design, shown in Table 2.8.

Sign in the slides	Sign in the question	
	Stop	Yield
Stop	Group 1	Group 2
Yield	Group 3	Group 4

Table 2.8

Finally, participants had a forced-choice recognition test where they had to pick the slide they had seen from a pair of slides.

Results
Participants who received misleading post-event information (groups 2 and 3) recognized the slide they had seen correctly in 41% of the cases, while participants who received consistent post-event information (groups 1 and 4) were able to do so in 75% of the cases.

Conclusion
Misleading post-event verbal information can get integrated with visual memory, alter it and affect performance on a visual recognition task. This has great practical significance because visual recognition tasks are a common practice in police investigations.

Essential understanding
✪ *The phenomenon of reconstructive memory is not found in highly naturalistic settings involving strong emotional reactions while witnessing an event. However, in such cases we could be dealing with a separate memory mechanism (flashbulb memory) that overrides reconstructive memory.*

Aim
To investigate whether eyewitness accounts get distorted as a function of misleading post-event information in a naturalistic setting.

Method
Interviews with elements of an experiment.

Participants
13 eyewitnesses to a real crime (a gun store robbery) in Vancouver.

Procedure
- In this real-life robbery, a thief entered a gun store, tied up the owner, stole money and guns, and left. The owner managed to untie himself, take a gun and run outside. This was followed by a gun shooting in which the robber was killed. The shooting was witnessed by 21 people from various viewpoints. All the witnesses were interviewed by the police.
- Four months after the incident researchers conducted interviews where they also used experimental elements (some participants were asked leading questions with misleading information, others were not).
- To determine the accuracy of participants' memories, they were compared to official police records.

Results
Misleading questions had very little effect on recall. Participants were able to accurately recall a large number of details.

Conclusion
The results have two potential explanations.
- Reconstructive memory is a phenomenon that is only found in artificial conditions of laboratory experiments.
- The study actually tapped into a different memory phenomenon—flashbulb memory. It occurs when the witnessed event is accompanied by a strong emotional experience, so memory of the event gets "imprinted" with a high degree of accuracy. See "**2.3.1 The influence of emotion on cognitive processes**".

2.2.2 Biases in thinking and decision-making

- **Cognitive biases**—systematic deviations from normative models that can result from heuristics
- **Confirmation bias**—the tendency to focus on information that supports a pre-existing belief and ignore information that can potentially contradict it
- **Expected utility theory**—a normative theory of choice; claims that choices should be made based on a calculation of expected outcome for each option and then selecting the option with maximum expected outcome
- **Framing effect**—a heuristic of making a choice under risk; describes how the choice depends on whether the

problem is formulated (framed) in terms of potential gains or in terms of potential losses

- **Heuristics**—mental shortcuts that people take when there is no time or resources to analyse the situation thoroughly
- **Illusory correlation**—a cognitive bias where people see a relationship between things or event that are not actually related
- **System 1 and system 2**—hypothetical systems of thinking that describe the relationship between intuitive thinking and rational analysis

ESSENTIAL UNDERSTANDING

Normative and descriptive models of thinking and decision-making

- **Normative models** of thinking and decision-making describe the rules of "correct" thinking. They assume that a decision-maker is completely rational, has unlimited computational capacity, is uninfluenced by emotional factors, and considers all available information. However, in reality people do not possess those kinds of resources. They take shortcuts.
- Incomplete, simplified strategies (shortcuts) that people use to arrive at decisions are known as **heuristics**. Using heuristics may or may not lead to **cognitive biases**—systematic, predictable deviations of actual decisions from normative models.
- Models that attempt to explain human thinking and decision-making as they really are (even when they deviate from normative rules) are called **descriptive models**.

Two systems of thinking

The way heuristics and rational reasoning interact with each other may be described through the idea of system 1 and system 2 thinking (Kahneman 2003).

- System 1 is responsible for quick, intuitive decisions based on past experiences. Such decisions have evolutionary value.
- System 2 can check these decisions and override them if necessary. It is responsible for deep rational analysis and it developed later in the process of evolution. See "System 1 and system 2 thinking".

Examples

- Numerous cognitive biases have been identified. They can be loosely grouped on the basis of their

hypothetical causes. See "**Common causes of intuitive thinking**".

- One of such causes is a tendency to focus on a limited portion of available information. An example of this is systematic deviations of human decisions from expected-utility theory under risk described in the prospect theory (Kahneman, Tversky 1979). See "Prospect theory".
- Empirically prospect theory is backed up by the discovery of **framing effect**: in decision-making situations involving risk, people are more risk-aversive when the problem is described (framed) in terms of gains and less risk-aversive when it is described in terms of losses. See **Tversky and Kahneman (1981)**.
- Another possible cause of intuitive thinking is a tendency to seek out information that confirms pre-existing beliefs. Ignoring information that can potentially contradict an existing belief is known as confirmation bias. Confirmation bias violates rules of logic. It has been demonstrated (for example, by Wason, 1968) that this cognitive bias is common for human thinking. See "Confirmation bias".
- The tendency to seek out information that confirms one's beliefs can also be seen in illusory correlation—a cognitive bias leading people to see a connection between things or events that are not actually connected. As demonstrated by Chapman and Chapman (1969), illusory correlation underlies practising clinicians' interpretations of Rorschach ink-blot test. It can also be the mechanism of stereotype formation. See "Illusory correlation".

THEORY

SYSTEM 1 AND SYSTEM 2 THINKING

Essential understanding

✪ *Hypothetically there exist two systems of thinking, one quick and intuitive, the other one rational and more thorough.*

Kahneman (2003) differentiated between two hypothetical systems of thinking—system 1 and system 2.

- **System 1 thinking** is fast, instinctive, emotional, automatic and relatively unconscious. It is thought to be the system that developed first in the process of evolution. It enables individuals to make rapid decisions based on their past experiences, which is important for survival. However, this comes at the cost of such decisions not being always accurate or entirely rational. System 1 is where heuristics originate. It is also commonly referred to as "intuition".

- **System 2 thinking** is slower, more analytical, logical, rule-based and conscious. It is thought to have evolved later with the development of language and abstract thought. System 2 enables us to override immediate automatic responses and analyse the situation in greater depth. When we have the time, resources or the necessity to cross-check the first intuitive decisions, system 2 may be switched on to override possibly faulty thinking.

COMMON CAUSES OF INTUITIVE THINKING

Research in this area has identified numerous cognitive biases. They can be loosely grouped based on the factors that may cause them, such as:

- the tendency to focus on a limited portion of available information (for example, asymmetric dominance, framing effect)
- the tendency to seek out information that confirms pre-existing beliefs (for example, confirmation bias, illusory correlation)
- the tendency to avoid the mental stress of holding inconsistent cognitions (for example, cognitive dissonance).

THEORY

PROSPECT THEORY

Essential understanding

✪ *Prospect theory is a descriptive theory of decision-making under risk. It explains deviations from expected utility theory by suggesting that people think about utilities as changes from a reference point.*

Prospect theory by Kahneman and Tversky (1979) is a descriptive theory of decision-making under risk. It claims that individuals think about utilities as changes from a reference point. In its turn, the reference point may be manipulated by the way the decision problem is formulated.

- Problems formulated in terms of potential losses cause people to be more eager to take risks.
- Problems formulated in terms of potential gains cause people to be more risk-avoidant.

The counterpart normative model

The normative model that prospect theory is compared to is **expected utility theory**. In this theory utility of an outcome should be multiplied by the probability of that outcome, and then the outcome that yields the largest value is chosen as the preferred one.

In expected utility theory, the relationship between expected utility and the subjective value attached to an option is a linear function: the more utility we expect, the more we are willing to take a risk to pursue that option.

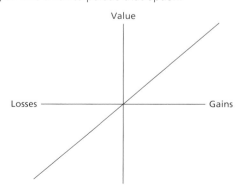

Figure 2.6 Value function in the normative expected utility theory

Deviations from the normative model

However, experiments showed that actual human decisions deviate from this linear function. Prospect theory suggests that people assign less subjective value to gains and more subjective value to losses, so that the choice function looks like Figure 2.7.

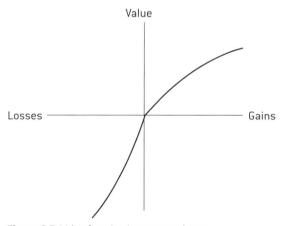

Figure 2.7 Value function in prospect theory

This tendency of human decision-makers to depend on whether the problem is formulated in terms of gains or losses is known as the framing effect.

Essential understanding
✪ *In decision-making situations involving risk, people are more risk-aversive when the problem is described (framed) in terms of gains and less risk-aversive when it is described in terms of losses. This is a systematic deviation from the predictions of the normative expected utility theory.*

Aim
To investigate the influence of the way a decision problem is framed on decisions in scenarios involving risk.

Method
Experiment; independent measures design.

Participants
307 university students who answered brief questionnaires in a classroom setting.

Procedure
Participants were given the following problem.

Imagine that the USA is preparing for an outbreak of an unusual Asian disease, which is expected to kill 600 people. Two alternative programs to combat the disease have been proposed. Assume that the exact scientific estimate of the consequences of the programs are as follows.

Group 1 was given the following options.

A: *200 people will be saved.*

B: *There is 1/3 probability that 600 people will be saved and 2/3 probability that no people will be saved.*

Group 2 was given the following options.

C: *400 people will die.*

D: *There is 1/3 probability that nobody will die, and 2/3 probability that 600 will die.*

Results
- Option A was chosen by 72% of participants (and option B by 28%).
- Option C was chosen by 22% of participants (and option D by 78%).
- Note that logically the problem given to the two groups was equivalent. If you assume that people make decisions rationally, you would expect choices in the two groups to be no different. However, we see that decisions were actually reversed.

Conclusion
The only difference between the two groups is in how the situation is described, either in terms of potential gains ("will be saved") or potential losses ("will die"). This should not matter for a rational decision-maker, so the observed reversal of choices is a deviation from the normative expected utility theory.

This has been called the framing effect: "Avoid risks, but take risks to avoid losses" (Baron 2008).

CONFIRMATION BIAS

Essential understanding
✪ *Confirmation bias is a tendency to focus on information that confirms a pre-existing belief and ignore information that contradicts it. Confirmation bias violates logic (which in this case is the normative model).*

Demonstration: Wason's four-card problem
Wason (1968) demonstrated this in the now classic four-card problem. Participants were given four cards and were told the following.
- Each of the cards has a letter on one side and a number on the other side.
- There is a rule: "If a card has a vowel on one side, then it has an even number on the other side".

The task was to "name those cards, and only those cards, that need to be turned over in order to determine whether the rule is true or false".

Suppose the four cards are "A", "K", "4" and "7". From the point of view of logic (the normative model), the correct answer is "A" and "7". This is why.
- Turning A or 7 can lead to either supporting the rule or refuting it. For example, if you turn A and there is an even number on the reverse side, that supports the rule, but if there's an odd number, that refutes the rule.
- Turning 4 can only lead to supporting the rule, but not refuting it. So, logically, turning card 4 is useless because it does not really test the rule.
- Similarly, turning K is useless because the rule will be neither supported nor rejected.

However, the most popular answers in Wason's study were "A only" or "A and 4". This shows that people attend selectively to information that can potentially support their expectations and at the same time ignore information that can potentially contradict their expectations.

ILLUSORY CORRELATION

Essential understanding
✪ *Illusory correlation violates norms of statistics. People may see a relationship between things that are not related if this goes in line with their prior beliefs. Illusory correlation is widespread—it was shown to be prevalent in thinking of practising clinicians and it is believed to be a mechanism of stereotype formation.*

Explanation
The tendency to seek out information that confirms pre-existing beliefs is also seen in illusory correlations. An illusory correlation is the belief that two phenomena are connected when in reality they are not. The normative model that is violated in this case is statistics.

Demonstration
Male homosexuality and responses on the ink-blot test.

Chapman and Chapman (1969) investigated how practising clinicians were using the Rorschach ink-blot test to diagnose, in particular, male homosexuality. Rorschach ink-blot test is a projective test where patients are given an unstructured ambiguous stimulus (an ink blot) and asked to say what they "see". It is believed that we can use the responses to gain an insight into the patient's personality. It had been demonstrated (statistically) that male homosexuals do in fact have a tendency to give particular responses for particular pictures. These statistically established tendencies are known as **clinically valid signs** of male homosexuality.

However, clinicians in the study failed to see these signs as indicative of male homosexuality despite actual frequent co-occurrence. Instead, they saw other signs of homosexuality—ones that might confirm prior expectations, but were not backed up by real evidence. For example, one of the clinically valid signs of homosexuality is seeing a "humanized animal", such as "a pigeon wearing mittens" in Card V.

Figure 2.8 Rorschach Card V

In contrast, one of the signs that clinicians incorrectly thought to be valid is humans with confused or uncertain sex, male or female genitalia.

Illusory correlation and stereotypes
Illusory correlation forms the basis of many other phenomena in psychology. For example, it may be the mechanism of formation of stereotypes. See "3.1.3 Stereotypes" in "Unit 3 Sociocultural approach to behaviour".

2.3 Emotion and cognition
2.3.1 The influence of emotion on cognitive processes

- **Covert rehearsal**—replaying the previously witnessed event in one's own memory
- **Flashbulb memory**—a special memory mechanism; vivid and highly detailed recollection of the circumstances surrounding witnessing or receiving the news of an unexpected and emotionally arousing event

- **Overt rehearsal**—discussing an event with other people
- **Personal consequentiality**—the extent to which an event is perceived as significant to oneself personally; if it is perceived as significant, it arouses an emotional reaction

ESSENTIAL UNDERSTANDING

Bidirectional relationship between cognition and emotion
- Emotion and cognition are closely interrelated. There exists a bidirectional relationship between them: cognition may influence emotion, and emotion may influence cognition.
- The way cognition influences emotion is through cognitive appraisal of stimuli that mediates a person's emotional reaction. The latest theories of emotion recognize cognitive variables as an integral part of emotional reactions.
- There are many examples of how emotion influences cognition. One of them is a special memory mechanism known as flashbulb memory. See **Brown and Kulik (1977)**.

Support for flashbulb memory
In their study Brown and Kulik (1977) investigated memories of a set of events and found that the more personally consequential the event, the more detailed and vivid its subsequent recollection. They also showed the role of overt rehearsal. See **Brown and Kulik (1977)**.

Further investigation of flashbulb memory
Further research in this area aimed to clarify certain issues surrounding the idea of flashbulb memory as a

special memory mechanism. Some of the issues are as follows.
- If it is a special memory mechanism, does it have a special neural basis?
- Is it encoding at the time the event occurs or rather subsequent rehearsal that creates the vividness characteristic of flashbulb memory?
- How does vividness of flashbulb memory compare to its accuracy? See "**Further exploration of the theory of flashbulb memory**".

To answer the first question, Sharot et al (2007) demonstrated that flashbulb memories trigger selective activation of the left amygdala. **See Sharot et al (2007)**.

For the second question, it has been demonstrated in some research (for example, by Neisser et al, 1996) that rehearsal may play a more important role than the experience of the event itself. See "**Is vividness of flashbulb memory the result of encoding or rehearsal?**"

For the third question, research by Neisser and Harsch (1992) showed that accuracy of flashbulb memories is questionable. There is evidence that accuracy of flashbulb memories decreases with the course of time at the same rate as accuracy of regular memories. See "**How accurate are flashbulb memories?**"

BROWN AND KULIK (1977)—THE THEORY OF FLASHBULB MEMORY

Essential understanding

✪ *The theory of flashbulb memory suggests the existence of a special memory mechanism that enables us to remember vividly the circumstances surrounding the receipt of surprising and emotionally arousing news.*

Flashbulb memories are vivid memories of the circumstances in which one first learned of a surprising and emotionally arousing event.

Two mechanisms

- **The mechanism of formation**: if an event is surprising and personally consequential, it will be emotionally arousing and will trigger a photographic representation. In other words, for flashbulb memories to be formed, the witnessed event needs to satisfy two conditions: it should be unexpected and it should create a strong emotional reaction (which occurs if the event is personally significant).
- **The mechanism of maintenance**: after the event has been imprinted in memory, it needs to be sustained.

Maintenance of flashbulb memories is achieved through overt and covert rehearsal.

- Overt rehearsal includes conversations with other people in which the event is reconstructed.
- Covert rehearsal is replaying the event in one's own memory.

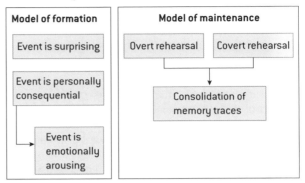

Figure 2.9 Flashbulb memory model

Brown and Kulik (1977)—determinants of flashbulb memories

Essential understanding

✪ *The two principal determinants of flashbulb memories were found to be a high level of surprise and a high level of personal consequentiality (the mechanism of formation). If these variables attain sufficiently high levels, they affect the frequency of overt and covert rehearsal (the mechanism of maintenance). Rehearsal affects how vivid and elaborate the memories are.*

Aim

To investigate the determinants of flashbulb memories about assassinations, highly newsworthy events, and personally significant events.

Method

Correlational data; based on a questionnaire centred around 10 very unexpected or novel events. There was an element of quasi-experiment: difference was investigated between white Americans and black Americans because it was hypothesized that assassinations of different public figures would have different consequences for these populations.

Participants

40 white Americans and 40 black Americans, aged 20–60.

Procedure

Participants filled out a questionnaire that was centred around 10 events. Nine of the events involved political figures (mostly assassinations) and the other event was a personal one that was unexpected and shocking. Participants were asked to write a free recall of circumstances in which they first received news of the event. They also rated each event on a five-point Personal Consequentiality scale and the frequency of rehearsal (the approximate number of times the participant had related the memory to somebody else).

Results

- Black participants were more likely to have vivid, elaborate flashbulb memories about those national leaders who were most involved with US civil rights (such as Martin Luther King or Malcolm X). Assassination of these leaders had more personal consequentiality to black participants than to white participants.
- Occurrence of flashbulb memories correlated (in both white and black participants) with ratings of personal consequentiality.
- Occurrence of flashbulb memories also correlated with frequency of overt rehearsal.

Conclusion

Results of the study match the predictions of the theory. They support the role of personal consequentiality in the formation of flashbulb memories (the model of formation). They also support the role of overt rehearsal in sustaining these memories (model of maintenance). However, the study did not directly test the role of eliciting surprise (all the events used in the questionnaire were just assumed to be sufficiently surprising) or covert rehearsal.

The theory sparked a lot of additional research in the area. These research initiatives can be broadly divided into three groups, depending on the key research question.

- Does there exist a unique neural mechanism of flashbulb memory? An attempt to discover this underlying neural mechanism was made by Sharot et al (2007). See **Sharot et al (2007)**.
- Is vividness of flashbulb memories created by characteristics of the event itself (surprise, consequentiality) or rather by subsequent rehearsal? See "**Is vividness of flashbulb memory the result of encoding or rehearsal?**"
- Although there is no arguing that flashbulb memories are vivid, how accurate are they? Brown and Kulik (1977) focused their research on vividness, but never assessed accuracy. See "**How accurate are flashbulb memories?**"

RESEARCH   Sharot *et al* (2007)—neural mechanism of flashbulb memory

Essential understanding

✪ *Selective activation of the left amygdala may be the neural mechanism of flashbulb memory—left amygdala is activated when the event that is being recalled is shocking and personally consequential.*

Aim

To investigate the neural mechanism of flashbulb memory by comparing brain response to recollecting the 9/11 attack as compared to control events.

Method

Experiment. Mixed design: independent measures because two separate groups of participants were compared; repeated measures because two types of memories were measured in each of the groups.

Participants

24 participants who had witnessed the 9/11 terrorist attacks in New York in 2001.

Procedure

Three years after the attacks participants were asked to retrieve memories of that day as well as memories of personally selected control events from 2001. Participants were split into two groups.

- The Downtown group (they had been in Downtown Manhattan, close to the World Trade Center, at the time of the attack)
- The Midtown group (they were a few miles away from the place of the attack).

Placed in an fMRI scanner, participants saw a series of 60 cue words, either "summer" or "September". On seeing the word "September" they had to provide a memory related to the terrorist attack. On seeing the word "summer" they had to provide an autobiographical memory from the preceding summer of 2001.

Results

- Selective activation of the left amygdala occurred when participants were recalling events from 9/11, but not control events.
- The rates of this selective activation were different in the two groups: it was observed in 83% of participants from the Downtown group and only 40% of participants from the Midtown group.
- During 9/11 trials the Downtown group showed higher amygdala activation than the Midtown group, but there was no difference across groups for summer trials.
- Selective activation of the left amygdala correlated with the proximity of the participant to the World Trade Center during the attacks ($r = 0.45$, $p < 0.05$).

Conclusion

It was concluded that selective activation of the left amygdala may be the neural mechanism of flashbulb memories. The pattern of results confirms that activation is higher when the participant is closer to the place of the attack (so the event is more personally consequential). At the same time, this pattern is specific to 9/11 memories and not to control memories, so it only characterizes surprising, shocking events.

RESEARCH   Is vividness of flashbulb memories the result of encoding or rehearsal?

Essential understanding

✪ *Some researchers emphasize the importance of rehearsal in flashbulb memories, claiming that it is rehearsal, and not experience of the event itself, that makes the largest contribution to how detailed and vivid flashbulb memories are.*

- For example, **Neisser et al (1996)** investigated flashbulb memories of the 1989 Loma Prieta earthquake in California. Some of the participants were from California (close to the earthquake) and some from Atlanta (the opposite coast of the USA). Further, participants were divided into those who had relatives in the affected area and those who did not. They were also required to report the level of their emotional arousal during the event as well as estimate the number of times they discussed the event with other people.
- Results of the study showed that ratings of emotional arousal did not correlate with recall significantly. In fact, some Californian participants reported low levels of emotional arousal. On the other hand, participants who had relatives in the affected area (including participants from Atlanta) also had more vivid and detailed memories of the event; so did participants who reported discussing the event more often with other people.
- It was concluded that rehearsal influences flashbulb memories to a greater extent than the emotional arousal experienced at the time of the event.

Essential understanding

⊛ *Unlike vividness, accuracy of flashbulb memories is questionable.*

Rationale

If we admit that subsequent rehearsal has a large impact on flashbulb memory, we should also acknowledge that accuracy of such memories can be compromised, because in discussing the event with other people we may be exposed to leading questions and other forms of post-event misinformation. From what we know about reconstructive memory (see "2.2.1 Reconstructive memory"), such post-event information may be integrated with the original information, distorting it. Does flashbulb memory suffer from the same bias? Classic research studies in this area focused on how detailed and vivid flashbulb memories are, but never assessed their accuracy.

Neisser and Harsch (1992) investigated participants' memory of the Challenger Space Shuttle explosion. A questionnaire was given to 106 participants asking them to describe the circumstances surrounding receiving the news (where they were at the moment, what they were doing, and so on). Participants answered the same questions twice: the day after the incident and three years later. Results showed the following.

- Participants' confidence about the correctness of their memory was high. The mean self-reported rating of confidence was 83%.
- Consistency of responses between the two points of time was low. On average only 42% of the questions were answered three years later in the same way.
- Participants were very confident in their responses on both occasions, and when shown their own questionnaire from three years earlier and asked to explain the discrepancies in answers, they were extremely surprised, but could provide no explanation.

This shows how we can have a very detailed and vivid memory about something, while at the same time this something did not happen exactly the way we remember.

2.4 Cognitive processing in the digital world (HL only)

- **Empathy**—the ability to understand or feel what another person is experiencing; includes both a cognitive component (perspective-taking, processing of emotional information) and an emotional component

- **Induced media multi-tasking**—switching back and forth between various tasks rather than focusing on one task at a time, induced by digital technology

- **Minute-by-minute assessment of behaviour**—a special type of structured observation where a checklist of behaviours is used every minute over and over again for the duration of the observation period

- **Neurological correlates**—areas and processes of the brain established (by neuroimaging research) to be associated with a certain psychological process or function

ESSENTIAL UNDERSTANDING

Background

We know that experience shapes neuronal connections through neuroplasticity. Since humanity is becoming increasingly exposed to digital technology, it would be reasonable to assume that the brain and hence cognitive processing undergo some changes as a result of that.

Effects of digital technology on cognitive processes

Some research studies show that interaction with digital technology can improve cognitive processing skills. For example, Rosser *et al* (2007) found that playing first-person shooters helped surgeons become faster and more accurate in surgery simulations. See **Rosser *et al* (2007)**. This seems easy to explain because both first-person shooters and surgery operations use the same set of visuospatial abilities and eye–hand coordination skills.

However, it has also been demonstrated that effects of playing videogames can be transferrable to a wider domain. For example, Sanchez (2012) showed that playing videogames that require spatial abilities (such as first-person shooters) may enhance students' understanding of abstract scientific concepts that also involve spatial reasoning (such as plate tectonics). See **Sanchez (2012)**.

These are all positive effects. However, digital technology may impact cognitive processes negatively. We consider this on the example of induced media multi-tasking and its detrimental effects on attention and academic performance. For a summary, see "**The positive and negative effects of modern technology on cognitive processes**".

Digital technology and reliability of cognitive processing

Induced media multi-tasking is an essential dimension of interacting with digital technology. Multi-tasking can have detrimental effects on attention and focus, resulting in lower academic achievement. See "**Reliability of cognitive processes in the context of digital technology**".

Using the experience sampling method, **Moreno *et al* (2012)** showed that media multi-tasking is highly prevalent among students. See "**Experience sampling method**".

Rosen, Carrier and Cheever (2013) showed that students who surrounded themselves with more technology while studying at home and engaged in more media multi-tasking, especially using Facebook, had lower average grade point average (GPA) scores (which are used as a measure of school achievement). See **Rosen, Carrier and Cheever (2013)**. This can probably be explained by reduced attention.

However, Rosen *et al* (2011) demonstrated that these detrimental effects of multi-tasking on attention and school performance can be overcome, to an extent, by using metacognitive strategies. See **Rosen *et al* (2011)**.

Finally, it has been demonstrated that being prone to media multi-tasking correlates with lower grey matter density in the anterior cingulated cortex (ACC). The same area is involved in cognitive control and emotional regulation. See **Loh and Kanai (2014)**.

Digital technology, cognition and emotion
In the context of digital technology, emotion and cognition can be considered using the example of empathy. Empathy has both emotional and cognitive components. See

"Emotion and cognition in the context of digital technology".

There has been a decline in empathy scores in tests, and this decline coincides with the onset of the digital era. Researchers have linked it to the appearance of social networking websites. See **Konrath, O'Brien and Hsing (2011)**.

However, this negative impact is not true for all online activities. Research showed that online activities that enhance face-to-face communication may actually lead to an increase in empathy (both cognitive and emotional). See **Carrier *et al* (2015)**.

It is generally believed that it is not digital technology as such that influences empathy, but the way technology is used. See "Digital technology and empathy: summary".

At the end of the section there is a summary of "**Methods used to study the interaction between digital technology and cognitive processes**".

RESEARCH   Rosser *et al* (2007) – videogames and surgeons

Essential understanding
✪ *Playing videogames that involve rapid visuospatial coordination may enhance related skills in performing real-life tasks.*

Aim
To investigate whether playing videogames results in better surgery performance in laparoscopic surgeons.

Method
Correlational study.

Participants
33 laparoscopic surgeons.

Procedure
- As part of their regular training, surgeons participated in a series of drills. For example, they lifted and moved triangular objects from one point to another by putting a needle through a small loop at the top of each triangle.
- The researchers measured the number of errors made and the completion time. This served as an indicator of performance during surgery.
- Playing videogames was assessed in two ways.

○ A self-report questionnaire was used to assess **videogame experience** outside of the research.
○ Participants were asked to play 3 games for 25 minutes, and the total score obtained in these games was used as an indicator of **game mastery**. The three games were selected so that they required fast reaction and precise movements.

Results
- Videogame mastery was highly correlated with less time and fewer errors in performing the surgery drills.
- Surgeons who played videogames for more than three hours a week made 37% fewer errors in surgery drills, and performed surgery 27% faster than their non-playing colleagues.

Conclusion
The researchers explain that when playing videogames participants improved their fine motor skills and attention, and were subsequently able to transfer these skills to a new situation. However, these are highly specific tasks and it is not known whether interacting with digital technology has any effects on cognition in a wider domain.

RESEARCH   Sanchez (2012)–effects of videogames on science learning

Essential understanding
✪ *Effects of playing videogames are transferrable to wider contexts not immediately related to the tasks performed in the game.*

Aim
To investigate how transferrable the effects of playing videogames are to wider domains such as science learning.

Method
Experiment; independent measures design.

Participants
60 university students.

Procedure
Participants were randomly divided into two groups.

- The spatial training group played a first-person shooter game (*Halo: Combat Evolved*)
- The non-spatial training group played a verbal game involving combining letters to form words (*Word Whomp*).

After playing their allocated game, participants read a complex text about plate tectonics that contained 3,500 words with no illustrations. It described a theoretical model of volcanic eruptions. After reading, participants were required to write an essay. Independent scorers read the essay and assessed the extent to which it demonstrated understanding of the important concepts of plate tectonics.

Results

Participants who played a first-person shooter game (the spatial training group) gained higher scores on the essay—these participants showed better understanding of plate tectonics.

Conclusion

Reading about a model of plate tectonics without illustrations requires one to encode verbal information and translate it into abstract spatial representations. Although that is somewhat different from what is required when playing a first-person shooter game, this research demonstrates that skills acquired in the game are to some extent generalizable to wider domains.

RELIABILITY OF COGNITIVE PROCESSES IN THE CONTEXT OF DIGITAL TECHNOLOGY

Reliability of cognitive processes refers to their accuracy and performance.

- Lack of **accuracy** leads to biases. We have seen examples in the theories of reconstructive memory (see "2.2.1 Reconstructive memory") and heuristics and cognitive biases (see "2.2.2 Biases in thinking and decision-making"). In these examples we remember something that is not true or we make decisions that are not rational. Research into how digital technology may influence accuracy of cognitive processes is still in its infancy.
- Lack of **performance** leads to a failure to store or process information, for example, for memory that would mean easier forgetting and shorter retention

in a memory store. We will be looking at the example of attention. Can digital technology lead to reduced attention? If the answer is positive, that would imply a lot of other effects too, because attention is a basic process. Even memory depends on attention when information is transmitted from sensory memory to the STM store (see "2.1.1 Models of memory").

One aspect of technology use that has been often linked to attention is **induced media multi-tasking**. Induced multi-tasking is an essential aspect of using digital technology. Modern devices allow us to do multiple things at once (multiple tabs open in the browser, real-time updates from social media, and so on).

EXPERIENCE SAMPLING METHOD

To assess the degree of multi-tasking in college students **Moreno et al (2012)** used the experience sampling method to get a "snapshot" of everyday activities in a sample of university students. They found that students were multi-tasking more than half the time they were using the internet, the most popular off-task activity being social networking.

The researchers sent out messages to a group of participants at random times during the day and immediately on

receiving the message participants had to answer a brief questionnaire with questions such as "What are you doing right now?", "How interested or engaged are you?" Typically, participants received 6–10 messages a day for the duration of a week. This method allows researchers to gain an insight into how participants structure their time, as well as what experiences they have in response to their daily activities.

RESEARCH   Rosen, Carrier and Cheever (2013)—the influence of induced multi-tasking on cognitive processes

Essential understanding

✪ *Multi-tasking induced by the use of digital technology is highly prevalent among students and negatively correlated with school achievement.*

Aim

To investigate the relationship between the use of digital technology, multi-tasking and school achievement.

Method

Correlational study.

Participants

263 students.

Procedure

On-task behaviour and off-task technology use was assessed using a checklist of activities such as "email", "Facebook", "talking on the telephone", "music on", "reading a book", "reading a website", "writing on the computer", "stretching/walking around". These activities were noted every minute during the observation period.

After the observation participants filled out a questionnaire containing their self-reported GPA.

Results

- On average participants maintained on-task behaviour only for 6 minutes before switching to off-task behaviour and averaged only around 10 minutes on-task in total.

- Four variables that had the strongest correlations with reduced on-task behaviour were: technology available at the start of studying; stretching/walking; texting; using Facebook.
- Off-task behaviour was associated with reduced school achievement. Those students who accessed Facebook at least once during the 15-minute study period had lower GPAs.

Conclusion

The incidence of off-task behaviour among students is high, with at least 1/3 of the study time spent off-task. Such multi-tasking is associated with lower school achievement. This involves Facebook use in particular.

Notes

The study demonstrates that multi-tasking induced by the use of digital technology correlates with school achievement (GPA). The assumption here is that school achievement is a reflection of cognitive abilities as well as such processes as attention. The most plausible explanation is perhaps that induced media multi-tasking is detrimental to attention and focus while studying.

Follow-up research

This explanation is corroborated by further studies, for example, **Swing et al (2010)** who showed in longitudinal research that the amount of screen entertainment time predicted attention problems in class.

- The study involved 4 measurements over a 13-month period.
- Observational data was collected from teachers who reported incidences of staying off-task, interrupting others, not paying attention, and so on.
- The study showed that playing games and watching television for more than two hours a day (at the beginning of the study period) predicted an increase in attention problems with the course of time.
- The researchers concluded that excessive use of digital technology may be linked to attention deficit.

RESEARCH　　Rosen *et al* (2011)—compensating for the negative effects of multi-tasking

Essential understanding

✪ *Metacognitive strategies can be used to compensate for the negative effects of induced media multi-tasking. Metacognitive strategies are used when you consciously monitor and regulate your cognitive processes.*

Aim

To investigate the effects of amount of multi-tasking and response delay on attention and academic performance.

Method

Experiment; independent measures design.

Participants

185 college students.

Procedure

Students viewed a videotaped lecture and were then given a test to assess their understanding. During the lecture, all students received text messages that required a response. There were three groups of participants depending on the number of text messages they received: small, medium or large.

Results

- The more text messages a student received during the lecture, the worse the student performed on the test.
- However, this also depended on response delay: students who chose to read and respond to the messages immediately after receiving them did significantly worse on the test than students who chose to read and respond some time (up to 5 minutes) later.

Conclusion

We can consciously override the automatic tendency to get distracted and switch to off-task behaviour by delaying the response to the distractor. To some extent this may compensate for the negative effects of induced media multi-tasking. However, such metacognitive strategy requires a lot of cognitive effort.

RESEARCH　　Loh and Kanai (2014)—neurological correlates of media multi-tasking

Essential understanding

✪ *Low grey matter density in the anterior cingulated cortex (ACC) may be the physiological basis of being prone to induced media multi-tasking.*

Aim

To investigate the physiological correlates of media multi-tasking.

Method

Correlational study; variables were measured by a questionnaire and fMRI.

Participants

75 healthy adults.

Procedure

Participants went through fMRI scans of their brain and filled out a self-report measure of media multi-tasking.

Results

There was a correlation between reported multi-tasking and grey matter density in the ACC.

Explanation

The ACC is known to be involved in:

- cognitive control (for example, it is active in tasks that require selective attention)
- emotional and motivational regulation.

This seems to suggest a reasonable explanation: people who are prone to media multi-tasking also demonstrate reduced cognitive control (over their attention) and a reduced ability to regulate their emotion (for example, the urge to open a message immediately on receiving it in anticipation of emotional gratification).

Note

The study is correlational, so the result can be potentially explained in both directions.
- Individuals with lesser grey matter volume in the ACC are more susceptible to media multi-tasking.
- Engaging in multi-tasking affects grey matter density in the ACC through neuroplasticity.

SUMMARY: THE POSITIVE AND NEGATIVE EFFECTS OF MODERN TECHNOLOGY ON COGNITIVE PROCESSES

Research discussed so far in this section highlights both positive and negative influences of digital technology on cognition. Here is a summary.

Positive influences
- Videogaming may enhance visuospatial skills that may be further applied in related real-world tasks (Rosser *et al* 2007)—the study of laparoscopic surgeons).
- Such skills acquired in videogames may even be transferred to wider domains such as science learning (Sanchez 2012—study of students learning about plate tectonics).

Negative influences
- Induced media multi-tasking, and increased consumption of digital media in general, leads to attention problems, see Swing *et al* (2010).
- This may result in lower school achievement: Rosen, Carrier and Cheever (2013)—media multi-tasking negatively correlated with GPA.
- This is corroborated by neuroimaging—media multi-tasking affects areas that are responsible for cognitive control and emotional regulation: Loh and Kanai (2014).

EMOTION AND COGNITION IN THE CONTEXT OF DIGITAL TECHNOLOGY

As we know, cognition is closely linked to emotion. Emotional variables are an integral part of cognitive processes such as thinking and decision-making. See the "**Adaptive decision-maker framework**" in "**2.1.3 Thinking and decision-making**". Emotional reactions can modify our memory and even trigger special memory mechanism. See "**Flashbulb memory**" in "**2.3 Emotion and cognition**". Conversely, cognitive appraisal modifies emotional reactions and influences the way we experience emotion.

Another example of a phenomenon that is a product of interaction of emotion and cognition is **empathy**.
- The cognitive dimension of empathy includes one's ability to process emotional information: take

perspectives of other people, understand what they feel and analyse a situation through their eyes. Perspective-taking is a major component of a special cognitive ability known as Theory of mind. See "**7.1.3 Development of empathy and theory of mind**" in "**Unit 7 Developmental psychology**".
- The emotional dimension of empathy is feeling what other people feel. It can probably be viewed as a consequence of the cognitive dimension: to feel what other people feel, you first need to understand it.

The question is, does interaction with digital technology influence the way people cognitively process emotional information?

RESEARCH Konrath, O'Brien and Hsing (2011)—decline in empathy scores over time

Essential understanding
✪ *The average empathy scores in US college students have been falling with the course of time, and the trend is consistent with the onset of the digital era (especially social networks and mobile phones).*

Aim
To examine changes in empathy scores in US college students over time.

Method
A cross-temporal meta-analysis; correlational study; Interpersonal Reactivity Index (IRI—Davis 1980) was used in

the research studies to measure empathy (both its cognitive and emotional components).

Participants
72 samples of US college students who completed a self-report measure of empathy some time between 1979 and 2009 (the total number of participants is almost 14,000).

Procedure
The Interpersonal Reactivity Index (IRI) is a personality scale that measures both emotional and cognitive components of empathy, such as empathic concern (emotional) and perspective-taking (cognitive).

Scores on the IRI were correlated with the year of data collection.

Results

- More recent generations of college students progressively reported lower scores, both on empathic concern and perspective-taking.
- The most dramatic changes occurred between 2000 and 2009. This coincides with the time when major social network sites became popular, as well as with the wide use of cell phones.

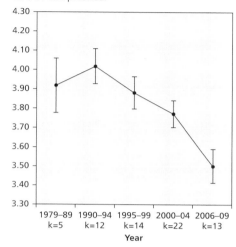

Figure 2.10 College students' empathic concern scores by period
Source: Konrath, O'Brien and Hsing (2011: 186)
Note: Capped vertical bars denote ± 1 *SE*.

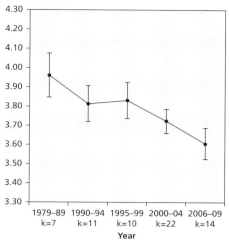

Figure 2.11 College students' perspective-taking scores by period
Source: Konrath, O'Brien and Hsing (2011: 186)
Note: Capped vertical bars denote ± 1 *SE*.

Conclusion

Discussing the possible reasons behind the observed trends, the authors point at the fact that this decline in empathy scores coincides with the onset of the digital era: "younger people more frequently remove themselves from deep interpersonal social situations and become immersed in isolated online environments" (Konrath, O'Brien, Hsing 2011).

RESEARCH **Carrier *et al* (2015)—different types of digital activity have different effects on empathy**

Essential understanding

✪ *Some digital activities provide opportunities for the development of virtual empathy and predict increased face-to-face communication. Such activities are associated with higher real-world empathy. Other activities (such as videogaming) have opposite effects.*

Aim

To investigate the relationship between digital activities, virtual empathy and real-world empathy.

Method

Correlational study.

Participants

1,726 participants born in the digital era (after 1980).

Procedure

The researchers used an anonymous online questionnaire that collected information on daily media usage and empathy scores. Both emotional and cognitive components of empathy were measured.

Results

- Engaging in online activities that eventually led to face-to-face communication was shown to be associated with higher real-life empathy scores.
- Such activities that predicted increased amounts of face-to-face communication (that was in turn associated with higher real-life empathy) were: social networking sites; browsing websites; using email; using a computer for purposes other than being online.
- Conversely, such activities as videogaming did not predict more face-to-face communication and reduced real-world empathy scores.

Conclusion

In investigating the relationship between digital activities and empathy we need to consider the exact digital activity. Some digital activities may lead to an increase in real-world empathy, while some others (such as videogaming) affect it detrimentally.

As a summary of research in this area, it is generally believed that it is not digital technology as such that influences empathy, but the way technology is used.

- For example, if online communication is used for supporting existing friendships, it can produce positive effects. We will be exposed to more personal stories,

share more with each other both online and offline, and in this sense our mutual understanding and perspective-taking will be enhanced.

- On the other hand, activities that are not associated with face-to-face communication and virtual empathy (such as gaming) can affect empathy scores negatively.

METHODS USED TO STUDY THE INTERACTION BETWEEN DIGITAL TECHNOLOGY AND COGNITIVE PROCESSES

Research studies mentioned in this section utilized a variety of methods. Each method has both strengths and limitations in the context of investigating the effects of digital technology on cognitive processes. Table 2.9 gives is a summary of the key points.

Method	Strengths	Limitations	Research study	Notes
Observation	This uses in-depth data; measurements can be done in a natural environment; many different parameters can be measured at once.	It is subject to biases and depends on the expertise of the observers.	Rosen, Carrier and Cheever (2013): observation was used to measure various aspects of interaction with digital technology. Swing et al (2010): observation was used to measure attention problems.	Observation cannot be used to test hypotheses in this area, but it can be used to measure variables.
Minute-by-minute assessment of behaviour	This provides detailed data that is especially useful in the study of multi-tasking.	We can assess the actions (for example, "opens Facebook"), but not the content (for example, exactly what the participant does on Facebook).	Rosen, Carrier and Cheever (2013)	This is a special type of structured observation. We mention it separately because it is well suited for the study of multi-tasking.
Experience sampling method	Unlike other observational methods, this allows researchers to gain an insight into participants' experiences (questions can be asked regarding how they experience what they are doing). This has high ecological validity—participants are living their daily lives.	It is time-consuming and difficult to collect and process data. Enough time points need to be used for it to be a reliable "snapshot" of participants' daily activities. Participants need to be motivated to follow instructions.	Moreno et al (2012)	This may be considered another special type of observation. If it includes open-ended questions, it is followed by content analysis.
Survey or questionnaire	Allows us to measure a broad variety of parameters at the same time; can measure both observable variables (behaviour) and unobservable ones (attitudes, values).	Relies on self-report, which makes it subject to biases such as social desirability. Participants may also give distorted estimates when it comes to such parameters as the number of hours spent playing games.	Rosser et al (2007): a survey was used to measure background gaming experience. Carrier et al (2015): an anonymous online questionnaire was used. Loh and Kanai (2014): a questionnaire was used to measure media multi-tasking.	This is used to measure variables.
Longitudinal study	This is especially helpful because the effects of digital technology on cognition are most likely postponed, not immediate. Longitudinal data allows us to see how the effects of digital technology unfold in time.	It is time-consuming and difficult to collect data. Although we can make inferences "A predicts B", we still cannot infer that "A causes B". The latter is only possible in experiments.	Swing et al (2010): repeated testing was used over a 13-month period. Konrath, O'Brien and Hsing (2011): generational cohorts were compared. This is a special type of longitudinal study (the cohort method).	There is a lack of longitudinal studies in this area.
Neuroimaging technology	This allows us to establish neurological correlates of increased usage of digital technology; this in turn allows us to explain how cognition may be affected.	Data is still correlational.	Loh and Kanai (2014)	When it is used as a method of measuring variables, it may be considered a type of technology-assisted observation.

Meta-analysis	This provides more accurate estimates where potential biases get cancelled out.	Requires a large body of research studies all of which used a similar procedure (for example, the same questionnaire)	Konrath, O'Brien and Hsing (2011): 72 studies that used the Interpersonal Reactivity Index	Meta-analyses usually require a long history of research in a certain area.
Correlational study	It is easy to collect data. It is the most widely used method in this area.	A cause–effect relationship cannot be established.	Rosser *et al* (2007) Rosen, Carrier and Cheever (2013) Rosen *et al* (2011): response delay was correlated with test performance. Loh and Kanai (2014) Carrier *et al* (2015) Swing *et al* (2010)	This is a method of testing hypotheses.
Experiment	The only method that allows researchers to make cause-and-effect inferences of the type "A influences or causes B".	This requires careful isolation of one IV and rigorous control of potential confounding variables (of which there are plenty).	Sanchez (2012) Rosen *et al* (2011): the number of texts sent to the students was manipulated.	This is a method of testing hypotheses.

Table 2.9

EXAM TIP

This HL extension includes three topics that can be applied to any of the three parts of the cognitive approach to behaviour. Combining these gives you nine potential areas from which exam questions may be asked.

Parts of cognitive approach to behaviour	a. Cognitive processing	b. Reliability of cognitive processes	c. Emotion and cognition
1. The influence of digital technology on cognitive processes	1a	1b	1c
2. The positive and negative effects of modern technology on cognitive processes	2a	2b	2c
3. Methods used to study the interaction between digital technology and cognitive processes	3a	3b	3c

Table 2.10

There is considerable overlap in these areas. The blocks we have covered in this section address all nine areas holistically.

Topics

3.1 The individual and the group
3.1.1 Social identity theory

- **In-group favouritism**—behaviour that is biased towards the benefits of the in-group
- **Minimal group paradigm**—the experimental procedure where trivial group differences are created artificially to investigate the effects of social categorization on intergroup discrimination
- **Out-group discrimination**—behaviour that creates disadvantages for the out-group

- **Social categorization**—the cognitive process of categorizing people into in-groups and out-groups
- **Social comparison**—the process of comparing the in-group to out-groups ("us" versus "them")
- **Social identity**—the part of self-concept that is based on group membership

ESSENTIAL UNDERSTANDING

Social identity theory
Social identity theory is a theory of intergroup conflict. Previously existing theories of intergroup conflict included:
- theories of aggressive personality
- realistic group conflict theory (Sherif 1966).

The claims of social identity theory are based on such interconnected concepts as:
- social categorization
- social comparison
- positive distinctiveness
- self-esteem
- out-group discrimination
- in-group favouritism.

Some of the theory's claims have been supported by research using the **minimal group paradigm**. See Tajfel *et al* (1971).

The mere fact of belonging to two different groups (even on the basis of trivial criteria) can trigger in-group favouritism and out-group discrimination.

Evaluation of minimal group studies
Minimal group studies have been criticized for being artificial in their procedure: group allocation is not random enough and the matrices involve forced choice. However, further research does not support this criticism. See **Locksley, Ortiz and Hepburn (1980)**.

Evaluation of social identity theory
The theory has great explanatory power. However, it does not explain individual differences.

THEORY

SOCIAL IDENTITY THEORY
Social identity theory is a theory of intergroup conflict. It aims to explain why conflict and discrimination occur.

Context
Social identity theory is better understood when placed in the context of previously existing explanations of intergroup conflict, including the following.
- Theories that stressed intrapersonal reasons (that is, factors within the personality). These theories of aggressive personality largely ignored social variables.
- Realistic group conflict theory (Sherif 1966). This suggested that intergroup conflict is caused by real conflict between group interests (competition over scarce resources). This theory emphasized social variables

and did not pay enough attention to the psychological variables. See "**6.2.1 Cooperation and competition**".

Claims of social identity theory
1. Competition over resources is not always necessary for the development of conflict between groups.
2. The mere perception of belonging to two groups (**social categorization**) is sufficient to trigger **out-group discrimination** and **in-group favouritism**.
3. Social categorization provides individuals with a means of building their **social identity**. People define themselves in social terms, in terms of being similar to or different from, "better" or "worse" than members of other groups.

4. Individuals strive to achieve a positive social identity because it increases their **self-esteem**.
5. Positive social identity is based on distinctiveness: the in-group must be perceived as positively different from ("better than") certain out-groups. This involves the process of **social comparison**.
6. When social identity is not positive, individuals will try to either leave the group or make the existing group more positively distinct.

Some of these claims have been supported by research studies using the so-called **minimal group paradigm**. In this experimental paradigm participants are randomly classified as members of two groups on the basis of a very trivial criterion. The groups are purely cognitive as there is no objective reason for the group members to compete.

RESEARCH   Tajfel *et al* (1971)—minimal group experiment 1

Essential understanding
✪ *The mere fact of belonging to two different groups (even on the basis of trivial criteria) can trigger in-group favouritism and out-group discrimination.*

Aim
To investigate effects of social categorization on intergroup behaviour in a minimal group paradigm.

Minimal group paradigm
To create minimal groups—that is, to investigate the effects of social categorization *per se*— the following conditions have to be satisfied.
- There should be no face-to-face interaction between participants.
- There should be anonymity regarding group membership.
- Criteria for social categorization should be very trivial and completely unrelated to what the participants are required to do in the experiment.
- Responses should not have any economic value to the participants (that is, one response should not be economically preferable to the others).
- The strategy of in-group favouritism should be in competition with a strategy based on rationality and common sense, for example, more benefit to all.
- Decisions made in the experiment should involve some real outcomes. For example, real money should be used, not just symbolic tokens.

Participants
64 male students of a school in Bristol (England), aged 14–15. They were tested in eight groups of eight participants. They came from the same school and knew each other well.

Procedure
- **At stage 1** (categorization) participants were shown 40 slides (each for less than a second) with clusters of dots on a screen and requested to estimate the number of dots.
- Following this, experimenters told participants that the researchers were also interested in a completely different kind of judgment, and that they would investigate those as well, taking advantage of the participants' presence. Participants were told that for convenience they would be divided based on the previous task—a group of four "overestimators" and a group of four "underestimators".
- **At stage 2** (distribution of rewards) participants were taken to another room one by one where they worked on their own in separate cubicles. They had to distribute rewards and penalties in real money to others. For this they were given a booklet with 18 matrices. Table 3.1 shows an example of a matrix.

You are in the group of: overestimators														
Rewards and penalties for:	1	2	3	4	5	6	7	8	9	10	11	12	13	14
Member number 2 of your group	−25	−21	−17	−13	−9	−5	−1	0	2	4	6	8	10	12
Member number 4 of the other group	12	10	8	6	4	2	0	−1	−5	−9	−13	−17	−21	−25

Table 3.1 Example matrix

Based on: Tajfel *et al* (1971)

- Some matrices in the booklet involved two members of the different groups (as in the example above). In some matrices the choice was between two anonymous members of the in-group, in some it was two members of the out-group. In the example above, the choice that gives maximum profit to an in-group member is 14, and the point of maximum fairness is 7.5.
- Participants always allotted money to others, never to themselves. All participants were anonymous because names were replaced by codes. They were told that at the end of the task they would be given whatever amount of money others had allocated to them (one point was worth 1/10 of a penny).

Results
- The mean choice in the different-group matrices was 9.2 (compared to 7.5 as the point of maximum fairness).
- The choices in the same-group conditions (two members of the in-group or two members of the out-group) were more closely clustered around the point of fairness (7.5).

Conclusion
Participants demonstrate in-group favouritism and out-group discrimination when categorized into groups based on trivial criteria.

Essential understanding

✪ *Participants sacrifice group and personal gain to achieve favourable intergroup differences.*

Aim

To clarify the strategy used by participants when making between-group choices.

Participants

48 boys of the same age and from the same school as in the first experiment.

Procedure

The design of the second experiment was based on the results of the first experiment. The procedure was largely the same, but the criterion for categorization and the matrices used in the booklets were different.

Participants were shown slides with pairs of abstract paintings—one by Kandinsky and one by Klee—and asked to choose the one they liked better. They were told that they would be split into groups based on whether they preferred Klee or Kandinsky, whereas in reality the allocation was random.

Different matrices were used, and this allowed experimenters to distinguish three types of strategy, which were:
- **maximum joint payoff (MJP)**: the choice that corresponds to the highest total number of points
- **maximum in-group payoff (MIP)**
- **maximum difference in favour of the in-group (MD)**: the point in the matrix that maximizes the difference between the payoffs for the members of the two groups.

Matrices were manipulated in such a way that the three strategies (MJP, MIP and MD) would contradict each other. For example, in the matrix shown in Table 3.2 as participants move from the left to the right MJP and MIP are maximized but MD is minimized. A "pure" MD choice would dictate choosing option 1, while an MJP+MIP strategy would dictate choosing option 13.

Rewards and penalties for:	1	2	3	4	5	6	7	8	9	10	11	12	13
Member number XYZ of your group (Klee)	7	8	9	10	11	12	13	14	15	16	17	18	19
Member number XYZ of the other group (Kandinsky)	1	3	5	7	9	11	13	15	17	19	21	23	25

Table 3.2

Based on: Tajfel *et al* (1971)

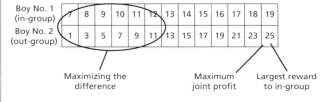

Maximizing the difference   Maximum joint profit   Largest reward to in-group

Results

Participants demonstrated a clear preference for MD. This means they preferred their group to get less money if this meant that their group would compare favourably to the other group.

Conclusion

Subjects sacrifice group and personal gain to achieve favourable intergroup differences. Note that the findings of this study lend support in particular to the idea of positive distinctiveness (claim 5 as given in "Theory: social identity theory").

Strengths
- A major strength of the procedure was the high level of control over confounding variables.
- Although separate studies can be criticized for lack of ecological validity and limited samples (for example, all school boys from the same country), social identity theory is now supported by a large body of empirical research, so accumulated evidence is strong.

Limitations
- The minimal group studies have been criticized for being artificial in their procedure. Teenage boys may be naturally competitive, and the matrices involved forced choice that was suggestive of competition. This may trigger demand characteristics.

- However, social categorization effects remained even when researchers made the groups explicitly random and removed forced choice from the matrices. **Locksley, Ortiz and Hepburn (1980)** conducted a series of experiments where they:
  - tossed a coin to allocate participants into groups so that participants could see that group membership was entirely random
  - gave participants a certain number of poker chips to allocate to group members, thus removing the forced choice associated with using matrices.

- Findings of Tajfel's original studies were replicated even in these conditions.

- Tajfel's theory has large explanatory power. It can be applied to many real-life phenomena such as behaviour of teenagers in cliques or behaviour of football fans. In both examples people belonging to a group have a tendency to value the products of the in-group and look down upon out-groups. According to social identity theory, these people's self-esteem is based on the belief that their group is superior to others.

- Social identity theory offers an explanation for why discrimination occurs even when there is no competition over resources.
- Social identity theory does not explain individual differences: why do some people rely on social identity for building their self-esteem more than others? Additional theories are required to explain these observed differences.

3.1.2 Social cognitive theory

DEFINITIONS

- **Human agency**—the belief that people are agents of their own behaviour; includes intentionality, forethought, self-reactiveness and self-reflectiveness
- **Observational learning**—learning that occurs as a result of observing other people perform actions as well as the consequences of these actions

- **Reciprocal determinism**—a model of three interacting factors: personal factors (physical, cognitive and emotional), behaviour and environment
- **Self-efficacy**—the extent to which individuals believe they can master a particular behaviour

ESSENTIAL UNDERSTANDING

Cultural norms are transmitted from individual to individual in the process of socialization. How exactly does this transmission occur? In other words, how do people learn from other people?

An influential theory that answers this question is social cognitive theory, proposed by Albert Bandura. Social cognitive theory is a development of its previous version—social learning theory, also proposed by Bandura.

Social learning theory rests on the idea that learning can occur indirectly (observational learning). This idea is supported in Bandura's Bobo doll experiments. See **Bandura, Ross and Ross (1961)**.

Social cognitive theory is an extension of social learning theory that also includes the following major aspects:
- reciprocal determinism

- the idea of human agency
- identification
- self-efficacy.

Social cognitive theory is supported in a variety of research studies.
- Most of them are correlational in nature and do not directly test the idea of "reciprocity". However, the sheer amount of these studies and the fact that results fit well into the theoretical explanation lend support to the model. An example is the study of **Perry, Perry and Rasmussen (1986)**.
- Some studies use large cross-cultural data sets and apply complex techniques of statistical modelling. These studies also provide support for the idea of reciprocal determinism. See **Williams and Williams (2010)**.

THEORY

THE IDEA THAT LEARNING CAN OCCUR INDIRECTLY (OBSERVATIONAL LEARNING)

In his social learning theory, Bandura suggested that there are two types of learning.
- **Direct learning** occurs when an individual performs an action and experiences its consequences (positive or negative), which reinforces or inhibits further repetition of this action.
- **Indirect learning** occurs when an individual observes another person's actions and their consequences.

When Bandura first suggested social learning theory as a way to explain learning, the predominant theory of learning was behaviourism, which made the implicit assumption that all learning is direct. In other words, the learning described in the behaviourist approach was all trial and error. Bandura felt that this was not enough to explain the complex process

of socialization including learning such things as language or religious practices. The advantage of social learning theory was that it was able to incorporate and explain indirect learning.

The idea that learning can occur indirectly though observing others (observational learning) has the following implications.
- It is not necessary to demonstrate the actual behaviour for learning to occur.
- In our learning we depend on available models—people whose behaviour we observe.

The idea that people learn from watching others was tested in a series of Bandura's famous Bobo doll experiments.

The first of the Bobo doll experiments was **Bandura, Ross and Ross (1961)**.

Aim
To find out how observing an adult model behaving aggressively towards an inflatable doll (Bobo doll) influences children's subsequent aggressive behaviour.

Method
The key method is a laboratory experiment (the IV was manipulated, the DV was measured). The way researchers measured the DV (children's subsequent behaviour) was structured observation through a one-way mirror.

Participants
72 children (36 girls and 36 boys) aged 3–6.

Procedure
The children were split up randomly in a number of groups (see below). First, they were allocated to one of the following three groups.
- Aggressive role model (24 children)—in this group the adult model behaved aggressively towards the Bobo doll by following a script.
- Non-aggressive role model (24 children)—in this group the adult model followed a similar script, but aggressive actions were replaced by non-aggressive actions.
- Control group— this group had no model.

Stage 1
A child was seated in one corner of a room and an adult model in another corner. The child was given prints and stickers to play with, and the model had a Tinkertoy set, a mallet and a 1.5-metre tall inflatable Bobo doll. The script that the adult model followed in the aggressive condition was to spend some time playing with the toy set and then to turn to the Bobo doll and behave aggressively towards it, both verbally and physically. In the non-aggressive condition the model just played quietly with the toys.

Stage 2
The child was taken to another room and a frustrating situation was created to "instigate" the child's aggression. The child was given attractive toys, but when the interest was sparked and the play began, the child was separated from the toys and taken to a third room instead.

Stage 3
The DV was measured in the third room, which contained a one-way mirror. The room contained toys similar to those in the first rooms, including a slightly smaller version of the Bobo doll. Observation at this stage lasted for 20 minutes.

The researchers had a checklist of behaviours to observe, including such categories as imitative aggression (aggressive acts copied from the distinctive behaviour of the adult model at stage 1), non-imitative aggression (aggressive acts that were not modelled by the adult, for example shooting a dart gun at the Bobo doll).

Results
- Exposure of children to the aggressive model increased the frequency of aggressive behaviour among the children.
- Imitation in same-sex role model conditions was more likely than in the conditions where the sex of the child and the sex of the model were different.
- Boys were more likely to be aggressive than girls across all groups.
- Boys were more likely to imitate physical aggression while girls were more likely to imitate verbal aggression.

Conclusion
The main conclusion from the study (apart from additional gender-related findings) was that the idea of observational learning was supported: learning can indeed be indirect and new behaviours can be learned by simply observing others.

THEORY
SOCIAL COGNITIVE THEORY AS AN EXTENSION OF SOCIAL LEARNING THEORY

Of course, to say that simply observing a behaviour automatically leads to learning this behaviour would be an oversimplification. There are many cognitive factors that mediate this influence. Bandura claimed that cognition needs to be viewed as a mediator between environmental stimuli and behaviour. So, instead of the classic behaviourist formula "stimulus—reaction", he assumed a more complex formula "stimulus–cognition– reaction". Bandura (1986) expanded on social learning theory and created the broader version (social cognitive theory) to account for all these nuances.

Apart from the idea of observational learning inherited from social learning theory, social cognitive theory included other major aspects. These were:
- reciprocal determinism
- the idea of human agency
- identification
- self-efficacy.

RECIPROCAL DETERMINISM
Reciprocal determinism is a model of three interacting factors: personal factors (physical, cognitive and emotional), behaviour and environment.

The concept of reciprocity implies that the three factors influence each other mutually, in a bidirectional way. For example, a person's emotional state (personal factor) may influence that person's behaviour, which in turn will influence the behaviour of others (environment). This environmental factor will then continue to influence the person's emotional state (personal factor), and so on. An example of this may be how aggression escalates in a conflict.

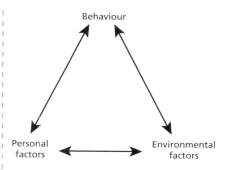

Behaviour

Personal factors ←→ Environmental factors

Figure 3.1 Reciprocal determinism

HUMAN AGENCY

Human beings do not simply react to environmental influences—they are agents of their own behaviour.

This means that human beings are self-regulating, self-reflecting and proactive.

IDENTIFICATION

Learning is more likely to occur if the observer can closely identify with the model. Identification is enhanced when there is perceived similarity between the model and the observer. This may explain why children were more likely to imitate the same-sex model in Bandura, Ross and Ross's (1961) study.

SELF-EFFICACY

Self-efficacy is the extent to which individuals believe they can master a particular skill or behaviour. In other words, it is the belief "I can do it". The theory claims that self-efficacy is an important prerequisite for modelling observed behaviour. If there is a lack of self-efficacy, the observer may not even attempt to replicate the observed behaviour.

RESEARCH   Perry, Perry and Rasmussen (1986)—aggression and self-efficacy in children

Essential understanding
✪ *Self-efficacy and expected consequences are both important as cognitive determinants of aggressive behaviour in schoolchildren.*

Aim
To explore the links between aggression and two cognitive factors that might influence children's decisions about whether to behave aggressively.

Method
Correlational study (questionnaires).

Participants
Elementary schoolchildren (mean age 11.3 years), split into an aggressive and a non-aggressive group.

Procedure
Children responded to two questionnaires. One of them measured children's perceptions of self-efficacy (in this case perceptions of their ability to perform aggression). The other one measured children's beliefs about the reinforcing and punishing consequences of aggression (their beliefs about positive and negative consequences of aggressive behaviour).

Results
Aggressive children reported that it is easier to perform aggression. They were also more confident that aggressive behaviour would lead to rewards, for example, protecting oneself from aversive treatment by others.

Conclusion
Children's perceptions of their self-efficacy and children's knowledge of the consequences of their actions are factors that contribute to aggressive behaviour.

Notes and evaluation
- Bandura's model of reciprocal determinism is difficult to test in an experimental setting. Perry, Perry and Rasmussen (1986) is a typical example of a study in this area. It uses a correlational design to examine the relationship among several variables relevant to the model, but of course the evidence only provides indirect support to the idea of reciprocal determinism.
- It is the large number of correlational studies (all looking at various aspects of the model) and the fact that correlational evidence fits well into the theoretical explanation that lends support to social cognitive theory.

RESEARCH   Williams and Williams (2010)—reciprocal determinism in mathematics

Williams and Williams (2010) attempted to get more direct evidence for the idea of reciprocal determinism (A influences B, but B also influences A). The design was correlational, but the researchers:
- collected a large data set (data on mathematics self-efficacy and mathematics achievement in 15-year-old schoolchildren across 33 nations)
- applied complex techniques of statistical modelling to see if the reciprocal model fits the data better than other simple models.

Results of this analysis were supportive of reciprocal determinism in 24 of the 33 nations, suggesting that reciprocal determinism is a universal phenomenon that transcends cultural differences. schoolchildren who believe they can cope well with mathematics indeed tend to perform well in mathematics tests. At the same time, performing well on mathematics tests further increases their self-efficacy.

3.1.3 Stereotypes

- **Illusory correlation**—a cognitive mechanism that leads a person to perceive a relationship between two events when in reality they are not related
- **Self-fulfilling prophecy**—a change in an individual's behaviour as a result of others' expectations about this individual
- **Stereotype**—a preconceived notion about a group of people; stereotypes are cognitive (beliefs), unlike

prejudice (attitudes) and discrimination (behaviour); stereotypes are intended to make generalizations about entire groups
- **Stereotype threat**—the anticipation of a situation that can potentially confirm a negative stereotype about one's group

---

ESSENTIAL UNDERSTANDING

Stereotypes are biased

Sometimes the sources of stereotypes are the actually existing differences between groups. In these cases stereotypes are no different from other schemas that we develop about objects and situations. They are simplified in that they ignore certain details, but otherwise there is no reason to suspect that they represent reality inaccurately. However, other stereotypes actually provide a biased or distorted representation of reality, suggesting the existence of group differences when there are none. It is this second kind of stereotype that has been the focus of psychological research.

Formation of stereotypes

Several theories have been proposed for the formation of the second kind of stereotype outlined above. The most prominent are:

- illusory correlation—see **Hamilton and Gifford (1976)**
- social categorization (which links to social identity theory)—see **Johnson, Schaller and Mullen (2000)**.

Illusory correlation occurs during encoding of serially presented stimuli. It can explain formation of negative stereotypes about minority groups. However, it only occurs in memory-based judgments and only when enough attentional resources are available (Hilton, Hippel 1996).

Social categorization enhances the formation of illusory correlations.

Effects of stereotypes on behaviour

Stereotypes have a range of effects on behaviour.

- People who hold a stereotype may influence the behaviour of the stereotyped group (self-fulfilling prophecy). See **Rosenthal and Jacobson (1968)**.
- Members of the stereotyped group itself may inadvertently reinforce the stereotype by changing their behaviour (stereotype threat). See **Steele and Aronson (1995)**.

FORMATION OF STEREOTYPES

The following ideas are often used to explain the origin of stereotypes: illusory correlation and social categorization.

Illusory correlation is a cognitive mechanism that leads a person to perceive a relationship between two events when in reality they are not related. This is a type of cognitive bias that takes place when two statistically infrequent events co-occur. The frequency of this co-occurrence is overestimated. It so happens that encountering a person from a minority group is statistically less frequent, and negative behaviours (such as crime) are also statistically less frequent than

acceptable behaviours. So when the two events (belonging to a minority group and negative behaviour) co-occur, the frequency of this co-occurrence is exaggerated, which gives rise to a negative stereotype about the minority group. For a classic study of illusory correlation see **Hamilton and Gifford (1976)**.

Social categorization has been shown to interact with illusory correlation in the formation of stereotypes. See **Johnson, Schaller and Mullen (2000)**.

RESEARCH   Hamilton and Gifford (1976)—illusory correlation

Essential understanding

✪ *Illusory correlation occurs during the encoding of serially presented stimuli.*

Aim

To investigate illusory correlations based on the co-occurrence of infrequent events.

Participants

104 undergraduates.

Procedure

Participants read a series of sentences describing desirable and undesirable behaviours performed by members of groups A and B. The groups were abstract because researchers did not want any previously existing associations or stereotypes to interfere with the task.

Table 3.3 summarizes the 39 sentences given to the participants.

	Group A	Group B	Total
Desirable behaviours	18	9	27
Undesirable behaviours	8	4	12
Total	26	13	39

Table 3.3

Based on this information, the following is clear.
- Group B was the minority (sentences featuring members of this group were half as likely).
- Undesirable behaviours in the sentences, just as in real life, were less frequent.
- The ratio of desirable to undesirable behaviours in group A and group B was exactly the same (18/8 = 9/4). So, there was no real correlation between behaviours and group membership.

Participants read these statements one by one, for example: "Bruce, a member of group A, did volunteer work for a church" (desirable behaviour).

After reading all the sentences, participants were asked to estimate how many members of each group performed desirable and undesirable behaviours.

Results
Participants overestimated the frequency with which members of the minority group performed negative behaviours.

Conclusion
There was a perceived association (correlation) between undesirable behaviour and group membership. The researchers argued that the illusory correlation was caused by event distinctiveness: encountering a member of the minority group is a distinct event, and so is encountering an instance of undesirable behaviour. Co-occurrence of two distinct events, according to Hamilton and Gifford, is overestimated.

LIMITATIONS OF ILLUSORY CORRELATION

Illusory correlation effects were found in many research studies with a variety of samples and experimental situations. However, limitations of these effects have been discovered as well.
- Illusory correlation effects disappear when judgments about groups are made **simultaneously** with the presentation of stimulus material. It is only when subjects retrieve information about groups from their memory that the effect occurs. So, illusory correlation as a mechanism of stereotype formation is limited to situations where people evaluate groups in a memory-based fashion.
- Illusory correlation formation is also inhibited when there are excessive demands on one's attention. For example, illusory correlation effects disappeared in studies where there was **increased cognitive load** on the participants (Hilton, Hippel 1996).

RESEARCH Johnson, Schaller and Mullen (2000)—social categorization in the formation of stereotypes

Essential understanding
✪ *Social categorization enhances the formation of illusory correlation.*

Procedure
A procedure like the one used in Hamilton and Gifford's (1976) study was combined with a social categorization manipulation.

Participants either knew nothing about their group membership or learned that they were a member of one of the groups.

Those who were assigned to one of the groups learned about their group membership either before or after the stimulus presentation (sentences with desirable or undesirable behavioural).

Results
Social categorization into the minority group before stimulus presentation eliminated the illusory correlation.

Social categorization into the minority group after stimulus presentation had no effect on the formation of stereotype.

Social categorization into the majority group (either before or after stimulus presentation) had little effect on illusory correlations.

EFFECTS OF STEREOTYPES ON BEHAVIOUR

There is a range of effects of stereotypes on behaviour.
- First, people who hold a stereotype may influence the behaviour of the stereotyped group. An example of this is found in the phenomenon of self-fulfilling prophecy and demonstrated in the study of **Rosenthal and Jacobson (1968)**.
- Second, members of the stereotyped group itself may inadvertently reinforce the stereotype by changing their behaviour as a result of increased anxiety or apprehension. This has been demonstrated in research of stereotype threat. See **Steele and Aronson (1995)**.

Essential understanding

⭐ *Steele and Aronson (1995) define stereotype threat as "being at risk of confirming a negative stereotype about one's group". Stereotype threat triggers an individual to unintentionally demonstrate behaviour that supports the existing stereotype.*

Aim

To investigate test performance as a function of stereotype threat in white and black participants.

Participants

114 male and female, black and white Stanford undergraduates.

Method and procedure

Black college students and white college students were given a 30-minute verbal test that was difficult enough for most participants to find it challenging.

In the experimental (stereotype-threat) condition participants were told that the test diagnosed intellectual ability: "a genuine test of your verbal abilities and limitations" (Steele, Aronson 1995).

In the control condition participants were told that the purpose of the research had nothing to do with intellectual ability: "to better understand the psychological factors involved in solving verbal problems" (Steele, Aronson 1995).

The assumption was that linking the test to ability would activate the existing racial stereotypes, so black participants faced the threat of fulfilling the stereotype.

Results

- White participants performed equally in the diagnostic and the non-diagnostic condition.
- Black participants performed as well as white participants in the non-diagnostic condition.
- However, black participants performed worse than white participants in the diagnostic condition.

Conclusion

Linking the test to diagnosing ability depresses the performance of black students through stereotype threat. When the test is presented as less reflective of ability, black participants' performance improves and matches that of white participants. The researchers suggest that this may be explained by increased apprehension of black students over possibly conforming to the negative group stereotype. Faced with this possibility, participants become anxious, which affects their test performance.

Essential understanding

⭐ *People who hold a stereotype may influence the behaviour of the stereotyped group.*

Aim

To investigate whether students of whom greater intellectual growth is expected will actually show greater intellectual growth in a period of one year or less.

Participants

320 students from the same public school, grades 1 to 6 (255 in the control group, 65 in the experimental group).

Procedure

Teachers in the school were told that certain students were expected to be "growth spurters", based on the results of their IQ test. In reality the test was fictitious and students designated as "spurters" were chosen at random.

Results

- In the year of the experiment, control-group students gained on average 8.4 IQ points, while students from the experimental group gained 12.2 IQ points.
- This expectancy advantage was most obvious in young students: for example, in grade 1 the average gain was 12 IQ points versus 27.4 IQ points in the control and the experimental groups respectively.
- The advantage of favourable expectations was more visible in reasoning IQ as compared to verbal IQ.

Conclusion

Changes in teachers' expectations produce changes in students' achievement. Stereotypes we have about other people may affect their behaviour through the process of self-fulfilling prophecy.

3.2 Cultural origins of behaviour and cognition

3.2.1 Culture and its influence on behaviour and cognition

- **Cultural norms**—the unique set of attitudes, beliefs and behaviours specific to a particular culture

- **Culture**—a "unique meaning and information system, shared by a group and transmitted across generations" Matsumoto (2007)

ESSENTIAL UNDERSTANDING

The three aspects to this topic are:
- defining culture and related concepts
- the influence of culture on behaviour
- the influence of culture on cognition.

Culture and related ideas
- The origin of culture may be explained evolutionarily: environmental context influences culture and cultural norms.
- Related concepts are cultural transmission, socialization, social learning, enculturation, acculturation and globalization.

The influence of culture on behaviour
This is covered in other topics such as:
- 3.2.2 Cultural dimensions
- 3.3.2 Acculturation
- 3.4. The influence of globalization on individual behaviour

The influence of culture on cognition
- There are cultural differences in the way people process information (cognitive style). See **Chiu (1972)**.
- In bilingual individuals the language that they are speaking triggers a change in decision-making processes. See **Briley, Morris and Simonson (2005)**.
- The mechanism through which culture influences cognition is an individual's conscious desire to conform to cultural norms.

ORIGIN OF CULTURE

Essential understanding
✪ *Environmental context can influence culture and cultural norms.*

According to Matsumoto (2007), "Culture is a solution to the problem of how to survive, given the problems in the environment, the physical and social needs that must be addressed, and the tools available". Based on this, the origin of culture can be explained as evolution: culture is a response of a group of people to the demands of their environment.

Specific environmental contexts engender certain expectations regarding appropriate cultural norms. **Cultural norms** are the unique set of attitudes, beliefs and behaviours specific to a particular culture.

CULTURE AND RELATED CONCEPTS

Related concepts covered in this unit are cultural transmission, socialization, social learning, enculturation, acculturation and globalization.
- **Cultural transmission** is the process of passing cultural norms from one generation to another.
- **Socialization** is the process by which social norms are incorporated by individuals.
- **Enculturation** is immersion in your own culture and acquisition of the cultural norms—that is, becoming part of your origin culture. Margaret Mead clarified the difference like this: socialization is "learning as a universal process" while enculturation is the "process of learning a culture as it takes place in a specific culture" (Mead 1963). Sometimes, however, the terms "socialization" and "enculturation" are used interchangeably. In a sense, cultural transmission is like "teaching", and socialization/enculturation is like "learning". They are two sides of the same process.
- **Social learning** is a mechanism of enculturation that involves observing other people perform actions as well as the consequences of these actions (see "**3.1.2 Social cognitive theory**").
- **Acculturation** is acquiring the cultural norms of a different culture (for example, when a person moves to a different country).
- **Globalization** is the increasing interconnectedness among all cultures and increasing cross-cultural influence. Psychologically this can be viewed as the process of "acculturation to a global culture".

The influence of culture on behaviour
The influence of culture on behaviour is covered in other topics. For example, see:
- cultural dimensions of behaviour and their influence on behaviours such as conformity and cooperation (see "**3.2.2 Cultural dimensions**")
- acculturation and its influence on attitudes, values and identity (see "**3.3.2 Acculturation**")
- globalization and its influence on identity and such behaviour as cooperation. (see "**3.4 The influence of globalization on individual behaviour**")

The influence of culture on cognition
- There are cultural differences in the way people process information (cognitive style). See **Chiu (1972)**.
- In bilingual individuals the language that they are speaking triggers a change in decision-making processes. See **Briley, Morris and Simonson (2005)**.
- This can be explained by a motivation to conform to the norms of potential observers. In other words, motivation to conform to cultural norms is the mechanism through which culture influences cognition.

Essential understanding
⭐ *There are cultural differences in the way children process information (cognitive style). The cognitive style of Chinese students is more holistic and contextual, whereas that of US students is more analytic and categorical. This may be explained by the differences in socialization practices and cultural values.*

Aim
To carry out a cross-cultural comparison of cognitive styles in Chinese and US students.

Participants
221 Chinese students in grades 4 and 5 from rural communities—all students came from middle-class families; 316 US students of the same grades sampled from rural districts of Indiana, comparable to the Chinese sample in terms of the socio-economic status.

Method
A 28-item cognitive-style test was used. Each item consisted of three pictures (for example, "cow", "chicken" and "grass"). The task was to select any two out of the three objects that were alike and went together, leaving the third one out.

Results
- US students scored significantly higher than Chinese students in **analytic** style: they grouped objects more often on the basis of separate components, for example, classifying human figures together because "they are both holding a gun".
- US students also scored significantly higher in the **categorical** style, for example a cow and a chicken were grouped together "because they are both animals" (leaving grass unpaired).
- On the contrary, Chinese students demonstrated a much higher prevalence of the **contextual** style, for example, classifying pictures together on the basis of contextual commonality. When given "cow", "chicken" and "grass" as the three objects, they would group cow and grass together because the cow eats grass, and the chicken would be left out.

Conclusion
Chinese students process stimuli holistically rather than analytically. They prefer to categorize objects on the basis of interdependence or relationships, while US students prefer to focus on components of the stimulus and categorize on the basis of membership in abstract groups.

Notes and evaluation
Chiu suggested that cognitive styles are end products of socialization processes. He carried out a review of published evidence and reported the following cultural differences in socialization relevant in the context of this research.
- Chinese parents emphasize mutual dependence in the family (as opposed to US parents who emphasize independence).
- Chinese students are more tradition-oriented ("living under their ancestors' shadows").
- Chinese students are more situation-oriented and sensitive to the environment.

Essential understanding
⭐ *Language-induced shifts in bicultural individuals influence their decision-making.*

Aim
To investigate the effect of language manipulation (Cantonese versus English) in bicultural individuals on decision-making processes.

Participants
Chinese undergraduates at a major Hong Kong university where all courses are taught in English. English and Cantonese are both official languages in Hong Kong, taught from early childhood. Students in this population are fluent in both languages and have substantial exposure to both cultures.

Method
Experiment, independent measures design; IV was language, DV was decision-making strategies.

Procedure
Study 1 (61 participants) involved **choice deferral**. Such decisions are relevant in situations such as considering the purchase of a new television to replace the old one that still works. A person who is deferring a choice, while choosing from the new options, will decide to buy none of them in an attempt to avoid potential disappointment. Such decisions are more in line with traditional Chinese values than western values.

An example of the decision-making scenario given to the participants was choosing between two restaurants. Each of the restaurants had two favourable features (the same for both the restaurants) and two unique unfavourable features. By making the unfavourable features unique to the options, researchers expected participants to focus on the potential losses.

Option A	Option B
Long wait (45 min)	Good variety of foods on the menu
Good variety of foods on the menu	Staff is not particularly friendly
High quality of food (4 stars)	View is not very attractive
Service is very slow	High quality of food (4 stars)

Table 3.4

Source: Briley, Morris and Simonson (2005: 356)

In each scenario participants could choose option A, option B or neither. If they chose neither it was referred to as "choice deferral".

Study 2 (90 participants) involved **compromise choices**. It included shopping scenarios with two extreme options and one compromise alternative. For example, in one of the scenarios participants had to choose one of three cameras: the cameras were characterized by two dimensions; options A and C had high values on one dimension and low values on the other dimension, while option B had moderate values along both dimensions (that is, option B was the compromise choice).

	Reliability rating of expert panel	Maximum autofocus range
Typical range	**40–70**	**12–28 mm**
Option A	45	25 mm
Option B	55	20 mm
Option C	65	15 mm

Table 3.5

Source: Briley, Morris and Simonson (2005: 356)

Participants were randomly split into two groups. In one of them the experiment was conducted in English, in the other in Chinese.

Results

- Choice deferral was more likely when the language of communication was Chinese (44% of participants in this condition chose neither of the two options, compared to 29% in the English language condition).
- Participants who were in the Chinese language condition were more likely to select compromise options: in the camera scenario 77% of participants chose the compromise option when the experiment was conducted in Chinese and only 53% chose the compromise option when it was conducted in English.

Conclusion
Culture affects decision-making processes through language; even the same bilingual individuals may prefer to make different decisions depending on which language they are speaking.

RESEARCH   **Briley, Morris and Simonson (2005)—follow-up studies**

Essential understanding
✪ *Language-induced shifts in bilingual individuals can be explained by a motivation to conform to observers' norms (individuals use language as an indicator of the identity of the audience that is likely to observe their behaviour).*

Aim
The authors wanted to test two potential explanations of the results of their study.
- Spoken language automatically triggers certain cultural schemas or cognitions.
- The changes in decision-making are the result of impression management.

Results
Further research by Briley, Morris and Simonson lends more support to the second explanation. For example, language manipulation effects tended to disappear when participants were given a demanding cognitive task (with the aim to increase cognitive load and hence give them no time to think about impression management).

Conclusion
The researchers argue that their bilingual participants adjusted their decision-making processes to the potential audience that would observe them; language spoken during the experiment might have been used as a clue that the audience would be English or Chinese. So, impression management and the desire to conform to cultural norms may be the **mechanism** through which culture influences cognition.

3.2.2 Cultural dimensions

DEFINITIONS

- **Cultural dimensions**—general factors underlying cross-cultural differences in values and behaviour; they have been identified on the basis of massive cross-national surveys
- **Emic approach**—examining a specific culture from within; enables an in-depth understanding of the unique culture without "imposed etic", but comparison with other cultures is difficult
- **Etic approach**—studying cultures from an outside perspective; enables cross-cultural comparisons, but requires the identification of universal phenomena that will serve as comparison criteria

ESSENTIAL UNDERSTANDING

Each culture is unique, so to compare them on a large scale is not an easy task. One needs to identify universal phenomena that are present in every individual culture. These phenomena will then become criteria for comparison.

Geert Hofstede (1973) conducted an extensive study involving participants from more than 70 countries and identified 5 such universal phenomena, or cultural dimensions. See **Hofstede (1973)** and "**Hofstede's cultural dimensions**".

Cultural dimensions have a wide range of influences on behaviour.

- Individualism–collectivism may influence rates of conformity. See **Berry and Katz (1967)**.
- Individualism–collectivism may influence volunteering. See **Finkelstein (2010)**.
- Power distance influences patterns of patient–doctor communication. See **Meeuwesen, van den Brink-Muinen and Hofstede (2009)**.
- Power distance influences people's reactions to empowerment in the workplace. See **Eylon and Au (1999)**.

RESEARCH   Hofstede (1973)—the multinational survey

Aim
To identify dimensions underlying cultural differences in values, attitudes and behaviour.

Participants
117,000 IBM employees (Hofstede founded the personnel research department of IBM Europe).

Method and procedure
A worldwide survey of values was conducted between 1967 and 1973. Results of the survey were statistically analysed to identify hidden dimensions underlying observed patterns of responses (a statistical technique known as factor analysis).

In order to confirm original findings and to generalize them to other populations, a series of follow-up studies were conducted between 1990 and 2002. The samples included commercial airline pilots, students and civil service managers. Around this time countries were also profiled against the value dimensions (value scores were established for each country).

Results
Originally Hofstede identified four dimensions: individualism versus collectivism, uncertainty avoidance, power distance, masculinity versus femininity. Later research refined the theory and added two more dimensions: long-term versus short-term orientation and indulgence versus self-restraint.

THEORY

HOFSTEDE'S CULTURAL DIMENSIONS

Individualism versus collectivism. In individualist cultures people define their personality in terms of their own personal characteristics, their success and their unique features. Among the strongest values in society are personal autonomy, competitiveness and self-sufficiency. In collectivist cultures identity is linked to the social group, and values associated with belonging to a group take priority over personal values.

Power distance index (PDI). A higher PDI score indicates that hierarchy between the less powerful and the more powerful is firmly established in the society and rarely questioned. A lower PDI score indicates that people question authority and believe that authority figures are not particularly superior to themselves.

Masculinity versus femininity. Masculine values include achievement, autonomy and competitiveness; feminine values include caring, cooperation, modesty and compassion.

Uncertainty avoidance index. This refers to the extent to which people can tolerate ambiguity. Cultures that rank high on this index tend to avoid risk-taking and are intolerant of events that are unexpected or unknown. Cultures that rank low on this index are more tolerant of uncertainty and embrace new situations more easily.

Long-term versus short-term orientation. Cultures that score low on this dimension (short-term orientation) are conservative, they rely on the past for guidance and they value traditions highly. A high score (long-term orientation) indicates a culture that is pragmatic and oriented towards the future and future challenges.

Indulgence versus restraint. Societies that promote indulgence allow a free gratification of basic and natural human desires, such as having a holiday or just having fun. Societies that promote restraint regulate gratification of needs with strict social norms.

RESEARCH — Berry and Katz (1967)—the influence of individualism and collectivism on conformity

Essential understanding
✪ *Collectivism is associated with higher conformity to group norms.*

Aim
To investigate whether cultural differences in individualism versus collectivism affect conformity.

Participants
This study looked at individuals from the Temne people of Sierra Leone and the Inuit people of Northern Canada. The Inuits live as a hunting and fishing society. This way of life promotes individualism. People are responsible for their survival on a daily basis, and there is little accumulation of food in the society. The Temne are a food-accumulating society whose way of life promotes collectivism. They are rice farmers who harvest one crop a year. In order to survive until the next harvest they rely on sharing food among group members.

Procedure
The researchers measured conformity using the Asch paradigm: participants are shown a series of lines of varying length, with one target line on top of a page and several other lines below. Participants are then asked to identify which of the other lines is of equal length to the target line. They are also tricked into believing that most of the other participants (Temne or Inuits, respectively) pick a particular line as the correct answer; however, this line is actually not equal to the target line. The measure of conformity in this procedure is whether or not the participant will accept the suggestion of the "majority" and pick an incorrect response because most other group members have chosen it.

Results
- The Temne had a significant tendency to accept the suggestion of the group and select the incorrect response.
- Participants from the Inuit group were mostly unaffected by this suggestion of the "majority".

Conclusion
The researchers concluded that the individualist Inuit participants conform less often than the collectivist Tenme because conformity to group norms is ingrained as a cultural value in the Temne society, which depend on tight social relations.

RESEARCH — Finkelstein (2010)—the effect of individualism and collectivism on volunteer behaviour

Essential understanding
✪ *People in individualist societies volunteer for different reasons from people in collectivist societies.*

Aim
To examine the effect of culture on volunteer behaviour.

Method
Online self-report questionnaires that measured a variety of possible reasons for volunteering including:
- altruistic motivation to help
- the desire to strengthen social ties
- role identity (volunteering for the sake of consistency with one's self-image)
- career-related reasons.

Participants
194 undergraduates at a US university who participated in exchange for extra course credit.

Results
- Collectivism was more strongly related than individualism to altruistic motivation and the desire to strengthen social ties.
- Collectivism, but not individualism, correlated with helping in order to sustain role identity.
- On the other hand, individualism was most closely associated with engaging in volunteering for career-related reasons.

Conclusion
The researchers concluded that individualists and collectivists differ in why they choose to volunteer, but not in the willingness to volunteer itself.

RESEARCH — Meeuwesen, van den Brink-Muinen and Hofstede (2009)—patient–doctor communication

Essential understanding
✪ *Patient–doctor communication in cultures with greater power distance is more one-sided.*

Aim
To investigate how cross-national differences in medical communication can be understood from Hofstede's cultural dimensions.

Method and procedure
Patient-doctor communication sessions were videotaped and analysed against a checklist of criteria (structured observation). Additional context information was gathered by using questionnaires.

Participants
307 general practitioners (GPs) and 5,807 patients from 10 European countries (Belgium, Estonia, Germany, United

Kingdom, the Netherlands, Poland, Romania, Spain, Sweden and Switzerland).

Results

- A large nation's power distance index (PDI) was associated with less unexpected information exchange and shorter consultation sessions. Communication was more one-sided, with the doctor speaking and the patient listening.
- In countries with a low PDI score, doctors shared more information, were more open to questions and generally

more flexible in their communication style. Sessions also lasted longer.

Conclusion

In nations with a high PDI score, roles of the patient and the doctor are more clearly described and fixed, and communication between them follows an established protocol more closely. Understanding of these differences is important to prevent intercultural miscommunication and, at a larger scale, to pursue integration of European healthcare policies.

RESEARCH   Eylon and Au (1999)—power distance and empowerment in the workplace

Essential understanding

✪ *Individuals from cultures with high PDI scores do not perform as well when empowered as when disempowered.*

Aim

To investigate the relationship between power distance and empowerment in the workplace.

Participants

135 MBA students from a Canadian university.

Procedure

Participants were divided into high power-distance and low power-distance groups based on their language and country of origin. They participated in a management simulation. At different point of the simulation all participants found themselves in situations where they were either empowered or disempowered.

Results

- Regardless of their cultural background, participants were more satisfied with their job in the empowered condition and less satisfied in the disempowered condition.
- Individuals from cultures with high PDI scores did not perform as well when empowered as when disempowered.
- Participants from cultures with low PDI scores performed similarly regardless of the condition.

Conclusion

High power-distance and low power-distance groups react differently to empowerment in the workplace (in terms of performance, but not in terms of work satisfaction). High power-distance groups may perform better while disempowered. Being disempowered in this context means having more structured tasks and well-defined responsibilities.

3.3 Cultural influences on individual attitudes, identity and behaviours

3.3.1 Enculturation

- **Cultural norms**—the unique set of attitudes, beliefs and behaviours specific to a particular culture
- **Cultural transmission**—passing cultural norms (attitudes, behaviours and beliefs) from one generation to the next

- **Enculturation**—the process by which people learn the necessary and appropriate norms in the context of their culture—that is, cultural transmission ("teaching") and enculturation ("learning") are two sides of the same process

ESSENTIAL UNDERSTANDING

There is a **bidirectional relationship** between cultural norms and the individuals who make up particular cultural groups. Cultural norms grow out of the behaviour of individuals but individuals' behaviour is shaped by cultural norms. This resembles the relationship between personal and shared knowledge in TOK.

The mechanism of enculturation is cultural transmission, which on the part of the child takes the form of learning. A research study that demonstrated how active learning leads to enculturation (using the example of musical enculturation) is **Trainor** *et al* (2012).

However, active learning might not be a universal mechanism of enculturation. In some non-western societies passive observational learning seems to be the predominant way. See **Odden and Rochat (2004)**.

Enculturation influences cognition (cognitive schemas) on a deep level. See **Demorest** *et al* (2008).

Enculturation interacts with acculturation to influence identity (and such related behaviours as self-esteem and the attitude toward one's social group). See **Kim and Omizo (2006)**.

Essential understanding

⭐ *Enculturation is the result of active learning.*

Trainor *et al* (2012) studied the phenomenon of musical enculturation. Music is an integral part of any culture, and enculturation necessarily entails becoming sensitive to music from one's culture. One example of cultural sensitivity to music would be how the same voice timbre may be considered pleasant in one culture and aversive in another.

Aim

To test the idea that musical enculturation occurs through active learning.

Method and procedure

38 western infants who were 6 months old were randomly assigned to one of two conditions:

- six months of active participatory music class
- six months of a class in which they experienced music passively while playing with toys.

DV 1 was sensitivity to western tonality. It was measured by examining infants' preferences to two versions of a sonatina by Thomas Atwood (1765–1838): the tonal version and the atonal version. The tonal version was the original while the atonal version had additional accidentals added. Infant preferences were measured in a head-turn preference procedure in which a light was flashed, illuminating an interesting toy, and once the infant looked at the toy, the music started playing. The music stopped once the infant looked away. It was assumed that the longer a child looks at the toy while the music is playing, the more the child likes the music.

DV 2 was social development of the infants. Making music with other people is a cultural activity involving interpersonal interaction, so it was predicted that infants in the active classes would show more social development than infants in the passive classes. Social development of the infants was measured by a questionnaire given to their parents.

Results

- Children in the active class group demonstrated a preference to the tonal version of the sonatina, while children in the passive group did not prefer one version to the other.
- The questionnaire showed that infants in the active condition by the age of 12 months showed significantly less distress to limitations, less distress when confronted with novel stimuli, more smiling and laughter, and easier soothability.

Conclusion

Active music making in a social context involving infants and parents promotes musical enculturation of infants, including their sensitivity to cultural tonality and social development.

Essential understanding

⭐ *Participatory learning might not be a universal mechanism of enculturation.*

Aim

To investigate the role of observational learning as a mechanism of children's enculturation in non-western cultural contexts.

Background

- Participatory learning is learning that occurs as a result of a child's active involvement in a learning activity. This idea is the legacy of Lev Vygotsky's influential views in developmental psychology. See "**7.1.2 Cognitive development**".
- Observational learning is learning that occurs when the child observes everyday activities without directly participating in them. This idea is the legacy of Albert Bandura's research. See "**3.1.2 Social cognitive theory**".
- Traditionally in theories of enculturation, participatory learning was believed to be the leading mechanism; observational learning was acknowledged as a starting point, but never the core process of cultural learning.

Method

Longitudinal naturalistic observation of children in key contexts of village life; semi-structured interviews with caretakers, teachers, pastors and chiefs; parental belief questionnaires. One of the researchers lived in the village for 20 months.

Participants

28 children aged 4–12 and their parents from a rural village in Samoa. Samoan society is hierarchical and socially stratified. This stratification influences practically all social practices.

Results

- Observations and interviews showed high specificity of Samoan attitudes towards education and enculturation. As there was a high distance to authority (power distance), questioning in class was discouraged as it was viewed as a sign of disrespect to the adult. Children were largely left to learn things on their own, and adults did not try to engage them or motivate them. Caretakers believed that children learn via observing and listening to their elders.
- Samoan houses are often built without walls (due to the hot and humid climate), and activities of nearby households may be easy to observe. Children and adults can freely observe the activities of others since the concept of privacy is not established in the society and can even be viewed as a form of secrecy or immorality.
- By age 15, adolescents spend a significant amount of time doing chores (such as washing clothes, feeding domesticated animals, child care, cooking). However, parents were never seen explaining the chore to the child or explicitly teaching the child in any other way. The same was true for fishing. By the age of 12, children were quite skilled fishermen, but never in their lives had

they been fishing under the supervision of an adult who would correct their mistakes. For example, if spear fishing was used, a boy would accompany his father, but there would only be one spear available and the child would never use it. Then after a certain age children would simply borrow the fishing equipment and start fishing by themselves.

- Knowledge of the intricate societal hierarchy, ritual practice and cultural concepts such as power and authority was also acquired in the same way.

Conclusion

Each culture may emphasize a different blend of mechanisms of enculturation. In the Samoan context observational learning plays a central role in children's enculturation.

Notes

These results are important for educators, especially in a multicultural classroom situation. Children who grow up in an environment that emphasizes observational learning as a mechanism of enculturation may be at a disadvantage in a western classroom which is typically focused on direct instruction, scaffolding and active participation.

RESEARCH   Demorest et al (2008)—the influence of enculturation on musical memory

Essential understanding

✪ *Enculturation influences cognition (cognitive schemas) on a deep level.*

Participants

150 trained and untrained participants from the USA and Turkey.

Procedure

Participants listened to several novel musical excerpts from both familiar and unfamiliar cultures (western, Turkish and Chinese) and then completed a recognition memory task.

Results

- Participants were significantly better at remembering novel music from their native culture.
- Musical expertise did not correlate with this result.

Conclusion

Enculturation influences musical memory on a deep level (cognitive schemas for musical information).

Note

In the broad sense, cognition also counts as "behaviour", so this research study may be used to demonstrate the effects of enculturation on behaviour.

RESEARCH   Kim and Omizo (2006)—enculturation, acculturation and identity

Essential understanding

✪ *Enculturation interacts with acculturation to influence identity.*

In the context of their research, acculturation is the process of adapting to the dominant group (European American), while enculturation is the process of retaining the norms of the indigenous group (Asian American).

Aim

To examine the relationship between Asian American college students' enculturation and acculturation in relation to the development of identity.

Method

Correlational study. All variables were measured through psychometrically validated questionnaires. Enculturation was operationalized as engaging in Asian American cultural behaviours; acculturation was operationalized as engaging in European American cultural behaviours.

Participants

156 Asian American college students aged 18–24.

Results

- Acculturation and enculturation scores did not correlate significantly. This lends support to Berry et al's (1997) model where acculturation and enculturation are presented as two independent dimensions and the combination of these two dimensions results in four distinct acculturation practices (see "3.3.2 Acculturation").
- Both enculturation and acculturation were related positively to participants' perception that they are good and worthy members of their cultural group.
- Enculturation was associated with increased positive feelings towards the Asian American social group and the belief that being a member of the Asian American group is an important aspect of one's self-concept.
- Acculturation was associated with self-efficacy, cognitive flexibility and the belief that others view the Asian American group positively.

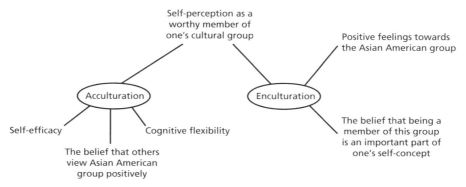

Figure 3.2 Results of Kim and Omizo (2006)

Conclusion

Enculturation and acculturation, being two relatively independent processes, may both contribute positively to the development of identity.

Notes

This study has all typical limitations of a self-report study with college students. Generalizability of findings is limited to a specific population of Asian American college students. Results are correlational, so no cause–effect relationship can be inferred from the data. Finally, the credibility of results depends on the psychometric properties of the questionnaires used to measure the variables.

3.3.2 Acculturation

DEFINITIONS

– **Acculturation**—internalizing the norms of the dominant culture where you have migrated
– **Enculturation**—internalizing the norms of your own culture of origin

Notes

Recognizing that the cultural influences in dominant and non-dominant groups are mutual, acculturation is now defined as the process of psychological and cultural change as a result of contact and interaction between cultures. It can result in changes to both cultures, not only the non-dominant one (Berry 2008). Specific research studies usually use the simplified approach and focus on how individuals change as a result of migration. Enculturation in this context refers to the ties with the heritage culture, while acculturation refers to adopting the norms of the host culture.

ESSENTIAL UNDERSTANDING

Strategies of cultural change

Individuals can adopt four strategies of cultural change. Each strategy is a combination of two independent dimensions—maintenance of heritage culture and seeking relationships with other groups. See **Berry (1997)**.

Limitations of acculturation effects

Research into acculturation has a number of typical limitations, including:
• reliance on self-report data
• correlational design
• the fact that acculturation design is biased in one direction (from poorer countries and more traditionalist societies to rich and more liberal countries).

Acculturation and health behaviour of migrants

Research into the effects of acculturation on health behaviour of migrants has identified two interesting effects: the healthy migrant effect and the negative acculturation effect.

• Acculturation contributes to unhealthy eating because migrants typically move into a culture that promotes less healthy eating behaviours than their own culture. See **Shah et al (2015)**.
• There are some protective factors that can serve as a buffer against developing obesity in migrants. See **Ishizawa and Jones (2016)**.
• Length of residence is associated with growing obesity. See **Da Costa, Dias and Martins (2017)**.
• In using such uni-dimensional measures as length of residence, this research ignores the complexities of acculturation strategies proposed by Berry (1997).
• Another criticism is that it is not the process of acculturation that seems to matter, but the culture to which one is acculturating. There were other studies that did not show a significant correlation between the risk of being overweight and the duration of residence. See **"Criticism of research into effects of acculturation on health"**.

BERRY (1997)—TWO-DIMENSIONAL MODEL OF ACCULTURATION

According to Berry (1997), individuals can adopt four strategies of cultural change.

- **Assimilation**—individuals are open to change and not concerned about the loss of connection with their original culture. They adjust their behaviour, attitudes and beliefs to the norms of the dominant culture.
- **Integration**—individuals preserve their original values and beliefs, but at the same time explore relationships with other cultures.
- **Separation**—individuals value their original culture, are afraid of losing it and, as a result, actively avoid contact with other cultures.
- **Marginalization**—individuals do not maintain their original culture, but neither do they seek contact with other cultures.

These four strategies can be visualized as a system of two independent dimensions: maintenance of heritage culture and seeking relationships with other groups.

In a way, the two dimensions can be thought of as enculturation (maintaining the heritage culture) versus acculturation (seeking relationships with the dominant culture). This idea has far-reaching implications: it means that enculturation and acculturation are not necessarily opposite

processes and can act together to pursue a common goal if cultural diversity is accepted in the society.

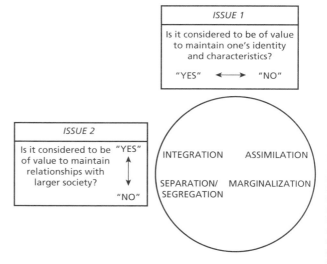

Figure 3.3 Acculturation strategies
Berry (1997)

TYPICAL LIMITATIONS OF ACCULTURATION RESEARCH

Acculturation is a process that occurs over a period of time, so it is important to conduct longitudinal studies. Ideally, studies should take into account changes in both the minority and the dominant culture. Since acculturation involves a wide range of attitudes, beliefs and behaviours, the common method of choice is self-report measures (questionnaires). Naturally, self-report data from questionnaires lends itself to a correlational design. This has implications in terms of wider coverage of variables, but limited scope for cause–effect inferences.

Since the majority of research studies look at samples of migrants, there is another limitation that must be accounted for.

- Most migration occurs from poorer countries to richer countries.
- Most migration occurs from traditional societies to more liberal societies.
- Migration in the opposite direction is very rarely studied due to limited availability of samples.

This makes acculturation research biased in one direction.

How does acculturation affect health behaviour of migrants?
Research in this area has identified two interesting effects.

- **The healthy migrant effect**—people who recently migrated have a tendency to be healthier than their counterparts who stayed in the country of origin. One potential explanation is that host countries are selective and they prefer to select healthy immigrants.

- **The negative acculturation effect**—the healthy migrant effect diminishes over time: migrants are becoming less healthy and more similar to their counterparts who stayed in the country of origin. One potential explanation is that the food environments in the migrant origin cultures tend to be healthier than food environments in the more "developed" host societies.

RESEARCH Shah *et al* (2015)—obesity in South Asian workers in the UAE

Essential understanding
✪ *Acculturation contributes to unhealthy eating because migrants typically move into a culture that promotes less healthy eating behaviours.*

Aim
To study the association between acculturation and obesity.

Participants
A random sample of 1,375 South Asian (from India, Pakistan and Bangladesh) male migrant workers in the UAE. Over half of them had lived in the UAE for six or more years. The most common occupations were drivers, labourers, agricultural workers and construction workers. There was

also a comparison group of men of the same age in their culture of origin.

Results
- Migrant workers in the UAE had significantly higher body mass index (BMI) than the comparison group.
- The longer they stayed in the UAE, the higher their BMI became.
- Prevalence of obesity was higher in migrants than in the comparison group; for example, it was more than double among Pakistani participants. At the same time, prevalence of obesity and being overweight in the migrant sample was also higher than in Emirati men.

Conclusion
Acculturation may contribute to unhealthy eating behaviours, resulting in obesity and being overweight. This may be explained by the fact that migrants are moving into a culture that promotes more unhealthy eating behaviour, compared to their culture of origin.

Evaluation
- A strength of the study is using random sampling because it increases representativeness of the sample. Participants were selected randomly from the mandatory health visa screening centre in Abu Dhabi.
- Years of residency is often used as an indicator of acculturation (the assumption is that the longer people live in a new country, the more they are acculturated to it). However, it is a crude measure susceptible to some bias. It does not take into account individual differences in terms of people's reaction to acculturative stress.
- This not being a true experiment, causation cannot be inferred.
- Results may be specific to migrant men and may not be applicable to South Asian women.

RESEARCH   Ishizawa and Jones (2016)—obesity in Asian migrants in the USA

Essential understanding
⭐ *There are some protective factors that can serve as a buffer against developing obesity in migrants.*

Aim
To compare obesity rates among second- and third-generation Asian migrants in the USA and identify potential moderating factors of developing obesity.

Method
Correlational study.

Participants
Asian migrants in the USA.

Results
Second- and third-generation migrants had a higher likelihood of obesity than first-generation migrants or people from their country of origin. However, there were moderating factors that protected against developing obesity, which were:
- living in a neighbourhood with a high migrant density
- living in a household that retained the original language.

Conclusion
Retaining some ties with the original culture may serve as a protective factor against developing obesity in migrants.

Evaluation
- The study took into consideration protective factors. It is a strength because just postulating that migrants are becoming more obese with the course of time is not too helpful from the practical viewpoint. Knowing what factors can potentially protect them is practical because we can enhance those protective factors to create healthier populations.
- The results of the study are formulated in terms of causation (moderating factors that protect against obesity), but we need to remember that it is still just an inference. It was observed, for example, that migrants who retained their original language were less likely to develop obesity with the course of time. The conclusion that retaining the original language protects from developing obesity seems plausible, but it is not certain. As in any correlational study, there could be other factors influencing the association of these two variables.

RESEARCH   Da Costa, Dias and Martins (2017)—obesity in migrants in Portugal

Essential understanding
⭐ *Length of residence is associated with growing obesity.*

Aims
To compare the prevalence of being overweight between immigrants and natives in Portugal; to study the correlation between length of residence and being overweight among immigrants.

Method
Correlational study.

Participants
31,000 people from Portugal, of whom 4.6% were migrants.

Results
Prevalence of excessive weight was higher in the sample of native Portuguese than in new migrants, but the length of residence was positively correlated with the prevalence of being overweight in migrants (those who stayed longer had a tendency to be more overweight).

Conclusion
The process of acculturation causes gradual changes in diet or lifestyle; these changes cause migrants to become more similar to the native Portuguese in terms of eating behaviours.

- As pointed out by **Schwartz _et al_ (2013)**, most studies of acculturation and health outcomes rely on a uni-dimensional understanding of acculturation—accultured versus non-accultured to the receiving culture, ignoring the second dimension proposed by Berry (1997), the ties with the original culture.
- As a result of this, it is not clear whether the observed effects of immigration on health are due to immigrants'

adaptation to the receiving culture, loss of connection with the heritage culture, or both.
- Another criticism is that it is not the process of acculturation that seems to matter, but the culture to which one is acculturating. There were other studies that did not show a significant correlation between the risk of being overweight and the duration of residence.

3.4 The influence of globalization on individual behaviour (HL only)

DEFINITIONS

- **Globalization**—the increasing interconnectedness of people worldwide through the growth of international exchange. Globalization is driven primarily by economic factors but has vast social, cultural and psychological

- consequences. In a sense, the effects of globalization on behaviour are related to the effects of acculturation on behaviour—in this case acculturation to the "global culture"

ESSENTIAL UNDERSTANDING

How globalization may influence behaviour
- The rapid increase in communication and interdependence in today's world may change people's behaviour, making it more cosmopolitan.
- However, there is an opposing hypothesis which suggests that globalization will trigger reactionary movements and people will more rigorously protect their local interests.
- This has been tested in empirical research. It was demonstrated that globalization influences people's cosmopolitan attitudes by weakening their identification with their group of origin, and this influences cooperation strategies that people choose, making them more global and less local. See **Buchan _et al_ (2009)**.

Effects of the interaction of global and local influences on behaviour
- Berry (2008) argues that it is essential to distinguish globalization as a process and outcomes of this process. The outcomes of globalization, according to him, depend on the predominant acculturation strategy (integration, assimilation, separation or marginalization). In its turn, the acculturation strategy is formed by an interaction of local and global influences. See **Berry (2008)**.

- Supporting this theoretical framework, Adams (2003) demonstrated that cultural values of the USA and Canada, contrary to common expectations, do not converge over time. In some aspects they are even becoming increasingly different, as if the two cultures were trying to emphasize their uniqueness. See **Adams (2003)**.
- Also in accordance with this theoretical framework, globalization influences adolescents' identity in one of three possible directions: development of a bicultural identity, identity confusion or formation of self-selected cultures. See **Arnett (2002)**.

Methods used to study the influence of globalization on behaviour
- Correlational research
- Cross-cultural comparisons

Weaknesses of these methods are that it is not easy to isolate the effects of globalization when depending on common metrics (self-report surveys) and when generalizing from a relatively small sample to a whole nation.

RESEARCH   Buchan _et al_ (2009)—globalization and cooperation

Essential understanding
✪ _Globalization influences behaviour. The more individuals or a whole society are included in the global network of interactions, the more likely they are to choose cooperation strategies that prioritize the global over the local._

Aim
To investigate the effects of globalization on cooperation strategies. In this, two alternative hypotheses were investigated.
(a) Globalization prompts reactionary movements, and large-scale cooperation takes the form of defending the interests of one's ethnic, racial or language group.

(b) Globalization strengthens people's cosmopolitan attitudes by weakening their identification with their group of origin.

Method and procedure
- To measure cooperation strategies the researchers used multilevel sequential cooperation experiments. In a typical trial subjects would be given 10 tokens and required to distribute the tokens among three accounts—personal, local and world.
- Each token placed in the personal account was saved.
- Each token placed in the local account was added to local contributions of three other individuals from the same country, the sum was multiplied by two and each of the four participants received 1/4 of that amount. For example, if Mike placed one token in the local account, and so did three other people from his country, the total would become 4 × 2 = 8, and each of the four participants would get two tokens.
- Each token placed in the world account was added to the contributions from the same three local people plus two other groups of four people from different countries. The sum was tripled by the experimenter, and the participant received 1/12 of the resulting amount. Placing tokens in the world account is potentially the most profitable decision, but only if it is shared by other players— so it is the riskiest.
- In these experiments the amount of an individual's contributions to the world account was taken as an operationalization of cosmopolitan interests (cosmopolitan cooperation strategy). Contributions to the local account were taken as an operationalization of parochial interests (parochial cooperation strategy).
- Globalization was measured by a standardized questionnaire (the Globalization Index) which asks a variety of questions tapping into the degree to which an individual takes part in the network of global economic, social and cultural relations. An example of a question is "How often do you watch a television programme or a movie from a different country?"

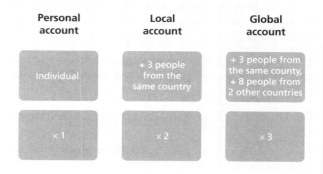

Figure 3.4 Personal, local and global accounts

Participants
Samples from six countries were used: the USA, Italy, Russia, Argentina, South Africa and Iran. There were approximately 190 participants per country.

Results
- The study lent support to the hypothesis that globalization strengthens people's cosmopolitan attitudes. People who had higher scores on the Globalization Index were also more likely to cooperate on the global level—that is, contribute more to the world account in the cooperation experiment.
- In order of increasingly cosmopolitan (and decreasingly parochial) cooperation the countries ranked as follows: Iran, South Africa, Argentina, Russia, Italy, the USA.

Conclusion
Higher levels of globalization are associated with stronger cosmopolitan cooperation strategies—a preference of global interests to the local interests. Globalization probably influences an individual to reduce perceived social distance with geographically remote others.

THEORY

BERRY (2008)—GLOBALIZATION AND ACCULTURATION

Essential understanding
✪ *Globalization is closely connected to acculturation. In its turn, choosing one of the four acculturation strategies (integration, assimilation, separation or marginalization) is the result of the interaction between the influences of the local culture and the global culture. The choice of acculturation strategies is fateful for the outcomes of globalization.*

Acculturation and globalization
Berry (2008) describes how the concepts of acculturation and globalization are related to each other. Both acculturation and globalization are initiated by intercultural contact and lead to change both on the individual and on the cultural level.

Assumptions that need to be rejected
Two assumptions used to be predominant in research and popular thinking.

- Acculturation and globalization induce more change in non-dominant peoples.
- The ultimate result of these processes is the loss of uniqueness of non-dominant group members and establishing a homogeneous society.

Both of these assumptions have been challenged. Berry's two-dimensional model of acculturation strategies, for example, incorporates the opportunity for multicultural societies to be established on the basis of integration as the acculturation strategy that embraces both the original culture and the new culture.

Possible outcomes of globalization
Berry (2008) claims that we need to differentiate between the process of globalization and the outcomes of this process. Globalization as a process refers to societies engaging in international contact, establishing an interconnected network of relations. Globalization is the

contact that provides the starting point for acculturation. This process, according to Berry, can have four possible outcomes, each outcome being the ultimate result of the adopted acculturation strategy.

- Globalization will lead to a homogeneous world culture, most likely based on the values and norms of the dominant cultures, with non-dominant societies adopting (**assimilating**) these norms.

- Mutual change will occur where societies share some common qualities but at the same time retain unique distinctive features (**integration**).
- Non-dominant groups will end up rejecting the growing influence of the dominant societies (**separation**).
- Globalization can lead to the destruction of non-dominant cultures, leaving these groups essentially with no culture (**marginalization**).

RESEARCH   Adams (2003)—do cultural values of the USA and Canada converge over time?

Essential understanding
✪ *Supporting Berry's (2008) theoretical framework, it has been demonstrated that the outcome of globalization is not necessarily convergence of cultural values.*

Aim
To investigate whether cultural values of Canadians would gradually assimilate US values. (Note that the USA is the most dominant society—for example, most of the films shown in Canada are US films).

Method
A survey consisting of 86 value statements.

Participants
Representative samples from both populations with a total of 14,000 participants.

Procedure
Adams (2003) studied cultural values of citizens of the USA and Canada at three points in time: 1992, 1996 and 2000.

Results
The initial expectations were not confirmed.
- The cultural value profiles of the two countries did not converge with the course of time—they remained distinctly different, and in some cases the differences became even larger.
- An example is the statement "The father of the family must be master of his own house". The percentage agreeing with this statement in the Canadian national sample from 1992 to 2000 decreased from 26% to 18%, while the percentage agreeing in the US national sample increased from 42% to 49%.

Conclusion
Globalization is not necessarily a straightforward process in which the dominant culture subsumes non-dominant cultures. The outcomes of globalization depend on the acculturation strategy chosen.

HOW DOES GLOBALIZATION INFLUENCE ADOLESCENTS' IDENTITY?

Essential understanding
✪ *Also in accordance with Berry's (2008) theoretical framework, the influence of globalization on identity may differ depending on the strategy chosen.*

Arnett (2002) argues that the primary psychological influence of globalization is on individuals' identity—how individuals think about themselves in relation to social groups. He also claims that the most affected group is adolescents: they are still discovering their identity, and they are usually more interested in global media (such as music and television), which is the driving force of globalization. He distinguishes **four main influences** of globalization on adolescents' identity.

- Many people in the world develop a **bicultural identity**: part of their identity stems from the local culture, and another part from the global culture. This is similar to the kind of identity developed by immigrants and members of ethnic minority groups.
- **Identity confusion** may be increasing, especially among adolescents in non-western societies. This happens if the development of a bicultural identity has not been

successful. For these individuals, the norms of the global culture undermine their belief in the local culture. At the same time, the global culture for them is too alien and out of reach. Identity confusion may lead to further problems such as substance use, depression and suicide.
- In response to globalization some people choose to form **self-selected cultures** with like-minded individuals and develop an identity that is not dependent on the global culture. Self-selected cultures may be diverse, ranging from religious fundamentalism to musical subcultures. What unifies them is an attempt to find an identity that is different from the mainstream global culture.
- The age period for identity formation increases, and **identity explorations**, which used to end typically by age 18, are being extended to a later life period (18–25).

In conclusion, Arnett (2002) points out that identity in today's world is based less on prescribed social roles and more on individual choices. Some people react to this with identity confusion, but others succeed in embracing the diversity and assimilating both the global and the local culture.

METHODS USED TO STUDY THE INFLUENCE OF GLOBALIZATION ON BEHAVIOUR

Essential understanding

✪ *Mainly correlational methods are used, and they involve cross-cultural comparisons. This implies a number of limitations.*

- As we have seen, multiple methods can be used to measure the variables involved in research. For example, Buchan *et al* (2009) measured cooperation through an experiment where participants allocated tokens to bank accounts.
- However, the methods used to establish the influence of globalization on behaviour are **correlational**. It is impossible to conduct a true experiment in this area. As a result, cause–effect inferences should be made with caution.
- Research into globalization involves the idea of multiple cultures interacting with each other, so a common choice is the method of **cross-cultural studies**. Success of cross-cultural studies depends on the existence of common metrics that can be applied equally to each culture in the research sample. An example of such a metric is Hofstede's cultural dimensions. Surveys have been developed to operationalize these constructs, and results of the surveys may be used to compare cultures with each other against a set of common dimensions. Another use

of these surveys is to look at how scores of a particular culture change over the course of time as the society gets involved in more and more globalization processes.
- There are two major weaknesses in using these survey scores. First, they rely on **self-report data** which is not always reliable as it is open to such biases as social desirability or acquiescence. Second, a **generalization** is made from the scores of a group of people (a sample taking part in the research) to the whole nation, which is a long leap. It is not easy to select a sample that will be representative of a whole culture. Nation scores are therefore only crude estimates.
- A major challenge in studying the influence of globalization on behaviour is the fact that cultures are **fluid and changeable**. They are in a constant state of dynamic interaction, so any changes to individual behaviour occurring within a culture may be a result of globalization as well as some other factors (for example, a natural development within a culture that would have occurred even in the absence of globalization). To isolate the effects of globalization is not an easy matter, especially since experimentation in this area of research is not possible.

EXAM TIP

This HL extension includes three topics that can be applied to any of the three parts of the sociocultural approach to behaviour. Combining these gives you nine potential areas from which exam questions may be asked.

Parts of sociocultural approach to behaviour	a. The individual and the group	b. Cultural origins of behaviour and cognition	c. Cultural influences on individual attitudes, identity and behaviours
1. How globalization may influence behaviour	1a	1b	1c
2. The effect of the interaction of global and local influences on behaviour	2a	2b	2c
3. Methods used to study the influence of globalization on behaviour	3a	3b	3c

Table 3.6

There is considerable overlap in these areas. The blocks we have covered in this section address all nine areas holistically.

Topics

4.1 Factors affecting diagnosis

4.1.1 Normality versus abnormality

DEFINITIONS

- **Abnormality**—not easy to define; this section describes various existing approaches
- **Abnormal psychology**—a study of patterns of behaviour that deviate from the accepted norms; however, abnormal psychology does not study all deviations, only those severe enough to be classified as mental disorders

ESSENTIAL UNDERSTANDING

How do we decide whether a behaviour is abnormal? The history of abnormal psychology has witnessed many approaches to answering this question. The most influential approaches are as follows.

- **Abnormality as a deviation from social norms**. This approach is appealing because it is based on common sense. However, it raises the question of defining social norms in various social contexts.
- **Abnormality as inadequate functioning**. Rosenhan and Seligman (1989) proposed seven criteria of abnormality and suggested that degrees of abnormality can be established based on combinations of these criteria.
- **Abnormality as a deviation from ideal mental health**. Jahoda (1958) defined six characteristics of mental health, thus focusing on the positive side of human existence. While it is a balanced description of what it means to be healthy, many elements of the model are difficult to quantify.
- **Abnormality as statistical infrequency**. This approach equals abnormal to statistically unusual. It provides a rigorous way to quantify abnormality based on conventions of social sciences. However, statistical norms themselves may change with the course of time.
- **The medical model** of abnormality avoids a single definition of abnormality altogether and instead defines each individual disorder by the system of symptoms. Classification systems are used in the medical model to provide clinicians with guidance in diagnosing disorders and delineating between them.

THEORY

ABNORMALITY AS A DEVIATION FROM SOCIAL NORMS

This approach does not belong to any particular author; rather it is a common-sense approach of defining abnormality as something that is not "acceptable" in the society.

Evaluation of the approach

Strength
It suggests a simple and intuitively appealing definition of abnormality based on common sense.

Limitations
- Abnormality is defined relative to social norms, but social norms themselves are changeable (both cross-culturally and in time).

- This approach to defining abnormality may be convenient for societies to impose control over citizens. If an individual behaves in a way that does not meet the interests of the society, this individual may be easily labelled as abnormal and even isolated. Since such a possibility exists even in theory, this approach may be ethically dangerous.
- There are cases when a behaviour is socially acceptable and yet harmful to the individual. Not including such behaviours is a drawback of the definition.
- Social norms differ depending on the context (for example, the same behaviour will be perceived differently at a rock concert and at a business meeting).

ROSENHAN AND SELIGMAN (1989)—ABNORMALITY AS INADEQUATE FUNCTIONING

Rosenhan and Seligman (1989) proposed seven criteria that can be used to establish abnormality:
- suffering
- maladaptiveness (for example, inability to achieve major life goals)
- unconventional behaviour (that is, not like that of most people)
- unpredictability of actions or loss of control over actions
- irrationality (others cannot understand why the person behaves in this way)
- observer discomfort (it makes others uncomfortable to witness the behaviour)
- violation of moral standards.

Evaluation of the approach

Strengths
- It embraces more dimensions of abnormality, for example, socially acceptable behaviour that causes individual suffering.
- It operationalizes abnormal behaviour in a way that can be established by observation.

Limitations
- The definition seems to be over-inclusive. For example, public displays of affection may cause observer discomfort (especially in some cultures), but is this enough to classify it as abnormal behaviour?
- Very few behaviours meet all seven criteria.
- Sometimes criteria may contradict each other. For example, unconventional behaviour may sometimes help an individual achieve major life goals.

To account for these limitations, Rosenhan and Seligman (1989) suggested that abnormality is a continuum rather than a black-and-white phenomenon; there exist degrees of abnormality based on how many criteria are met.

JAHODA (1958)—ABNORMALITY AS A DEVIATION FROM IDEAL MENTAL HEALTH

Jahoda (1958) used the idea of mental health as the starting point. She believed it was much more important to define healthy behaviour than disorders.

The six characteristics of ideal mental health that Jahoda (1958) proposed were:
- efficient self-perception
- realistic self-esteem
- voluntary control of behaviour
- accurate perception of the world
- positive relationships
- productivity.

Evaluation of the approach

Strengths
- It is more humanistic—it focuses on health rather than disorders.
- It provides a balanced description of what it means to be healthy.

Limitations
- It seems impossible for a person to achieve all six criteria, so most people would be classified as "not entirely healthy" in this framework.
- Some parameters are difficult to measure. For example, it may require a subjective opinion of the clinician to establish that the client's perception of the world is "accurate".

ABNORMALITY AS STATISTICAL INFREQUENCY

This approach looks at separate traits and behaviours rather than deciding if "the whole person" is normal or abnormal. Traits and behaviours are considered abnormal if they are defined as statistically unusual. The definition requires thresholds after which we would consider behaviour to become "unusual". These thresholds have been defined somewhat arbitrarily in statistics for social sciences, and they link to the following thresholds of statistical significance:
- $p < 0.05$ (rarer than 5 cases out of 100)
- $p < 0.01$ (rarer than 1 case out of 100)
- $p < 0.001$ (rarer than 1 case out of 1,000).

Evaluation of the approach

Strengths
- It is very quantifiable: traits and behaviours are compared to those of a large representative population.
- It labels behaviours and traits, not people.
- It links to statistical criteria used elsewhere in social research.

Limitations
- Statistical norms themselves are changeable because they are defined relative to the population, and the population does not remain the same. For example, overt homosexuality is more prevalent today than it was several decades ago; the average IQ in the world gradually increases (the Flynn effect).
- Statistically infrequent behaviours are not always undesirable—one example is unusually high IQ.

THE MEDICAL MODEL OF ABNORMALITY

The medical model of abnormality assumes that abnormal behaviour, much like a physical disease, has a set of symptoms and a set of causes behind those symptoms (symptomology and etiology). Symptoms may be observed, causes may be inferred and treatment should target these inferred causes.

This model avoids the need for a general definition for abnormal behaviour altogether. Instead it focuses on mental disorders one by one, defining them descriptively by a system of symptoms. All these descriptions are then brought together in a **classification system**. Such classification systems assume that each disorder is characterized by a defined set of symptoms that can be differentiated from other sets of symptoms (disorders). See "**4.1.2 Classification systems**".

Evaluation of the approach

Strengths
- It makes diagnosis independent of clinicians' beliefs regarding what causes the disorder. Psychiatrists may

disagree on the origin of a disorder, but they should be able to use the common language of observable symptoms to agree on the presence of a disorder.
- It is flexible and testable. Like any model, it can be tested against empirical observations and refined if the fit is not perfect (this takes the form of new editions of classification systems being published).

Limitations
- Many symptoms of mental illness are not as easily observed as symptoms of physical disease.
- One symptom may be an indicator of multiple disorders, and any single disorder manifests itself in a variety of symptoms. This is a difficulty that classification systems must tackle.
- The problem of threshold is relevant for this approach as well. For example, if some symptoms are present and others are not, do we still diagnose a disorder?

4.1.2 Classification systems

- **Classification system**—a diagnostic manual providing a system of diagnostic categories, a set of symptoms for each diagnostic category, and rules for making a diagnosis based on these sets of symptoms.

- **Psychoanalytic tradition**—the approach to diagnosing mental illness, based on the works of Sigmund Freud and his followers, focused on identifying unconscious drives and theorizing about childhood experiences

ESSENTIAL UNDERSTANDING

Classification systems are the foundation of the medical model of abnormality.

Examples of classification systems
- The *Diagnostic and Statistical Manual* (DSM) is published by the American Psychiatric Association (APA). It is currently in its fifth edition (DSM-5) and is widely used in the USA.
- The *International Classification of Diseases* (ICD-10) is published by the World Health Organization and is widely used in European countries.
- The *Chinese Classification of Mental Disorders* (CCMD-3) is also widely used.

History
- Views on mental illness have gradually changed as a result of scientific advances and social movements, and these changes are reflected in the history of classification systems (for example, the DSM).

- In the DSM, there was a major shift from establishing causes of disorders based on the clinician's interpretation of the client's behaviour to describing a set of observable symptoms and trying to create classification categories that would not overlap. In this way, the role of theory in diagnosis was gradually reduced. This might have made diagnosis more superficial, but it also allowed clinicians with diverse theoretical backgrounds to use a common language and arrive at similar diagnoses.

Challenges
Someone designing a classification system faces a variety of challenges, some of which are: explanation versus description; validity versus reliability; cross-cultural applicability.

Research
Empirical research of classification systems takes the form of investigating their validity and reliability. See "**4.1.3 Validity and reliability of diagnosis**".

History of the DSM		
Edition	**Year**	**Characteristics**
DSM-I	1952	This edition was heavily based on psychoanalytic traditions: clinicians looked for origins of abnormal behaviour in childhood traumas. The focus was on establishing causes, which involved a lot of interpretation on the part of the psychiatrist.
DSM-II	1968	The publication itself was triggered by attacks from scientists (for example, behaviourists criticized using unobservable constructs such as "trauma" or "unconscious drives") and social activists (for example, the anti-psychiatry movement viewed psychiatry as a form of social manipulation). However, DSM-II still retained a lot of psychoanalytic features; it was focused more on explaining and interpreting disorders than describing them.
DSM-III	1980	The publication was the result of doubts raised in the scientific community regarding the ability of psychiatrists to reliably differentiate between normality and abnormality. Studies such as Rosenhan (1973) questioned the validity of diagnosis. Diagnostic categories had to be made more "scientific", and this was done by a change of focus from explaining and interpreting disorders to describing them. With a focus on describing sets of observable symptoms, DSM-III included 265 disorders organized in 5 groups (the multi-axial system).
DSM-IV	1994	DSM-III was criticized for overdiagnosis (too many people could be diagnosed with a mental disorder). In response, the diagnostic categories were revised and DSM-IV included the clinical significance criterion: symptoms were considered clinically significant if they created major distress or interfered with daily functioning.
DSM-5	2013	The multi-axial system was criticized for being artificial and not reflecting the reality of things. Ultimately, it was eliminated. Cultural variability of symptoms was emphasized and tools such as the "Cultural formulation interview" were included to help clinicians avoid cultural bias in diagnosis.

Table 4.1

CHALLENGES IN DESIGNING A CLASSIFICATION SYSTEM

Challenges involve:
- explanation versus description
- validity versus reliability—when explanation is eliminated from the process of diagnosis, it makes diagnosis more consistent across clinicians (more reliable), but leaves less room for consideration of unique individual circumstances (which may reduce validity)
- discrete diagnostic categories versus degrees of abnormality
- delineation between categories
- cross-cultural applicability
- medicalization of the population (percentage of the population that can be categorized as mentally ill).

RESEARCH   Empirical research of classification systems

Empirical research of classification systems takes the form of establishing their validity and reliability. A good classification system should:
- allow different clinicians using it to arrive at the same diagnoses, even if their theoretical orientations are not the same
- allow a diagnosis that corresponds to the real problem experienced by the patient
- take into account cultural differences regarding reporting, demonstrating and interpreting symptoms of abnormal behaviour
- minimize potential biases in the diagnostic process.

All these aspects are investigated in multiple research studies. The medical model is just that—a model, a construct that we design to describe reality. We conduct numerous checks of how well the construct fits the observed data, and if the fit is not perfect, we modify the model and repeat the cycle of checks.

Using the example of the DSM, this research into reliability and validity of classification systems is discussed in "4.1.3 Validity and reliability of diagnosis".

4.1.3 Validity and reliability of diagnosis

- **Comorbidity**—co-occurrence of two or more diagnoses
- **Diagnosis** ("dia" = differentiating, "gnosis" = knowledge; telling apart)—relating a pattern of abnormal behaviour (symptoms) to a certain category in the classification system
- **Misdiagnosis**—when a person is diagnosed with a disorder that does not match the actual behaviour
- **Predictive validity**—the ability of diagnosis to predict how the disorder will respond to treatment; if diagnosis

is valid, the development of the disorder should be predictable
- **Reliability of diagnosis**—the extent to which different clinicians using the same classification system arrive at the same diagnosis for the same patient; also known as "inter-rater reliability"
- **Validity of diagnosis**—the accuracy of diagnosis; that is, the extent to which the diagnosis reflects the real nature of the patient's problem

ESSENTIAL UNDERSTANDING

Validity and reliability are two essential characteristics that define the quality of diagnosis.

There are two ways to establish **inter-rater reliability of diagnosis**: the audio-/video-recording method and the test-retest method. See "**Establishing inter-rater reliability of diagnosis**".

A diagnosis is **valid** if it corresponds to the actual disorder.

Trade-off

There is usually a trade-off between validity and reliability of classification systems. As interpretation is eliminated from the process of diagnosis in an attempt to increase consistency across clinicians, some nuances and individual circumstances may be ignored, meaning that the diagnosis is not perfectly valid for a particular individual. See "**Relationship between validity and reliability of diagnosis**".

Reliability of the DSM

Reliability of the various editions of the DSM reflects the attempts to improve consistency of diagnosis by different clinicians.

- Reliability of the early editions (DSM-I and DSM-II) was found to be very low (for example, **Beck et al 1962**), which triggered an initiative to make diagnostic categories more observable and eliminate interpretation from the diagnostic process.
- Reliability of DSM-III was higher, but some diagnostic categories were shown to be more reliable than others; the spread was considerable. See **Di Nardo et al (1993)**, **Williams et al (1992)**.

- The tendency was continued, but paradoxically reliability estimates of DSM-5 became typically lower. They even dropped for some diagnostic categories that remained largely unchanged from the earlier editions, such as MDD—**Regier et al (2013)**.
- This paradox may be explained by the fact that research in this area has become more rigorous. The test-retest method is now almost always preferred to the audio-/video-recording method, thus reliability estimates may be more conservative, but at the same time more realistic—**Chmielewski et al (2015)**.

Validity of diagnosis

The key problems related to establishing validity of diagnosis are:
- heterogeneity of clinical presentation
- diagnosis based on symptomology rather than etiology
- the issue of comorbidity
- stability of symptoms
- choosing appropriate treatment.

Validity cannot be directly quantified. There are two approaches commonly used to assess validity of diagnosis.
- Assessment of systematic biases in the diagnostic process. See "**4.1.4 The role of clinical biases in diagnosis**".
- Assessment of psychiatrists' ability to detect the mental disorder when the disorder is objectively known. A classic study by Rosenhan (1973) brought into question the ability of psychiatrists to tell mentally healthy people from the mentally ill (at the time when DSM-II was in use). See **Rosenhan (1973)**.

| **RESEARCH** | **Establishing inter-rater reliability of diagnosis** |

There are two ways to assess inter-rater reliability of diagnosis.
- **The audio-/video-recording method**—one clinician conducts a clinical interview with the patient; this interview is recorded and the recording is given to a different clinician who then makes a diagnosis independently. The two diagnoses are compared.
- **The test-retest method**—two clinicians conduct interviews with the same patient independently.

The limitation of the first method is its artificiality. The diagnosis may depend, for example, on the nature of questions asked during the clinical interview or how the patient responds to non-verbal reactions of the clinician.

In a natural situation two clinicians conducting the same interview will conduct it differently, which will contribute to variance in diagnosis. However, in the audio-/video-recording method the clinicians observe exactly the same behaviour—a scenario that is very unlikely in real life. As a result, estimates of reliability of diagnosis may be somewhat inflated.

The second method is much less artificial. However, the limitation is the necessity to keep the time interval between the two interviews short. If the interval is too long, the patient's symptoms may change naturally. Inconsistencies in diagnosis will partially reflect the real changes in the patient's behaviour, and reliability of diagnosis in this case will be underestimated.

Validity and reliability of classification systems tend to be **inversely related**: as reliability increases, validity has a tendency to decrease, and vice versa.

How can this trade-off between validity and reliability be explained? To increase reliability of a classification system we need to ensure that all clinicians, irrespective of their theoretical backgrounds and personal biases, notice the same symptoms and attribute them to the same categories. For this to be possible, the symptoms need to be very observable and "objective" (independent of the clinician's interpretation). In an attempt to achieve this, classification systems focus on more obvious symptoms and ignore subtle individual differences. However, ignoring individual circumstances may mean that the diagnosis does not fit the patient perfectly. In this sense, when subjective interpretation is eliminated from the process of diagnosis, validity may (or may not) be compromised.

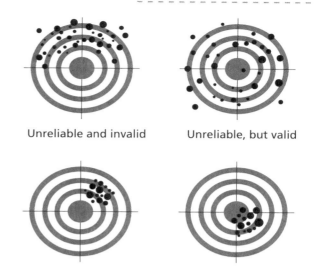

Unreliable and invalid   Unreliable, but valid

Reliable, not valid   Both reliable and valid

Figure 4.1 Validity and reliability of diagnosis represented as targets

---

RESEARCH   Reliability of the DSM—history

DSM-I and DSM-II

At first, reliability of the DSM was found to be extremely low. For example, **Beck et al (1962)** found that for DSM-I agreement on a specific diagnosis between two psychiatrists was only 54% on average. Reliability of DSM-II was shown to be similarly low. This caused the APA to start an initiative to make diagnostic categories in the DSM more observational and thus "scientific".

DSM-III and DSM-IV

Research studies confirmed that there was a visible improvement to reliability of diagnosis using DSM-III. This was also enhanced by the addition of the Structured Clinical Interview for DSM (SCID)—a standardized interview that allowed all clinicians to follow the same protocol.

However, although the improvement in reliability was obvious on average, it was not universal—reliability of diagnosis became acceptable and even excellent for some mental disorders, but remained low for some others.

- **Di Nardo et al (1993)** found excellent reliability for such diagnostic criteria as simple phobias and obsessive-compulsive disorder (OCD), but poor reliability for generalized anxiety disorder (GAD).
- **Williams et al (1992)** showed that test-retest reliability for different diagnostic categories in DSM-III varied from "almost perfect" to "moderate" and "weak". This seemed to depend mostly on whether or not a disorder has clear behavioural manifestations. For example, substance abuse has more obvious behavioural manifestations than a social phobia.

Since progress was nonetheless obvious, this line was continued and the new editions (DSM-IV and DSM-5) further refined diagnostic categories to increase consistency of diagnosis, especially for the disorders that had been associated with low reliability of diagnosis.

DSM-5

Paradoxically, recent studies show that reliability of DSM-5 is often lower than that of the earlier editions, even for the diagnostic categories that remained largely unchanged.

- **Regier et al (2013)** summarized data from field trials for the DSM-5 and reported mixed results. On the one hand, out of 23 diagnostic categories that were studied, more than half demonstrated moderate to strong reliability. On the other hand, six categories were in the weak range and three categories were in the unacceptable range. Major depressive disorder (MDD) was among the categories that had "weak" reliability of diagnosis, which is surprising because this category did not change much from the earlier editions of the DSM.
- **Chmielewski et al (2015)** explained this paradox by observing that modern studies of reliability of diagnosis use more rigorous methods and research procedures, as compared to earlier studies. Most importantly, field trials for DSM-5 almost exclusively used the test-retest method of establishing reliability, while earlier studies often used audio-/video-recordings. As we know, estimates of reliability in the test-retest method are more conservative, but probably closer to the reality of clinical diagnosis.

Current issues

- Results of current research studies and earlier research studies are not directly comparable, but we can assume that estimates obtained from the recent studies are more realistic.
- The DSM has succeeded in increasing reliability of diagnosis on average, but this remains inconsistent across diagnoses. Further work needs to be done to enhance reliability of certain diagnostic categories.

Validity is the extent to which diagnosis corresponds to the reality (that is, reflects the real nature of the patient's problem).

Key problems related to validity of diagnosis
- Heterogeneity of clinical presentation—one and the same disorder can manifest itself differently in different patients, so the diagnostic manual should allow for some flexibility.
- Classification is based on symptomology rather than etiology. This means that diagnostic categories will overlap, because two disorders that have distinct causes may manifest themselves in similar symptoms.
- Comorbidity—this is an issue because if disorders A and B frequently occur together, it raises the question: can they be just symptoms of a more general disorder C? In other words, the problem is where to draw the line between symptoms of the same disorder versus two different disorders.
- Stability of symptoms—some symptoms are not stable, and making a diagnosis on their basis would be incorrect, so clinicians have to ensure that the symptoms they observe are stable in time.

- Selecting treatment—diagnosis determines the type of treatment that will be prescribed, and it is important that this treatment targets the real cause of a disorder. In a sense, effectiveness of treatment is a test for validity of diagnosis.

Validity of diagnosis cannot be directly quantified, but it can be assessed through research of clinical biases. To achieve this, **two ways** are commonly used.
- Assessment of the extent to which diagnosis is affected by various sources of clinical bias. For example, two clinicians with different cultural backgrounds should arrive at the same diagnosis for the same patient using the same classification system.
- Assessment of psychiatrists' ability to diagnose the disorder when the disorder is objectively known (but not disclosed to the psychiatrist).

The first approach links to a variety of clinical biases in diagnosis. See "**4.1.4 The role of clinical biases in diagnosis**". The second approach is a more direct test of validity. This approach was used in **Rosenhan's (1973)** study.

| RESEARCH | Rosenhan (1973)—sane in insane places |

Essential understanding
✪ *Results of this classic study questioned the ability of psychiatrists to differentiate between mental health and mental illness. The study triggered the process of modifying the DSM to make diagnostic criteria more observable.*

Aim
To investigate whether psychiatrists in a naturalistic setting could tell the difference between sane and insane people.

Method
Field study with elements of participant observation.

Procedure
Eight mentally healthy subjects tried to gain admission to psychiatric hospitals. In the interview with the psychiatrist the pseudo-patients followed a standard script where they complained of hearing voices that said "empty", "hollow" and "thud". This was the only symptom they made up; they were instructed to answer all the other questions about themselves honestly.

Upon admission, the pseudo-patients stopped simulating symptoms and behaved normally. They told the staff they did not experience any symptoms any longer and sought to be discharged from the hospital. At the same time, they secretly wrote down their observations.

Results
- Seven out of eight patients were admitted to hospital with a diagnosis of schizophrenia.
- When discharged, they were all diagnosed with "schizophrenia in remission".
- It took the patients on average 19 days to get out of the hospital by their own means (range from 7 to 52 days).

- None of the hospital staff ever suspected that the pseudo-patients were in fact healthy.
- The normal behaviour of the pseudo-patients was often misinterpreted as symptoms of a disorder.
- The patients were largely ignored by the staff. The average amount of time spent by members of the staff with each patient was under seven minutes a day.

Follow-up study
Since the professional community was highly sceptical of Rosenhan's results, he conducted another study with a hospital that was informed beforehand that pseudo-patients would be sent to seek admission there. In fact, Rosenhan did not send anyone. Staff members used a 10-point scale with each new patient to rate how likely they were to be a pseudo-patient. Results showed that psychiatrists and staff members often rated the real patients as pseudo-patients quite confidently.

Conclusion
Rosenhan concluded that psychiatrists lacked the ability to distinguish mental disorders from sanity, which questions the validity of psychiatric diagnoses. He suggested that this alarming situation could be explained by the effect of labelling: once someone is labelled with a disorder, everything he or she does is interpreted through the lens of that disorder.

Notes
Rosenhan provided the first direct test of validity of psychiatric diagnosis (DSM-II was used at the time of the study). The study has sparked extensive research into clinical biases.

4.1.4 The role of clinical biases in diagnosis

- **Clinical bias in diagnosis**—a systematic deviation from accuracy in diagnosis caused by misinterpretation of the patient's behaviour; clinical bias may be associated with clinician variables and patient variables
- **Clinician variables**—professional background, beliefs, attitudes and other characteristics of the clinician that may cause systematic deviation in diagnosis
- **Cultural syndrome**—a set of symptoms specific to a particular culture (that does not exist outside of that culture)

- **Patient variables**—characteristics of the behaviour of certain groups of patients in the clinical situation that may cause misdiagnosis
- **Reporting bias**—differential rates of reporting symptoms of mental disorders in different cultures
- **Somatization**—expressing symptoms of mental illness in the form of physical malfunction

ESSENTIAL UNDERSTANDING

All clinical biases in diagnosis may be broadly divided into three groups.

- Clinician variables (characteristics of the clinician that may cause certain systematic biases in diagnosis). See "**Clinician variables in diagnosis**".

- Patient variables (biases related to the patient's age, gender, race, and so on). See "**Patient variables in diagnosis**".
- Cultural factors in diagnosis (which result from the clinician and the patient having different cultural backgrounds). See "**Cultural factors in diagnosis**".

CLINICIAN VARIABLES IN DIAGNOSIS

Sources of bias associated with the clinician include:

- the clinician's theoretical orientation—as demonstrated, for example, in **Langwieler and Linden (1993)**
- the clinician's abilities (such as perspective-taking, tolerance for uncertainty, tolerance for differences)

- the clinician's cognitive biases (such as confirmation bias or illusory correlation)—see "**Unit 2 Cognitive approach to behaviour**" for more on cognitive biases.

RESEARCH Langwieler and Linden (1993)—the clinician's theoretical orientation

Essential understanding

✪ *Diagnosis may be influenced by the theoretical orientation and personal attitudes of the clinician.*

Aim

To find out if biases associated with clinicians' professional background exist in real-life medical decision-making processes when the clinicians do not suspect they are participating in a study.

Method

The study focused on individual differences between clinicians while keeping the patient variables constant. The study used a combination of qualitative methods including covert observation, interviews and content analysis.

Procedure

- A pseudo-patient was trained and presented to four clinicians during the regular working hours. The pseudo-patient was a 30-year-old female physician who pretended to work as a clerk; the story she presented was designed according to DSM-III symptoms of major depressive disorder (MDD).
- Four clinicians were selected, each with a different professional background (for example, psychoanalytic training versus behaviourist). All of them gave informed consent to participate in a study on medical decision-making where a pseudo-patient would come to their

office unannounced and record the whole session on a concealed tape recorder.

- After the study clinicians listened to the session recording with the researchers and recalled their thoughts during the interview. Their comments while listening to the recordings were transcribed and submitted to a content analysis.

Results

- All clinicians arrived at slightly different diagnostic conclusions. For example, medication was prescribed in some cases and not prescribed in others. Suicidal thoughts were investigated by some clinicians but not others.
- The initial diagnosis was formed very early (in less than three minutes) in the process of the interview. In theory, assessment should come first and conclusions second, but analysis of transcripts revealed that these processes actually appeared to be interdependent: an initial conclusion was made early in the process and influenced the subsequent assessment procedures. In all cases the early diagnosis was identical to the final diagnostic conclusion.

Conclusion

There are marked individual variations in the diagnostic process carried out by clinicians of varying professional and theoretical backgrounds. This therapist individuality contradicts the idea of a standardized diagnostic process and can be regarded as a bias.

PATIENT VARIABLES IN DIAGNOSIS

Patient variables are related to the fact that different groups of people behave differently in a diagnostic process. Patient variables may take many forms; some examples follow.

- Reporting bias—some groups experience symptoms of a disorder but fail to acknowledge them and report to professionals. See **Furnham and Malik (1994)**.

- Somatization—some groups experience symptoms of a mental disorder in a physical form; they will report the symptoms to a physician rather than a psychiatrist. This is especially prevalent in societies where mental disorders are stigmatized. See **Lin, Carter and Kleinman (1985)**.

RESEARCH   **Furnham and Malik (1994)—reporting bias for depression in British Asians**

Essential understanding
✪ *Cultural differences in the way mental disorders are perceived may influence the rate at which they are reported.*

Aim
To investigate cross-cultural beliefs about depression.

Background
Statistically British Asians (immigrants from Bangladesh, India and Pakistan) are rarely diagnosed with depression. One possible explanation is that British Asians have depression but fail to report it (reporting bias).

Participants
152 female subjects in two age groups: young (aged 17–28) and middle-aged (35–62). Half of the participants were Native British, the other half were of Asian origin (born and educated in India, Pakistan or Bangladesh).

Method and procedure
This was a quasi-experiment. Participants filled out questionnaires about their symptoms of mental illness and their beliefs about depression. Responses were compared across groups (the two IVs were culture and age).

Results
- Perception of depression differed among Asian and British participants. For example, Asian participants (but not British participants) believed depression is temporary and can be fixed by having a job outside the home.
- These differences were less pronounced in the group of younger women.
- Asian middle-aged women reported being depressed significantly less than the younger group.

Conclusion
Cultural differences exist in the way depression is perceived. These differences may be attributed to underlying cultural dimensions (such as individualism versus collectivism).

These cultural differences influence the rates at which disorders are reported: people from traditional collectivistic societies tend to report depression more to relatives and less to professionals. Globalization gradually erases these cultural differences, with younger generations having less reporting bias.

RESEARCH   **Lin, Carter and Kleinman (1985)—somatization in refugees and immigrants**

Essential understanding
✪ *Somatization may be prevalent among certain social groups. It prevents patients from accurately reporting symptoms of mental illness.*

Aim
To determine the presence of somatization in certain cultural groups.

Method
Analysis of clinical record; quasi-experiment (comparison of pre-existing groups).

Participants
Chinese, Filipino, Vietnamese and Laotian patients that were undergoing treatment in US hospitals. Half of the patients were refugees (they had been forced to move due to the war in Vietnam). The other half were immigrants (it was their conscious decision to emigrate).

Procedure
The researchers analysed clinical records of patients in US primary care. They were looking for signs of somatization, which was defined as vague somatic symptoms in the absence of a clear etiology. Rates of somatization were compared across groups.

Results
- Somatization was diagnosed in 35% of patients.
- Refugees were more likely to have somatization than immigrants.
- Patients with somatization were more likely to come from a "traditional" background (with larger household sizes and lower levels of education).
- Patients with somatization were more likely to be less proficient in English.

Conclusion
Somatization is prevalent among certain social groups, such as Asian refugees and immigrants. People from traditional societies (where mental disorders tend to be stigmatized) are more prone to somatization. Refugee status also contributes to somatization, probably due to the added stress of forced relocation and acculturation.

CULTURAL FACTORS IN DIAGNOSIS

Cultural dimensions started making their way into the DSM in its fourth edition. It included a "cultural formulation interview" in an appendix and a glossary of "culture-bound syndromes" (later renamed as "cultural syndromes"). More attention was given to cultural variables in DSM-5.

"Cultural syndromes" are sets of symptoms that are only recognized as illness in a particular culture. In fact, these symptoms may only exist in a given culture and nowhere else. Some examples of cultural syndromes follow.

- *Ataque de nervios* ("attack of the nerves") is a syndrome found mostly among Hispanic people. Symptoms include uncontrollable screaming, trembling and partial loss of consciousness. It may be a culturally acceptable form of reaction to extreme stress.

- *Shenjing shuairuo* (neurasthenia) includes symptoms of fatigue, anxiety, depressed mood and general weakness. This is a diagnosis specific to Asia (especially China), and it may be a culturally accepted form of depression. Traditional medicine describes this syndrome as loss of vital energy.
- *Taijin kyofusho* is a syndrome specific to the Japanese and the Korean cultures. It involves a fear of interpersonal relationships based on an irrational belief that others will not be pleased about one's physical appearance or body odour.

It is important for clinicians to be trained in a way that increases their awareness about cultural syndromes.

4.2 Etiology of abnormal psychology

4.2.1 Prevalence rates and disorders

DEFINITIONS

- **Bereavement exclusion**—a condition that existed in DSM-IV and stated that depression cannot be diagnosed if the symptoms occur less than two weeks after a significant loss, such as the death of a close person (this condition was removed in DSM-5)
- **Onset age of a disorder**—the average age when individuals in a given population are first diagnosed with the disorder

- **Period prevalence**—the proportion of people in a given population who have the disorder within a given time interval; typically used periods are 12-month prevalence, lifetime prevalence
- **Point prevalence of a disorder**—the proportion of people in a given population currently diagnosed with the disorder

ESSENTIAL UNDERSTANDING

It is important for practical reasons to characterize the spread of a disorder in a population. The main parameters used for this purpose are prevalence rate (point prevalence and period prevalence) and onset age (see "Definitions").

Major depressive disorder (MDD) has high prevalence rates. The World Health Organization (WHO) forecasts depression to be the second leading cause of disability in the world by 2020.

Prevalence rates of MDD vary across cultures. The highest prevalence estimates are found in some of the wealthiest countries in the world. At the same time, age of onset and sociodemographic correlates of major depression do not vary substantially across cultures. See **Kessler and Bromet (2013)**.

It is not easy to separate true prevalence of disorders from variations of estimates associated with:
- the classification system in use
- reporting bias
- cultural variations in the expression of symptoms—see "**Factors influencing prevalence rate estimates**".

Since we can only establish prevalence rates of disorders through estimates, and our estimates are influenced by the currently used classification system and a variety of clinical biases, the topics "**4.1.2 Classification systems**" and "**4.1.4 The role of clinical biases in diagnosis**" are an indispensable part of a discussion of prevalence rates of disorders.

Kessler and Bromet (2013)—cross-national study of prevalence rates of depression

Essential understanding

✪ *Available data indicates that there is considerable cross-cultural variability in prevalence of depression. However, other parameters such as onset age and sociodemographic correlates are found to be quite consistent across cultures.*

Aim

To compare prevalence of depression across cultures.

Method

Review of publications containing epidemiological data (epidemiological surveys).

Results

- MDD is a commonly occurring disorder in all countries where epidemiological surveys were carried out.
- Lifetime prevalence estimates for MDD ranged widely from 1% (Czech Republic) to 16.9% (USA).
- The 12-month prevalence estimates ranged from 0.3% (Czech Republic) to 10% (USA).

- The age of onset, on the other hand, does not vary substantially. For example, the median age of onset is similar in high income and low-middle income countries (25.7 versus 24 years, respectively).
- Sociodemographic correlates of depression are also fairly consistent across cultures. For example, women's risk for developing MDD is typically twice that of men.

Conclusion

Prevalence rates of MDD vary considerably across cultures. This may be due to a variety of factors including the classification system in use, the survey used to establish the symptoms, representativeness of samples used in research, as well as true prevalence.

The highest prevalence estimates are found in some of the wealthiest countries in the world. The authors suggest that this may be due to income inequality, but this requires further exploration.

FACTORS INFLUENCING PREVALENCE RATE ESTIMATES

It is important to understand that true prevalence of depression (and mental disorders in general) may be obscured by a variety of factors. In epidemiological surveys we only arrive at estimates, and these estimates may be affected by the following.

- Classification system—there is no diagnosis independent of the classification system, and any changes in the diagnostic manual will be reflected in estimates of the prevalence of disorders. For example, in DSM-5 the bereavement exclusion for depression was removed, making the diagnosis more inclusive and potentially increasing the frequency of diagnosing people with depression.

- Reporting bias—for example, some populations may fail to report symptoms of depression because mental illness is stigmatized in their society.
- Cultural variations in the expression of symptoms—even if people do report their symptoms, they may present them differently in the clinical situation, which (depending on the training of the psychiatrist) may lead to bias in diagnosis.

In this sense the topic "Prevalence rates and disorders" is closely linked to two other sections: "**4.1.2 Classification systems**" and "**4.1.4 The role of clinical biases in diagnosis**". Relevant material from these sections can be used to answer questions about prevalence of disorders.

4.2.2 Explanations for disorders: Biological explanations for depression

- **5-HTT**—serotonin transporter gene: a gene involved in the regulation of reuptake of serotonin at brain synapses
- **Etiology** of a disorder—a set of factors that caused it; we may distinguish between biological, cognitive and sociocultural etiologies
- **Gene-environment correlation (rGE)**—the idea that genetic predisposition can influence the environment itself and so, when viewed in development, environment is not completely independent of genotype

- **Gene-environment interaction (G × E)**—the idea that individuals having different genotypes will react to the same environment in different ways; for example, some people may have a genetic predisposition to depression that will make them more vulnerable to stressful life events
- **Selective serotonin reuptake inhibitors (SSRIs)**—a class of drugs that act by preventing the reuptake of excess serotonin in the synapse, increasing its concentration

ESSENTIAL UNDERSTANDING

Biological explanations for depression include genetic factors and neurochemistry (neurotransmitters and hormones).

Genetic factors

- Research into genetic etiology of depression uses the same approaches as genetic research elsewhere in psychology. Genetic heritability of depression cannot be measured directly but it can be estimated from data obtained in such methods as twin studies, family studies, adoption studies and molecular genetics.
- In twin studies, the Falconer model has been traditionally used to estimate heritability. See "**1.3.1 Genes and behaviour, genetic similarities**" in "**Unit 1 Biological approach to behaviour**".
- Using this approach, Kendler *et al* (2006) demonstrated that heritability of depression was significantly higher in women (A = 42%) than in men (A = 29%), and that the relative contributions of genetic and environmental factors did not change from generation to generation. See **Kendler *et al* (2006)**.

Gene-environment interaction

- These variable results in men and women highlight the importance of considering **gene-environment interactions (G × E)**. Genes may create a susceptibility to certain environmental influences. In other words, genes may create a predisposition to depression, but it will depend on environmental factors whether or not this predisposition will be triggered. To uncover such interactions, one needs to conduct longitudinal studies.
- Silberg *et al* (1999) demonstrated in a longitudinal study that genetic predisposition causes girls to be more vulnerable to stressful life events. If these events occur, they are more likely than boys to respond with depression. See **Silberg *et al* (1999)**.

Pinpointing a specific gene

Can we pinpoint a specific gene that is responsible for this vulnerability to stressful life events? Caspi *et al* (2003), using methods of molecular genetics, suggested that a functional polymorphism in 5-HTT (serotonin transporter gene) determines how strongly stressful life events will influence depressive symptoms. See **Caspi *et al* (2003)**.

Gene-environment correlation

Gene-environment interaction (G × E) describes the situation when individuals with different genetic predispositions react differently to the same environment. However, genetics can also influence the environment itself. This is known as gene-environment correlation (rGE). There are three types: passive rGE, evocative rGE and active rGE (also known as niche picking). See "**Gene-environment correlation**".

Biological explanations other than genetics

Genetic explanations for mental disorders are linked to other biological explanations: evolution, neurotransmitters, hormones. One of the most influential theories that currently describes the role of neurotransmitters in depression is the "serotonin hypothesis". See "**The role of neurotransmitters in depression**". It is closely linked to research on treatment of depression because it implies that certain drugs that increase the level of serotonin in the brain (such as SSRIs) can be effective for reduction of symptoms. See "**4.3.2 Biological treatment of depression**".

RESEARCH — Kendler *et al* (2006)—the Swedish national twin study of depression

Essential understanding

✪ *In twin studies using the Falconer model, heritability of major depression is estimated at 38% on average. There are notable sex differences in heritability of depression. At the same time the estimates are stable across generations.*

Aim

To compare genetic heritability of major depression in men and women as well as across historical cohorts.

Participants

42,161 twins located through the national Swedish Twin Registry. This is a nearly complete registration of all twin births in the country. Birth cohorts spanned nearly 60 years, which enabled researchers to compare results across generations.

Method

To assess lifetime major depression, a personal computer-assisted telephone interview was conducted with all participants using modified DSM-IV criteria.

Procedure

Informed verbal consent was obtained prior to the interview. Trained interviewers with adequate medical background collected data. Efforts were made to reach both members of a pair within one month.

Results

- Prior studies (meta-analyses) of genetic heritability of depression showed quite similar results, estimating heritability of depression at 37% on average.
- The estimated heritability of major depression for the entire sample in Kendler *et al* (2006) was 38%—very similar to prior results.
- No evidence was found that shared environment was of any importance as a factor of developing major depression (C = 0%).
- Heritability estimates for men were: A = 29%, E (individual environment) = 71%.
- Heritability estimates for women were: A = 42%, E =58%.
- These estimates did not differ significantly across age cohorts.

Conclusion

The researchers concluded that major depression was moderately heritable.

Men and women have different rates of genetic susceptibility for depression. However, we should remember when interpreting this finding that genes and environment are in constant interaction. For example, as the researchers suggest, genes may exist that increase the risk of depression in response to variations in the hormonal environment. Such genes would increase the risk of depression in women (during menstrual cycles and pregnancy) but not in men.

Essential understanding

✪ *Genetic predisposition makes adolescent girls more vulnerable to certain stressful life events than adolescent boys. This is an example of gene-environment interaction (G × E) because genotype only creates a predisposition that requires an environmental event to be triggered.*

Aim

To investigate what causes the differences in heritability of depression in males and females. With this end, to investigate the development of depressive symptoms among boys and girls from childhood to adolescence.

Participants

The data used was taken from the Virginia Twin Study of Adolescent Behavioural Development—a longitudinal four-wave study of more than 1,400 male and female juvenile twin pairs who were between 8 and 16 years of age at the time of the first assessment.

Method

A longitudinal twin study.

Procedure

- Depressive symptoms were assessed using the Child and Adolescent Psychiatric Interview. This interview

is administered to both twins and at least one of the parents.
- A list of 39 potentially stressful past-year life events was created. These included such events as failing a grade or losing a close friend through arguments. Ratings for these events were obtained in interviews with the mothers.

Results

- The life events most associated with depression were similar in boys and girls. Examples included increased quarrelling between parents and failing a grade.
- Boys and girls have similar levels of depression before the age of 12, but girls' rates of depression increase significantly faster after that age.
- Analysis showed that stressful life events had a greater impact on depressive symptoms of girls than boys, especially during and after puberty.

Conclusion

The effect of negative life events on depressive symptoms in adolescent girls is stronger than in boys. This suggests a genetic predisposition to experiencing particular stressful life events. In other words, girls have a genetic predisposition that makes them more vulnerable to stressful life events, at least in adolescence.

Essential understanding

✪ *A functional polymorphism in 5-HTT moderates the influence of stressful life events on depression.*

Aim

To investigate the relationship between stressful life events and depression in individuals with different functional polymorphisms (alleles) of the 5-HTT gene.

Participants

A representative birth cohort of 1,037 children from New Zealand.

Method

A longitudinal study. Quasi-experimental comparisons—the sample was divided into three groups:
- both short alleles of 5-HTT (s/s)—17%
- one short allele and one long allele (s/l)—51%
- both long alleles (l/l)—31%.

Procedure

- Participants were followed longitudinally and assessed at ages 3, 5, 7, 9, 11, 13, 15, 18, 21, 25.
- A "life history calendar" was used to assess stressful life events. It included 14 major events (such as employment, health, relationship stressors) and was administered to

participants twice at age 21 and 25 (immediately before the 26th birthday).
- Participants were assessed for past-year depression with an interview based on DSM-IV criteria. This was combined with informant reports from persons nominated by each participant as "someone who knows you well".

Results

- There were no differences between the three groups in the number of stressful life events they experienced.
- However, it was found that participants with a short allele of 5-HTT (s/l and especially s/s) reacted to stressful life events with more depressive symptoms. For example, participants who had a stressful life event at age 21 demonstrated an increase in their depressive symptoms by age 26, but only if they carried a short allele of 5-HTT (s/l or s/s). Conversely, depressive symptoms of participants in the l/l group stayed on the same level.

Conclusion

The researchers concluded that 5-HTT does not influence exposure to stressful life events, but influences an individual's reaction to these events. The study demonstrated that genetic predisposition can moderate a person's reactivity to stressful life events—an instance of gene-environment interaction (G × E).

GENE-ENVIRONMENT CORRELATION (RGE)

Gene-environment interaction (G × E) describes the situation when individuals with different genetic predispositions react differently to the same environment. The reality is more complex, however, because if we look at it dynamically, genetics can influence the environment itself. This is known as gene-environment correlation (rGE), and there are three types.

- **Passive rGE**—this is when parents pass on to the child both the genes and some corresponding environment, so genes and environment are not entirely independent. For example, parents may give the child genetic predisposition to depression as well as a highly demanding environment that places the child under a lot of stress.
- **Evocative rGE**—this is when a person's genotype evokes a particular environmental response. For example,

a person with depression may be constantly gloomy, so people at work may stop interacting with him or her. This lack of interpersonal interaction may in turn become the environmental factor that further contributes to the person's depression.

- **Active rGE** (also known as **niche-picking**)—this is when an individual actively selects certain environments that better match his or her genetic predisposition. For example, a child predisposed to depression may seek high-demanding situations where it is hard to succeed.

Existence of gene-environment correlations is a challenge to current research because it is not easy to study them in all their complexity. Study of them requires longitudinal research with large samples and sophisticated statistical modelling.

THE ROLE OF NEUROTRANSMITTERS IN DEPRESSION

There have been a variety of research studies that tried to establish the role of neurotransmitters in depression by comparing depressive symptoms in clients with varying concentrations of neurotransmitters in the brain. Among neurotransmitters that were said to influence depression, the most influential candidate is serotonin, and the idea that its imbalance in the brain is a factor that causes depression is known as the "**serotonin hypothesis**".

This hypothesis has been supported by evidence of two types.

- Certain drugs that were known to deplete levels of serotonin in the brain were also found to have depression-inducing effects.
- Certain drugs that were known to increase the levels of serotonin in the brain were also found to relieve symptoms of depression. For example, a class of drugs known as selective serotonin reuptake inhibitors (SSRIs) were shown to be effective against depression. SSRIs prevent reuptake of excess serotonin from the synapse, increasing its concentration in the synaptic gap.

For some of these research studies see "4.3.2 Biological treatment of depression".

4.2.3 Explanations for disorders: Cognitive explanations for depression

ESSENTIAL UNDERSTANDING

As in any other aspect of human behaviour, biological factors of depression interact with cognitive and sociocultural factors.

Theory

Cognitive explanations for depression suggest that the patterns of information processing (how an individual interprets various life events) influence the development of the disorder. See the most influential of cognitive explanations (Beck 1967).

Research

The core premise of the theory—the idea that depression is linked to faulty thinking patterns—is supported by empirical research. Here are two examples.

- Alloy, Abramson and Francis (1999) demonstrated that negative cognitive styles predict the development of depression. See **Alloy, Abramson and Francis (1999)**.
- Caseras *et al* (2007) showed that individuals suffering from depression exhibit negative attention biases. See **Caseras *et al* (2007)**.

Criticism of the empirical studies that support cognitive explanations for depression have focused on their correlational nature: it is difficult to separate thinking that causes depression from thinking that is caused by depression.

However, major support for this area of research comes from the studies of cognitive behavioural therapy (CBT) and its effectiveness compared to other methods of treatment. See "4.3.3 Psychological treatment of depression".

BECK (1967)—COGNITIVE THEORY OF DEPRESSION

This theory suggests that cognitive factors are the major cause of depression. It highlights the importance of automatic thoughts—the semi-conscious sub-vocal narrative that naturally occurs in people's minds to accompany their daily activities. The central claim of the theory is that a change in automatic thoughts can lead to a change in behaviour. The theory identifies three **elements of depression**.

- The cognitive triad: negative beliefs about the self, the world and the future—these negative beliefs are deeply rooted and they influence automatic thoughts to be irrationally pessimistic.
- Negative self-schemata: when negative beliefs about the self become generalized, individuals start seeing their

own fault in everything that happens to them, even if they cannot control it.
- Faulty thinking patterns: these are logical fallacies and irrational conclusions that people make because the way they process information is biased.

Cognitive theory of depression forms the basis of cognitive behavioural therapy (CBT). The core idea of this approach to treatment is that confronting the client's faulty thinking patterns with the objective reality of the situation will replace the irrational elements with more logical thinking, which will in turn affect behaviour. CBT is an influential approach to treatment. See more on its effectiveness in the section "**4.3.3 Psychological treatment of depression**".

RESEARCH   Alloy, Abramson and Francis (1999)— negative cognitive style

Essential understanding
✪ *Negative cognitive styles increase vulnerability to depression when people confront stressful life events. The researchers define cognitive styles broadly as "the way people typically interpret or understand events in their lives" (Alloy, Abramson, Francis 1999).*

Aim
To investigate whether a particular cognitive style (positive or negative) in freshmen is associated with subsequent development of depressive symptoms.

Method
Quasi-experiment (comparison of two pre-existing groups); longitudinal study.

Participants
Non-depressed college freshmen.

Procedure
At the start of the study, participants were given a questionnaire that determined their cognitive style and

split into two groups based on results: low risk versus high risk for depression. Participants with a negative cognitive style (allocated to the high-risk group) typically believed that negative life events were catastrophic and that the occurrence of such events meant that they (the participants) were flawed or worthless.

Participants were then followed longitudinally for 5.5 years. Assessments included self-report measures and structured interviews.

Results
- During the first 2.5 years of follow-up, high-risk freshmen were more likely to develop major depressive disorder than low-risk freshmen (17% versus 1%).
- High-risk freshmen were also more likely than low-risk freshmen to develop suicidal thoughts and behaviour (28% versus 13%).

Conclusion
Negative cognitive styles may influence the development of major depression.

RESEARCH   Caseras *et al* (2007)—attention bias

Essential understanding
✪ *Major depression is associated with biased attention—depressed people find it harder to disengage their attention from negative stimuli.*

Aim
To investigate whether attention to positive versus negative stimuli is different in depressed versus non-depressed participants.

Method
Quasi-experiment (comparison of two pre-existing groups); eye-tracking technology was used to measure the variables.

Participants
43 participants recruited through a university website.

Procedure
- Depressive symptoms were assessed using a questionnaire (the Beck Depression Inventory). On the basis of the scores, participants were split into two groups—those with depressive symptoms and non-depressed.
- Participants were shown a series of 32 picture pairs with negative, positive and neutral stimuli. Each pair of pictures was presented for three seconds. The negative pictures presented images of sadness and loss, whereas the positive pictures showed people engaging in enjoyable activities. Using eye-tracking technology, researchers measured two components of visual attention:
  - initial orienting (which of the two pictures the participant looks at initially)

- o maintenance of attention (the duration of looking at this picture before switching to the other one).

Results
- Participants with depressive symptoms demonstrated a bias in maintenance of attention to negative pictures—but no differences were found in initial orienting.

- In other words, once depressed participants started looking at a negative picture, they found it harder to switch their attention to the other picture.

Conclusion
Negative attention bias potentially is one of the mechanisms of major depression.

4.2.4 Explanations for disorders: Sociocultural explanations for depression

ESSENTIAL UNDERSTANDING
Sociocultural explanations for depression focus on environmental factors that may increase an individual's susceptibility to depression.

Social vulnerability factors
In an influential classic study, **Brown and Harris (1978)** outlined vulnerability factors that may increase the risk of developing depression: having three or more children, lack of an intimate relationship, lack of employment and loss of mother. These claims were supported in other independent research studies, with the overall conclusion that social factors are involved in the development of depression along with personal factors.

For example, Kivelä et al (1996) demonstrated that social factors such as early loss of a parent or lack of participation in religious activities predict the onset of depression in elderly people. See **Kivelä et al (1996)**.

Spreading of symptoms in the social network
Apart from identifying social vulnerability factors, researchers also investigate how depression may be affected by the structure of an individual's social network. The major finding in this area is that symptoms of depression may spread from person to person, affecting people up to three degrees of separation away. See **Rosenquist, Fowler and Christakis (2011)**.

Effects of culture
Although culture probably cannot cause depression and in this sense is not a factor of depression etiology, cultural variables certainly play an important moderating role both in development and expression of depressive symptoms. For example, depression in certain traditional societies is stigmatized, which may cause people to misinterpret their symptoms and either fail to report them (reporting bias) or report them as symptoms of physical illness (somatization). See **"4.1.4 The role of clinical biases in diagnosis"** for more on reporting bias and somatization.

RESEARCH   Kivelä et al (1996)—social predictors of depression in elderly people

Essential understanding
✪ *Social factors play a role in the etiology of depression in old age.*

Aim
To investigate (in a longitudinal study) the extent to which various social factors predict occurrence of depression in an elderly Finnish population.

Method
Longitudinal study; quasi-experimental comparison of two groups.

Procedure
- A clinical study of depression in old age was completed in Finland in 1984–85 with 1,529 participants aged 61 or older. DSM-III was used to determine the occurrence of depression.
- Those participants who were not depressed in 1984–85 were clinically interviewed and examined again in a follow-up study in 1989–90 (N = 679).
- Social variables and the occurrence of certain life events in the period 1984–89 were measured through questionnaires.

- Two groups were compared: depressed versus non-depressed in 1989–90.

Results
- In 1989–90, 8.2% of the men and 9.3% of the women in the sample were diagnosed with depression.
- Comparison with non-depressed men revealed the most powerful predictors of depression in men: poor relationship with the spouse; a negative change in the relationship with the spouse and with the neighbours; the loss of mother while under 20 years of age; a grandchild's divorce; moving into institutional care; an alcohol problem of a close person.
- The most powerful predictors of depression in women were: the loss of father while under 20 years of age; low activity in religious events; worsening of relationships with neighbours; a decline in the social participation rate during the follow-up period; an alcohol problem of a close person; living with one's husband but without other people.

Conclusion
Social factors and changes in social ties may predict the onset of depression at old age. There are certain sex differences in the social factors of depression in old age, probably associated with differences in experiencing marital stress.

Rosenquist, Fowler and Christakis (2011)—symptoms of depression in the social network

Essential understanding
✪ *Symptoms of depression may spread from person to person, affecting people up to three degrees of separation away.*

Aim
To investigate if depressive symptoms can spread from person to person (like an infectious disease).

Method
Statistical analysis of social networks, longitudinal data.

Participants and procedure
- Data was taken from an earlier Framingham Heart Study, a longitudinal study of risk factors for heart disease initiated in 1948 and involving 12,067 participants. To keep track of participants, the researchers collected information that would help them locate participants later: names of their friends, neighbours, co-workers and relatives. Since Framingham was a small town, many of these nominated contacts also participated in the study.
- A questionnaire for measuring depression was administered three times between 1983 and 2001 to one of the cohorts in this longitudinal study.
- Rosenquist, Fowler and Christakis (2011) computerized all data, with a focus on levels of depression in each

individual as well as friends, relatives, neighbours and co-workers.
- Data was analysed using statistical methods of social network analysis.

Results
There was a significant correlation in depressive symptoms between people up to three degrees of separation away. Participants were:
- 93% more likely to be depressed if a person they were directly connected to (such as a friend) was depressed
- 43% more likely to be depressed if a person within two degrees of separation (such as a friend's friend) was depressed
- 37% more likely to be depressed if a person within three degrees of separation (such as a friend's friend's friend) was depressed.

Changes in social ties (for example, acquiring new friends) predicted changes in depressive symptoms, but not vice versa.

Conclusion
Depression in one person may cause depression in people the individual is socially connected to (friends, relatives, co-workers). In this sense, symptoms of depression may spread along the network of social connections somewhat like an infectious disease.

4.3 Treatment of disorders

4.3.1 Assessing the effectiveness of treatment

- **Meta-analysis**—statistical analysis of data aggregated from a large number of published research papers

- **Psychotherapy**—psychological approaches to the treatment of mental disorders; this section excludes treatment by medication from the concept of psychotherapy and focuses purely on psychological approaches

ESSENTIAL UNDERSTANDING

Challenges
There are many challenges in assessing the effectiveness of treatment of disorders. These are some of the factors that need to be considered.
- **Severity of the disorder**—some treatments work better with mild disorders, others may be more effective in severe cases.
- **Treatment outcomes**—indicators of effectiveness could be an observable reduction of symptoms, self-reported improvement of quality of life, improvement of social adjustment as reported by close friends and relatives.
- **The time frame** may be short-term or long-term. Some treatments may be more effective in the short term, some in the long term.
- **Method of measuring** the therapy outcome—observable changes in a patient's behaviour are the most reliable indicators, but they do not capture the complexity of the patient's experiences. Self-report measures capture more aspects, but are less reliable.

- **The exact mechanism of change**—our knowledge of therapy effectiveness will be incomplete if we do not know which elements exactly cause the positive change in the client.
- **Placebo effects**—we can only conclude that a treatment is effective if it outperforms a placebo. This requires more sophisticated research designs.

Research questions
Assessing the effectiveness of psychotherapy implies answering two broad questions. Meta-analysis allows us to attempt to answer these.
- Is psychotherapy effective on average?
- What elements of psychotherapy exactly are responsible for its effectiveness?

See "**Is psychotherapy effective on average?**" and "**What elements explain the effectiveness of psychotherapy?**"

Current evidence

Current evidence suggests that psychotherapy in general is effective, but common (non-specific) factors may play a larger role than specific therapeutic techniques. However, due to the nature of meta-analyses, this conclusion is not applicable to all treatments and in all circumstances.

All the evidence discussed in this section deals with psychological treatment and excludes treatment by medication (such as antidepressants). For a discussion of the effectiveness of drug treatment, see "**4.3.2 Biological treatment of depression**".

RESEARCH   Is psychotherapy effective on average?

Eysenck (1952) reviewed available data and arrived at the conclusion that psychotherapy does not work. More specifically, his analysis showed that 67% of patients spontaneously recovered in two years without any treatment, and that the rate of success with patients undergoing psychotherapy was not larger than that. However, methodological quality of research studies at that time was low: RCTs were not yet used and often the allocation to treatment and control groups was not random; meta-analysis as a method was not yet developed. This research led to multiple attempts at testing the effectiveness of psychotherapy more rigorously and improving the methodology of research itself. Meta-analysis was developed and new methods of treatment emerged.

Smith and Glass (1977) conducted a meta-analysis of 375 studies (carefully selected on the basis of their methodological quality) and concluded that psychotherapy is in fact effective. The typical therapy client in their analysis was healthier than 75% of untreated individuals (compared to 50% expected by random chance).

To further quantify the effectiveness of psychotherapy, **Wampold (2007)** conducted a meta-analysis comparing psychotherapy with medicine. It was demonstrated that effectiveness of psychotherapy was in fact comparable to that of some established medical practices, such as the influenza vaccine or cataract surgery. We need to keep in mind, however, that those are average estimates across all possible types of psychotherapy and many different types of mental disorders.

RESEARCH   What elements explain the effectiveness of psychotherapy?

Classic meta-analyses (such as Eysenck or Smith and Glass) observed very little difference between various approaches to psychotherapy in terms of their overall effectiveness. For example, in Smith and Glass (1997) the type of therapy explained only about 10% of the variance in outcome measures.

This suggests that there should exist some common elements that are present in all (or most) approaches to psychotherapy and are responsible for its effectiveness. These elements are known as non-specific factors of psychotherapy. They are contrasted with specific factors of psychotherapy—elements that are unique to a given approach to treatment.

To analyse which elements of psychotherapy exactly are responsible for patient improvement, research studies sometimes employ the so-called "**dismantling design**". In these studies some patients undergo the full treatment programme while other patients undergo incomplete programmes where one of the elements of treatment is removed. Patient outcomes in complete and incomplete programmes are then compared.

Wampold (2007) suggested that three non-specific factors of psychotherapy effectiveness are especially salient: client's willingness to trust the therapist; formation of a working alliance between the therapist and the client; placebo effects. See "**Non-specific factors of psychotherapy**".

RESEARCH   Jacobson *et al* (1996)—dismantling CBT

Essential understanding
✪ *Full CBT was not found to be any more effective than its individual components (such as behavioural activation alone), and this may suggest that there are other non-specific factors at work that make therapy effective even in the absence of specific therapeutic techniques.*

Aim
To explain the effectiveness of CBT for depression by pinpointing the components responsible for therapy outcomes.

Participants
152 outpatients with major depression according to DSM-III-R criteria.

Method
Experiment; matched pairs design.

Background
The full CBT treatment includes three major components:
* behavioural activation (such as home assignments to rehearse certain patterns of behaviour, role-plays, monitoring of daily activities)

- the teaching of skills to modify automatic thoughts (such as learning to notice automatic thoughts, analysing how rational they are)
- modification of core schemas (changing one's deep beliefs about the self, the world and the future).

According to the cognitive theory of depression, modification of core schemas is the ultimate goal of the therapy, so all three elements work together to ensure positive change in the patient.

Procedure
Participants were randomly assigned to one of three conditions:
- the full CBT treatment (including all three core components)
- treatment that combined behavioural activation and the teaching of skills to modify automatic thoughts (the first two components)
- the behavioural activation component only.

The outcome measures were depressive symptoms, assessed through self-report questionnaires and semi-structured clinical interviews. Apart from these measures of overall effectiveness researchers also looked at measures of change in three separate domains: increased behavioural activation;

decreased negative thinking; changes in core schemas. All these elements were measured by questionnaires.

Results
- There was no evidence that the complete treatment produced better outcomes than any of the two incomplete treatments.
- This was true for such outcome variables as "altering the patient's negative thinking patterns". Patients in all three conditions showed improvement in all three domains—increased behavioural activation, decreased negative thinking, and a positive change to the core schemas. This was puzzling because clearly the complete treatment targets negative thinking patterns and core beliefs to a much greater extent than incomplete treatments.

Conclusion
No evidence was found that full cognitive treatment is more effective than any of its components.

Discussion
One of the potential explanations of this puzzling finding is the presence of non-specific factors. Perhaps these factors were present even in the incomplete treatment protocols, rendering the therapy effective despite the absence of specific therapeutic techniques.

RESEARCH **Non-specific factors of psychotherapy**

Non-specific factors of psychotherapy could potentially explain such puzzling findings as:
- no difference between a full treatment programme and its separate components in Jacobson *et al* (1999)
- lack of variation between approaches to psychotherapy in terms of their overall effectiveness in Eysenck (1952) and Smith and Glass (1977).

Wampold (2007) reviewed empirical evidence and suggested that three non-specific factors of psychotherapy effectiveness are especially salient.
- **Client's willingness to trust** that the therapist will provide an explanation that will help them ("I believe you

will help me")—therapists who are capable of inspiring this kind of trust may end up being more effective, and this may outweigh the effect of a particular method of treatment.
- Formation of a **working alliance** with the client—this entails the readiness of the client to take responsibility and work together with the therapist.
- **Placebo effects**—while research tries to separate placebo effects from the "real" effect of psychotherapy, in practical terms therapists may make use of placebo effects to make their clients more responsive to treatment.

4.3.2 Biological treatment of depression

- **Antidepressants**—drugs that target depressive symptoms by affecting the levels of neurotransmitters in the brain
- **Fluoxetine**—an antidepressant; one of the chemicals that function as an SSRI (selective serotonin reuptake inhibitor)

- **Publication bias**—the tendency for successful trials to be published more often than unsuccessful trials
- **Response rate**—one of the indicators of the effectiveness of treatment; the percentage of participants who showed at least a 50% decrease in the scores on a standardized depression scale

---

ESSENTIAL UNDERSTANDING

Mechanism
Biological treatment of depression is based on the assumption that the major cause of depression is a chemical imbalance in the brain. To restore balance, we can use antidepressants—drugs that modify the level of neurotransmitters available in the synaptic gaps. There are

various types of antidepressants, and their physiological mechanism is different. See "Antidepressants".

Effectiveness
- A complete evaluation of effectiveness should take into account various factors such as long-term versus

- short-term effects and a comparison to alternative methods of treatment. For example, it has been shown that antidepressants are effective for the reduction of symptoms of depression and provide a quick result, but psychotherapy may reach the same levels of effectiveness in the long term. See "**Treatment of adolescents with depression study (TADS)**".
- Conclusions on the effectiveness of antidepressants have been questioned on the grounds of the possibility of publication bias. Kirsch (2014) and Kirsch *et al* (2002) demonstrated that effectiveness of antidepressants is not so obvious when published and unpublished data are combined, so there may be publication bias. See "**Criticism of biological treatment**".
- This criticism, however, is only relevant to the aggregate estimates of effectiveness that average across types of patients, types of disorder, and so on. Elkin *et al* (1989) demonstrated, for example, that antidepressants are more effective than other treatment methods with severe depression, but not with mild and moderate depression. See "**Counter-arguments to criticism**".
- Overall, it may be concluded that antidepressants are effective in a variety of situations (most notably severe symptoms that must be reduced urgently), but decisions regarding antidepressant treatment should be made after a careful cost-benefit analysis. See "**Conclusion: are antidepressants effective?**".

ANTIDEPRESSANTS

Antidepressants are drugs that modify the level of neurotransmitters that have been shown to be associated with depressive symptoms.
- **Tricyclic antidepressants (TCA)** inhibit the reuptake of certain neurotransmitters, such as serotonin and noradrenaline, in the synaptic gap. This increases the concentration of this group of neurotransmitters available in the synaptic gap.
- **MAO inhibitors** decrease the activity of monoamine oxidase (MAO): a chemical that breaks down excess monoamine neurotransmitters (such as serotonin, dopamine, noradrenaline) in the synaptic gap.
- **Selective serotonin reuptake inhibitors (SSRIs)** are probably the most widely used class of antidepressants. They target serotonin specifically. This also makes them ideal for scientific research into the effectiveness of antidepressant drugs. Several different chemicals function as SSRIs, the most popular of these is fluoxetine. A popular trade name for fluoxetine is Prozac.

RESEARCH   Treatment of adolescents with depression study (TADS) (2004–2007)

Essential understanding
✪ *Antidepressants are effective for the reduction of symptoms of depression and provide a quick result, but psychotherapy may reach the same levels of effectiveness in the long term.*

Aim
To examine the short-term and long-term effectiveness of drug treatment and psychotherapy for the treatment of depression in adolescents.

Method
Randomized control trial; longitudinal study.

Participants
13 clinics in the USA were involved in the project with 439 participants in total—adolescents aged 12–17. All participants were diagnosed with major depression.

Procedure
TADS was a multi-site study in the USA funded by the National Institute of Mental Health (NIMH). The study lasted 36 weeks in total and was conducted in three stages.

Stage 1: acute treatment (12 weeks). Participants were randomly assigned to one of four conditions:
- fluoxetine alone
- CBT alone
- a combination of fluoxetine and CBT
- placebo and clinical management.

Stage 2: consolidation treatment (six more weeks). At the end of stage 1 clients from the placebo group were informed that they had been taking a placebo and allowed to choose any of the other three treatment conditions, but they did not participate in the study any more. Therefore stage 2 only included three groups of participants.

Stage 3: continuation treatment (18 weeks). This stage was meant to assess long-term effectiveness of treatment.

Response rates were used as the indicator of effectiveness. Response rate is the percentage of participants who showed a 50% decrease (or more) in the scores on a standardized depression scale such as the Hamilton Depression Rating Scale (HAM-D).

Results
- At the end of stage 1 combination treatment had the best response rate (71%). The response rate of fluoxetine alone was slightly lower (61%). These treatments outperformed CBT (44%) and placebo (35%).
- At the end of stage 2 CBT "caught up with" medical treatment (response rate 65% for CBT and 69% for fluoxetine). Combination treatment, however, was still slightly more effective (85%).
- At the end of stage 3 the effectiveness of combination treatment was still the same, but both other groups almost equalled combination treatment in effectiveness (81% both for fluoxetine and CBT conditions).

Conclusion
All three active treatments of depression outperform placebo, so both medical treatment and psychotherapy can be considered effective. The effectiveness of antidepressants

for reducing the symptoms of depression supports the idea that depression is caused by a chemical imbalance in the brain.

If continued, CBT gradually reaches the same level of effectiveness as medication and even combination treatment. Therefore medication is more effective than psychotherapy in the short term, but not in the long term.

It may be suggested based on these results that antidepressants should be recommended, especially when a quick response is important (for example, when there are suicidal thoughts).

Response rate	12 weeks	18 weeks	36 weeks
Placebo	35%	Discontinued	Discontinued
Fluoxetine	61%	69%	81%
CBT	44%	65%	81%
Fluoxetine + CBT	71%	85%	86%

Table 4.2 Based on information available on the TADS website

RESEARCH Criticism of biological treatment

Essential understanding

✪ *There is doubt about the validity of the conclusions about effectiveness of antidepressants. One of the largest limitations is the existence of publication bias.*

Kirsch (2014) reviewed both published and unpublished data and formulated several arguments against the effectiveness of antidepressants.

- Different antidepressants show very similar clinical effect irrespective of their physiological mechanism. This may suggest that some other non-physiological factors actually cause improvement.
- There may be publication bias in the estimates of effectiveness: successful trials tend to be published

more frequently, and unsuccessful trials may be under-represented in scientific literature.

- There is a possibility of an "enhanced placebo effect": as side effects are present in antidepressant drugs but not in placebo, both clinicians and patients can work out which condition they are assigned to.

Kirsch *et al* (2002) conducted a meta-analysis that combined both published and unpublished data from clinical trials of antidepressants sponsored by pharmaceutical companies. Results showed that 82% of the effect of antidepressants was duplicated by placebo. The researchers concluded that when published and unpublished data are combined they fail to demonstrate effectiveness of antidepressants.

RESEARCH Counter-arguments to criticism of antidepressants

The main counter-argument to the criticism of antidepressants is that average estimates of effectiveness may be misleading and we should look at more specific types of problem instead. For example, it has been argued that severity of the disorder is important.

In support of the idea that severity of depression needs to be taken into account when determining the effectiveness of antidepressants, **Elkin *et al* (1989)** conducted a study in which 250 patients were randomly assigned to one of four conditions (placebo, drugs and two types of psychotherapy):
- interpersonal psychotherapy
- CBT

- antidepressant medication and clinical management
- placebo and clinical management.

Treatment in all groups was continued for 16 weeks. Results were as follows.
- All three active treatment conditions outperformed placebo.
- For mild and moderate depression, the three conditions did not differ substantially among themselves. However, there was a clearer advantage of medication over psychotherapy in cases of severe depression.

It can be concluded that drugs are more effective than psychological treatment for severe depression.

CONCLUSION: ARE ANTIDEPRESSANTS EFFECTIVE?

The problem with this question is that it invites the use of aggregate estimates of antidepressant effectiveness that will average across:
- the types of antidepressants
- outcome variables (for example, short-term effects versus long-term effects)
- characteristics of the disorder (such as severity, the presence of suicidal thoughts)
- characteristics of the patient (such as age, cultural background).

When we do try to arrive at such aggregate estimates, we depend on results of meta-analyses combining a large number of research studies. Findings from such meta-analyses have been inconclusive: most of them suggest that antidepressants are significantly more effective than placebo, but Kirsch *et al* (2002) and Kirsch (2014) raised doubts and argued that these results may be due to publication bias.

However, this concerns the aggregate estimates. There may be considerable variations depending on specific outcome variables, characteristics of the patient, characteristics of the disorder, and so on. For example, it has been demonstrated that the effectiveness of antidepressants becomes increasingly superior to other methods when the disorder is more severe initially. So, antidepressants may be the preferred method of treatment in cases of severe depression (Elkin *et al*, 1989).

Similarly, it has been demonstrated that antidepressants are more effective than other methods of treatment in the short-term (see **"Treatment of adolescents with** **depression study (TADS)"**. Therefore they may be the preferred method in cases where quick results are necessary, for example, when suicidal thoughts are present.

It may therefore be concluded that antidepressants are effective in a variety of situations (most notably severe symptoms that must be reduced urgently), but decisions regarding antidepressant treatment and its duration should be made on a case-to-case basis after a careful cost-benefit analysis.

4.3.3 Psychological treatment of depression

– **Relapse rate**—recurrence of a past condition (developing symptoms of depression again a while after the treatment was discontinued)

– **Remission rate**—the percentage of participants who show little or no symptoms of depression after the treatment period

– **Response rate**—the percentage of participants who show at least a 50% decrease in the scores on a standardized depression scale

ESSENTIAL UNDERSTANDING

CBT

• CBT is perhaps the most extensively studied, well-established and evidence-based method of psychological treatment of depression. It is based on Beck's cognitive theory of depression with its assumption that depression is caused by irrational automatic thinking patterns that lead to irrational behaviour.

• CBT targets both the automatic thoughts (making them more logical) and behaviour (making it more rational and more adjusted to the environment). So the two major goals of CBT are **cognitive restructuring** and **behavioural activation**.

• Unlike many other forms of psychotherapy, CBT is highly focused on specific, well-defined problems. It is a relatively short process. The client is expected to be an active participant in the process of therapy.

Effectiveness of CBT

In characterizing the effectiveness of CBT, we should look at various outcome variables. Three commonly used measures are response rates, remission rates and relapse rates.

• In terms of response and remission rates, it has been demonstrated in some research studies that CBT may be as effective as medication. For example, DeRubeis

et al (2005) showed that CBT equals medication in effectiveness after 16 weeks of treatment. However, this success may be dependent on the skills of the therapist. See **DeRubeis *et al* (2005)**.

• In terms of relapse rates, it has been shown that the effect of CBT is more enduring than the effect of medication—it lasts longer after the therapy is discontinued. See **Hollon *et al* (2005)**.

• Effectiveness of cognitive therapy could also depend on which symptoms in particular are being targeted. Some symptoms may be more responsive to CBT, some to medication. For example, Fournier *et al* (2013) demonstrated that medication and CBT targeted slightly different clusters of depressive symptoms. See **Fournier *et al* (2013)**.

Mechanism of CBT

Effects of CBT have been substantiated in research that revealed physiological changes in patients who went through CBT sessions. For example, Goldapple (2004) demonstrated a specific pattern of brain changes in CBT patients as compared to medication patients. See **Goldapple (2004)**.

RESEARCH   DeRubeis *et al* (2005)—response and remission rates at 8 weeks and 16 weeks

Essential understanding

✪ *CBT is as effective as medication for moderate to severe depression at 16 weeks, but this depends on the skills of the individual therapist.*

Aim

To investigate response and relapse rates of CBT as compared to medication in the short term (8 weeks) and long term (16 weeks) for moderate to severe depression.

Method

Randomized control trial.

Participants

240 patients diagnosed with MDD, moderate to severe symptoms.

Procedure

Participants were randomly assigned to three groups:

• 16 weeks of antidepressant medication

• 16 weeks of CBT

• 8 weeks of placebo.

Research took place at several different research sites (with several different therapists). Depression symptoms were measured before and after therapy by the Hamilton Depression Rating Scale (HAM-D).

Results

- At 8 weeks both the active treatments outperformed placebo, but the response rate was slightly higher in the medication group.
- At 16 weeks response rates reached 58% both for medication and CBT.
- Remission rates at 16 weeks were also similar.
- However, results were not uniform across research sites. At one site in particular, medication turned out to be more effective than CBT.

Conclusion

CBT can be as effective as medication for the treatment of moderate to severe depression—but this is contingent on the therapist's skill and experience.

| | 8 weeks | 16 weeks | |
	Response rate	Response rate	Remission rate
Medication	50%	58%	46%
CBT	43%	58%	40%
Placebo	25%	-	-

Table 4.3 Findings from DeRubeis et al (2005)

RESEARCH   Hollon et al (2005)—relapse rates

Essential understanding

✪ Cognitive therapy has a more enduring effect than medication.

Method and procedure

Three groups of patients with moderate to severe depression were compared. They were:
- patients who responded positively to cognitive therapy and were withdrawn from treatment for 12 months
- patients who responded to medication and continued medication
- patients who responded to medication and continued to take a placebo.

Results and conclusion

Results showed that relapse rates were the smallest in the cognitive treatment group. This shows that CBT has an enduring effect that extends beyond the end of treatment. It also suggests that medication mainly targets the symptoms of depression but not the cause.

Group	Relapse rate in 12 months
Responded to CBT, withdrawn from treatment	31%
Responded to medication, continued medication	47%
Responded to medication, continued placebo	76%

Table 4.4 Findings from Hollon et al (2005)

RESEARCH   Fournier et al (2013)—clusters of depressive symptoms

Essential understanding

✪ CBT and medication target slightly different clusters of symptoms; to increase effectiveness treatments should be matched to specific symptoms (rather than "depression" in general).

Procedure

Patients were randomly assigned to three conditions—medication, CBT and placebo. Results were measured separately for:

- mood
- cognitive symptoms (suicidal thoughts)
- anxiety
- vegetative symptoms (such as insomnia).

Results

It was found that CBT was more effective for reducing vegetative symptoms, but medication had a faster effect on cognitive symptoms (suicidal thoughts).

RESEARCH   Goldapple (2004)—brain changes in CBT patients

Essential understanding

✪ There is a specific pattern of brain changes in patients that undergo cognitive treatment. These changes are different from those observed in patients taking medication because cortical areas are affected to a much greater degree.

Method and procedure

PET scans were used to compare patients in CBT and medication conditions. The starting scores on the HAM-D scales in both groups were similar, as well as the reduction in scores by the end of the treatment.

Results

The two treatments were similar in that they both affected the cortical-limbic pathways—structures that connect the cortex to the limbic system. However, in addition, CBT was associated with metabolic changes in the cortex and medication was associated with changes in the lower areas of the brain (the limbic system and the brain stem).

Conclusion

The researchers concluded that CBT acts in a "top–down" way whereas medication produces more "bottom–up" changes.

4.3.4 The role of culture in treatment

- **Compliance with treatment**—willingness of the patient to follow the recommendations from the clinician, such as regularly taking the prescribed medicine

- **Internal model of illness**—a culturally determined schematic representation of a mental disorder (that is, the way the patient perceives his or her illness); being a type of schema, it influences the way information about the disorder is processed by the patient

ESSENTIAL UNDERSTANDING

Effects of cultural factors

The role of culture in treatment is manifold. It stems from the cultural differences in how symptoms of mental disorders are experienced, presented and perceived (see "**4.1.4 The role of clinical biases in diagnosis**"). Since culture affects these aspects of mental disorders, treatment is also affected.

- Cultural factors can influence compliance with treatment. For example, it was shown in a study by Kinzie *et al* (1987) that cultural perceptions of antidepressant medication influence the rates of compliance with treatment among Southeast Asian patients in US clinics. See **Kinzie *et al* (1987)**.
- Cultural factors can influence the patient's internal model of illness. This model will in turn mediate all treatment efforts, so a culturally sensitive psychiatrist must strive to understand the patient's internal model and adjust the interventions accordingly. For example, Naeem *et al* (2012) showed that it is possible to design a culturally sensitive version of CBT for local use in developing cultures such as Pakistan. See **Naeem *et al* (2012)**.

Culturally sensitive treatment

- Culturally sensitive treatment may be designed using either a top–down or a bottom–up approach. The difference is in how substantially the cultural variables are incorporated into the treatment programme. See "**Culturally sensitive treatment**".
- The effectiveness of culturally sensitive treatment has been demonstrated in meta-analyses such as Griner and Smith (2006). The researchers showed that cultural adaptations are effective especially when they specifically target a particular cultural group. See **Griner and Smith (2006)**.

RESEARCH   **Kinzie *et al* (1987)—compliance with antidepressant treatment**

Essential understanding

✪ *When the patient and the therapist belong to different cultural backgrounds, patients may fail to follow the therapist's prescriptions because these prescriptions clash with their culturally determined beliefs about mental illness. This situation may be remedied by openly discussing the issue with the patient.*

The researchers examined 41 depressed Southeast Asian patients who underwent long-term treatment of depression in US clinics. All patients had been prescribed tricyclic antidepressants (TCA). The patients' TCA blood levels were examined to determine whether they were actually taking the prescribed medicine. Results showed no detectable medicine levels in 61% of the patients.

The researchers explain this result by social stigma associated with taking antidepressants.

At the same time, cultural attitudes towards authority may cause such patients to pretend that they are following the prescription so as not to offend the doctor.

However, after a doctor–patient discussion about the problems and benefits of antidepressants, the rates of compliance significantly improved. This shows how an open discussion about the client's cultural beliefs may positively affect treatment.

RESEARCH   **Naeem *et al* (2012)—internal model of illness**

Essential understanding

✪ *In certain traditional communities there exist internal models of illness that could be taken into account to develop versions of CBT that account for local needs and values.*

Aim

To develop a culturally sensitive CBT programme and assess its effectiveness in the developing world (with Pakistan as an example).

Method

Qualitative research study using data from interviews and field observations.

Participants

Nine patients attending a psychiatric outpatient clinic in Pakistan.

Procedure

In interviews, participants were asked about their thoughts on their illness and the course of the treatment. Interviews were conducted in Urdu and tape recorded; transcripts were made later based on the recordings.

This data was combined with field notes from one of the authors during his clinical field practice. Inductive content analysis was applied to derive common themes emerging in the patients' subjective interpretations.

Results
Four themes emerged in the content analysis.
- Patients' perceptions of depression—patients tended to mention physical symptoms much more often than mental symptoms, did not use "depression" as a label for their illness and used expressions such as "illness of poor sleep" and "tension".
- Patients' beliefs about the causes of depression—they attributed their illness to "problems in the environment", "thinking too much" and "worries".
- Modes of referral for help—the majority of patients were referred to the clinic by relatives.
- Patients' knowledge about treatment of depression—they believed that they could be cured by "good quality medicine" or magicians.

Conclusion
Based on the results of this investigation, the authors were able to develop a culturally sensitive version of CBT that took local needs into account. This version of CBT used the language appropriate for the context (for example, "tension") and focused on re-interpreting somatic symptoms as signs of depression.

CULTURALLY SENSITIVE TREATMENT

Results of research which demonstrates that taking cultural perceptions into account may enhance the effectiveness of treatment in certain cultural contexts raise the question: what are the rules we should follow to design culturally sensitive treatments?

The adaptation of a treatment to a cultural context can be done using either a top–down approach or a bottom–up approach.
- **Top–down adaptations** involve relatively superficial changes to the original treatment programme, such as changing the language of delivery or hiring bicultural support staff.
- **Bottom–up adaptations** involve deeper changes to the way treatment is delivered. Such adaptations typically start with a research phase where qualitative studies are conducted to understand the nature of patients' interpretations of the illness and the treatment (see Naeem et al 2012). Culturally sensitive treatments are then designed based on this information, sometimes going as far as acknowledging and incorporating the help of local healers (magicians).

RESEARCH   Griner and Smith (2006)—effectiveness of culturally sensitive treatment

Essential understanding
✪ *Cultural adaptation increases effectiveness of treatment, and this is especially true for specific adaptations that target a specific culture.*

Aim
To examine the effectiveness of culturally adapted treatments of mental disorders.

Method and procedure
- A meta-analysis of 76 studies was conducted; only the studies that had a quantitative estimate of effectiveness were included.
- The types of cultural adaptations used in these research studies ranged from consultations with individuals familiar with the client's culture to cultural sensitivity training for staff.

Participants
The total sample in the research studies included in the analysis was around 25,000 participants

Results
- There was a "moderately strong" benefit of culturally adapted interventions.
- The benefit was four times stronger for same-race groups of clients than for mixed-race groups of clients.
- When the therapist spoke the client's native language, therapy was more effective than when the therapist spoke English.

Conclusion
Cultural adaptations carried out for specific sub-populations (groups of clients) are much more effective than making treatment more culturally flexible in general.

Topics

Option: obesity

5.1 Determinants of health
- 5.1.1 Prevalence rates of health problems
- 5.1.2 Biopsychosocial (BPS) model of health and well-being

5.2 Health problems
- 5.2.1 Biological explanations of health problems
- 5.2.2 Psychological explanations of health problems: Dispositional factors and health beliefs
- 5.2.3 Social explanations of health problems
- 5.2.4 Risk and protective factors

5.3 Health promotion
- 5.3.1 Effectiveness of health promotion programmes

EXAM TIP

Note that the grouping of topics in this book is somewhat different from what you find in the IB psychology guide. The "official" grouping of topics is shown below.

Determinants of health
- Biopsychosocial model of health and well-being
- Dispositional factors and health beliefs
- Risk and protective factors

Health problems
- Explanations of health problem(s)
- Prevalence rates of health problem(s)

Promoting health
- Health promotion
- Effectiveness of health promotion programme(s)

This is important to note because in the final exam you will be given three essay titles to choose from, one for each of the three components above (determinants of health, health problems and promoting health).

5.1 Determinants of health

5.1.1 Prevalence rates of health problems

- **Body Adiposity Index (BAI)**—a measure of obesity, calculated on the basis of height and hip circumference
- **Body mass index (BMI)**—a measure of obesity: body weight divided by height squared
- **Comorbidity**—the presence of additional diseases co-occurring with the primary disease
- **Incidence**—the development of new cases of a disease during a specified period of time in previously healthy individuals

- **Morbidity**—the rate of a population affected by a disease; includes incidence and prevalence
- **Mortality**—the number of deaths caused by a disease, per place and time
- **Prevalence**—the percentage of individuals in the population (in a given time period) who are experiencing a disease or a health problem

ESSENTIAL UNDERSTANDING

Definitions and classification

The basic measurements used in epidemiology are:
- mortality (death)
- morbidity (incidence, prevalence). (See "**Definitions**".)

To estimate epidemiological parameters of obesity we first need to establish a way to classify people as being of a normal weight, overweight and obese. Several approaches may be used for this including the absolute value of BMI, BMI percentiles and non-BMI measures such as Body Adiposity Index (BAI). See "**Classification of obesity**".

Prevalence and incidence

The WHO monitors obesity in the world by maintaining the Global Database on BMI. Prevalence rates for obesity have been invariably increasing for the past 50 years, leading to an obesity pandemic. There is considerable variation from nation to nation, ranging from 1% to 80%. Obesity and overweight currently affect over one third of the world's population. See "**Prevalence of obesity**" (Hruby, Hu 2015; Nguyen, El-Serag 2010).

Prevalence rates of obesity differ by gender, geographical region, age and income groups. See "**Prevalence of obesity in sub-groups**".

Obesity increases the risk of comorbidities such as type 2 diabetes, cardiovascular disease and certain types of cancer. This makes obesity a costly problem and a pressing global issue. See "**Costs of obesity**".

Incidence is a useful epidemiological metric complementary to prevalence. It is especially useful to inform prevention initiatives. Pan *et al* (2011) in a US study of BMI changes between 2008 and 2009 estimated the incidence of obesity at 4% per year. See **Pan *et al* (2011)**.

Body mass index (BMI)

The most widely used approach to classifying obesity in adults is on the basis of body mass index (BMI). This is calculated as body weight in kilograms divided by height in metres squared. The criterion of obesity that is commonly used worldwide is BMI ≥ 30, and the criterion for overweight is BMI ≥ 25.

Obesity classification for children is more difficult, however, because body composition fluctuates a lot as a child grows. For this reason, the WHO publishes BMI-for-age references for individuals under 19 years.

BMI percentile

Another approach to classifying obesity is to use percentiles rather than absolute values of BMI. The Centers for Disease Control and Prevention (CDC) in the USA use statistical data to determine age- and sex-specific percentiles. For example, obesity is defined in children as BMI ≥ 95th percentile (for the same sex and age group). This means that a child will be classified as obese if their BMI exceeds that of 95% of other children from the sex and age sub-population (Hruby, Hu 2015).

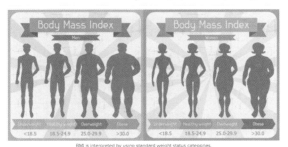

BMI is interpreted by using standard weight status categories.

Figure 5.1 BMI

Source: www.medicalnewstoday.com

Non-BMI measures

However, using BMI is not without pitfalls (Malterud, Tonstad 2009).
- Association between obesity (as measured by BMI) and mortality is non-linear. It means we cannot claim that as BMI increases, so does the risk of mortality (for example due to heart failure). In fact, it was even shown that starting with a certain level of BMI the risk of heart failure starts decreasing.
- The association between BMI and mortality also becomes weaker with age.

There is increasing evidence suggesting that abdominal obesity (rather than total body fat) is a better predictor of some cardiovascular or cancer-related outcomes. Abdominal obesity may be measured by waist circumference, hip circumference or waist–hip ratio. For example, an alternative to BMI is Body Adiposity Index (BAI), which is based on a person's height and hip circumference and does not take into account body weight.

PREVALENCE OF OBESITY (HRUBY, HU 2015; NGUYEN, EL-SERAG 2010)

The WHO monitors obesity around the world by maintaining the Global Database on BMI. This database builds on data available from published literature and a network of collaborators. A limitation is that there is a lack of nationally representative samples. However, the database covers approximately 86% of the world's population.
- **In the USA** the prevalence of overweight and obesity has invariably increased for the past 50 years. The prevalence rate of obesity in Americans is currently about 35%. The rising trend has levelled off, but there is much variation among sub-populations. For example, gender distribution is disproportional: there are far more cases of extreme obesity (BMI ≥ 35) among women than men.
- Prevalence rates **in Europe** are comparable to those in the USA. There was a smooth increase over several decades, rising up to around 30% for a number of European countries. This has some rare exceptions, for example, Denmark and Saudi Arabia showed a decrease in prevalence rates of obesity for men.
- **Globally** obesity and overweight affect over one third of the world's population. It is estimated that if the current trends continue, by 2030 this figure will reach 58% for the adult population in the world on average and 85% in the USA. There are wide variations in prevalence of obesity worldwide, ranging from 1% in India to 80% in some regions of the Pacific Islands. The highest rates of obesity have been seen in the Pacific Islands and the lowest have been reported in Asia.

PREVALENCE OF OBESITY IN SUB-GROUPS

Here are some points raised in the WHO's "Global Status Report on Noncommunicable Diseases" (WHO 2014).
- Throughout the world women are more likely to be obese than men. For example, in Africa and Southeast Asia obesity prevalence for women is roughly double the obesity prevalence for men. The exception is high-income countries, where prevalence rates of obesity for men and women are similar.
- The prevalence rate of overweight in high-income countries is more than double that of low-income countries. For obesity this difference more than triples.
- The prevalence of childhood overweight is increasing everywhere in the world, but especially in Africa and Asia.

- Obesity greatly increases the risk of comorbidities such as depression, type 2 diabetes, cardiovascular disease and certain types of cancer.
- It is estimated that obesity in middle years shortens life expectancy by 4–7 years. Studies show that obesity is associated with excess risk of total mortality, death from cardiovascular disease, diabetes, cancer or accidental death (Hruby, Hu 2015).
- Obesity is costly to the national economy because of its morbidity. Therefore, the problem of overweight and obesity has become a pressing global issue.

RESEARCH   Pan *et al* (2011)—incidence of obesity in the US adult population

Essential understanding
✪ *Prevalence rates are useful to identify high-risk populations and plan interventions. However, prevalence rates do not make a distinction between individuals who have been obese for a long period of time and individuals who recently became obese. As such, incidence rates are complementary to prevalence statistics: prevalence shows the magnitude of the problem, and incidence shows the rate of development. This is important for prevention initiatives.*

Participants
More than 400,000 US adults.

Method and procedure
The researchers used data from an ongoing, state-based US telephone survey conducted annually by state health departments. The survey used random-digit dialling to select a representative sample.

Obesity was defined as having a BMI $\geq$ 30. Incidence of obesity was calculated by dividing the number of adults who developed obesity during a one-year period (between 2008 and 2009) by the number of adults who were non-obese.

Results
- The estimated incidence of obesity in the US sample in 2009 was 4%. This means that during the year 4% of previously non-obese individuals became obese. Note that the opposite process also occurs: some obese individuals lost weight and moved back to the non-obese category.
- Incidence of obesity was significantly higher among young age groups.
- College graduates had lower incidences of obesity than groups with a lower education level.

Conclusion
The high incidence of obesity over a one-year period shows the importance of implementing prevention programmes. Initiatives to prevent obesity are most likely to be effective among young adults, particularly young women. Adults with lower education are also a risk group.

Incidence is a useful epidemiological metric complementary to prevalence.

5.1.2 Biopsychosocial (BPS) model of health and well-being

DEFINITIONS

- **Biomedical model of health**—the traditional model of health that considered biological malfunction the only cause of illness
- **Biopsychosocial (BPS) model of health**—the alternative holistic model of health
- **Circular causality**—a pattern of causal relationships wherein A influences B, B influences C, but C influences A
- **Holism**—the philosophical idea that the whole cannot be reduced to the sum of its part and so has to be studied in its entirety
- **Psychosomatic phenomena**—experiencing physical (somatic) symptoms without a physical cause, due to psychological factors only
- **Reductionism**—the philosophical idea that complex phenomena can be reduced to their simple components; it forms the foundation of many research studies attempting to establish determinants of health

ESSENTIAL UNDERSTANDING

The biomedical model versus the biopsychosocial (BPS) model
The biomedical model of health that used to be predominant in health research and practice assumed a fundamental division between mind and body and reduced health to biological factors. See "The biomedical model".

The BPS model is the currently accepted alternative which claims that health is multi-determined (biological, psychological and social factors). See "The biopsychosocial (BPS) model".

A biopsychosocial approach to the treatment of obesity was shown to be more effective than less holistic approaches in the study of **Nguyen *et al* (2016)**.

Implications and criticism of the BPS model
The BPS model has some important implications: the importance of subjective experiences, the necessity to

recognize the active role of the patient in treatment, and the idea of circular causality. See "**Implications of the BPS model**".

The BPS model is an overarching idea rather than a concrete testable scientific model. Concrete research studies almost inevitably resort to reductionism. There is also a concern about how far the model has made its way into actual everyday medical practices. See "**Criticism of the BPS model**".

Links to other topics

- Explanations of health problems (biological, psychological and social)
- Dispositional factors and health beliefs (this topic is a zoom-in on psychological explanations)
- Protective and risk factors

THE BIOMEDICAL MODEL

The traditional **biomedical model of health** has its roots in the strict division between mind and body and considers disease primarily as a failure within the body. The model leaves no room for the idea that psychological or social factors may influence health. Accordingly, health in the model is seen simply as the absence of disease. Many researchers claim that the biomedical model is reductionist. However, due to its tremendous successes the model was universally accepted until the 1970s.

THEORY

THE BIOPSYCHOSOCIAL (BPS) MODEL

In contrast to the biomedical model, it is now generally accepted that illness and health are the result of interaction between biological, psychological and social factors. This is known as the BPS model of health. It was pioneered by **George L Engel (1977)**. The model is a holistic alternative to the biomedical model.

The BPS model is a paradigm based on the overarching idea that health sciences become more holistic and less dehumanizing. Engel did not deny that the traditional biomedical model was based on rigorous science and led to major advancements in medicine, but he also protested the tendency of clinicians to regard patients as objects and ignore their subjective experiences and interpretations. As a result, the BPS model views health as a product of multiple interacting determinants including the patient's beliefs, social environment, and so on.

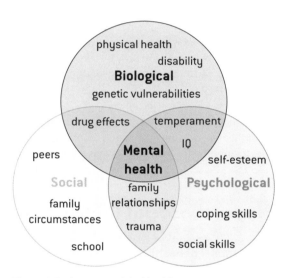

Figure 5.2 The BPS model of health

In line with the BPS model, in 1948 the WHO officially defined health as "a state of complete physical, mental and social well-being and not merely the absence of disease or infirmity". This definition has not been changed since then.

IMPLICATIONS OF THE BPS MODEL

Borrell-Carrió, Suchman and Epstein (2004) noted some of the important implications of the BPS model.

- The patient's subjective experiences should be considered along with objective biomedical data; they may play a role in the development of disease through **psychosomatics** (the influence of psychological factors on physical symptoms).
- In any disease there are usually multiple interacting causes and contributing factors. It may be complicated by **circular causality**, for example, a disease causes a change of lifestyle, and the change of lifestyle in its turn aggravates the disease. However, to plan treatments we need to make linear approximations ("A causes B").
- Patient–clinician interaction should recognize the role of patients in the process of treatment as more active and powerful.

Essential understanding

✪ *Using a complex treatment programme based on the BPS model for the treatment of obesity is effective for weight loss.*

Aim

To investigate the effectiveness of a treatment programme designed on the principles of the BPS model.

Method

Retrospective review of data from a weight loss programme at an outpatient clinic.

Participants

142 patients, mean age 40 years; their average weight at the start of the study was 210.2 lbs (95.3 kg).

Procedure

The BPS programme combined the medical knowledge of insulin with cognitive behavioural therapy (CBT) (to reframe thinking) and behavioural therapy (to break unhealthy eating habits).

Participants were taught about insulin and its role in fat storage. They studied the food groups that affect insulin and were advised to limit the intake of these products in order to keep insulin low.

Phentermine—a drug that suppresses appetite while maintaining energy and alertness—was prescribed to participants and CBT techniques were also incorporated into the programme to help participants change their thinking patterns. Table 5.1 gives examples of the key thinking patterns that were reframed.

Participants were asked to follow an eating schedule with five meals a day. They were instructed never to starve themselves, but to avoid sweets and artificial sweeteners. Behavioural interventions were aimed at breaking old eating habits and developing new ones.

Faulty thinking pattern	Correct thinking pattern
Weight loss is about eating less	Weight loss is about lowering insulin (so you need to know what kind of foods spikes insulin levels and eat accordingly)
I am on a diet	I am mindful about insulin ("diet" is not the right word because it has the connotation of deprivation and hunger)
I enjoy eating	I eat for enjoyment (enjoyment is important in life, but I control it and I can have my enjoyment after I have had my breakfast, lunch and dinner)

Table 5.1 Key thinking patterns reframed

Results

- There was a 10.8% decrease in weight on average from the baseline to completing the programme over 86 days (from 210.2 lbs to 187.4 lbs; 95.3 kg to 85.0 kg).
- Over the same time, BMI decreased from 34.6 to 30.1.

Conclusion

A biopsychosocial approach to the treatment of obesity may be effective in outpatient clinic settings, even with monthly short visits. While the majority of weight loss programmes focus only on one or two aspects such as dieting, weight loss medication or CBT, a holistic combination of approaches seems to be more effective.

CRITICISM OF THE BPS MODEL

The idea that illness is multi-determined seems intuitively obvious today and a humanistic approach is accepted more widely than previously. Many research studies have demonstrated that a variety of biological, psychological and sociocultural factors influence health and health-related behaviour.

However, the following needs to be taken into account.
- The BPS model is a paradigm or overarching idea rather than a concrete theory.
- It is rarely possible for a specific research study to be holistic. We can measure a large number of variables that potentially determine health-related behaviour and correlate everything with everything, but this "sea of correlations" will not give us a clear idea about cause–effect relationships. Conversely, in an experiment we can establish cause and effect, but we can only manipulate a small number of IVs. As a result, when it comes to research, we usually have no choice but to resort to some form of reductionism.
- While the BPS model is intuitively attractive, it remains to be seen to what extent it has actually made its way into everyday medical practices around the world. The researchers point out that a lot of ideas of the BPS model continue to be postulated on paper, but when it comes to everyday practice, many professionals still seem to assume the biomedical model of health.

THE BPS MODEL IN RESEARCH

To see how the BPS model is applied (and tested) in research, we will consider:
- **explanations of health problems** (biological, psychological and social)
- **dispositional factors and health beliefs** (this topic is a zoom-in on psychological explanations)
- **protective and risk factors**. See "**5.2 Health problems** and its sub-sections.

We will use the example of **obesity**.

EXAM TIP

Note that to answer exam questions on the BPS model of health, you can use the material from these three topics to provide research evidence supporting your arguments.

5.2 Health problems

5.2.1 Biological explanations of health problems

ESSENTIAL UNDERSTANDING

The BPS model of health considers it necessary to look at the full range of variables that may be causing disease ("determinants of health"). We apply this approach to obesity.

The biological determinants of obesity often considered in research are: genetic factors; leptin and insulin; patterns of brain activation; biological processes of addiction.

Leptin is a hormone that signals fat to the brain. Lower levels may mean lack of regulation of fat storage. Leptin is an RNA messenger for the ob gene. It has been discovered, however, that it is not the level of leptin as such that might be the problem, but how responsive brain receptors are to an increase in leptin levels. See "**The role of leptin**".

Biological processes of addiction may also be involved in obesity because fat and sugar lead to the production of dopamine and this is linked to the brain reward system. See "**Biological processes of addiction**".

If obesity is biologically determined, it also has to be inherited, at least to a certain degree. Haworth *et al* (2008) demonstrated in a twin study that genetic factors play a major role, explaining 60–74% of variation in obesity. Additionally, they argued that there are no specific genes for obesity beyond those that regulate BMI. See **Haworth *et al* (2008)**.

DelParigi *et al* (2005) using PET scans showed that obese people have a specific pattern of brain activation in response to tasting food after a fasting period. This shows the neurological basis of behaviours related to overeating. See **DelParigi *et al* (2005)**.

THE ROLE OF LEPTIN

In the search for biological factors responsible for obesity, leptin is a promising candidate. Leptin is a hormone that binds to specific receptors in the hypothalamus to alter the regulation of energy intake and expenditure. Leptin is believed to mediate the body's response to food deprivation. Leptin is a messenger RNA for the **ob gene**—a gene discovered using mouse models of obesity and cloning techniques.

Figure 5.3 A normal-weight mouse and a genetically obese mouse

Leptin levels have been found to reflect the amount of fat stored in the body: fasting dramatically depletes the levels of leptin while overeating boosts them. This is how the body signals to the brain that fat is being stored.

The level of scientific interest in leptin increased exponentially after Mantzoros (1999) discovered that administering leptin to mice with a mutation to the ob gene (which reduced the amounts of leptin produced naturally) had positive effects on their obesity symptoms. It suggested that human obesity may also be linked to leptin deficiency and hence treatable by medication.

However, further investigations in this area showed that only a minority of obese humans are in fact leptin-deficient. Mantzoros (1999) found that most obese humans actually have increased leptin levels, which prompts the following suggestions.
- Most cases of obesity produce leptin resistance, so leptin treatment will only be effective for a small number of individuals.
- The biological mechanism of obesity may be linked to leptin receptors rather than production of leptin (in other words, it is not the level of leptin that is the problem, but the fact that the brain does not respond to increased leptin levels).

All food in general, but especially high-sugar and fatty food, causes the **brain reward system** to release **dopamine**, which creates the feeling of pleasure. As with addiction to other substances, excessive consumption of food causes the brain to regulate itself and reduce the amount of dopamine released in response to intake. As a result, we require more food to reach the same level of dopamine (and therefore the feeling of pleasure or satisfaction). This is known as developing **tolerance**.

RESEARCH Haworth *et al* (2008)–twin study of obesity

Essential understanding
✪ *As evidenced in twin studies, both BMI and obesity are to a large extent influenced by genetic factors.*

Aim
To investigate heritability of BMI and obesity.

Method
Twin study.

Participants
A large UK representative sample of twins—more than 2,000 same-sex pairs at 7 years old and more than 3,500 same-sex pairs at 10 years old.

Procedure
Parents of the twins filled out questionnaires with measures of the children's height and weight. From this data BMI was calculated for each child. Based on their BMI, participants were categorized into groups of normal weight, overweight and obese. BMI correlations between monozygotic (identical—MZ) twins were then compared to BMI correlations between dizygotic (fraternal—DZ) twins.

Results
- Results were similar for both variables—obesity and normal individual variations of the BMI within the population.
- Genetic inheritance played the major role, explaining 60–74% of variation.

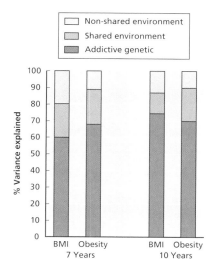

Figure 5.4 Results from the twin study (BMI and obesity)

Source: Haworth *et al* (2008: 1588)

Conclusion
Obesity and BMI are to a large extent, but not exclusively, genetically determined. The fact that heritability of obesity and normal BMI variation within the population are so similar implies that obesity is simply a quantitative extreme of some continuous trait and that there are no specific genes for obesity beyond those that regulate BMI.

RESEARCH DelParigi *et al* (2005)—obesity and patterns of brain activation

Essential understanding
✪ *Obese people (as compared to lean people) have a specific pattern of brain response to a meal after a prolonged fast. This shows that obesity can be associated with a specific pattern of brain activation in response to food stimuli.*

Aim
To compare patterns of brain activation in obese and lean individuals following the sensory experience of food.

Method
Quasi-experiment (comparison of pre-existing groups). PET was used to measure the variables.

Participants
21 obese (BMI > 35) and 20 lean (BMI < 25) individuals.

Procedure
Participants were given 2 millilitres of a liquid meal after a 36-hour fast. PET was used to measure changes in regional cerebral blood flow (rCBF) in response to this sensory experience of food.

Results
Differences in rCBF were observed in several regions of the brain. In particular, obese individuals demonstrated (as compared to lean individuals):
- greater increases in the middle-dorsal insula and the midbrain
- greater decreases in the posterior cingulate, temporal and orbitofrontal cortices.

Table 5.2 gives details based on prior knowledge of functions localized in these areas.

Area	Function
The insular cortex	This area participates in many aspects of eating behaviour including the response to flavour, food texture, smell, hunger for food and thirst. The middle-dorsal insula in particular has been associated with the sensitivity to the fat content in food (it is activated when fat is detected on the palate) .
The midbrain	The midbrain is one of the most ancient brain structures. It is a part of the brain system that produces dopamine so it plays a role in increasing overall excitation and motivation.
The posterior cingulate cortex	This area has been associated with processing emotional stimuli, both positive and negative. This showed that the reaction of the brain to the sensory sensation of food was more "emotional" in obese individuals and more neutral in lean individuals.
The orbitofrontal cortex	The same areas of the orbitofrontal cortex that were shown to be active in obese individuals in this study had been shown to be activated in response to a symbolic monetary value gain (and proportional to this gain). So this area is associated with an overall reward response.

Table 5.2 Areas of the brain and their functions

Conclusion

Obesity is associated with a specific pattern of brain response that is not confined to one particular area.

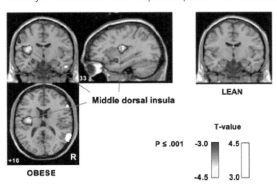

Figure 5.5 PET showing brain response to sensory experience of food

Source: DelParigi et al (2005: 438)

5.2.2 Psychological explanations of health problems: Dispositional factors and health beliefs

- **Attrition**—gradual dropping out of a treatment or prevention programme
- **Cognitive restraint**—a stable, consciously controlled intention to limit food intake
- **Disinhibition**—loss of an inhibition; an episode of "giving in" to the impulse
- **Dispositional factors**—a wide range of characteristics "internal" to an individual that influence the individual's behaviour, including genetic set-up, personality traits, attitudes and beliefs; dispositional factors are commonly opposed to situational factors
- **Health beliefs**—personal convictions about health and illness that influence health behaviours; individual health beliefs can also be influenced by a wider social and cultural context
- **Observed variation in health-related behaviour**—observed individual differences; we can quantify the percentage of this "observed variation" that is explained by a particular model
- **Predictive power**—the quantifiable ability of a scientific model to predict behaviour in real-life settings

ESSENTIAL UNDERSTANDING

Psychological determinants of health problems

Health-related behaviours (such as overweight and obesity) are influenced by biological factors as well as environmental factors. But there is also something in between—psychological variables that influence how environmental stimuli are perceived and interpreted. Psychological determinants of health-related behaviour may moderate the influences of both biological and environmental factors.

Psychological explanations of health have focused on dispositional factors such as personality traits and health beliefs. See "Dispositional factors and health beliefs". They have also involved various cognitive variables mediating environmental effects.

Personality traits and obesity

In a meta-analysis, Jokela et al (2013) demonstrated that conscientiousness (as a personality trait) was most strongly related to a lower risk of obesity. See **Jokela et al (2013)**.

In a longitudinal study, Sutin et al (2011) demonstrated that the combination of personality traits most predictive of obesity was high neuroticism and extraversion and low conscientiousness. See **Sutin** *et al* **(2011)**.

Cognitive variables

One of the commonly suggested psychological explanations is that obese individuals crave food; that is, they associate food (especially fatty food) with pleasure and satisfaction. However, Craeynest *et al* (2008) in a study involving an implicit association test (IAT) demonstrated that this is not the case. Craving fatty foods appears normal for people. It may be that obese individuals lack inhibitory control (that is, the ability to suppress this craving), but this requires further research. See **Craeynest** *et al* **(2008)**.

Another psychological factor contributing to obesity is the individual's perception of his or her weight and related health risks. Lewis *et al* (2010) in a qualitative research study demonstrated that perceptions of weight and health risks were indeed deviating from reality. The researchers also showed that these perceptions were different for moderately and severely obese individuals. See **Lewis** *et al* **(2010)**.

Health beliefs: models of health-related behaviour

The large number of cognitive variables that contribute to determining health engenders a need for an integrated model that will bring them all together to better predict individuals' health behaviour. Three of the most influential models are the health belief model (HBM), the theory of reasoned action (TRA) and the theory of planned behaviour (TPB). Each model can be characterized by its predictive power. See **"Models of health-related behaviour"**.

The health belief model (HBM)

The health belief model (HBM) views health behaviour as the result of a set of beliefs grouped into two categories (perceived threat of the illness and perceived effectiveness of the health behaviour). It also takes into account moderator variables: health motivation and cues to action. See **Rosenstock (1974)**.

Predictive power of the HBM was investigated in a study by Deshpande, Basil and Basil (2009). These researchers demonstrated a good overall fit of the model with the data. They also pointed out that the relative contributions of HBM components were different for men and women, which may have implications for designing prevention strategies. See **Deshpande, Basil and Basil (2009)**.

Although these studies have demonstrated that the HBM is useful for explaining and predicting health-related behaviour, the question is to what extent. Reviews and meta-analyses (Taylor *et al* 2006; Zimmerman, Vernberg 1994) have shown that the predictive power of the HBM is quite weak. Critics have also pointed out limitations of the model such as ignoring some important variables and assuming that people are rational decision-makers. See **"Evaluation of the HBM"**.

An influential alternative to the HBM is the theory of planned behaviour (TPB), which is a later extension of the theory of reasoned action (TRA). You are familiar with both these theories from **"2.1.3 Thinking and decision-making"** in **"Unit 2 Cognitive approach to behaviour"**.

The theory of planned behaviour (TPB)

The theory of planned behaviour (TPB) views behaviour as a result of intention, and intention is in turn predicted by a set of beliefs: attitudes, perceived social norms and perceived behavioural control. See **"The theory of reasoned action (TRA) and the theory of planned behaviour (TPB)"**.

Both the theories have been criticized for their exclusive focus on cognitive variables and it has been suggested to expand them to include additional factors. However, the TPB has also shown better predictive power than the HBM. See **"Evaluation of the TPB"**.

Godin and Kok (1996) showed that the TPB model explains about one third of the observed variation in health-related behaviours (not limited to obesity). See **Godin and Kok (1996)**.

Back to the BPS model

Overall, the models of health beliefs and health-related behaviour have been helpful in summarizing the influence of psychological factors on health. However, they are often criticized for the same sort of reductionism that can be seen in biological explanations. For example, research in the area of belief models rarely incorporates biological variables. The reason may be that, while the BPS model is necessary as the overarching ideology driving research, a specific research study must be intentionally reductionist in order to isolate variables and quantify their effects. See **"Back to the BPS model: interaction of factors"**.

DISPOSITIONAL FACTORS AND HEALTH BELIEFS

Behaviour is influenced by dispositional factors and situational factors. Using a very broad categorization, dispositional factors are factors internal to the individual, and situational factors comprise environmental influences. Examples of dispositional factors are:
- genetic predispositions
- personality traits
- stable (dispositional) beliefs
- attitudes.

Dispositional beliefs are stable beliefs that manifest themselves in a variety of situations. They are distinct from situational beliefs that arise momentarily in a specific situation and can be easily changed.

A number of dispositional health beliefs can influence health-related behaviour. An example is health self-efficacy (the belief that you can succeed in becoming healthier by changing your lifestyle).

Jokela *et al* (2013)—meta-analysis of personality traits and obesity

Essential understanding
✪ *Conscientiousness (as a personality trait) is associated with a lower risk of obesity.*

Aim
To investigate the association between personality traits and the development and persistence of obesity.

Method
Meta-analysis.

Participants
78,931 men and women, mean age 50 years.

Procedure
Combined data on the participants was used. A sub-set of the studies was longitudinal. The average follow-up period in these studies was 5.4 years.

Personality was assessed using questionnaires built on the Big Five model of personality, which includes the five traits of extraversion, neuroticism, agreeableness, conscientiousness and openness to experience.

Results
One of these five personality traits—conscientiousness—was shown to play a role in obesity. Conscientious reflects high self-control, orderliness and adherence to social norms. High conscientiousness was associated with:
- lower obesity risk in general
- lower obesity risk in initially non-obese individuals (a follow-up period of 5.4 years)
- greater likelihood of reversion to non-obese in initially obese individuals.

Conclusion
Conscientiousness is the only broad personality trait that is associated with obesity. However, this shows that dispositional factors play a role both in the development and persistence of obesity.

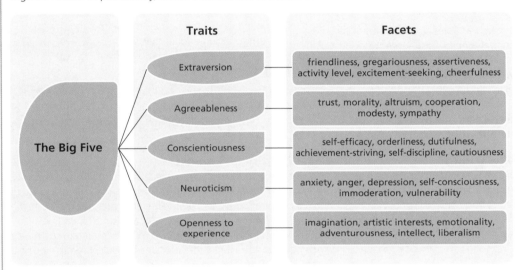

Figure 5.6 The Big Five traits

Sutin *et al* (2011)—longitudinal study of personality traits and obesity

Essential understanding
✪ *High neuroticism and extraversion and low conscientiousness is the combination of traits most strongly associated with adiposity.*

Aim
To investigate whether there is a concurrent association between personality and adiposity; whether personality predicts fluctuations in adiposity (across the adult life span).

Method
Longitudinal study, correlational.

Participants
1,988 volunteers.

Procedure
The study began in 1958. The researchers used data from the Baltimore Longitudinal Study of Aging. The longitudinal data used in the study spanned more than 50 years, with up to 32 assessments of height and weight and up to 16 assessments of personality.

Personality traits were assessed with a questionnaire built on the Big Five model of personality. As Figure 5.6 shows, this model groups all personality traits into five large independent domains: neuroticism, extraversion, conscientiousness, agreeableness and openness to experience. Each of these general traits contains a number of more specific sub-traits.

Results
Concurrent associations
- Overweight and obese participants had higher scores on scales of neuroticism and extraversion and lower scores on conscientiousness.
- At the level of more specific sub-traits, overweight and obese individuals scored higher on impulsivity and excitement-seeking (among some other traits).

Obese participants also tended to be happier ("positive emotion"), but less disciplined ("self-discipline").

Longitudinal associations

- Individuals who were more impulsive had greater fluctuations in weight over time. By contrast, participants who scored high on conscientiousness were able to maintain a steady weight.
- Individuals scoring low on agreeableness (or, conversely, high in antagonism) increased more in BMI over time.

Impulsivity was also associated with a greater increase in adiposity over time.

Conclusion

This research may have implications for the design of treatment and prevention programmes. For example, with individuals high on impulsivity and low on conscientiousness such programmes may stress menu planning and regular meal schedules. Interventions in a group setting may be more effective for extraverts than for introverts.

RESEARCH   Craeynest *et al* (2008)—craving for food and inhibitory control

Essential understanding

✪ *It is commonly suggested that one of the cognitive determinants of obesity is craving for food when the individual comes to associate food with feelings of pleasure and satisfaction. However, research produces counter-intuitive results: it may be the case that craving for food is "normal" for all people, but obese people are less capable of inhibiting this natural craving reaction.*

Aim

To compare implicit and explicit associations between fat food and arousal in groups of overweight and normal-weight teenagers.

Method

Quasi-experiment: comparison of pre-existing groups.

Participants

12–16-year-old overweight and normal-weight individuals, some of whom could be categorized as obese.

Procedure

The following variables were measured and compared in overweight and normal-weight participants.

- Implicit associations—an implicit association test (IAT) was used that quantified the association between food and arousal. For an explanation of IATs see "6.2.2 Prejudice and discrimination" in "Unit 6 Human relationships". In these tasks six pictures of fat food (such as French fries) and six pictures of "lean food" (for example, fruit) were coupled with high-arousal words (such as "excited", "nervous") and low-arousal words (for example, "calm", "lazy"). Participants were required

to classify as quickly and accurately as possible stimulus words or pictures into the categories "fat food", "lean food", "active" and "calm". Reaction times were used to measure whether there was any implicit association between high-arousal stimuli and fat food.

- Explicit associations—participants rated food pictures (presented one by one using presentation software) for emotional arousal.

Results

- Counter to the hypothesis, there was no difference in IAT results between overweight and normal-weight participants. However, for both groups of participants fat food was associated significantly more with high arousal than with low arousal.
- The same result was obtained for self-report measures: both groups rated pictures of fat food as more emotionally arousing than pictures of lean food.

Conclusion

The researchers concluded that associating fat food with arousal is "normal" for people, so the urge to eat fat food (and the anticipation of pleasure from the process) is not unique to overweight people. It should be something else that causes excessive weight.

If nearly all people show associations between high arousal and fat food, what other process can cause excessive food consumption? The researchers hypothesized that this could be **lack of inhibitory control**: everyone experiences arousal when exposed to fat food, but only overweight or obese individuals act on it because they cannot inhibit their first impulse. This hypothesis requires further testing.

RESEARCH   Lewis *et al* (2010)—health beliefs and obesity in Australian adults

Essential understanding

✪ *Moderately and severely obese individuals have different perceptions of their weight and associated health risks.*

Aim

To compare health beliefs in moderately and severely obese adults.

Method

Qualitative study.

Participants

141 Australian adults with moderate (BMI $\geq$ 30) and severe (BMI $\geq$ 40) obesity.

Background

Research shows that obese individuals often underestimate their weight and as a consequence deny some of the possible health risks, which in turn affects their behaviour. At the same time, most prior research studies treated obese individuals as a homogeneous group, ignoring the possible impact of severity of obesity on health beliefs.

Procedure

In-depth semi-structured telephone interviews were conducted with all participants. The duration of an interview was 60–90 minutes. The interviews were transcribed and subject to content analysis. As the transcripts were read and re-read and emergent themes identified and grouped, researchers also noted differences and similarities between the two weight groups.

Results

The commonalities in responses between the two groups included two major themes.

- They believed that they were personally responsible for changing their behaviours and losing weight.
- Failed attempts to lose weight decreased motivation.

Table 5.3 shows some of the key differences.

Moderately obese participants	Severely obese participants
described themselves as "overweight" and "fat"	used medical terminology ("obese")
distanced themselves from stereotypes associated with obese people	described themselves in stereotypical language
did not believe that their weight posed a serious health risk	acknowledged the seriousness of the risk
believed that their excessive weight is caused by environmental factors	blamed themselves
felt empowered to change their weight, and a sense of personal responsibility encouraged them	felt powerless and a sense of personal responsibility only added to that
The main motivation to lose weight was the social pressure.	The main motivation to lose weight were the health risks.

Table 5.3 Differences in responses from the two groups

Conclusion

Moderately obese individuals tend to underestimate the problem, attribute it to environmental factors, and feel empowered to change weight. Severely obese individuals are more accurate in their perceptions, but they are also more powerless. Prevention and treatment programmes should take these differences into account.

MODELS OF HEALTH-RELATED BEHAVIOUR

Research studies such as Craeynest et al (2008), Lewis et al (2010) and Dalle Grave, Galugi and Marchesini (2014) demonstrate a variety of cognitive variables that may contribute to determining health-related behaviour. However, the more such variables are discovered, the more there is a need for an integrated model that will bring them all together to better predict individuals' health behaviour.

Such models have been proposed and extensively researched. Three of the most influential ones are the health belief model (HBM), the theory of reasoned action (TRA) and the theory of planned behaviour (TPB). Each of these models can be characterized by predictive power: to what extent can the combination of variables included in the model explain the observed individual variation in health-related behaviour?

THEORY

ROSENSTOCK (1974)—HEALTH BELIEF MODEL (HBM)

The health belief model (HBM) was designed in the 1950s originally to explain why people failed to take part in disease prevention programmes, particularly for tuberculosis. In this model there are two major predictors of health behaviour:

- perceived threat of the illness
- perceived effectiveness of the health behaviour.

Perceived threat consists of a combination of two beliefs:

- perceived susceptibility ("How likely am I to get it?")
- perceived severity ("If I get it, how bad will it be?").

Perceived effectiveness of a health behaviour consists of beliefs about costs (barriers) and benefits of this behaviour. So, the idea is that individuals will engage in health behaviours if: they feel threatened by the illness; they think that the health behaviour is effective against this illness; costs associated with this behaviour are low while benefits are high.

Effects of these two major predictors are moderated by:

- cues to action
- health motivation (self-efficacy).

Cues to action are various events that may trigger health behaviour. Examples include noticing symptoms, advice from a family member and public health campaigns.

Health motivation is the overall dispositional readiness to engage in health behaviours. As part of the normal variation of personality traits in the population, some people are more attentive to their health and some less.

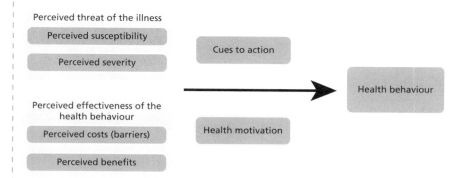

Figure 5.7 HBM factors affecting health behaviour

The HBM can be used both to predict behaviour of obese individuals (such as exercise and dieting) and to design strategies to prevent obesity. For example, the fact that obesity itself is a risk factor for developing a range of diseases such as diabetes or heart disease may be used in fear appeals. Through fear appeals we increase the perceived threat of obesity, thus increasing the probability of health behaviours. Simply educating people about the scientifically established health risks of obesity does the same job.

RESEARCH Deshpande, Basil and Basil (2009)—HBM and healthy eating habits among college students

Essential understanding

⭐ *The HBM demonstrated a good overall fit with data, as demonstrated by an HBM-based survey.*

Aim
To investigate how health beliefs impact eating behaviours of college students.

Method
An HBM survey; a correlational study.

Participants
A convenience sample of 194 undergraduate students at a Canadian university, aged 18–25. The average BMI of the participants in the study was 23.

Background
Transitioning to college life usually implies starting to make your own food decisions for the first time, so the population of college students is highly relevant for a study of health beliefs and their influence on eating behaviour.

Procedure
A number of independent measures were incorporated into the survey, mostly as questions on a seven-point Likert scale. Components of the HBM were all reflected in the survey. The DV in the study was the likelihood of eating healthily, and it was operationalized as a combination of self-report items such as "I intend to eat a nutritious diet most of the time in the next two weeks".

Results
- The HBM demonstrated a good overall fit with the data.
- In particular, perceived severity, perceived susceptibility and cues significantly predicted the perceived effectiveness of eating a healthy diet. In turn, perceived effectiveness of eating a healthy diet, along with perceived barriers (costs), predicted the likelihood of healthy eating in the next two weeks.
- The relative contributions of these factors into healthy eating differed between males and females.

Conclusion
The HBM was helpful in explaining observed variations of healthy eating behaviour among college students.

Since the HBM revealed gender differences, men and women deserve tailored healthy eating promotion campaigns. For females these campaigns should focus on the severity of not eating healthy diets. For males the focus should be on increasing their perceptions of susceptibility.

EVALUATION OF THE HBM

Research studies such as Deshpande, Basil and Basil (2009) show that the HBM is helpful in explaining and predicting people's health behaviour. However, the exact predictive power is important—it is helpful, but to what extent?
- **Taylor *et al* (2006)** conducted a review of available evidence and claimed that the HBM's predictive power is quite weak in most areas of health-related behaviours.
- **Zimmerman and Vernberg (1994)** in a similar research project spanning 30 research studies, found that the HBM was able to explain an average of 24% of observed variation in health behaviour. This means that after the HBM components have been taken into account, 76% of individual differences in health behaviour remain unexplained.

Critics have also argued that the HBM has several limitations.
- Some research studies demonstrated that these additional components (such as self-efficacy) actually have larger predictive power in relation to health behaviours than the core components, so it is not clear why these factors are not included in the model.
- The model is mainly focused on cognitive factors (beliefs), ignoring surrounding environmental influences, which is a limitation from the point of view of the BPS model.
- The model also assumes that people are rational decision-makers driven in their health behaviour by a cold cost-benefit analysis.

THE THEORY OF REASONED ACTION (TRA) AND THE THEORY OF PLANNED BEHAVIOUR (TPB)

These two theories have been proposed to explain human decision-making in a variety of domains, not only health-related behaviour. However, they have been extensively applied in health psychology as well.

For an introduction to the TPB see "**2.1.3 Thinking and decision-making**" in "**Unit 2 Cognitive approach to behaviour**".

The TRA (Fishbein 1967) argues that future behaviours are best predicted by the presence of a behavioural intention, and that the behavioural intention is in turn predicted by

two sets of beliefs—attitudes ("behavioural beliefs") and perceived social norms.

The TPB essentially was an extension of this framework that added one more dimension to it—perceived behavioural control (Ajzen 1985). This was to a large extent due to Bandura's work on self-efficacy at that time, which showed self-efficacy to be an important predictor of future behaviour.

In both these models behavioural intention is essentially a combination of a number of prior beliefs, this is why they are both **belief models**.

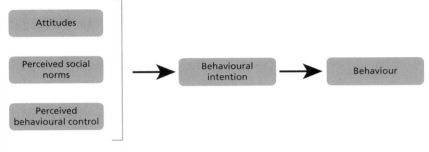

Figure 5.8 TPB factors affecting health behaviour

EVALUATION OF THE TPB

The TRA and TPB have been criticized for their focus on cognitive variables: they talk about "perceived" social norms, and one may claim that there may be some observable social facts that are not perceived by the individual yet exert influence on the individual's behaviour. Such factors are ignored in the models that emphasize the cognitive over the

social. There has been a lot of debate around whether or not the TPB should be extended to include additional variables.

Overall, there is evidence that the TPB is a better predictor of health-related behaviours than the TRA, which in turn is a better predictor than the HBM (Taylor *et al* 2006). This is supported by **Godin and Kok (1996)**.

RESEARCH Godin and Kok (1996)—predictive power of the TPB for health-related behaviours

Essential understanding
✪ *Across a range of health behaviours the TPB model provides good explanation (about one third) of the observed variation. Correlations are consistent with what is predicted by the model.*

Procedure and results
Godin and Kok (1996) carried out a systematic review of existing evidence for the efficacy of the TPB in explaining and predicting health-related behaviours. In a synthesis of 56 research studies they established the overall average correlations as:
- between intention and attitudes: 0.46
- between intention and perceived social norms: 0.34

- between intention and perceived behavioural control: 0.46
- between intention and behaviour: 0.46.

Collectively the first three variables explained 32% to 46.8% in behavioural intention (the lowest estimate was obtained in the domain of eating behaviours, the highest in oral hygiene behaviours).

Conclusion
The overall conclusion from the study was that the TPB could explain about one third of the observed variations in health-related behaviours. At the same time there was considerable dispersion of results depending on which health-related behaviour is predicted exactly.

In light of the BPS model, we can view health-related behaviour as the result of a complex interaction of variables. Roughly, social factors create an environment where we are exposed to a large number of fatty foods. Certain genetic predispositions may exist that influence metabolic processes (for example, through the regulation of leptin) and this causes some people's brains to be more aroused by food-related reward or less sensitive to cues of satiety. However, between the environmental and biological variables there is a layer of mediators—cognitive variables (beliefs) that can influence how the organism reacts to the environmental stimuli. These mediators are described in belief models (such as HBM, TRA, TPB).

However, it is extremely difficult to study multiple factors in their complex interaction with each other. Investigation of

biological influences on health-related behaviour, for example, has been based almost entirely on a sort of reductionism where biological variables are assumed to be the primary cause of behaviour. The same is true for research in the area of belief models. They rarely incorporate biological variables and look directly at the interaction between factors rather than considering factors one by one.

A study that combines psychological and biological variables could, for example, investigate the role of self-efficacy (perceived behavioural control, cognitive variable) in mediating the response of individuals with low and high leptin resistance (biological variable) to increased availability of high-fat foods (socio-environmental variable). However, such a study would be very difficult to implement, and the complex interactions would be difficult to quantify.

5.2.3 Social explanations of health problems

DEFINITIONS

– **Added sugar**—sugars and syrups added to food during its preparation or processing (does not include naturally occurring sugars)

– **Energy density**—the amount of energy stored in a particular weight of food (typically measured in kilocalories per gram)

ESSENTIAL UNDERSTANDING

Two of the most important social determinants of obesity are a sedentary lifestyle and consumption of added sugars. Foods with added sugars tend to be cheaper, so this links to an individual's SES status. See "**Social determinants of obesity**".

This is evident, for example, from the currently reported obesity epidemic in many tiny states of Oceania. This has been attributed to westernization processes: local foods

were replaced by imported canned products, and physical labour was gradually replaced by desk jobs. See **Curtis (2004)**.

Of course, there is a much greater variety of environmental factors that can contribute to obesity, apart from the two broad groups of factors mentioned above. For additional environmental factors that influence obesity and for additional research support, see "**5.2.4 Risk and protective factors**".

SOCIAL DETERMINANTS OF OBESITY

Essential understanding
✪ *The sedentary lifestyle that is encouraged by our social environment and the amount of added sugar in food available to us are both social factors that may contribute to overweight and obesity.*

Hill and Peters (1998) point out that evolution does not protect us against obesity: humans have evolved mechanisms to protect them against body weight loss, but nothing to defend against body weight gain when food is abundant. Two of the most important social determinants of obesity are a sedentary lifestyle and the type of food we consume.

A sedentary lifestyle means less energy spent; the amount of energy consumed from food may become much larger than the amount of energy spent, in which case the excess energy will be stored by the body in the form of fat. Sedentary behaviours include screentime activities, using a car to commute, passive rest and lack of exercise. Advances in technology and transportation, and availability of screen entertainment are environmental factors that contribute to obesity.

Type of food
• A change in the type of food we consume may lead to an increase in consumption of calories. Given the high amount of added sugars in processed food and drink, calorie consumption may exceed our everyday needs. The primary source of added sugars is soft drinks or sugar-sweetened beverages (SSBs). Added sugars can also be found in most processed products such as pasta sauces, potato chips or ketchup. Added sugars are sometimes called "empty calories" because they do not have any nutritive value.

• Access to products with added sugar may be considered a social determinant of obesity because food high in added sugar tends to be cheaper and one's SES determines the type of food consumed. Drewnowski (2004) claimed that the **energy density** of food is inversely related to its cost—diets based on added sugars and fats tend to be cheaper than more healthy diets based on lean meats, vegetables, fruit and fish.

Essential understanding

⭐ *Obesity rates in many island states in Oceania are extremely high. This can be attributed to westernization during and after the Second World War: physically demanding jobs were traded for desk jobs, and local products were replaced by imported canned foods.*

Curtis (2004) reports that the island populations of Oceania face some of the highest levels of obesity in the world. In Nauru, Samoa, the Cook Islands and Tonga rates of obesity have been reported to reach as high as 75%. The two main contributory factors are believed to be a decrease in physical activity and a transition to the western diet.

Many of the islands in Oceania (examples are Pitcairn, Vanuatu, Tuvalu, Fiji, Nauru and Kiribati) were colonized or taken under protection by such countries as the USA, Australia and France during the Second World War. During and after the war food aid from these countries eliminated the need for domestic fishing and farming. Most islands in

Oceania are still economically dependent on these countries. Large numbers in the island populations have traded farming for desk jobs, and domestic products have been replaced by imported food.

Observations also show that within these tiny island states, prevalence of obesity is higher in urban areas and lower in rural areas. In fact, groups that have maintained a traditional diet have lower obesity rates compared to western populations.

Military personnel based in the Pacific islands during and after the Second World War introduced the islanders to the western lifestyle and caused rapid changes. Traditional islanders' food (such as fresh fish and meat, fruits and vegetables) were replaced by rice, sugar, canned products, flour and soft drinks. These replacement products contain many calories but do not have a high nutritional value. In addition, the introduction of modern technology and new ways to commute (as opposed to traditional agricultural labour and long journeys by canoe) led to decreased physical activity.

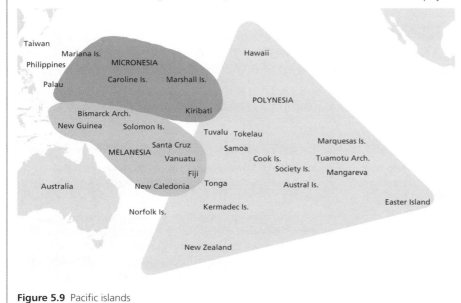

Figure 5.9 Pacific islands

OTHER ENVIRONMENTAL VARIABLES

Of course, apart from the two broad groups of factors mentioned above, there is a much greater variety of environmental factors that can contribute to obesity. For

more on these factors and for additional research support, see "5.2.4 Risk and protective factors".

5.2.4 Risk and protective factors

– **Confounding variables**—when A is a risk factor and C is the chance for developing a disease, a confounding variable is any third variable B, such that when it is taken into account the association between A and C weakens or disappears

– **Protective factors**—factors that reduce the chance of developing a disease or illness

– **Risk factors**—factors that increase the chances of developing a disease or illness

ESSENTIAL UNDERSTANDING

Risk and protective factors

All factors influencing health and well-being are typically organized into two groups: risk factors and protective factors.

- A risk factor is anything that increases the chances of developing a disease.
- A protective factor is anything that can reduce such chances.

For some of the commonly mentioned risk and protective factors for obesity, see "**Risk and protective factors for obesity**". How is this supported by research?

Risk and protective factors for obesity

Padez et al (2005) found in a cross-sectional study with 7–9-year-old children that family variables make an important contribution to childhood obesity. Parental education, parental obesity, duration of sleep and breastfeeding were shown to be important. See **Padez et al (2005)**.

Haines et al (2006) showed in a longitudinal study with adolescents that a range of personal, behavioural and socio-environmental variables serve as risk and protective factors in the development of obesity. Separate analyses were conducted in this study for each of the potential risk and protective factors. See **Haines et al (2006)**.

Separating confounding variables

When we correlate potential risk factors with BMI and obesity one by one, we are likely to find a significant correlation, but in many cases this could be explained by confounding variables. It is therefore important to conduct research with large samples where complex statistical techniques are used to estimate the effect of a risk factor over and above a range of potentially confounding variables. In a study like this, Chaput (2009) found that the risk factors most predictive of BMI were short sleep duration, low calcium intake, restraint and disinhibition. This suggests that obesity prevention programmes should target a wider range of "non-traditional" risk factors. See **Chaput (2009)**.

RISK AND PROTECTIVE FACTORS FOR OBESITY

Table 5.4 shows some commonly mentioned risk and protective factors for obesity.

Risk factors	Protective factors
Parental obesity	Breastfeeding for the first six months of life
Endocrine disorders	High intake of dairy products (calcium)
High birth weight	Eating breakfast
High-energy density in the diet	Regular physical activity
Sedentary activity	Sufficient duration of sleep
Poor sleep	Accessibility of sporting venues
Unhealthy eating habits of parents	Reinforcement of healthy behaviours by parents (parental influence)
Availability of foods with high amounts of added sugar	Self-efficacy
Low SES	Realistic knowledge and expectations about weight loss
Body dissatisfaction	

Table 5.4

RESEARCH   Padez et al (2005)—risk and protective factors for overweight and obesity in children

Essential understanding

⭐ *Family variables are the most important predictors of obesity among Portuguese children. Parents' obesity, being a single child in the family and short sleep duration were all risk factors for obesity, while breastfeeding and parents' education turned out to be protective factors.*

Aim

To identify risk and protective factors for overweight and obesity in Portuguese children.

Method

Cross-sectional study.

Participants

4,511 Portuguese children (aged 7–9), all of whom attended public schools.

Procedure

Height and weight were measured for each child. Parents filled out a questionnaire that collected information on the following factors: parents' weight, height, educational levels and occupation, child's birth weight, number of months spent breastfeeding, number of children in the family, order of birth, time allocated to watching television, physical activity, sleeping time on school days and at weekends.

Results

- In the sample, 20% of children were classified as overweight and 11% as obese.
- Fathers' and especially mothers' levels of obesity were found to be the most important risk factors.
- A high level of education of parents was found to be associated with lower obesity in children.
- Being a single child in the family was associated with increased risk of obesity. Conversely, children from large families and children who were born later than siblings presented a lower risk for being overweight or obese.
- More hours of television viewing increased the risk of obesity.

- Breastfeeding children for more than six months had a protective effect against obesity.
- Fewer hours of sleep were associated with higher likelihood of overweight and obesity.
- Interestingly, time spent on physical activity and mean energy intake were not associated with overweight or obesity.

Conclusion
Overall the study shows that, at least in the Portuguese childhood population, family variables are the most important predictors of obesity. This suggests that intervention programmes should be designed taking the family context into account.

Note
Separate analyses were conducted in this study for each of the potential risk and protective factors.

RESEARCH **Haines *et al* (2006)—risk and protective factors for obesity in adolescents**

Essential understanding
✪ *A range of personal, behavioural and socio-environmental variables serve as risk and protective factors in the development of obesity. Body dissatisfaction and unhealthy weight control behaviours are among the most important risk factors.*

Aim
To examine a range of possible risk and protective factors of overweight among adolescents. All the potential factors were combined into three groups—personal, behavioural and socio-environmental.

Method
Longitudinal study.

Participants
A diverse sample of 2,516 adolescents who participated in the Project Eating Among Teens (EAT) study.

Procedure
Participants completed surveys twice, at time 1 (1998–9) and time 2 (2003–4).
The measures in the survey included:
- outcome variables: BMI (calculated based on self-reported weight and height)
- personal variables: body satisfaction; depressive symptoms; weight concern
- behavioural variables: dietary intake, frequency of fast food consumption, frequency of breakfast consumption, hours spent engaging in physical activity, sedentary behaviours, disordered eating behaviours (behaviours targeted at losing weight such as fasting, eating little food, using a food substitute, using laxatives, smoking more cigarettes than usual, taking diet pills or inducing vomit)
- socio-environmental variables: home availability of healthy foods, weight-related teasing, parental weight-related concerns and behaviours (when either or both of the parents are trying to lose weight or encourage their children to do so), peer dieting behaviours
- demographic variables: sex, ethnicity, age, SES status.

Results
- Personal factors: body dissatisfaction and weight concerns at time 1 predicted overweight at time 2. This was a positive correlation: the more body dissatisfaction and weight concern there was, the more overweight the participant was five years later.
- Behavioural factors: dieting and use of unhealthy weight control behaviours was also predictive of overweight at time 2.
- Protective factors against overweight were greater frequency of breakfast consumption, higher levels of weight-related teasing, higher levels of parental weight-related concerns.
- This also implies that the rest of the factors (listed above) were not significantly associated with overweight.

Conclusion
The positive association between body dissatisfaction and weight concern and overweight may be explained by dietary restraint: weight concerns lead to dieting and other restrictive behaviours, these restrictive behaviours lead to hunger, and this leads to disinhibition and overeating.

Dieting was shown to lead to increased overweight, which may be explained using the same logic: dieting to lose weight leads to cognitive restraint, and this leads to disinhibition and binge eating.

Overall, factors within all three domains (personal, behavioural and socio-environmental) were significantly associated with overweight.

The findings suggest that interventions that increase adolescents' dissatisfaction with their bodies and put pressure on them to lose weight by engaging in dieting will not be effective. Instead, an effective intervention will be to enhance a positive self-image and a motivation to engage in healthy behaviours such as eating breakfast regularly.

Note
Separate analyses were conducted in this study for each of the potential risk and protective factors.

Essential understanding

✪ *It is essential to see whether a risk factor contributes to obesity over and above other potentially confounding variables. This may be done with the use of statistical techniques on large data sets. In Chaput (2009), application of such techniques resulted in identifying a set of "non-traditional" risk factors, whereas some "traditional" ones were shown to be insignificant.*

Aim

To determine the contribution of a range of risk factors to adult overweight and obesity.

Participants

White two-parent families, French Canadians from the greater Quebec City area.

Background

The Quebec Family Study was started in 1978 and was conducted in three phases, with the third phase ending in 2001. Its major objective was to investigate the role of genetics in obesity, fitness and diabetes.

Method and procedure

For the purposes of the study, Chaput (2009) used a sub-set of the Quebec Family Study data. Longitudinal analysis was conducted with participants over a six-year follow-up period.

Height, weight and BMI were measured along with several potential risk factors such as:
- lipid, alcohol and calcium intake
- mean daily caloric intake
- eating behaviour traits (assessed with a questionnaire):
  o cognitive dietary restraint (a person's intent to control the amount of food intake)
  o disinhibition (occasional excessive eating in response to certain cues)
  o susceptibility to hunger (food intake in response to experiencing hunger)
- daily physical activity
- the number of hours of sleep
- demographic variables: SES status, employment status, the level of education and annual family income.

Although all these factors had been shown in prior research to be significantly associated with the risk of obesity, Chaput (2009) argues that such studies usually look at risk factors one by one, and rarely assess the unique contributions of a certain risk factor over and above the others. For example, imagine you split the sample into two groups based on the amount of calcium intake and compare rates of obesity in these two groups. You might discover that rates of obesity are higher in the group consuming more calcium, and conclude that calcium intake is a risk for developing obesity. However, you might also end up in a situation where the two groups also differ considerably in other variables, for example family income. Suppose that families with lower income tend to consume less calcium. In this case you should wonder what the observed differences in the rates of obesity actually reflect—calcium intake or family income. Researchers should be looking for effects of risk factors on obesity after statistically correcting for the effects of other associated variables—for example, is calcium intake associated with rates of obesity over and above what can be explained by variations in family income?

Chaput (2009) used statistical techniques that allowed these types of questions to be answered.

Results

When analysed one by one, most of the factors were significant. However, after statistical adjustment, the only factors significantly associated with a higher BMI were:
- short sleep duration
- low dietary calcium intake
- high disinhibition eating behaviour
- restraint eating behaviour.

Discussion

It is interesting that the relationship between body weight and such "traditional" risk factors as physical exercise intensity or lipid and alcohol intake turned out to be confounded by other factors, because with statistical adjustment these relationships were lost. Instead, some "non-traditional" factors appeared to be important. This suggests that health professionals may need to address a wider range of "non-traditional" risk factors (such as sleep duration) to increase the effectiveness of prevention programmes.

Researchers say that the issue of sleeping time is particularly pertinent because there has been a decrease in the average number of sleeping hours by more than one hour over the past several decades. The effect of calcium intake suggests the importance of dairy foods, particularly skimmed milk.

Findings also suggest that cognitive restraint may have a negative impact. Cognitive restraint may lead to being constantly under stress, which may lead to higher frequency of disinhibition episodes (when an individual "gives up" to food), which may result in guilt and lower self-efficacy.

5.3 Health promotion

5.3.1 Effectiveness of health promotion programmes

- **Acceptability** (of a health prevention programme)—participants and stakeholders of the programme welcome data obtained and believe that it causes positive change

- **Ecological approach to health promotion**—an approach that takes into account multiple layers of influence, from the individual level to the community and policy level

- **Fidelity (of a health programme)**—participants of the programme actually implement the recommended activities; this can be measured as the average percentage of the prescribed activities conducted

- **Social marketing**—mass media and advertising campaigns, designed to achieve social change

- **Sugar-sweetened beverages (SSBs)**—drinks with added sugar, such as non-diet soft drinks, flavoured juice drinks and energy drinks

ESSENTIAL UNDERSTANDING

Ecological approach to health promotion

As we have seen, obesity (as well as any other health problem) is a biopsychosocial phenomenon, so it is reasonable to expect prevention programmes to target a range of biological, psychological and social factors. A holistic problem requires a holistic solution.

Health promotion can be defined as "the process of enabling people to increase control over, and to improve, their health" (WHO 2005).

Ecological approach to health promotion suggests that there are multiple layers of environmental determinants of health that need to be addressed holistically: individual, interpersonal, organizational, community and policy level. See "Ecological approach to health promotion".

Interpersonal level

An example of health promotion on the **interpersonal level** is the Challenge! health promotion model. It is based on the idea of mentorship. See "Challenge! health promotion model".

Research has demonstrated effectiveness of this programme in terms of preventing BMI gain and reducing consumption of unhealthy foods. However, the key effects of the programme were delayed and only became visible in 24 months. See Black *et al* (2010).

Organizational level

An example of health promotion on the **organizational level** is the Health Promoting Schools (HPS) framework. The three elements targeted in this health promotion strategy are curriculum, school environment, and family involvement. See "Health Promoting Schools (HPS) framework".

In research, this framework was shown to be generally effective and interventions acceptable. However, fidelity of interventions varied, and family involvement appeared to be the weakest element of the programme. See Langford *et al* (2015).

Community level

An example of health promotion on a **community level** is social marketing. See "Social marketing: Canada on the Move".

Craig, Tudor-Locke and Bauman (2006) investigated the effectiveness of "Canada on the Move", a social marketing campaign to promote walking, and found that a combination of motivational messages and dissemination of easy-to-use pedometers was effective at increasing average walking time. See Craig, Tudor-Locke and Bauman (2006).

Policy level

An example of health promotion on the **policy level** is the introduction of specially designed taxes on sugar-sweetened beverages (SSBs) combined with subsidies on fresh fruits and vegetables. See "Health and taxes".

Challenges

Health promotion strategies against obesity face a number of challenges such as the fact that different sub-groups in a population are differentially vulnerable to weight gain. See Malterud and Tonstad (2009).

THEORY

ECOLOGICAL APPROACH TO HEALTH PROMOTION

Broadly, there are two approaches to health promotion: the individual-based approach and population-based approach.

The population-based approach focuses on promoting programmes and policies that affect the health of an entire population. In the long run, healthy populations contribute more to the economy, so policy-makers have recognized the importance of such health promotion programmes. Individual-based approaches target specific groups of people, taking into consideration their unique circumstances.

However, the most successful health promotion programmes would probably adopt the so-called ecological approach where multiple layers of environmental determinants of health are recognized and addressed. Table 5.5 gives examples.

Level	Examples of action
Individual	Education to change attitudes and beliefs
Interpersonal	Social networking campaigns that encourage physical activity and healthy diets
Organizational	Healthy lunch initiatives at school; workplace exercise facilities
Community	Mass media campaigns
Policy level	Legislation on food labelling; taxes or incentives for businesses

Table 5.5 Environmental determinants and actions taken

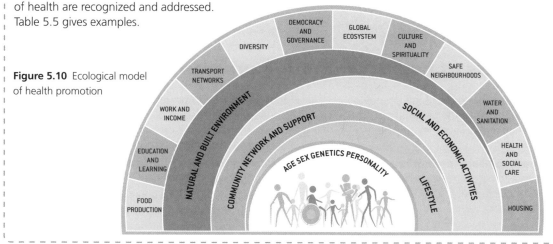

Figure 5.10 Ecological model of health promotion

Challenge! is a 12-session health promotion and obesity prevention programme based on the idea of mentorship. Mentorship is built on the principles of role modelling and support. Mentors for the programme are selected in a way that makes them relatable to the participants (approximately the same age and social background, same gender and race). Each participant is paired with a mentor. Mentors then visit participants at home and accompany them on trips, for example, to convenience stores or parks.

Each session has a challenge, for example, to persuade someone to drink water instead of soda. Each participant also sets a personal goal related to physical activity and eating habits (for example, to eat two portions of vegetables every day).

The mentors help participants to formulate realistic goals and increase motivation. During the regular sessions participants discuss their successes and failures, barriers that they have encountered and ways to overcome them. Such discussions are based on the HBM—reflecting on one's motivation, identifying benefits and barriers, and so on.

Each session also includes making and tasting healthy snacks, taste tests, and sharing recipes for healthy food (Black *et al* 2010).

RESEARCH — Black *et al* (2010)—effectiveness of Challenge! health promotion model

Essential understanding

✪ *This health promotion programme is effective in preventing an increase of BMI and reducing snacks and desserts. Many of the key effects of the programme are delayed and only become visible after 24 months.*

Aim

To evaluate the 12-session Challenge! programme in terms of changes in BMI status, body composition, physical activity and diet.

Participants

235 black adolescents aged 11–16, from low-income urban communities, of whom 38% could be classified as overweight or obese.

Method

Randomized controlled trial.

Procedure

Baseline measures included weight and height, body composition, physical activity and diet.

Participants were randomly assigned to either health promotion or control. The health promotion programme was delivered by college-aged black mentors of the same gender.

Evaluations were conducted after 11 months (post-intervention) and 24 months (delayed follow-up). Precise measurements were taken of the key variables. For example, body composition (percentage of body fat) was measured by a radiograph absorptiometry scanner. Physical activity was assessed by placing a uniaxial accelerometer on each adolescent's ankle with a non-removable hospital band. Dietary patterns were measured with a questionnaire. Overweight was categorized as BMI ≥ 85 percentile, and obesity as BMI ≥ 95 percentile.

Results

- In the intervention group the percentage of overweight or obese participants declined whereas in the control group it increased. Such trends suggest that there was a tendency (perhaps especially in the heaviest adolescents) to increase fat percentage and fat mass, whereas the intervention protected them from this tendency.

- Intervention was effective in dietary improvements, especially the reduction of snacks and desserts. Most other dietary effects faded away, but the effect on snacks and desserts was stable over the two-year follow-up period.

- There was no effect on adiposity in 11 months, but in 24 months some delayed effects on body composition were observed among the heaviest participants. This suggests that changes in adiposity are delayed. They follow behavioural changes.

Conclusion

Overall, the researchers concluded that the Challenge! promotion programme was effective in preventing an increase in BMI and in reducing snacks and desserts. This shows that behavioural interventions in general can lead to sustainable changes in diet and body composition.

The fact that most of the effects of the intervention on dietary choices faded away in the two-year follow-up period suggests that a more intensive intervention may be necessary to maintain these changes.

The researchers also note that effects of such intervention programmes (for example, changes in adiposity) sometimes may not be detected straight away, but become visible after a delayed follow-up.

THE HEALTH PROMOTING SCHOOLS (HPS) FRAMEWORK

The WHO recognizes the link between health and education: healthy children achieve better education, and better education results in better health. With this in mind, the WHO's subdivision in the Western Pacific Region developed a framework for Health Promoting Schools (HPS). The HPS framework aims to create school environments that will encourage healthier lifestyles. The HPS is a multi-component programme including:

- health education classes in the school curriculum
- changing the school's physical environment
- working with families and the wider school community.

The HPS framework suggests a number of guidelines that schools have to follow in order to deserve the title of a "Health Promoting School". The overall purpose is to create schools that constantly strengthen their capacity to function as a healthy environment. The framework is a holistic approach that involves multiple stakeholders in the process of gradual transformation. The framework also provides a monitoring tool for the stakeholders to assess their progress (WRPO).

The HPS framework has been shown to be generally effective at increasing physical activity and fruit and vegetable intake in school students.

| RESEARCH | Langford *et al* (2015)—effectiveness of the Health Promoting Schools (HPS) framework |

Essential understanding

✪ *The Health Promoting Schools (HPS) framework is generally effective, but the weakest of the three elements is family involvement. There are also issues with fidelity of interventions due to lack of institutional support, which points toward the need for a closer integration between education and health.*

Aim

To summarize research studies investigating the effectiveness of the HPS framework.

Participants

Students aged 4–18 attending schools.

Method

A combination of (quantitative) meta-analysis and (qualitative) inductive content analysis. The former was used for such data as target age group, study duration and programme outcomes (BMI, fruit and vegetable intake, and so on). The latter was used to read the "discussion" section in research papers and identify the specific elements of the HPS that were or were not effective. In total, 26 studies were included in the analysis because these studies included both process and outcome data.

Procedure

Inductive content analysis identified the themes of:

- intervention acceptability
- implementation fidelity
- family involvement
- barriers to implementation
- facilitators of implementation.

Results

- Where reported, **acceptability** of the intervention was generally high. Students, teachers, parents and catering staff all reported that they mostly enjoyed the

changes and welcomed their positive effects. It was also observed that initially teachers were often resistant to the innovations in the curriculum, but with the course of time resistance lessened.

- Reports on intervention **fidelity** varied. Fidelity is the extent to which all stakeholders involved in the health promotion programme take it seriously. It is often expressed as the percentage of intervention activities successfully implemented. In Langford *et al* (2015) it ranged from 21–90%.
- **Family involvement** was consistently shown to be the weakest of the three HPS elements. Parental attendance at meetings was poor, which was especially true for low SES areas.
- Tailoring the programme to the context of a particular school (including working with the school itself to develop the programme) was shown to **facilitate** success of the mission.
- In contrast, the most commonly identified **barriers** to implementation were lack of institutional support and the emphasis on academic subjects over PE. Offering unfamiliar and potentially unpopular healthy foods was also risky for catering services, which explains why they were usually reluctant to do so.

Conclusion

The following implications for policy and research have been suggested based on this review.

- Greater integration is needed between health and education.
- The importance of family involvement needs to be carefully considered.
- More process evaluations need to be published in research papers to enable identification of elements of the prevention programme most responsible for success.

SOCIAL MARKETING: CANADA ON THE MOVE

Social marketing

Social marketing is often used as a tool to prevent and control obesity. It includes using various marketing and promotion strategies (using television and other advertising campaigns) to increase public awareness about health.

Canada on the Move

- The WHO's Global Strategy for Diet and Physical Activity developed in 2004 (WHO 2004) recommended motivating the mass public to undertake at least 30 minutes of moderate-intensity activity most days of the week. When applied to walking and added to normal walking that we do anyway, this translates into the recommendation of at least 60 minutes of daily walking time.

- Canada on the Move was a national campaign aimed at promoting walking and the use of pedometers (step counters). A web-based platform was created to collect and monitor walking data. Pedometers and increased walking were promoted through advertisements in mass media, with the message "add 2,000 steps". At the same time, pedometers were mass-distributed in malls via cereal boxes. The message was to "donate your steps to health research", and users were directed to the project's website.

RESEARCH Craig, Tudor-Locke and Bauman (2006)—effectiveness of the Canada on the Move programme

Aim

To investigate the impact of the Canada on the Move programme on physical activity (walking).

Participants

9,935 adults.

Method and procedure

Telephone interviews and questionnaires were used to collect data. The questionnaire was used to assess walking and physical activity in the previous seven days. Participants were also asked whether they:

- had heard of the campaign brand Canada on the Move
- had heard the messages "add 2,000 steps" and "donate your steps to health research"
- owned a step counter.

Results

- Awareness of the brand Canada on the Move was associated with 13% higher odds of sufficient walking.
- Recognizing the specific tagline "donate your steps to health research" was associated with 23% higher odds of sufficient walking, compared to participants who did not recognize this tagline.
- Participants owing a pedometer were 14% more likely to engage in sufficient walking than those not owning one.

Conclusion

Health promotion through the increase of walking may be achieved by combining motivational messages with dissemination of easy-to-use tools for self-monitoring.

HEALTH AND TAXES

Legislation in the sphere of health can include such initiatives as taxation and subsidies, food labels, age limits on consumption and geographic limitation of sales.

In 2016, the WHO published the meeting report "Fiscal policies for diet and prevention of non-communicable diseases". This meeting and report were the result of a large number of requests from member states for guidance on how to design fiscal policies on diet. During the meeting, existing evidence was reviewed and the following conclusions were made.

- Specially designed taxes on SSBs (resulting in retail prices increasing by 20% or more) can be effective to reduce consumption.
- Subsidies for fresh fruits and vegetables (resulting in a reduction of retail prices by 10–30%) can be effective for increasing fruit and vegetable consumption.

- Consumers from low-SES backgrounds are most responsive to such policies and benefit the most from changes.

For example, Mexico in 2012 had the highest worldwide consumption of SSBs, and the rate of overweight and obesity was 71% among adults. In 2014, Mexican authorities implemented two taxes affecting non-alcoholic beverages with added sugar. This resulted in a decrease in household purchases of such beverages. Purchases decreased by up to 12% in the course of one year. Reductions were higher among families of lower SES status—as we know from the WHO (2016), these families are most vulnerable to environmental risk factors of obesity because they cannot afford healthy food.

ANALYSIS: CHALLENGES TO HEALTH PROMOTION STRATEGIES AGAINST OBESITY

Malterud and Tonstad (2009) analysed major challenges to health promotion attempts (with a focus on the Norwegian context). They identify the following major challenges.

- Different sub-groups in a population are **differentially vulnerable** to weight gain. For example, rates of obesity vary considerably with ethnicity (immigrant women from non-western cultures have a higher prevalence of obesity than women born in Norway). This could mean that a specific health promotion strategy needs to be designed for each of the key sub-groups.
- Health promotion programmes currently largely **ignore biological variables** such as genetic inheritance, operating on the assumption that changing environmental influences will lead to a change in health-related behaviour. However, we know from research that genetic heritability explains most of the variation in BMI (heritability coefficients around 0.7). Health promotion strategies should take genetics into account, but how?
- The opportunity to make healthy choices is **unequally distributed** among people (with richer people having more opportunities). However, campaigns emphasizing personal responsibilities of individuals regarding their eating behaviours may underestimate this fact, and this may lead to stigmatization of the low-SES victims of the obesity epidemic as "irresponsible".

Topics

6.1 Personal relationships
6.1.1 Formation of personal relationships

DEFINITIONS

- **Familiarity**—the cognitive state of knowing a person well because of meeting him or her on multiple occasions
- **Major histocompatibility complex (MHC)**—a group of genes that are involved in the formation of the immune system

- **Mere exposure effect**—the cognitive effect of being presented with the same stimulus repeatedly multiple times
- **Proximity**—closeness in physical space

ESSENTIAL UNDERSTANDING

Personal relationships take many forms. We will focus on romantic relationships—being attracted to another person, forming romantic bonds, getting married.

Biological origins of romantic relationships are mainly relevant to attraction. **Biological explanations** of attraction include:
- evolutionary explanations
- genetic explanations
- neurochemical explanations.

Evolutionary explanations—evolutionary theory predicts that females will find desirable males who can provide better economic care for future offspring while males will look for females who are healthy and can produce healthy offspring. If evolutionary explanations for attraction are true, these patterns should be universal across cultures. See **Buss (1989)**.

Genetic explanations—these are linked to evolutionary explanations and suggest that the basis of interpersonal attraction may be biological markers of genetic compatibility. This is demonstrated in the "Dirty T-shirt study". See **Wedekind et al (1995)**.

Neurochemical explanations—these have included research on pheromones, hormones such as oxytocin and neurotransmitters such as dopamine. You will find this research in other topics:
- 1.2.2 The influence of pheromones on behaviour

- 1.2.1 The influence of hormones on behaviour
- 1.1.3 Neurotransmitters and behaviour.

Cognitive explanations of attraction and romantic relationships have included several prominent theories including the following.
- Similarity-attraction hypothesis (Byrne 1961) claims that we are attracted to others who resemble ourselves and we perceive people more positively if we believe that they share our attitudes to important issues. **See Byrne (1961).**
- Matching hypothesis suggests that individuals seek contact with people whose attractiveness is similar to their own. Walster *et al* (1966) and Berscheid *et al* (1971) demonstrated that people do indeed try to match their attractiveness to that of their potential mates, at least at the initial stages of a relationship. See **Walster *et al* (1966), Berscheid *et al* (1971).**

Social explanations of attraction and romantic relationships have focused on such factors as:
- familiarity and the mere exposure effect, see **Zayonc (1968), Moreland and Beach (1992)**
- proximity (being close to each other in physical space), see **Festinger, Schachter and Back (1950)**
- social proof (being more attracted to people who we perceive to be more well-accepted in society), see **Jones *et al* (2007)**.

BIOLOGICAL EXPLANATIONS OF ATTRACTION
Biological explanations of attraction include evolutionary, genetic and neurochemical explanations. These three groups of factors are closely connected with each other.

Essential understanding
✪ *Patterns of mate preference in males and females are similar cross-culturally and are consistent with the predictions of evolutionary theory.*

Aim
To investigate cross-cultural similarities and differences in mate preferences in males and females.

Method
A survey:
- questions on the age at which the participant preferred to get married, the desired age difference between self and spouse, the desired number of children
- a section requesting participants to rate each of 18 characteristics (such as dependable character, chastity, intelligence) in how desirable it would be in a potential mate.

Participants
37 samples from 33 countries located on 6 continents with over 10,000 participants in total.

Results
- In all samples females valued "**good financial prospect**" in a potential mate more highly than males. This supports the evolutionary explanation of attraction because females may be trying to maximize the survival chances of their offspring.
- Males valued **physical attractiveness** in potential mates more than females, consistent with the evolutionary explanation that men find traits associated with fertility to be desirable.
- In each of the samples males preferred mates who are **younger**, which is also consistent with the evolutionary hypothesis (younger females have higher reproductive capacity).
- Females preferred males who are older (possibly due to this being a cue of longevity, maturity or experience).

Conclusion
- Researchers concluded that gender differences in mate preference were consistent across cultures and fit well into the evolutionary explanation of attraction.
- Females appear to be maximizing their reproductive success by seeking resources for self and offspring.
- Males appear to be looking for more fertile females.

Notes
Researchers acknowledge that the samples obtained cannot be viewed as representative of respective populations in all countries. Sample sizes varied in different countries: they ranged from 1,491 in the USA to 55 in Iran. Rural and less educated individuals were underrepresented.

Essential understanding
✪ *Sexual attraction may have an evolutionary basis because female preferences for male sweat are correlated with similarities in male and female major histocompatibility complex (MHC).*

Aim
To investigate the influence of MHC genes on females' ratings of attractiveness of male sweat odour.

Background
MHC is a group of genes that plays an important role in the immune system. Dissimilar MHC in parents produces a stronger immune system in the offspring. MHC information may be encoded by body odour.

Participants
49 female and 45 male students (mean age 25) typed for their MHC.

Procedure
- Female participants were asked to report if they were using oral contraceptives.
- The men were asked to wear a cotton T-shirt on a Sunday and Monday night.
- The T-shirts were given to female participants who were asked to rate the odour of six T-shirts each: three worn by men with MHC dissimilar to their own, and three worn by MHC-similar men.
- Each T-shirt was placed in a box and women sniffed the contents through a hole in it.
- On a scale from 0 to 10, women scored the odour of every T-shirt for intensity, pleasantness and sexiness.

Results
- Women who did not take oral contraceptives rated the odour of MHC-dissimilar men as more pleasant than that of MHC-similar men.
- In women who were taking oral contraceptives this tendency was reversed: body odour of MHC-similar men was rated more pleasant than that of MHC-dissimilar men.
- Ratings of intensity did not differ.
- Body odours of MHC-dissimilar men reminded women of their own mates or ex-mates.

Conclusion
- Researchers concluded that MHC similarity may indeed be a factor of sexual attraction.
- Oral contraceptives imitate steroids that are naturally released during pregnancy. The authors explain this by saying that this may lead to the reversal of odour preferences so that women prefer relatives (probably because they help take care of the baby).

OTHER BIOLOGICAL EXPLANATIONS

There is a variety of other biological explanations for the development of attraction (and therefore the formation of romantic relationships). Many of these link to topics that you know from other parts of the course.

- Pheromones—the search for human pheromones is still in progress and research in this area is inconclusive, but the idea of pheromones signalling biological cues of attractiveness links to biological origins of attraction. See "1.2.2 The influence of pheromones on behaviour".

- Hormones such as oxytocin—for example, Scheele et al (2012) found that oxytocin is involved in promoting fidelity in monogamous men; they are more reluctant to approach an attractive woman if they were injected with a dose of oxytocin. See "1.2.1 The influence of hormones on behaviour".

- Neurotransmitters such as dopamine—for example, Fisher, Aron and Brown (2005) in an fMRI study found that when people are looking at pictures of their loved ones, certain areas of their brain are selectively activated. These brain areas are part of the dopaminergic reward pathway: they are rich in dopamine and implicated in feelings of euphoria. See "1.1.3 Neurotransmitters and behaviour".

COGNITIVE EXPLANATIONS

Psychologists have looked for cognitive mechanisms that would explain why and how personal relationships are formed.

Several theories have been proposed, some of which are:
- similarity-attraction hypothesis
- matching hypothesis.

RESEARCH Byrne (1961)—similarity-attraction hypothesis

Essential understanding

✪ *According to this hypothesis, perceived similarity is a predictor of attraction. It claims that we are attracted to others when they somehow resemble ourselves (for example, in appearance, personal background, personality, values and attitudes).*

Aim
To investigate the relationship between interpersonal attraction and attitude similarity.

Method and procedure
Researchers asked participants to rank a number of issues on their importance (from most important to least important). Examples included a range of issues from God and premarital sex to Western movies. Two weeks later they were shown an anonymous questionnaire from another student. In fact, the questionnaire was faked so that responses were one of the following:
- identical to that of the participant on all issues

- opposite to that of the participant on all issues
- similar on important issues and dissimilar on unimportant ones
- similar on unimportant issues and dissimilar on important ones.

Participants were asked to indicate their feelings towards the stranger and rate this person on such characteristics as intelligence and morality.

Results
- Participants provided more positive ratings towards the stranger when their attitudes were similar.
- Similarity in important attitudes was more closely associated with positive ratings than similarity in less important attitudes.

Conclusion
Perceived similarity of attitudes indeed increases interpersonal attraction.

RESEARCH Walster *et al*, 1966—the matching hypothesis: Hatfield

Essential understanding

✪ *The matching hypothesis was first proposed by Elaine Hatfield (formerly known as Elaine Walster). It states that people are more likely to form a relationship with someone who is equally socially desirable.*

Aim
To investigate whether people are more likely to date someone of a similar level of physical attractiveness.

Participants
376 men and 376 women (freshmen).

Method and procedure
Participants were randomly paired with one another at a "Computer Dance"—they were told that if they provided some information about their interests and personalities, the computer would match them with a date. As they were purchasing tickets for the dance, four confederates secretly rated their physical attractiveness. After that the participants filled out a set of questionnaires.

Two days after completing questionnaires, participants were randomly assigned to a date. When they got to know their date's name, they were told to meet their date at the dance.

Participants' attitudes toward their dates were assessed during the intermission. Several weeks after the dance participants were also contacted to find out if they actually started to date their partner "in real life".

Results

Some observations that supported the matching hypothesis. Since partners were randomly assigned, we can assume that attractive and less attractive participants were assigned on average to partners of similar attractiveness. Data showed that attractive individuals were harsher in their standards and rated their dates as less attractive. They also expressed less desire to date their partner again.

However, other observations did not support the hypothesis. Participants' own attractiveness did not influence their desire (and attempts) to date more attractive partners. If the partner was attractive, participants would try to date him or her irrespective of how attractive they were themselves.

Conclusion

The matching hypothesis was not supported in this study. Participants sought relationships with the most attractive dates, not the ones that were similar to them in the level of attractiveness.

Notes

– The measure of physical attractiveness in this study is not highly reliable: raters saw the participant only for a few seconds as they were standing in line.
– Desirability of the partner was reduced to physical attractiveness for the purposes of this research.
– Findings could be limited to large group situations where young people are in very brief contact with one another.

RESEARCH Berscheid *et al* (1971)—another test of the matching hypothesis

Essential understanding

✪ *The matching principle is a determinant of the initial contact but not of maintaining an already established relationship.*

Aim

To replicate Walster *et al's* (1966) study with some modifications.

Method and procedure

Participants were randomly split into two groups: high probability of rejection (POR) and low POR.

The high POR participants were told that there would be a preliminary meeting with their tentative date prior to the dance where their date would be given a chance to either accept or reject them as a partner. The low POR participants were told that their dates had agreed to attend the dance with whoever was chosen by the computer algorithm.

After this, participants were requested to specify characteristics that they desired in a date—how intelligent, outgoing, attractive and popular they wished their date to be.

Results

– Attractive participants chose more physically attractive and popular dates than unattractive participants did. This supports the matching hypothesis.
– It was not different in high and low POR groups. In other words, increasing fear of rejection had no effect on the choosing strategy.

Conclusion

– Why did their study support the matching hypothesis while prior studies did not? Researchers suggest that the timing of expressing dating preferences is important. In Berscheid *et al* (1971) participants made a choice before they met their date. In Walster *et al* (1966) they made the choice after meeting the date and interacting with him or her for some time.
– They concluded that the matching principle may be a determinant of initial contact (whether or not you will approach the potential date), but not of maintaining already established relationships.

SOCIAL FACTORS IN THE FORMATION OF RELATIONSHIPS

Formation of relationships is essentially a social phenomenon, so it is not surprising that various social factors influence it.

– **Proximity** is one such factor. Being close to each other in physical space means increased chances of meeting each other (mere exposure effect) and therefore familiarity. Familiarity may lead to better liking. In this way what starts as a social factor becomes cognitive.
– **Social proof**: we may be more attracted to people who we perceive to be more well-accepted in society.

SOCIAL EXPLANATIONS: PROXIMITY

Essential understanding

✪ *Proximity increases likelihood of friendship*

Festinger, Schachter and Back (1950) studied residents of a large apartment complex (Westgate West). Residents did not choose where to live—they were assigned apartments as they became available. All residents were asked to indicate which people from the same apartment complex they were friends with. Results showed that proximity (literally the distance from door to door) was related to establishing friendship:

– 41% of residents who lived next door to each other indicated that they were friends

– 22% of those who lived two doors apart were friends
– only 10% of residents who lived on opposite ends of the hall were friends.

Proximity effect may have several potential explanations.

– Friendship may be induced by simple courtesy norms: you run into each other, so you must engage in some sort of polite interaction.
– Friendship may be the result of the expectation of future interactions: you will keep running into each other, so for things not to be awkward you need to establish a friendly relationship.

SOCIAL EXPLANATIONS: FAMILIARITY

Essential understanding

✪ *Familiarity increases liking. It is easier to like something we are used to than something we don't have any experience with.*

Zayonc (1968) experimentally supported the existence of mere exposure effect: merely being exposed to an object repeatedly produces a preference for that object. In his study participants were shown a selection of photographs of faces in a random order, and some faces were shown more frequently than others. After some time participants rated how they liked each of the faces, and it was observed that faces which had been shown more frequently were reported to be liked more.

Moreland and Beach (1992) conducted a similar study in a more natural setting. Four female confederates of similar appearance attended a large lecture class in college. One of them attended 5 sessions, another 10 sessions, another 15 sessions, and the fourth one actually did not attend any classes. At the end of the term students were shown photographs of these four women and asked to rate them on a number of dimensions (such as interesting, attractive, intelligent, honest). As predicted, the more frequently the confederate appeared in class, the higher the ratings.

RESEARCH   Jones *et al* (2007)—social proof

Essential understanding

✪ *Mate preferences may be socially transmitted. Women rate men as more desirable when the men are shown surrounded by women, as opposed to when they are shown alone or surrounded by other men.*

Procedure

Female participants in the study were shown pairs of male faces and asked to rate their attractiveness. Later they were shown the same pairs of faces again, but this time one picture in each pair had a female face at the side. The female face was shown staring at the man's face with either a smile or a neutral expression.

Participants were then asked to rate the attractiveness of the faces again.

Results

- The second round of ratings did not change for the faces that were not accompanied by a female face staring at it.
- Ratings in the second round were higher for the pictures that had a smiling woman staring at the male face.
- Ratings were lower for pictures where the woman was staring at the man's face with a neutral expression.

Conclusion

Researchers conclude that when forming attraction women may use social clues and mimic the attitude of other women to men.

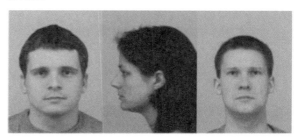
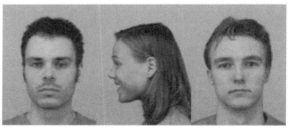

Figure 6.1 Photographs used in the experiment

Jones *et al* (2007)

6.1.2 Role of communication in personal relationships

- **Attribution**—the process of explaining other people's behaviour by assigning causes to it (either situational or dispositional)
- **Attributional style**—a preference for attributing situational/dispositional causes to a partner's positive/ negative behaviours
- **Patterns of accommodation**—shifts in communication styles that occur between partners to better adapt to each other in the course of interaction; they can be thought of as strategies of resolving interpersonal conflict
- **Self-disclosure**—purposeful disclosure of personal information (such as feelings, concerns, fears) to another person

ESSENTIAL UNDERSTANDING

Once a personal relationship has been established, it needs to be maintained. Relationships sometimes break apart, and constructive communication is a major means of preventing this. Several approaches have tried to explain how exactly communication is used in personal relationships:

- social penetration theory
- approaches focusing on attributional styles
- approaches focusing on patterns of accommodation.

Social penetration theory (Altman, Taylor 1973) claims that as relationships develop, individuals progressively move from superficial layers of interaction to intimacy through self-disclosure. Sheldon (2009) demonstrated that the theory can be applied to describe communication patterns between Facebook friends. See **Sheldon (2009)**.

Approaches focusing on attributional styles build on the theory of attribution proposed by Heider (1958) and claim that there are individual differences in how attributions are typically made in a relationship. Research shows that negative attributional styles (that is, attributing dispositional

factors to negative behaviour and situational factors to positive behaviours of the partner) are associated with less enduring relationships. For example, Stratton (2003) in a qualitative study demonstrated that negative attributional styles were predominant in distressed families that sought therapeutic help. See **Stratton (2003)**.

Approaches focusing on patterns of accommodation demonstrate that using communication strategies which acknowledge the disagreement and try to resolve it constructively can be associated with more sustainable relationships, as opposed to destructive and/or passive strategies.

- Rusbult and Zembrodt (1983) conceptualized four possible patterns of accommodation (voice, exit, loyalty, neglect). See **Rusbult and Zembrodt (1983)**.
- Gottman and Krokoff (1989) demonstrated that couples who did not avoid conflict but solved it constructively were more satisfied with their relationship. See **Gottman and Krokoff (1989)**.

THEORY

Altman and Taylor (1973)—social penetration theory

Social penetration theory proposed by Altman and Taylor (1973) claims that individuals in a relationship move from a shallow level of communication to a more intimate level. Intimacy is characterized by greater self-disclosure: individuals start sharing their deep emotions and concerns with each other.

The act of **self-disclosure** has been shown to have a range of effects (Collins *et al* 1994).

- People disclose more to those they initially like.
- When you disclose to another person, that person tends to like you more.
- When you disclose to another person, you tend to start liking that person more.

In other words, the act of self-disclosure produces increased liking in both actors in the process. Since this is so, self-disclosure may be an important component of communication that is responsible for maintaining relationships.

The onion metaphor is sometimes used to illustrate social penetration theory. In this metaphor, as interpersonal relationships develop, layer after layer of an individual's personality is peeled off, moving from the layer of superficial social self to the layer of the personal core ("the real me").

Figure 6.2 Layers of an onion are similar to the layers of a person's personality

---

RESEARCH   Sheldon (2009)—self-disclosure on Facebook

Essential understanding

✪ *Social penetration theory can explain communication patterns among Facebook users.*

Aim

To investigate self-disclosure, social attraction, predictability and trust as predictors of Facebook relationships.

Participants

243 undergraduate students (average age 20).

Method and procedure

Participants were given a set of questionnaires. When answering questions about interactions with another individual online, they were instructed to base their responses on one concrete individual, the person they talked to the most on Facebook.

Results

- The perception of attraction drives self-disclosure, especially the number of topics discussed with the person on Facebook.
- Increased disclosure was associated with higher predictability (less uncertainty) about the person, which

in turn was associated with greater trust. This supports the so-called uncertainty reduction theory: the more people talk with each other, the less uncertainty they experience and they are able to like each other more.

Conclusion

Researchers conclude that in online communication between Facebook friends people initially disclose to those they like. This disclosure leads to being more certain about the friend's behaviour (predictability). Predictability increases trust, trust increases likelihood of self-disclosure, and self-disclosure increases liking, which completes the circle.

THE ROLE OF ATTRIBUTIONAL STYLES

Attribution theory originally proposed by Heider (1958) claims that people are "naive psychologists" who try to understand the behaviour of others; with this end they assign causes to behaviours they observe. This makes the social world more predictable and thus easier to navigate. The causes assigned to the behaviour of others may be broadly divided into two types:

- **dispositional attributions** (when we decide that someone's personality is responsible for the behaviour, for example, "he must have exceeded the speed limit because he is reckless")
- **situational attributions** (when we decide that the behaviour was caused by external factors, for example, "he must have exceeded the speed limit because there was an emergency").

In interpersonal relationships, the way attributions are made and communicated may be important in establishing and maintaining mutual trust.

Healthy relationships are characterized by a positive attributional style where the partners assume best intent on the part of each other and refrain from automatically blaming the other person when a negative behaviour is observed. In a positive attributional style positive behaviours are attributed to the partner's personality while negative behaviours are attributed to adverse circumstances (situational factors).

RESEARCH   Stratton (2003)—attributional style in families that attended family therapy

Essential understanding

✪ *Distress in family relationships may be associated with negative attributional styles, especially towards the children.*

Aim

To observe attributional styles in troubled families that sought therapeutic help.

Method

A qualitative research study—observation and content analysis of transcripts.

Participants

Stratton (2003) analysed films of family therapy sessions from eight families with either step-parents or adoptive parents. All of the children in the household and both the parents attended the recorded sessions.

Procedure

All interactions observed in the recordings were coded using a comprehensive checklist for coding attributional behaviours. The total number of attributions analysed was 1,799, with around 4 attributions per minute per family (that is how common they are, at least in a family therapy situation).

Results

- Parents often used attributions which implied that their children cause bad outcomes.
- All of the parents in these families made more dispositional attributions for their children than themselves (for example, when children do something wrong it is because they want to, but when parents do something wrong it is because they are forced to by the situation).
- Negative behaviours of children were described as controllable more often than negative behaviours of parents.

Conclusion

Researchers concluded that for these troubled families (we assume they were troubled because they sought therapeutic help) the attributional style was consistent with "blaming the children"—describing the children as causing negative outcomes and the parents as being affected by these outcomes. This shows how distress in family relationships is associated with negative (blaming) atrributions.

Essential understanding

✪ *Patterns of accommodation that acknowledge the disagreement and try to resolve it constructively (voice) are associated with higher marital satisfaction over time, as opposed to destructive and/or passive strategies.*

In communication theory the concept of accommodation describes a situation in which shifts occur in the partners' speech styles to adapt more to each other.

Accommodation can also be thought of as a strategy for resolving interpersonal conflict.

Rusbult and Zembrodt (1983) analysed student self-report essays to identify four main communication strategies used to resolve conflict or disagreement in a relationship. The four strategies are:

- voice: acknowledge dissatisfaction and try to improve the situation
- exit: acknowledge dissatisfaction and try to end the relationship
- loyalty: not acknowledge dissatisfaction and passively wait for the situation to improve
- neglect: not acknowledge dissatisfaction and allow the relationship to deteriorate.

	Active	
Constructive	**VOICE:** acknowledge dissatisfaction and actively attempt to improve the situation	**EXIT:** acknowledge dissatisfaction and actively work to end or abuse the relationship
	LOYALTY: not necessarily acknowledge dissatisfaction and passively wait for situation to improve	**NEGLECT:** not necessarily acknowledge dissatisfaction and passively allow the relationship to deteriorate
	Passive	**Destructive**

Figure 6.3 Relationship conflict strategies

Gottman and Krokoff (1989) conducted longitudinal observational studies of couples. Couples were observed in their home environment or in a laboratory while engaging in a discussion on either a low-conflict or a high-conflict issue. Results showed that expressing anger and disagreement was not necessarily associated with marital dissatisfaction over time. In fact, couples who solved their conflict constructively were more satisfied with their relationship. On the contrary, couples who avoided conflict were less satisfied. Researchers explained that such couples do not have the opportunity to experience constructive conflict resolution together.

6.1.3 Explanations for why relationships change or end

ESSENTIAL UNDERSTANDING

This topic is a natural continuation of the previous topic, "6.1.2 Role of communication in personal relationships". Self-disclosure, positive attributional style and constructive conflict resolution through accommodation are all related to maintaining the relationship and preventing break-up.

However, researchers were also interested in creating a specific model of relationship break-up; that is, understanding the stages through which relationship dissolution progresses and identifying specific factors that trigger this process.

The prominent models that have been proposed in this area include the following.

- Gottman's Four Horsemen of relationship apocalypse— this is an evidence-based model that identifies four elements of a relationship that are most predictive of its deterioration: criticism, contempt, defensiveness and stonewalling. See "**Gottman's Four Horsemen of relationship apocalypse**".
- Rollie and Duck's (2006) five-stage model of relationship breakdown—this model views relationship breakdown as a continuous process that goes through a series of consecutive stages. See **Rollie and Duck (2006)**.

Supporting these models empirically in their entirety requires a large number of longitudinal studies, so it is difficult to illustrate this support with separate examples. However, specific research studies do support aspects of these theoretical models. Examples include the following.

- LeFebvre, Blackburn and Brody (2014) applied Rollie and Duck's (2006) model to investigate how Facebook users behave online both during and after a break-up. They found evidence for the last three stages of the model— social stage, grave dressing, resurrection. See **LeFebvre, Blackburn and Brody (2014)**.
- Flora and Segrin (2003) found that negativity in partners' accounts of their relationship history and lack of relational breadth predicted lower satisfaction and break-up in a six-month interval. See **Flora and Segrin (2003)**.

Research in the area typically relies on retrospective self-report measures which are open to a variety of biases such as social desirability or effects of reconstructive memory. There is also an ethical concern because participants may be required to recreate hurtful episodes in their memory.

Gottman's Four Horsemen of relationship apocalypse

The Gottman Institute, headed by husband and wife John Gottman and Julie Gottman, conducts longitudinal research into couples through observation, questionnaires and interviews and tries to predict how relationships will unfold.

Research at the Gottman Institute utilizes a rich combination of quantitative and qualitative data. Couples are invited into the laboratory ("the Love Lab") and their interaction is recorded with two remote-controlled cameras.

Biometric data from a polygraph is recorded simultaneously and projected on the same screen so that researchers can see both the people and their biometric data in real time. In addition to this, relationship history is studied through self-report measures and individual interviews.

The Four Horsemen is a popular name for the four main elements of relationships that have been proven to be predictive of relationship deterioration (for example, divorce).

- **Criticism**—this refers to a general statement that expresses a dispositional attribution about a person, for example, "you always forget to feed the dog".
- **Contempt**—treating someone with disrespect or mocking sarcasm, for example insulting the partner or eye rolling. It is considered the primary predictor of divorce.
- **Defensiveness**—when someone claims to be under attack for no reason, for example shifting the blame onto others.
- **Stonewalling**—essentially ignoring the partner, for example withdrawing from conversation and refusing to interact with the partner or pretending not to hear.

THEORY

Rollie and Duck (2006)—five-stage model of relationship breakdown

According to Rollie and Duck (2006), relationship breakdown is a process, not an event. They conducted longitudinal observations of couples which led them to formulate five stages of relationship breakdown. The assumption is that the stages are sequential; that is, a stage cannot be skipped.

- **The intrapsychic stage**—dissatisfaction is experienced internally by one or both partners, but is not shared with anyone. It may include social withdrawal, rumination or silent resentment.
- **The dyadic stage**—partners voice their discontent and discuss their issues with each other. Depending on their attributional styles and patterns of accommodation, conflict at this stage may either be constructively resolved or avoided and become latent.
- **The social stage**—partners start seeking support from others. Problems are shared with a wider community. Alliances may be built and partners can reinforce their discontent with each other.
- **Grave dressing**—stories are prepared that will be told to people in order to save face. Partners defend their decision to break up and come up with arguments to justify this decision to others.
- **Resurrection**—partners recover from the relationship. They redefine what they are looking for in future relationships

RESEARCH   LeFebvre, Blackburn and Brody (2014)—relationship dissolution on Facebook

Essential understanding
✪ *Online break-up behaviours broadly follow Rollie and Duck's (2006) stages.*

Aim
To apply Rollie and Duck's (2006) relationship dissolution model to investigate how Facebook users behave online both during and after a break-up.

Participants
226 college students.

Method and procedure
Participants completed an online survey that asked open-ended questions about a romantic relationship that had ended within the past two years. They rated the seriousness of that relationship, the frequency of face-to-face and online communication with the partner, reported on online communication with the partner and behaviours that occurred both during and after the break-up.

Inductive content analysis was used to analyse data.

Results
Researchers identified the most common online behaviours both during and after the break-up.

- **During relationship dissolution**: participants minimized their Facebook activity; cleared away the presence of their partner by removing their Facebook relationship status, untagging or deleting wall postings and pictures, and hiding other public displays of affection; observed online actions of their partners (that is, engaged in "stalking").
- **After relationship dissolution**: participants continued getting rid of the unwanted remains such as previous wall postings or other visible connections to their ex-partner. Some participants defriended, deleted or blocked Facebook access to their ex-partner and some of the associated social network. Impression management behaviours also became prominent. These included positive online self-presentation. Many behaviours were aimed to evoke jealousy or regret from previous partners.

Conclusion
Researchers claim that the results of this study support Rollie and Duck's (2006) model of relationship dissolution, especially the last three stages: the social stage, grave dressing and resurrection.

Flora and Segrin (2003)—relational history and satisfaction

Essential understanding

⭐ *Diverse experiences in relational history are necessary to maintain a relationship.*

Aim

To examine how perceptions of relational history predicted relational well-being in dating and married couples.

Participants

65 married couples and 66 dating couples, at least 20 years old and native speakers of English.

Method and procedure

– Measurements of relationship well-being (satisfaction and stability) were taken twice with a six-month interval.
– A semi-structured interview (oral history) was used where participants answered a set of open-ended questions in a story-like fashion while their partner was present in the same room. A coding scheme was used later to assess the interview transcripts against a set of scales such as fondness, affection and negativity toward the spouse, among others.

– In addition, relationship development was assessed through relationship development breadth—a questionnaire completed by the participants alone. Relationship development breadth is the extent to which partners have experienced specific behaviours (such as becoming sexually intimate), cognitions (such as thinking that the partner was the right person for them) and affect (such as feeling a deep emotional connection) in the course of the relationship. The more behaviours, cognitions and emotional reactions you experienced in the course of a relationship, the "broader" your relationship development has been.

Results

Break-up and lower satisfaction at time 2 (six months after the start of the study) were related to little relational development breadth and negative oral history appraisals.

Conclusion

Researchers concluded that a variety of behavioural, cognitive and affective experiences are necessary for long-lasting relationships.

Evaluation of research

Research in the area of relationship dissolution has been criticized in terms of methodological quality and ethical considerations.

– Research in this area typically relies on retrospective self-report measures that are open to a variety of biases

such as social desirability or effects of reconstructive memory.
– Such studies require participants to recreate hurtful episodes in their memory that can cause some level of psychological harm.

6.2 Group dynamics

6.2.1 Cooperation and competition

– **Competition**—interpersonal or intergroup behaviour that benefits the interests of the actor at the cost of the interests of another person or group. The outcome of competitive behaviour is "I win, you lose". When competition escalates and becomes explicit, it takes the form of a **conflict**
– **Cooperation**—interpersonal or intergroup behaviour that benefits the interests of another person or another group. The outcomes of cooperative behaviour are either "I win, you win" or "I lose, you win"
– Cooperation occurs both on the interpersonal level and the intergroup level. Interpersonal cooperation is also known as **prosocial behaviour**. Intrinsic interpersonal cooperation is known as **altruism**

ESSENTIAL UNDERSTANDING

While intergroup cooperation reflects cooperation between individuals, it cannot be simply reduced to it, because group behaviour is not simply a sum total of individual behaviours.

Why do individuals cooperate or compete?

From the evolutionary standpoint **competition** is more easily explained: individuals compete for resources to maximize their survival potential.

Theories to explain **cooperation** on the individual level include:

– kin selection theory (Hamilton 1964)
– reciprocal altruism theory (Trivers 1971)
– negative-state relief model of altruism (Cialdini, Kenrick 1976)
– empathy-altruism model (Batson 1981).

Some of these theories are covered in "**6.3.2 Prosocial behaviour**".

Why do groups cooperate or compete?

- A prominent theory to explain competition and cooperation between groups is **realistic conflict theory (RCT)** (Campbell 1965). It is supported by the Robber's Cave studies (Sherif *et al* 1961). It claims that intergroup conflict is the result of competition over scarce resources and cooperation is the result of superordinate goals. See **Sherif *et al* (1961)**.
- **Social identity theory** (Tajfel, Turner 1971) provides an alternative explanation, claiming that in-group favouritism and out-group discrimination are results of mere categorization into distinct groups. See "**3.1.1 Social identity theory**" in "**Unit 3 Sociocultural approach to behaviour**".

Behavioural game theory

In modern psychology cooperation and competition between individuals and groups is often studied as part of **behavioural game theory**.

Using behavioural game theory Burton-Chellew, Ross-Gillespie and West (2010) demonstrated that cooperation between humans within a group may be enhanced by competition between groups. See **Burton-Chellew, Ross-Gillespie and West (2010)**.

Biological correlates of intergroup conflict

Cooperative behaviour and intergroup conflict in humans have been linked to biological variables.

- De Dreu *et al* (2012) found that after taking a dose of oxytocin participants were more likely to pre-emptively compete with other groups. See **De Dreu *et al* (2012)**.
- Decety *et al* (2004) found distinct brain regions to be associated with cooperation and competition. See **Decety *et al* (2004)**.

THEORY

Why do individuals cooperate or compete?

Competition is easily explained from the point of view of evolution and natural selection. Individuals compete for resources to maximize their survival potential.

However, humans and non-human animals demonstrate a lot of **cooperative behaviour**, both extrinsic and intrinsic. This presents an evolutionary puzzle, especially intrinsic cooperation (altruism). There have been several prominent theories that offer a solution to this puzzle.

- **Kin selection theory (Hamilton 1964)** claims that organisms behave altruistically towards others when this behaviour maximizes the survival value of their genes. For example, someone may help a relative because they share common genes and this behaviour may increase the chance that the genes will be passed on to further generations.
- **Reciprocal altruism theory (Trivers 1971)** states that one organism may help another if a return favour is anticipated sometime in the future (I will help you, and you will help me in return when I need it).
- **Empathy-altruism model (Batson 1981)**—applied to humans, this model postulates the existence of "true" altruism caused by genuine empathetic concern for others.

Some of these theories are covered in "**6.3.2 Prosocial behaviour**".

THEORY

Why do groups cooperate or compete?

One of the first influential theories to explain intergroup competition and cooperation was **realistic conflict theory (RCT)** (Campbell 1965). This theory states that intergroup conflict arises when groups have opposing (incompatible) goals and are competing for scarce **resources**. These opposing goals, according to the theory, are the reason why groups develop in-group norms, display acts of in-group favouritism and discriminate against out-groups.

However, RCT claims that groups cooperate when they have **superordinate goals**; that is, their goals are compatible and they may be more successful if they work together. When this is the case, existing stereotypes, prejudice and discrimination will be reduced or eliminated.

RCT has been supported by classic research studies by Muzafer Sherif.

RESEARCH   Sherif *et al* (1961)—the Robber's Cave studies

✪ Essential understanding

- *Competition over scarce resources and opposing goals induces conflict and discrimination.*
- *Introduction of superordinate goals reduces conflict and encourages cooperation.*

Participants

24 white lower-middle-class 12-year-old boys. The boys did not know each other prior to meeting in the summer camp.

Procedure and results

These field studies were conducted in the realistic setting of a summer camp for boys (Robber's Cave was the camp's name) and included three stages.

Stage 1: group formation

Boys were placed into two groups that later took the names of the Rattlers and the Eagles. Each group was initially unaware of the other one because the two groups were staying at opposite ends of the camp site. Groups quickly developed internal norms, structure, traditions and rituals, and they started identifying themselves as "we".

Stage 2: inter-group conflict

The two groups came to know about each other's existence, and the researchers (who posed as the camp leaders) arranged a series of competitive activities such as tug of war. All activities were designed so that there were clear winners and losers; winners received an attractive prize and losers received nothing, so their goals were incompatible. As a result of this, boys clearly demonstrated:

- in-group favouritism—they focused on their similarities and always spoke positively about their in-group

- out-group discrimination—they traded insults, burned the flags of the other group and even raided their cabins.

Stage 3: conflict reduction

Researchers changed the nature of the activities by creating situations where group goals we are interdependent—one group could only succeed if it cooperated with the other. For example, a heavy truck that was used to drive the boys around the camp broke down and had to be pushed. It was too heavy for one team but when both teams worked together they managed to bump start the truck. In response to the introduction of such superordinate goals a reduction of conflict behaviour was observed.

Conclusion

The core cause of intergroup conflict is competition over scarce resources, and cooperation is possible when there are superordinate goals.

THEORY

Alternative explanation—social identity theory

Essential understanding

✪ *In-group favouritism and out-group discrimination may be the result of mere categorization into distinct groups.*

Gaps in RCT

RCT provides a powerful explanation of intergroup competition and cooperation, but it is not exhaustive.

- It has been observed that the first signs of in-group favouritism and out-group discrimination (in the form of derogatory verbal comments about the other team) were observed in the Robber's Cave studies when the boys had just learned about the existence of the other group. Technically no competition over resources had yet been created.
- There are cases when conflict is sparked even when groups do not compete over resources.

Social identity theory

Social identity theory (Tajfel, Turner 1969) provided an explanation for these gaps in RCT.

Social identity theory posits that in-group favouritism and out-group discrimination are both effects of **social categorization**—when individuals identify with a social group, their self-esteem becomes linked to the status of that group, so individuals pursue opportunities to increase positive distinctiveness of their group in relation to other groups ("us" versus "them"). For example, they will sacrifice the benefit of their own group if this sacrifice increases positive distinctiveness. See "3.1.1 Social identity theory" in "Unit 3 Sociocultural approach to behaviour".

THEORY

Behavioural game theory

In contemporary psychology cooperation and competition between individuals and groups is often studied as part of behavioural game theory.

Game theory is a mathematical approach to modelling the interaction of two or more rational "agents" (decision-makers). Being rational means that each of the agents chooses the course of action that maximizes its expected utility. The actions of one agent depend on the actions of the other agent or agents, which makes game theory suitable for describing many social processes such as bargaining,

stock market exchange and warfare. Game theory has found many applications in economics, business, marketing, political sciences and other areas.

Behavioural game theory looks at how people actually behave in typical interaction situations. Human behaviour is not always completely rational and therfore does not always coincide with the predictions of mathematical game theory. However, these deviations from rationality themselves may be predictable. In the words of Dan Ariely, we are "predictably irrational".

RESEARCH   Burton-Chellew, Ross-Gillespie and West (2010)—competition causes cooperation

Essential understanding

⭐ *Cooperation between humans may actually be the result of competition between groups.*

Aim

To study behaviour in a public goods game with an added competitive incentive for combined group performance.

Method

Experiment, independent measures design.

Procedure

A situation was modelled where groups competed with other groups for financial rewards (a so-called public goods game).

The sample was randomly divided into groups of four, and each group played a public goods game among themselves.

In the game each participant received an endowment of 20 monetary units (MU). They could then contribute any fraction of this sum (0–20 MU) to a group investment. They kept any MU they did not contribute. MU contributed for the investment were multiplied by two and evenly divided between the four participants, so investment was beneficial

for the group (a return of two MU for each one contributed), but costly for the individual (a return of 0.5 MU for each one contributed).

In the no-competition (control) group there were no other conditions.

In the competition (experimental) group participants were also given a chance to earn additional MU depending on the combined performance of their group. Groups were ranked according to the sum total of their contributions, and participants of the highest-ranking group each received an additional 16 MU.

Results

The presence of group competition resulted in participants repeatedly contributing more to the public fund. Importantly, results showed that collaborating more did not lead to higher individual rewards, but people increased collaboration anyway when group competition was introduced.

Conclusion

Researchers conclude that higher levels of cooperation within the group are caused by competition between groups.

RESEARCH   Biological correlates of intergroup conflict

Essential understanding

⭐ *Cooperative behaviour and intergroup conflict in humans have been linked to biological variables.*

De Dreu et al (2012), in a modified version of the prisoner's dilemma game, found that after taking a dose of oxytocin participants were more likely to pre-emptively compete with other groups out of fear that others will start competing first. In other words, they were more likely to engage in defence-motivated non-cooperation. This points to a role of oxytocin in increasing cooperation with the in-group and, as a side effect, increasing competition with out-groups.

Decety et al (2004) conducted an fMRI study where participants played a computer game either in cooperation with or in competition against another person. Distinct brain regions were found to be selectively associated with cooperation and competition:
– cooperation—orbitofrontal cortex
– competition—inferior parietal cortex and medial prefrontal cortex.

Researchers argue that this pattern reflects different mental frameworks involved in competition and cooperation: we need to process information differently depending on what we expect from others.

6.2.2 Prejudice and discrimination

– **Discrimination**—negative behaviour towards a group of people; it involves treating people in an unfair way based on their group membership
– **Prejudice**—a negative attitude towards an individual or a group of people
– **Social bias**—stereotypes, prejudice and discrimination are all types of social bias
– **Stereotypes**—generalized (and often biased) perceptions of typical characteristics of individuals based on their group membership

ESSENTIAL UNDERSTANDING

Prejudice and discrimination are closely linked to other topics such as:
– stereotypes—these form the cognitive basis of prejudice and discrimination (see "3.1.3 Stereotypes" in "Unit 3 Sociocultural approach to behaviour")
– social identity theory—categorization into social groups ("us" and "them") triggers in-group favouritism and outgroup discrimination (see "3.1.1 Social identity theory" in "Unit 3 Sociocultural approach to behaviour")

competition and cooperation—both prejudice and discrimination are enhanced when the groups are in a competitive relationship with each other; for example, competition over scarce resources causes groups to develop prejudice and discrimination against each other (see "6.2.1 Cooperation and competition").

Implicit prejudice
- Today people demonstrate prejudice less explicitly due to social desirability. However, they may still be prejudiced against certain groups without even realizing it. This is called **implicit prejudice**.
- Tests have been developed to measure implicit prejudice.
- One of the approaches is to use Implicit Association Tests (Greenwald, McGhee, Schwartz 1998). They are based on the idea that if a person has a strong automatic association between two mental representations, the reaction time taken to associate them will be shorter. It has been shown that implicit prejudice may exist where explicit prejudice doesn't. Implicit racial prejudice

may influence decision-making in legal contexts. See **Levinson, Cai and Young (2010)**.
- It was demonstrated in experimental research that implicit prejudice is malleable to an extent. In particular, exposing people to positive, non-stereotypical exemplars from social groups can decrease implicit prejudice towards those groups. This is demonstrated, for example, in the Obama effect. See **Columb and Plant (2011)**.

Out-group size and intergroup prejudice
- On the one hand, RCT predicts that an increase in the size of the out-group will increase the perceived threat and, as a result, prejudice. On the other hand, the contact hypothesis predicts that as the out-group size increases, contact between groups will become more frequent, reducing intergroup prejudice.
- This contradiction is resolved in the study of Savelkoul *et al* (2011) where it was shown that a curvilinear relationship exists between out-group size and the level of perceived threat. See **Savelkoul *et al* (2011)**.

Implicit prejudice

In recent years overt displays of prejudice have decreased due to the taboo that exists in developed societies. However, although people do not demonstrate prejudice explicitly, they may still be prejudiced against certain groups, sometimes even outside of their conscious awareness (that is, they may not realize that they are prejudiced). This is called implicit prejudice.

Since implicit prejudice, by definition, cannot be revealed in a self-report measure (such as a questionnaire), the challenge is to develop an instrument that will allow researchers to see prejudice even where participants themselves do not see it.

Implicit association tests (IATs)

IATs were introduced by **Greenwald, McGhee and Schwartz (1998)**.

They are based on the idea that if a person has a strong automatic association between two mental representations, the reaction time taken to associate them will be shorter. All these tests are computer-based. For example, a test to measure implicit racial bias might include the following trials:

Trial 1
Black/Unpleasant   White/Pleasant
Enjoyment

Trial 2
Black/Pleasant   White/Unpleasant
Enjoyment

Trial 3
Black/Unpleasant   White/Pleasant
African American

Trial 4
Black/Pleasant   White/Unpleasant
African American

Participants are required to classify the target words (Enjoyment, African American) as quickly as possible either to the left category, such as Black/Pleasant (by pressing E) or to the right category, such as White/Pleasant (by pressing I).

The idea is that if a participant has an implicit racial prejudice against African Americans, they will think less in trial 3 than in trial 4. They will also take less time to react in trial 1 than in trial 2. If you have a racial prejudice against black people, it may be cognitively harder for you to process the category "Black/Pleasant", so you will take a longer time to react.

There is a great variety of IATs today. For example, a gender-science IAT requires participants to quickly group male and female photographs together with science and liberal arts words.

RESEARCH   Guilty by implicit racial bias—Levinson, Cai and Young (2010)

✪ Essential understanding
- *Implicit prejudice may exist where explicit prejudice does not.*
- *Implicit racial prejudice may influence decision-making in legal contexts.*

Aim
To examine whether people hold implicit associations between African Americans and criminal guilt.

Participants
67 undergraduate and graduate students at the University of Hawaii eligible for jury duty.

Method and procedure
Researchers designed a "Black/White, Guilty/Not guilty" IAT.

Participants completed computer-based measures: the IAT, feeling thermometers (designed to evaluate explicit racial preferences, for example "How warm do you feel towards African Americans?") and a robbery evidence evaluation task.

The evidence evaluation task presented participants with a story of an armed robbery. After this they saw a series of crime scene photographs (pieces of evidence) and were primed with a picture of either a dark-skinned or a light-skinned perpetrator (skin colour was manipulated by software). For each piece of evidence participants then had to decide whether it indicated that the defendant was guilty or not guilty.

Results
It was found that participants held strong implicit associations between "Black" and "Guilty" (compared to between "White" and "Guilty").

Interestingly, scores on the IAT negatively correlated with scores on the feeling thermometer: participants who reported feeling warmly towards African Americans were also more likely to show an implicit "Guilty" bias against them.

These implicit associations predicted the way mock jurors evaluated evidence. Stronger implicit associations between "Black" and "Guilty" were linked to judgments of ambiguous evidence as more indicative of guilt.

Conclusion
Implicit attitudes of race and guilt may be different from explicit attitudes (found in self-report measures). At the same time, implicit associations between race and guilt may influence legal decision-making.

Implications
The authors claim that the findings have large implications in terms of compromising the legal principle of presumption of innocence: if not proven otherwise, people are assumed to be innocent. However, if implicit biases exist in this area, the principle that is postulated on paper may be compromised in practice.

RESEARCH   Implicit prejudice and the Obama effect—Columb and Plant (2011)

Essential understanding
✪ *Positive exemplars from social groups can decrease implicit prejudice towards these groups.*

Background
Barack Obama was the first black person to be elected as President of the United States.

Aim
To investigate if exposure to Obama can cause a decrease in implicit anti-black prejudice.

Method
Experiment, independent measures design.

Participants
51 non-black undergraduate psychology students.

Procedure
Participants performed a task where they had to decide whether a string of letters was a word or a non-word. They performed 2 sets of 24 trials. Before each trial they were primed with a name or a string of Xs. "Primed" means that the name was flashed on the screen for 55 ms. The names were either negative exemplars of black people, that is, people who were perceived negatively by the majority of participants at the time of the study (such as OJ Simpson), or the positive exemplar (Obama).

Participants were randomly assigned into one of three conditions.
- Negative: participants in this condition were primed with negative exemplars on the first set of trials and Xs on the second set of trials.
- Negative then Obama: participants were primed with negative exemplars on the first set of trials and "Obama" on the second set of trials.
- Control: participants were primed with Xs on both sets of trials.

After completing this procedure, all participants were given the Black/White implicit association test (IAT). This measured their implicit anti-black prejudice. A measure of explicit prejudice (a questionnaire) was also administered.

Results
Participants in the Obama condition demonstrated significantly less implicit prejudice than participants in the negative condition. There was no difference between the Obama condition and the control condition.

Explicit prejudice (measured by the questionnaire) was not affected by this experimental manipulation.

Conclusion
Exposure to Obama "undid" the harmful effect of negative exemplars on implicit racial prejudice.

Positive counter-stereotypic exemplars (such as Barack Obama) can decrease implicit anti-black prejudice.

Essential understanding

⊘ *Anti-immigrant prejudice is mediated by the relative size of the out-group.*

Background

One approach to explain anti-Muslim attitudes builds on realistic conflict theory (RCT) and suggests that the actual competition for resources between majority and minority groups induces negative attitudes and hostility towards the out-group.

Another approach is the intergroup contact theory which suggests that intergroup contact will reduce negative contact and hostility.

These are opposing explanations: one of them predicts that increased intergroup contact (through increased competition over resources) will increase prejudice; the other suggests that intergroup contact (through developing friendship) will decrease prejudice.

Aim

To investigate the effect of the relative out-group size on anti-Muslim attitudes.

Method

The researchers used unique data of the percentage of Muslims in geographical regions in the Netherlands. This was coupled with a national survey of anti-Muslim attitudes and perceived threat (1,375 participants). They used advanced statistical techniques to analyse this data.

Results

It was found that a larger out-group in a geographical region increases people's level of perceived stress in that region, which in turn **induces** anti-Muslim attitudes.

At the same time (a contradictory result) it was found that a larger out-group in a geographical region increases the likelihood that people will have friends and colleagues belonging to ethnic minority groups, which in turn **reduces** perceived threat and anti-Muslim attitudes.

A finding that reconciles these two results is the **curvilinear relationship** between out-group size and the level of perceived threat. For relatively small out-groups, an increase of the out-group size is associated with an increase in the level of perceived stress. However, as the out-group gets bigger, contact effects counteract these tendencies. At some point the direction of this relationship is reversed: the bigger the out-group, the more positive people's attitude towards it.

Conclusion

Prejudice towards immigrants may be mediated by perceived threat and the relative out-group size. Relatively small out-groups cause members of the majority to perceive threat, which leads to high levels of anti-immigrant prejudice (in line with RCT). However, as the out-group size increases, inevitable personal contacts with the members of the out-group reverse this tendency, and eventually anti-immigrant prejudice starts to become weaker (in line with the contact hypothesis of conflict resolution).

6.2.3 Origins of conflict and conflict resolution

DEFINITIONS

– **Competition**—interpersonal or intergroup behaviour that benefits the interests of the actor at the cost of the interests of another person or group. The outcome of competitive behaviour is "I win, you lose"

– **Conflict**—when competition escalates and becomes explicit, it takes the form of a conflict
– **Conflict resolution**—the process of reducing overt conflict through special intervention strategies

ESSENTIAL UNDERSTANDING

Conflict

Conflict is a continuum. On one end of the spectrum there are negative attitudes towards other people (prejudice); on the other end there is overt physical violence. Arguably, conflict has a tendency to escalate: it starts with weaker manifestations such as negative attitudes towards the out-group and, if supported by aggravating factors, takes more overt forms.

Conflict may occur between individuals and between groups. However, because our personal identities and group identities are closely tied together, it may be hard to tell them apart.

Origins of conflict

A number of theories have pointed to different factors that may serve as origins of conflict. The most prominent among them are:

– competition over scarce resources (see "Realistic conflict theory (RCT)" in "6.2.1 Cooperation and competition")
– the mere fact of being categorized into social groups (see "3.1.1 Social identity theory")
– a combination of resource stress and the perceived salience of a potentially competitive group (see "The instrumental model of group conflict").

Although not directly causing conflict, some factors can also aggravate already existing negative group dynamics. See Staub (1999).

Conflict resolution

Contact theory (Allport 1954) posits that contact between groups reduces intergroup conflict provided several conditions are met. See Allport (1954).

A meta-analysis supported this theory and highlighted additional aspects, for example, the fact that effects of intergroup contact generalize across situations. See **Pettigrew and Tropp (2006)**.

The effects of contact between groups on the reduction of conflict are asymmetric and depend on group membership.

Members of the dominant groups respond more positively to perspective-taking, while members of the non-dominant groups respond more positively to perspective-giving (expressing themselves and being heard). See **Bruneau and Saxe (2012)**.

THEORY

Origins of conflict

Essential understanding

✪ *A number of theories have pointed to different factors that may serve as origins of conflict: competition over scarce resources (see "realistic conflict theory (RCT)"); social categorization (see "3.1.1 Social identity theory"); a combination of resource stress and the perceived salience of an out-group (see "*The instrumental model of group conflict*").*

Prejudice and discrimination (the "weaker" side of the conflict continuum) are caused by:
- competition over scarce resources, as shown in RCT and the classic studies of Sherif (see "**Robber's Cave studies**" in "**6.2.1 Cooperation and competition**").
- the mere fact of being categorized into social groups, as shown in social identity theory (Tajfel, Turner 1979). See "**3.1.1 Social identity theory**" in "**Unit 3 Sociocultural approach to behaviour**".

The instrumental model of group conflict (Esses et al 2001) is a development of the RCT. This model suggests that perceived intergroup competition is the result of the following.
- Resource stress (perceptions of the availability of valued resources)—resources may be both economic and symbolic such as power or prestige. Resource stress is the perception that resources are not available to all groups in sufficient quantities.
- The salience of a potentially competitive out-group—some groups are more likely to be perceived as competitors than others.

In turn, this perceived intergroup competition produces the following responses.
- It produces negative affective and cognitive responses—cognitive responses involve zero-sum beliefs, the belief that the more one group obtains, the less there is available for the other group. Emotional responses may include anxiety and fear.
- It results in attempts to remove the source of competition by using one of the following strategies:
  o decreasing competitiveness of the out-group (discriminatory behaviour, negative stereotypes)
  o increasing competitiveness of the in-group
  o avoiding contact with the out-group (for example, denying access to a territory).

See **Esses *et al* (2001)**.

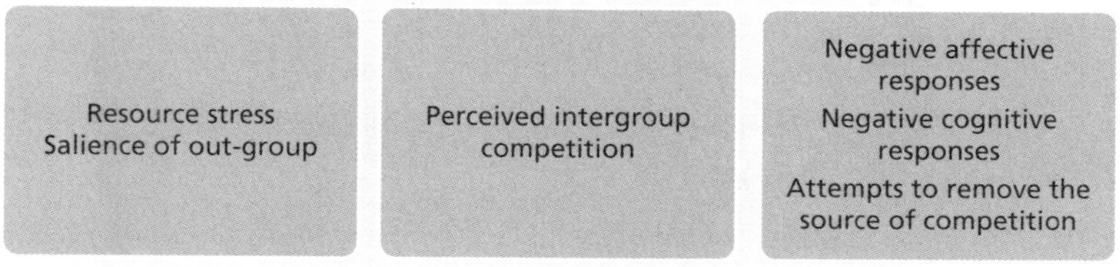

Resource stress Salience of out-group	Perceived intergroup competition	Negative affective responses Negative cognitive responses Attempts to remove the source of competition

Figure 6.4 The instrumental model of group conflict

Esses *et al* (2001)

Aggravating factors

Essential understanding
✪ *Although not directly causing conflict, some factors can also aggravate already existing negative group dynamics.*

Since conflict is a spectrum, it may start with milder forms such as prejudice and discrimination, and escalate with the course of time, taking more violent and overt forms. The aggravating factors that can deepen prejudice and discrimination and turn them into overt forms of conflict, according to **Staub (1999)**, are:

- difficult living conditions in a society (economic, political, and so on)
- frustration of basic human needs (feeling of security and control, the need for a positive identity, the need for connection with others)
- turning to the group for identity and connection
- scapegoating (claiming that some other group is responsible for life problems)
- adoption or creation of group ideologies.

Conflict resolution
Conflict resolution is the process of reducing overt conflict through special intervention strategies.

Examples of factors that promote conflict resolution are:
- intergroup contact
- perspective-taking and perspective-giving.

Conflict resolution—the contact hypothesis

Essential understanding
✪ *Contact between groups reduces intergroup conflict provided several conditions are met.*

Intergroup contact has been considered to be one of the most effective strategies for reducing intergroup conflict. In its original form, formulated by **Allport in 1954**, the contact hypothesis stated that contact between groups will improve intergroup relations if the following conditions are met:
- equal status of the groups within the contact situation
- intergroup cooperation (cooperative interdependence)
- common goals
- support of authorities, law or custom (intergroup contact occurs in the context of supportive norms).

Later the theory was refined and two additional factors were introduced (Dovidio, Gaertner, Kawakami 2003):

- opportunity for personal acquaintance between the members, especially in cases when the members do not conform to stereotypic expectations
- development of intergroup friendships.

First evidence for this theory came from the experiences of US soldiers in the Second World War. Although black and white units were usually segregated in the US army during the war, sometimes combat troops were combined due to necessity. It was observed later that soldiers from these troops had more positive racial attitudes.

The school context may be especially suitable for specially designed intergroup contact programmes because it is easier to create Allport's conditions of optimal contact in a school than anywhere else (Al Ramiah, Hewstone 2013).

RESEARCH   Pettigrew and Tropp (2006)— contact hypothesis

Essential understanding
✪ *A meta-analysis supports contact theory and highlights several additional effects of contact on intergroup attitudes.*

Pettigrew and Tropp (2006) conducted a meta-analytic review of research studies that tested the contact hypothesis (over 500 studies).

Results
- Intergroup contact that met Allport's four conditions was shown to produce significantly reduced intergroup bias.
- At the same time, these conditions are not necessary for the reduction of intergroup conflict: a small result is produced even when they are not met.
- They reported a significant negative correlation between contact and prejudice: r = –0.22, p < 0.0001. A correlation of this size is comparable to the relationship

between condom use and sexually transmitted HIV, and between passive smoking and the incidence of lung cancer (Al Ramiah, Hewstone 2013).
- Effects of intergroup contact generalize across situations. For example, contact with out-group members at work is associated with reduced prejudice towards members of the same out-group in one's neighbourhood.
- Contact with one out-group (for example, blacks) is associated with reduced prejudice towards secondary out-groups (for example, homosexuals, immigrants).

Note
Almost all the studies in this area are based on self-report measures of attitude change rather than behavioural criteria. However, many studies validate these self-reports with ratings from participants' close friends.

✪ Essential understanding
- *Members of the dominant group, unlike members of the non-dominant group, benefit from perspective-taking (it results in a positive change in the attitude towards the out-group).*
- *Members of the non-dominant group, unlike members of the dominant group, benefit from perspective-giving (expressing oneself and being heard).*

Aim
To examine the conditions under which a brief dialogue-based intervention could improve intergroup attitudes.

Participants
47 white Americans and 76 Mexican immigrants, mean age 33 in both groups.

Method and procedure
Participants were randomly assigned to one of two groups: senders and responders. The role of the sender was to write about a difficult problem faced by people from their ethnic group and then send this short essay to the responder. The role of the responder was to translate the essay using Google Translate, write a summary of the translated essay in their own words and send it back to the sender. This message was again translated. Participants thought they were assessing the effectiveness of the online translation tool.

For the responders, describing a difficulty or challenge faced by the members of the out-group in their own words is perspective-taking. For the senders, describing their problem and then reading its restatement in someone else's words is perspective-giving. Importantly, they experience "being heard" by the responder.

Interactions were conducted over a live video interface (Skype). Audio was disabled; participants communicated through the text chat window. Interaction lasted 20–30 minutes. The interaction partner was a member of an out-group confederate who was acting according to a standard script.

Both before and after the interaction, participants filled out a questionnaire measuring their attitudes towards the out-group.

Results
Members of the dominant groups benefited more from perspective-taking (79% of participants showed a positive change in attitude towards the out-group).

Members of the non-dominant group did not benefit much from perspective-taking, but responded positively to perspective-giving (63% of participants changed their attitude to a more positive one).

Conclusion
Effects of contact between groups on the reduction of conflict are asymmetric and depend on group membership: members of the dominant groups respond more positively to perspective-taking, while members of the non-dominant groups respond more positively to perspective-giving (expressing themselves and being heard).

Notes
In a follow-up study, a similar procedure was implemented with two modifications.
- Attitudes towards the out-group were assessed both immediately and one week after the intervention.
- The participants were Palestinian and Israeli.

Results of the previous study were replicated. However, it was also shown that changes in attitudes towards the out-group were transient. One week after the intervention the attitudes returned to their original state.

6.3 Social responsibility

6.3.1 Bystanderism

- **Bystander effect**—the phenomenon where a witness to an emergency situation is less likely to help the victim if other onlookers are present

ESSENTIAL UNDERSTANDING

The bystander effect
The bystander effect characterizes a situation where someone witnesses a critical situation yet does not help the victim because other people are also witnessing the same situation. Paradoxically, the more people witness the situation, the less likely the victim may be to get help.

Theory of unresponsive behaviour
Latané and Darley (1970) summarized their findings and formulated a theory of unresponsive behaviour. They suggested a five-step cognitive model of bystander intervention.
1. Noticing the event
2. Interpreting the event as an emergency
3. Assuming personal responsibility
4. Choosing a way to help
5. Implementing the decision.

Psychological mechanisms of bystanderism
The bystander effect refers to the observed behaviour (absence of help). The psychological mechanisms that cause this behaviour are as follows (Latané and Darley 1970).
- **Diffusion of responsibility**—the perception that you are not the only one who is responsible for intervening (the pressure to intervene is not focused on you). Especially when other onlookers' behaviours cannot be observed, people may convince themselves that somebody else is already taking action to intervene.

- **Evaluation apprehension**—the fear of being judged by others when acting publicly; this makes people more reluctant to intervene.
- **Pluralistic ignorance**—this is the tendency to rely on the reactions of others when defining an ambiguous situation.

Pluralistic ignorance is the key mechanism of bystanderism at step 2 of the cognitive model; evaluation apprehension and diffusion of responsibility are the key mechanisms at step 3.

Empirical support
Diffusion of responsibility was demonstrated in an intercom study where participants took much more time to report an emergency when they believed that there were other witnesses to the situation (although the emergency situation was not ambiguous). See **Darley and Latané 1968**. Pluralistic ignorance was demonstrated in a research study with a smoke-filled room. It was shown that the presence of passive others dramatically reduces the probability that the participant will interpret an ambiguous situation as an emergency. See **Latané and Darley 1968**.

RESEARCH   **Darley and Latané (1968)—diffusion of responsibility (the intercom study)**

Essential understanding
✪ *The perception that you are not the only one responsible for intervening reduces the likelihood of helping (diffusion of responsibility).*

Aim
To investigate the prediction—the more bystanders witness an emergency, the less likely any one bystander is to intervene and provide help.

Participants
59 female and 13 male students in introductory psychology courses participated in the experiment as part of a class requirement.

Method and procedure
- Each participant was taken to an individual room with an intercom system that enabled the person to talk to other participants. The individuals were told that they were going to take part in a discussion of personal problems associated with college life. They were also told that the discussion was held over the intercom to preserve anonymity of all participants and avoid embarrassment.
- Participants had to talk in turn. In round 1 they had to present their problems to the group. In round 2 each person in turn was expected to comment on what the others had said. Finally round 3 was meant for a free discussion. While someone else was speaking, the participant's microphone was off.
- In reality all the other voices in the discussion were pre-recorded and the participant actually heard recorded messages. One of these was the victim of a staged emergency situation.
- The future victim spoke first, saying that he found it difficult to adjust to college life in a big city. He also admitted with embarrassment that he was prone to seizures, especially when under stress. The other participants then spoke in turn, with the real participant last in the sequence. As round 2 began and it was the victim's turn to speak again, the victim underwent a serious nervous seizure similar to epilepsy (asked for help incoherently and made choking sounds, then turned quiet). As all the other microphones were off, it was impossible for the participant to know how the others were reacting to this emergency situation.

The independent variable was the number of other people that the participant believed were present in the discussion (that is, the number of voices they heard in the first round):
- participant alone with the victim (no confederates)
- participant, victim and one confederate
- participant, victim and four confederates.

The **dependent variable** was the time from the start of the seizure until the participant left the cubicle to look for help. If participants did not leave the cubicle within six minutes, the experiment was terminated. After being debriefed the participants also filled out a series of questionnaires.

Results
- Participants were visibly stressed by the situation; many of them had trembling hands and sweating palms.
- The perceived number of bystanders had a major effect on the likelihood of reporting the emergency.
- Response in smaller groups was also faster than in groups with many bystanders.

Group size	Percentage responding	Time it took to respond
Participant and victim	85	52 seconds
Participant, victim, 1 confederate	62	93 seconds
Participant, victim, 4 confederates	31	166 seconds

Table 6.1 Darley and Latané (1968)

Conclusion
Analysing participants' behaviour during the experiment and responses during the debriefing session, Darley and Latané concluded that participants did not decide not to help. Rather, they were in a state of conflict and could not decide what to do.

This may be explained by diffusion of responsibility. On the one hand, participants were trying to avoid the embarrassment of overreacting or destroying the anonymity of the experiment. On the other hand, they were trying to avoid the shame associated with not helping. With more participants present, the latter was weaker because responsibility was psychologically "distributed" among all of them.

Limitation
Participants were interacting over an intercom and could not see each other's reactions. This is a somewhat artificial situation. In real-life emergencies bystanders can often see each other, so other mechanisms apart from diffusion of responsibility may also contribute to bystanderism. This is why researchers conducted other studies such as the smoke-filled room study.

RESEARCH   Latané and Darley (1968)—pluralistic ignorance (smoke-filled room study)

Essential understanding

⭐ *Seeing other people remain passive in an ambiguous situation decreases the likelihood of intervening because participants do not interpret the situation as dangerous (pluralistic ignorance).*

Aim

To investigate if participants will report an ostensibly dangerous situation when other witnesses remain passive.

Method and procedure

The participant was seated in a small waiting room to fill out a preliminary questionnaire. After some time smoke began to enter the room through a wall vent.

There were three groups of participants **(independent variable)**.

- Some participants were in the waiting room alone.
- Some were in the room with two confederates acting as naive participants. Confederates were instructed to act indifferently and to pay little attention to the smoke, just carry on with the questionnaire.
- Some were in the room with two other real participants.

The **dependent variable** was the time it took the participant to leave the room to report the smoke. The experiment was terminated if the participant did not report the smoke within six minutes. Throughout the experiment participants were observed through a one-way mirror.

Results

- In the alone condition 75% of participants reported the smoke; it took them two minutes on average.
- In the condition with two passive confederates only 10% reported the smoke. The others coughed, rubbed their eyes and waved the smoke away from their faces, but continued to work on the questionnaire.
- In the condition with three naive bystanders, only 38% of the group reported the smoke.
- In post-experimental interviews participants reported that they thought the smoke looked "strange" and that they were not sure it was dangerous. They thought it could be steam or air-conditioning vapour, smog or even a "truth gas" filtered into the room to make them answer the questionnaire honestly.

Conclusion

When faced with an ambiguous event, a bystander is likely to look at the reactions of other people and be influenced by these reactions. This can lead to interpreting the situation as not dangerous and therefore not intervening. This phenomenon may be called "pluralistic ignorance".

6.3.2 Prosocial behaviour

- **Altruism**—selfless helping, that is, helping behaviour that occurs at no benefit, or even at some cost, to the helper
- **Prosocial behaviour**—any behaviour that is intended to benefit others, individual people or society on the whole. Helping, sharing, cooperating and volunteering are all examples of prosocial behaviour; such behaviour as obeying the rules is also considered prosocial

ESSENTIAL UNDERSTANDING

Evolutionary puzzle

Prosocial behaviour may be driven by a variety of motivating factors, including purely egoistic concerns. For example, a businessperson who runs a charity organization may benefit the society as a result of his or her activities, but may actually pursue self-interest.

When prosocial behaviour occurs as a result of egoistic motives, it is easy to explain it by existing theories such as the theory of evolution (the idea of survival of the fittest). Similar behaviour may also be observed in animals.

However, when prosocial behaviour occurs at some cost to the helper (altruism), it becomes more challenging to explain its origins. Darwin admitted that altruism presented an evolutionary puzzle. One of the approaches to solve this puzzle is to deny the existence of purely altruistic behaviour altogether, by asserting that all instances of seemingly altruistic behaviour actually have egoistic motives behind them. However, other psychologists do not agree. They claim that humans are capable of real altruism driven by pure empathy.

Theories of altruism

Examples of prominent theories that attempt to explain altruistic behaviour are:

- kin selection theory (Hamilton 1964)—this evolutionary theory suggests that organisms are driven by the desire to maximize survival of their genes (rather than themselves); it predicts that altruism will be likely if the target is young, healthy and closely related to the helper—see **Hamilton (1964)**—"**Kin selection theory**"
- empathy-altruism hypothesis (Batson *et al* 1981).

Empirical support

- Madsen *et al* (2007) provided support to kin selection theory by demonstrating that participants are more willing to endure pain when it benefits closer relatives. They also showed that this pattern repeats cross-culturally. See **Madsen *et al* (2007)**.

– Batson *et al* (1981) demonstrated that ease of escape does not affect participants' altruistic behaviour when empathy is induced through perceived similarity with the victim. This means that when empathy is activated, people behave unselfishly. See **Batson** *et al* **(1981)**.

Challenges

One of the main challenges in this field of research is that it is difficult to establish in an experimental setting whether the observed behaviour was driven by altruistic or egoistic motives. The only way to do so may be through self-report, but self-report is subject to social desirability bias, especially in sensitive topics like this one.

THEORY

Hamilton (1964)—kin selection theory

Essential understanding

✪ *Organisms are trying to maximize survival of their genes. Since their relatives have partially the same genotype, altruism is justified. This means that closer relatives are more likely to be the target of altruistic behaviour.*

Theory

Kin selection theory is an extension of evolutionary theory that suggests that organisms may be driven by the desire to maximize survival potential of their genes (rather than themselves). In other words, it is not our own survival that we desire (although we want that too), but the survival of our genetic material.

Hamilton coined the term "kin selection" as an addition to "natural selection" in Darwin's evolutionary theory, and "indirect fitness" as an addition to "direct fitness".

Predictions

Based on this starting idea, kin selection theory predicts that:
– relatives will be the target of altruistic behaviour more often than non-relatives, and closer relatives more often than distant relatives
– younger kin are more likely to be helped than older kin (because they are more likely to produce offspring and pass on the genes)
– healthy kin are more likely to be helped (for the same reason).

Limitations

– The theory relies on the assumption that both animals and humans are able to identify kin from strangers.
– Helping behaviour occurs between strangers, and these instances cannot be explained by kin selection theory.
– Competition between kin (found both in animals and humans) cannot be explained by the theory.

RESEARCH   Madsen *et al* (2007)—support for kin selection

✪ Essential understanding

Participants are willing to endure more pain when it benefits closer relatives. This pattern repeats cross-culturally.

Aim

To investigate the influence of kin selection on human altruism in an experimental design, thus avoiding the influence of social desirability. In addition, the researchers tested the theory in two different cultures. This is important because cross-cultural differences are not usually compatible with an evolutionary explanation of behaviour (if the behaviour truly evolved in humans as a species, there should be few or no cultural differences).

Method

Experiment, repeated measures design.

Participants

The experiments were conducted in two intentionally different populations: students in the UK and South African Zulu. This was done to see if the same patterns of behaviour will be observed despite the cultural differences in the idea of kinship.

Procedure

Participants were asked to provide a list of individuals of varied genetic relatedness, for example parents, cousins or siblings. They were then asked to adopt a painful position: sitting as though on a chair, with the back against a wall and calves and thighs at right angles. This position becomes increasingly painful with time. Participants were asked to hold it for as long as possible. The length of time a participant was able to maintain the position was then translated into a material benefit for the recipient, a person from the participant's list.

They had 5 trials with 15-minute breaks in between. In a random order, they had to maintain the difficult position for:
– themselves (co-efficient of relatedness r = 1)
– their parents or siblings (r = 0.5)
– their grandparent, aunt, uncle, niece or nephew (r = 0.25)
– their cousin (r = 0.125)
– a local charity organization (r = 0).

Every effort was made to ensure that participants and the recipients did not live together, to avoid confounding variables. The material benefit (a payment) was sent directly to the recipient. The payment for the UK participants was 1.50 GBP for every 20 seconds the position was held. The payment for the Zulu participants consisted of food hampers of the same monetary value. All Zulu participants came from extremely poor rural communities, so food was perceived as a necessity.

Results

- As a general trend, the amount of time spent in the painful position increased with the co-efficient of relatedness: participants were more ready to maintain this position for themselves than their parents, more for their parents than grandparents, and so on.
- This effect of kinship was transcultural.

Conclusion

The study provides experimental evidence that kinship plays a role in moderating altruistic behaviour. This is not to say that kinship is the only, or even the leading, factor in determining altruism, but the study demonstrates that kinship has an influence over and above other possible factors.

THEORY

Empathy-altruism hypothesis

Batson *et al*'s empathy-altruism hypothesis states that people may help others out of genuine concern for their well-being. If individuals feel empathy towards another person, they will help that person regardless of what they can potentially gain from it and even at a cost to themselves.

The empathy-altruism hypothesis is often opposed to evolutionary explanations of altruism because it denies that all altruism can be reduced to some form of selfish interest.

RESEARCH   Batson *et al* (1981)—the Elaine study

Essential understanding

✪ *When empathy is activated (induced through perceived similarity), people behave unselfishly.*

Aim

To investigate if empathy produces genuinely altruistic (unselfish) motivation to help.

Method

Experiment, 2 × 2 experimental design.

Participants

44 female introductory psychology students; 11 participants per group.

Procedure

On arriving at the venue participants were told to wait for the arrival of the second subject, Elaine, who was actually a confederate. It was determined through drawing lots that one of them (always Elaine) would be performing a task under aversive conditions—electric shocks at random intervals. The job of the other one (always the real participant) was to observe Elaine.

Participants were then taken to a separate room where they observed Elaine through CCTV (actually a recording). It was evident from the first trial that Elaine was finding the shocks extremely unpleasant.

After the second trial (out of ten) they were given a chance to volunteer to help her by taking her place.

Variables

Two **independent variables** were manipulated in the experiment.

- Cost of escaping without helping—easy escape versus difficult escape. In the difficult escape condition participants believed that if they did not take Elaine's place they would have to continue witnessing the situation. In the easy escape condition they believed they could just get up and walk away.

- Level of empathy—low versus high. This was manipulated through a values and interests questionnaire. All participants filled out this questionnaire before the experiment. Elaine's questionnaire was prepared in advance to be either very similar or very dissimilar to the participant's own responses. Elaine's questionnaire was then given to the participant as part of "impression formation", so the participant perceived Elaine as either similar or dissimilar to herself. Based on prior studies, Batson *et al* (1981) claim that perceived similarity increases empathy towards a person.

The **dependent variable** was whether or not the participant agreed to replace Elaine after the second trial.

Results

The lowest proportion of participants who agreed to help was observed in the low empathy–easy escape condition. Low empathy appeared to make the motivation to help egoistic, so ease of escape reduced helping dramatically (from 64% to 18%). Conversely, under high empathy–easy escape did not have any significant effect on the probability of helping; in fact, even more participants chose to help Elaine in the easy escape condition (91% versus 82%).

Probability of taking Elaine's place		
	Low empathy	High empathy
Easy escape	18%	91%
Difficult escape	64%	82%

Table 6.2

Batson *et al* (1981)

Conclusion

The motivation to help in high empathy conditions was altruistic, not egoistic. Ease of escape no longer affected participants' behaviour when the level of empathy was high, hence we can accept the empathy-altruism hypothesis and claim that genuinely altruistic behaviour in humans is caused by feelings of empathic concern.

6.3.3 Promoting prosocial behaviour

ESSENTIAL UNDERSTANDING

There should exist factors that would counteract bystanderism and increase the likelihood of prosocial behaviour. If we discover these factors, we can probably design strategies to enhance them, making society in general more prosocial.

Targeting the incentives

Some of these strategies target the **system of incentives** associated with helping and non-helping: they reduce the costs of helping and increase the costs of non-helping. An example is the so-called "Good Samaritan law" accepted in many countries. This law has been shown to be effective, for example, for quickly reporting cases of heroin overdose. See **Nguyen and Parker (2018)**.

Targeting psychological variables

Other strategies target the **psychological variables**. They are aimed at teaching people skills associated with prosocial behaviour or training people in ways that make them more responsive to the needs of others. Such strategies are often implemented with young children. (An example is **mindfulness-based kindness curriculum**.) However, they may also target adults (for example, **compassion training**).

- Flook *et al* (2015) demonstrated that a mindfulness-based kindness curriculum for pre-school children makes their behaviour more prosocial. See **Flook *et al* (2015)**.
- Hutcherson, Seppala and Gross (2008) demonstrated that a brief session of loving-kindness meditation may enhance general positivity toward strangers. See **Hutcherson, Seppala and Gross (2008)**.
- Leiberg, Klimecki and Singer (2011) in a specially designed Zurich Prosocial Game demonstrated that a brief compassion training has a significant effect on prosocial behaviour toward strangers in a novel situation. See **Leiberg, Klimecki and Singer (2011)**.

RESEARCH   Nguyen and Parker (2018)—effectiveness of Good Samaritan law

Essential understanding:

✪ *Good Samaritan laws protect people who help others in an emergency. Such laws have been shown to be effective, for example, for reporting heroin overdose.*

The law

Good Samaritan laws are designed to protect people who are trying to help others in an emergency situation but may face the possibility of failure. If they are not successful, or if the person gets hurt as a result of their trying to help, their prosocial behaviour may have negative legal consequences for them personally, and Good Samaritan laws are designed to counteract this. In some countries the law even requires punishment for bystanders if they witness an incident if the situation is not dangerous for themselves and yet they do not provide help to the victim.

Examples of Good Samaritan bills that have been endorsed can be seen in Australia, Argentina and Canada.

Effectiveness

In the USA accidental drug overdose has been reported to be a primary cause of death, even exceeding motor vehicle deaths (Nguyen, Parker 2018). In response to this growing threat, more and more states are accepting Good Samaritan laws that provide immunity from arrest to those who witness or experience an overdose and call an emergency service. Under the law such people cannot even be charged with possession of drugs.

To assess the effectiveness of adopting such laws for the reduction of drug overdose-related deaths, **Nguyen and Parker (2018)** analysed hospital admissions data (across 270 hospitals in New York and New Jersey) before and after the law was adopted. They found an overall increase in hospital admissions for heroin-related accidental overdose cases, but not for non-heroin accidental overdoses. This provided support for the effectiveness of Good Samaritan laws in increasing heroin-related hospital admissions.

RESEARCH   Flook *et al* (2015)—mindfulness-based kindness curriculum

Essential understanding

✪ *A mindfulness-based kindness curriculum for pre-school children is effective in terms of fostering prosocial attitudes.*

Aim

To investigate a mindfulness-based kindness curriculum as a means of promoting prosocial behaviour in pre-school children.

Participants

68 pre-school children.

Method and procedure

Mindfulness training involves enhancing awareness of a particular attentional object, be it breath, external stimuli, thoughts or emotions. Such training usually results in improved sustained attention and emotion regulation. In this particular training young children engaged in age-appropriate practices to extend care and well wishes to a mental image of a person.

Children were randomly assigned to either a mindfulness-based kindness curriculum (KC) or a wait-list control group. The KC was a 12-week intervention (two 30-minute lessons a week) using literature, music and movement to teach and reinforce concepts related to kindness and compassion.

A variety of variables were measured both before and after the intervention. They included a special experimental sharing task in which a child was given an envelope labelled "me", an envelope with a picture of another child and 10 stickers. The other child was either a most liked peer from the participant's class, a least liked peer from their class, an unfamiliar child or a child who the participant was told was sick. Children were told that they could keep as many stickers as they would like to themselves and give as many as they would like to the other person.

Results
Children in the control group kept significantly more stickers for themselves over time compared to children from the KC group.

Conclusion
Researchers concluded that implementing a mindfulness-based prosocial skills training curriculum in real-life settings is beneficial in terms of fostering values of helping, sharing and compassion.

RESEARCH   Hutcherson, Seppala and Gross (2008)—loving-kindness meditation

Essential understanding
✪ *A brief session of loving-kindness meditation may enhance general positivity toward strangers. Loving-kindness meditation is a meditative practice in which individuals direct compassion and wishes for well-being to real or imagined others.*

Aim
To investigate if it is possible to self-generate feelings of social connection and positivity toward others.

Participants
93 volunteers who rarely or never meditated in their daily life.

Procedure
Participants were randomly split into two groups: one group went through a 7-minute guided loving-kindness meditation; the other one went through neutral imagery induction. Both before and after this session researchers measured participants' explicit and implicit evaluative responses to six photographs:
- a picture of themselves
- a close other
- three neutral strangers
- a non-social object (for example, a lamp).

Explicit evaluative responses were assessed by a 7-point scale. Using this, participants rated each photograph indicating how connected, similar and positive they felt toward the subject.

To assess implicit responses to each picture, a procedure was used where each face was presented 18 times in random order, followed by a positive word (such as brilliant or loyal) on 9 trials; and followed by a negative word (such as cruel or immoral) on the other 9 trials. Participants had to quickly decide whether the word was positive or negative. An implicit positive response shows itself as a bias to respond more quickly to positive words after the presentation of the photograph.

Results
Loving-kindness mediation was effective in increasing feelings of social connection and positivity toward strangers on both explicit and implicit levels.

Conclusion
Researchers concluded that even this brief and easy technique may help decrease social isolation. However, it remains to be demonstrated that these effects are not only short-term.

RESEARCH   Leiberg, Klimecki and Singer (2011)—compassion training

Essential understanding
✪ *A brief compassion training can significantly affect prosocial behaviour toward strangers in a novel situation.*

Aim
To investigate the effects of compassion training on prosocial behaviour in adults (aged 18–35 years).

Participants
69 female volunteers from the University of Zurich recruited through advertisement.

Method
Experiment, mixed design.

Procedure
Prosocial behaviour was assessed with a novel game developed for the purposes of the study: the Zurich Prosocial Game.

In this computer-based procedure participants guided their character with mouse clicks as fast as possible through a maze. At the end of the maze there was treasure which was converted into real money.

They could also see one other player (ostensibly a person from a different university, but actually a pre-programmed algorithm) progress through another maze on the same screen. Importantly, the two mazes did not intersect in any way so theoretically it was possible to complete the game while absolutely ignoring the other player.

At some points during the game, red and blue gates appeared that blocked the participants' paths. Each participant had a number of red and blue keys that she could use to unlock the gates.

When the co-player ran out of keys, participants could use their own key to open the gate for the co-player. They could see how many doors of each colour were left, and how many keys of each colour they had as well as how many the co-player had.

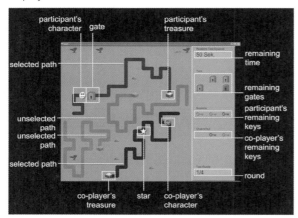

Figure 6.5 Screenshot from the Zurich Prosocial Game

Leiberg, Klimecki and Singer (2011)

Participants were randomly split into two groups: one underwent compassion training while the other received memory training. In each of the groups the Zurich Prosocial Game was played twice, once before the training and again five days after it.

- The compassion group attended a one-day training session to learn a Buddhist meditation technique called Metta. The training involved sitting in an upright position and concentrating on warm and positive feelings toward oneself, a beloved person, a neutral person and, ultimately, all human beings. Participants had to imagine the person while silently repeating phrases like, "May you be happy".

- The memory training group went through a session of similar duration where they were taught the method of loci. This involved a series of locations (for example, a well-known route in Zurich) and a series of items (words) to be memorized. Participants created mental associations between the locations and the words and in this way memorized the sequences.

Results

While there was no change in the frequency of helping observed in the Zurich Prosocial Game from pre- to post-training in the memory training group, compassion training significantly increased frequency of helping.

Conclusion

The researchers concluded that a brief compassion training has a significant effect on prosocial behaviour. They also noted that compassion training resulted in transfer of behaviour in a novel task (a task that was unrelated to the contents of the training). It remains to be observed if effects of such (or longer) training sessions also show in everyday life behaviour.

Topics

7.1 Developing as a learner
7.1.1 Brain development

DEFINITIONS

– **Differentiation**—development of the network of connections between neurons

– **Migration**—transportation of newly formed neurons to their correct location

– **Neurogenesis**—the production of new nervous cells

– **Pruning**—elimination of unnecessary connections and neurons that are rarely used

– **Structure-function relationships**—the correspondence between biological maturation of the brain and the development of cognitive functions

ESSENTIAL UNDERSTANDING

Structural and functional changes

One of the ways to study human development while considering the interaction between biological and cognitive factors is the study of structure-function relationships. If structural and functional changes coincide in time, we may infer that cognitive development and brain development are related, although this inference comes with limitations. See "Structure-function relationships".

The process of structural brain development can be broken down into four stages: neurogenesis, migration, differentiation and pruning. See "Structural changes in the brain".

Empirical studies of brain development

At first, research of the developing brain was confined to post-mortem studies that could only look at very crude features such as the size of the brain. With the invention of brain imaging technology, many more possibilities opened up. See "Empirical studies of brain development".

Chugani (1999) used PET scans to investigate how glucose metabolism in the brain develops during the first year of life. Results showed some correspondence between increasing glucose metabolism in various parts of the brain and behaviour that is becoming more complex. See Chugani (1999).

Empirical studies of structure-function relationships

Werker *et al* (1981) demonstrated that infants have an ability to discriminate between phonemes in Hindi even if they had never been exposed to this language. This ability is lost later, probably due to lack of linguistic experience and pruning. See **Werker *et al* (1981)**.

Kolb and Fantie (1989) showed that it is necessary to triangulate data to reach conclusions about structure-function relationships in the developing brain. In their research they looked at "categorization based on linguistic features" (the function) and how it depends on the maturation of frontal lobes (the structure). They combined five pieces of evidence, from studies with both adults and children, to claim that categorization based on linguistic features gradually develops with the development of frontal lobes. See **Kolb and Fantie (1989)**.

Limitations of developmental neuroscience

Research in developmental neuroscience has some inherent limitations, most notably the ability/strategy controversy, the maturation/learning controversy, the correlational nature of research and the fact that localization of function may change over time. See "Limitations of developmental neuroscience".

Structure-function relationships

Biological, cognitive and sociocultural approaches to understanding behaviour provide three different angles on the process of psychological development.
– Biological approaches focus on the structural changes in the brain (structure).
– Cognitive approaches focus on the development of cognitive functions (function).
– Sociocultural approaches focus on environmental influences on the process of development.

One of the ways to study these variables in their interaction is the study of structure-function relationships. This refers to looking at structural changes in the brain longitudinally and comparing them with the corresponding changes in cognitive functioning.

If structural and functional changes coincide in time, this can be taken as evidence that brain development and cognitive development are related.

Structural changes in the brain

The process of brain development has been broken down into four stages:

1. neurogenesis (production of new nervous cells)
2. migration of neurons to their correct location
3. differentiation (development of the network of connections between neurons)
4. pruning (elimination of connections and even neurons themselves).

Neurogenesis is finished in the period of gestation (before birth). Neurons are overproduced to account for the future normal process of cell death.

Migration starts at around nine weeks from conception. Neurons travel along special glial fibres that connect the innermost parts of the brain to the cortical layers. New neurons are formed deep inside the brain and they use these structures as pathways along which they "crawl" to their correct positions outside.

Differentiation starts shortly after conception and continues rapidly until the age of two, reaching the rate of 40,000 synapses per second at some point. This is followed by a plateau and then rapid reduction in the number of synapses.

By the end of puberty around 50% of the originally formed synapses are eliminated, and the rate of **pruning** can reach 100,000 synapses per second sometimes. This means that children have a larger number of neuronal connections than adults. However, pruning is useful because it makes the brain a more efficient system, a lot like replacing a network of secondary roads with a few major highways.

Empirical studies of brain development

Initially research into brain development was confined to post-mortem studies. Researchers were looking at the most obvious differences in brain structure depending on age, such differences as the size of the brain.

Brain imaging technology provided a possibility to study the developing brain in much more detail (including brain processes via fMRI), and research can now be conducted with living participants.

RESEARCH   Chugani (1999)—brain development in the first year of life

Essential understanding
⭐ *There is a correspondence between the structural development of the brain and patterns of behaviour in the first year of life.*

Aim
To investigate the correspondence between the structural development of the brain and the development of psychological functions in the first year of life.

Participants
Children aged 0–12 months.

Method
Observations assisted with PET scans.

Procedure
PET scans were used to investigate glucose metabolism.

Results
– **0–1 month**: glucose metabolism in the brain is confined to primary sensory and motor cortex, thalamus and brainstem. The behaviour of newborn babies is also very limited (mostly visual exploration of the world when they are awake).
– **2–4 months**: glucose metabolism increases in parietal, temporal and primary visual cortex. Children at this age also acquire a number of new functions, for example, they improve on tasks requiring integration of visual and spatial information (such as coordinating the hand and the eyes to grab a toy that they find interesting).
– **8–12 months**: there is an increase in glucose metabolism in the frontal cortex. This coincides with the appearance of some cognitively complex behaviours.

Conclusion
Results seem to imply that there is a certain correspondence between the structural changes in the brain and the development of psychological functions in the first year of life.

RESEARCH   Werker *et al* (1981)—Hindi phoneme discrimination in infants

Essential understanding
✪ *Infants have a natural ability to discriminate between phonemes, even for languages they are not exposed to. This ability is lost later, probably due to pruning.*

Aim
To compare the ability to differentiate between Hindi phonemes in infants, English-speaking adults and Hindi-speaking adults.

Participants
Hindi-speaking adults, infants of 6–7 months and English-speaking adults.

Method
Quasi-experimental comparison between groups.

Procedure
Pairs of stimuli were used, for example, /ta/ versus /Ta/ (Hindi). The critical difference in this pair of sounds is the place of articulation: the tongue is placed either on the alveolar ridge or on the back of the upper front teeth. This distinction between sounds is not used in English.

Participants were tested in a **discrimination paradigm**.
- For infants, this procedure involves first conditioning an infant to turn his or her head towards the loudspeaker when there is a change in the auditory stimulus. For this the infant is reinforced with the presentation of an interesting electronically activated toy animal each time he or she turns correctly.
- Adults pressed a button when they thought they detected a change in stimulus.

Results
Infants were just as able to discriminate between Hindi phonemes as Hindi-speaking adults.

English-speaking adults were not able to discriminate between Hindi phonemes.

Conclusion
- Up to a certain age, infants have the ability to discriminate between natural language sounds without prior language experience.
- A decrease in speech perceptual abilities may be due to linguistic experience—learning one language causes people to lose the ability to discriminate between phonemes that are not used in this language.

RESEARCH   Kolb and Fantie (1989)—structure-function relationship in the development of categorization based on linguistic features

Essential understanding
✪ *A combination of methods and evidence from various research studies are needed to make inferences about structure-function relationships in the developing brain.*

Aim
To aggregate evidence on the development of structure-function relationship for categorization based on linguistic features.

Participants
Children of various ages, healthy adults and adults with confined frontal lobe lesions.

Method
Summary of research evidence that came from a combination of methods (case studies, observations, neuroimaging research).

Procedure
- Categorization based on linguistic features was measured by the Chicago Word Fluency Test. In this test participants are given a letter (for example, S) and required to write as many words beginning with this letter as possible in the given time.
- Categorization based on non-linguistic features was measured by a modification of this test where participants were required, for example, to write the names of as many objects or animals as they could think of.
- Kolb and Fantie (1989) summarized research findings and observations involving participants' performance on both types of task.

Results
Adults:
- When healthy adult subjects performed the test, frontal lobe regions were active (as established by brain imaging techniques).
- Adult patients with confined frontal lobe lesions did very poorly on the test.
- At the same time, these patients performed normally on the non-linguistic modification of the test.

Children:
- Children performed poorly on the Chicago Word Fluency Test when they were very young, but gradually their performance improved with age.
- Even very young children performed well (as well as adults) on the non-linguistic modification of the test.

Conclusion
Taken together, these observations show that categorization based on linguistic features (the function) depends on the development of frontal lobes (structure).

This study is an example of how difficult it is to study structure-function relationship in a developing brain. It always requires data triangulation.

7.1.2 Cognitive development

- **Centration**—focusing on one aspect of the problem while ignoring the other aspects
- **Cognitive egocentrism**—the inability to understand that other people's viewpoints and perspectives are different
- **Irreversibility**—the inability to mentally reverse an operation
- **Lack of conservation**—the inability to understand that the object remains the same even if its physical appearance changes
- **More knowledgeable other**—an interaction partner (peer or adult) who is more informed about the subject of interaction
- **Object permanence**—understanding that an object exists even when it is not perceived
- **Scaffolding**—providing children with support that is minimally necessary for them to solve tasks in their zone of proximal development
- **Zone of proximal development**—the hypothetical potential of development comprised of everything a child cannot do on his or her own, but can do with the help of others

ESSENTIAL UNDERSTANDING

Multiple theories have existed to explain cognitive development of human children, but two theories that are often considered to be the most prominent are those of Piaget and Vygotsky.

Piaget's theory

Piaget's system of general principles about knowledge is known as genetic epistemology. In this framework, cognitive development is viewed as a type of adaptation, with two basic processes of assimilation and accommodation. More specifically, his theory of cognitive development claims that children move progressively through a series of stages. See "**Piaget's theory of cognitive development**".

Children's reasoning at the sensorimotor stage is subordinate to their motor development. An important phenomenon discovered by Piaget for this stage is object permanence. See "**Sensorimotor stage (birth to 2 years)**".

At the preoperational stage children's reasoning is characterized by cognitive egocentrism, centration, irreversibility and lack of conservation. These phenomena were demonstrated in Piaget's conservation tasks and Piaget and Inhelder's three mountains task. See "**Preoperational stage (2–7 years)**".

- Piaget's conservation tasks demonstrate the phenomena of centration, irreversibility and (lack of) conservation. See "**Piaget's conservation tasks**".

- Piaget and Inhelder's (1956) three mountains task demonstrates the phenomenon of cognitive egocentrism. See **Piaget and Inhelder (1956)**.
- However, the three mountains task has been criticized for its complexity. In a replication study, Borke (1975) demonstrated that children as young as 3 or 4 years old were able to perform well on the task if it was modified to make the instructions more accessible. See **Borke (1975)**.

Children at the concrete operational stage can only solve problems when they are applied to concrete objects, while at the formal operational stage abstract thought is fully developed. See "**Concrete operational stage (7–11 years)**" and "**Formal operational stage (11–16 years)**".

Piaget's theory is criticized for the notion of clear-cut stages, for the assumption that development is driven by biological maturation, and for ignoring certain variables such as individual differences. See "**Evaluation of Piaget's theory**".

Vygotsky's theory

Lev Vygotsky's sociocultural theory views cognitive development as a process of internalizing culture. It focuses on higher-order cognitive functions and emphasizes the role of social interaction, language and education. It also explains the role of signs as tools in mastering higher-order cognitive functions. See "**Vygotsky's sociocultural theory**".

Vygotsky's theory has many aspects so it cannot be supported by a single study. Research has focused on supporting such elements of the theory as the role of signs in mastering higher-order cognitive functions, the role of scaffolding and more knowledgeable others in promoting development, and so on. See "Empirical support for Vygotsky's sociocultural theory".

Vygotsky's theory is commonly criticized for being too philosophical in nature and lacking empirical support. However, it should be noted that some elements of the theory were intended to be philosophical and as such are not testable. See "Evaluation of Vygotsky's sociocultural theory".

THEORY

PIAGET'S THEORY OF COGNITIVE DEVELOPMENT

Essential understanding
✪ *Piaget's theory views cognitive development of a child as a form of adaptation that moves progressively through a series of clear-cut stages.*

Genetic epistemology
Piaget's views on cognitive development in general are that intellectual development is a form of adaptation. The two connected processes involved in adaptation are:
- assimilation: changing one's behaviour or perception of the world to better fit into already existing mental representations (schemas)
- accommodation: the opposite process—changing one's mental representation (schema) to better fit the world.

He referred to his approach as "genetic epistemology" to emphasize its fundamental relation to knowledge in a range of disciplines outside psychology.

Cognitive development of children
The theory of cognitive development of Jean Piaget (1896–1980) is based on the following ideas.
- Children's cognitive processes are qualitatively different from those of adults.
- In their cognitive development children progressively move through a series of clear-cut stages.

Stages of cognitive development
Piaget described a considerable number of stages of cognitive development that can be grouped into four major stages:
- sensorimotor stage (birth to 2 years)
- preoperational stage (2–7 years)
- concrete operational stage (7–11 years)
- formal operational stage (11–16 years).

Sensorimotor stage (birth to 2 years)
Children's reasoning at this stage is secondary to their movements and sensations—they perform some actions with their hands and observe the result, and that is how they think. They cannot perform operations in their mind.

An important phenomenon that characterizes this age is **object permanence**—the ability to understand that an object exists even when it is outside of your perceptual field. Object permanence is formed by around 8–12 months. Before that, when children do not see the object, they don't realize it exists.

Preoperational stage (2–7 years)
At this age children are able to perform some forms of reasoning in their mind, but these forms of reasoning are not yet fully-fledged operations.

Some central phenomena that characterize this stage are:
- cognitive egocentrism—the inability to take other people's perspectives
- centration—focusing all attention on one aspect of a situation while ignoring all other aspects
- irreversibility—the inability to mentally reverse the sequence of events
- lack of conservation—the inability to understand that an object physically remains the same even when its appearance changes.

Some of these phenomena were demonstrated in Piaget's famous conservation tasks. See "Piaget's conservation tasks".

Egocentrism was demonstrated in an experiment by Piaget and Inhelder (1956), which also later became known as the three mountains task. See **Piaget and Inhelder (1956)**.

RESEARCH   Piaget's conservation tasks

Essential understanding
✪ *Conservation tasks with children at the preoperational stage demonstrate centration, irreversibility and lack of understanding of conservation.*

Procedure
In a typical task the child is shown two equal glasses of water and asked to say which of the glasses has more water in it. The child will correctly say that the glasses have equal amounts of water. Then the experimenter pours water from one of the glasses into another glass, narrower but taller. The

child observes the process. Then the child is asked which of the two glasses has more water in it now.

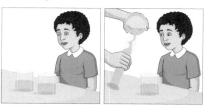

Figure 7.1 Piaget's conservation task using containers of water

Result
If understanding of conservation has not been acquired, the child will say that the taller glass has more water.

Interpretation
This shows lack of conservation (the inability to understand that the water remained the same, although its appearance changed). It also shows centration (the child focuses attention on one aspect of the situation—how tall the glass is—and ignores the other aspects). Irreversibility is also demonstrated (the child is not able to reverse the action mentally).

RESEARCH Piaget and Inhelder (1956)—the three mountains task

Essential understanding
✪ *Cognitive egocentrism is a function of age: most four-year-old children are egocentric while most seven-year-olds are not.*

Procedure
The child is shown a three-dimensional model of three mountains. The model includes some features (like snow, a tree, a cross) that are visible from some angles and not visible from others. The child spends some time looking at the model from where he or she sits, and then the researcher introduces a doll. The doll is positioned at the same table facing the mountains from a different viewpoint. The child is then asked to describe what the doll can see. To do this, the child is given a series of pictures showing the three mountains model from various angles, and asked to pick the picture that corresponds to what the doll can see.

Figure 7.2 Three mountains task

If the child picks a picture that corresponds to his or her own viewpoint, and not the doll's, that is a sign of cognitive egocentrism.

Results
Piaget and Inhelder (1956) observed that the ability to choose the picture corresponding to the doll's viewpoint is a function of age. In their studies four-year-old children almost always chose the picture that corresponded to their own (and not the doll's) viewpoint. Cognitive egocentrism is overcome by 7–8 years of age (children of this age almost always choose the correct picture).

RESEARCH Borke (1975)—criticism of the three mountains task

Essential understanding
✪ *The three mountains task has been criticized for its complexity. Critics have said that young children do not perform as well on the task because they do not understand the instructions, not because they are actually more egocentric.*

Procedure
Borke (1975) replicated the same procedure, but with a few modifications.
- The content of the task was changed to make it more relatable to children. Grover (a character from *Sesame Street*) was used instead of the doll; the "boring" three mountains were replaced by a farm area with details such as people, trees, animals, a lake and a house.
- Instead of picking one from a series of pictures, children were given two identical displays: one to look at and one on a turntable to provide their response. They were asked to turn the table to select the angle that they believed was seen by Grover.

Result
Children as young as 3–4 years were able to use the turntable to match Grover's viewpoint.

Conclusion
- Results of the original experiment (Piaget, Inhelder 1956) might have been biased because the nature of the task was cognitively complex and not engaging for children.
- The study of Borke (1975) does not dispute cognitive egocentrism itself—children are indeed egocentric, and they overcome cognitive egocentrism at a certain age—but according to Borke, this happens earlier than was originally thought.

PIAGET'S THEORY OF COGNITIVE DEVELOPMENT (CONTINUED)

Concrete operational stage (7–11 years)

Children at this stage are no longer egocentric. They understand reversibility and successfully pass conservation tasks. However, as the name suggests, they can only solve problems when the problems are applied to concrete objects. They cannot perform abstract operations (such as algebra). Inductive reasoning is well developed, but deductive reasoning is problematic.

Formal operational stage (11–16 years)

At this stage abstract thought is fully developed. Mental operations become abstract and fully reversible. This is the age of deductive reasoning abilities and metacognition.

EVALUATION OF PIAGET'S THEORY

Essential understanding

✪ *Piaget's theory is mainly criticized for the idea that development is driven by biological maturation and the notion of clear-cut stages in development.*

Criticism

– The notion of clear-cut stages has been challenged by some observations—sometimes children (especially with some help from adults) are capable of solving tasks from a higher stage.
– Piaget believed biological maturation to be the driving force of intellectual development. He has been criticized for this neglect of sociocultural variables and the role of learning.
– The theory does not take into account individual differences. It assumes that all children develop at approximately the same rate as dictated by biological factors.

Defence

These considerations weaken the theory but do not refute it. When a new theory is proposed, it is necessary to be reductionist in order to formulate hypotheses and test them. Piaget probably did not deny the existence of individual differences, but chose to ignore them for research purposes to test some more fundamental assumptions of the theory first.

Piaget changed the way scientists think about growing children. His research created a new paradigm where intellectual development of children was given importance.

VYGOTSKY'S SOCIOCULTURAL THEORY

Essential understanding

✪ *Vygotsky's sociocultural theory views cognitive development as a process of internalizing culture through language and interaction with more knowledgeable others (peers and adults). Higher-order cognitive functions are mastered using tools such as signs.*

Culture and language

– The development of a child cannot be viewed separately from the child's culture. In fact, development itself is nothing else but a process of **internalizing the culture**.
– Culture is internalized through social interaction. Language plays an important role in this process. Children internalize language in numerous interactions with peers and adults, and language becomes a tool for internalizing culture.

Higher-order cognitive functions

– All cognitive processes may be divided into "lower-order functions" and "higher-order functions". Higher-order functions are the key focus of the sociocultural theory because they are influenced the most by sociocultural factors and the least by biological factors.
– Higher-order cognitive functions include such processes as voluntary attention, semantic memory and conceptual thinking. The difference between lower-order and higher-order cognitive functions is in how voluntary or conscious they are.

Using tools

– Higher-order cognitive functions are mastered through the use of tools such as signs. For example, memorizing a list of words can be enhanced by using cards with associated pictures. These cards become signs for the words and can be used as a tool for memory.
– Language is a system of signs, and in this sense language becomes the tool for mastering abstract thinking and internalizing culture.

Zone of proximal development

In the development of a child there are three areas of potential achievement.

– The zone of actual development defines what the child can do independently, without the help from others.
– The zone of proximal development (ZPD) defines what the child can do with the help of a "more knowledgeable other" (for example, an adult).

– The out-of-reach zone defines what the child cannot achieve even with help from others.

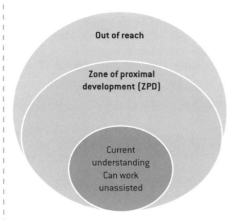

Figure 7.3 Zone of proximal development

Role of learning

Vygotsky suggested that learning should be one step ahead of development. For this, education should be focused on the ZPD: give students tasks that they cannot solve by themselves, but can solve with some help from adults. To achieve this adults provide **scaffolding**.

| RESEARCH | Empirical support for Vygotsky's sociocultural theory |

Essential understanding

✪ *Empirical support for Vygotsky's theory comes in the form of various experiments that show the role of signs in developing higher-order functions, the role of more knowledgeable others and scaffolding in promoting development, and so on. The theory also offers an alternative explanation for the conflicting findings in research such research as Piaget and Inhelder (1956) and Borke (1975).*

Alternative explanation for the findings of other researchers

Vygotsky's theory provides an explanation for some of the observed discrepancies in the findings of other researchers. For example, the differences in findings between Piaget and Inhelder (1956) and Borke (1975) could be attributed to the fact that the experimenter in Borke's study played a more active role. The experimenter provided children with a practice task and used a turntable as a "scaffold" instead of pictures. With this help, children were able to demonstrate a higher level of cognitive development.

Leontyev (1931): signs as a tool for mastering higher-order cognitive functions

AN Leontyev (1903–1979) conducted a series of experiments showing that higher-order cognitive functions are developed through the use of cultural tools (signs). For example, in one of the studies (Leontyev 1931), participants of different ages were required to memorize a list of 15 simple words read out by the experimenter. Experimental conditions were as follows.
– Participants were given 30 cards with pictures that they could use as a tool to help them to memorize words. When participants heard a word, they could look at the cards and put aside one that would help them remember the word later.

– In the no-cards condition, participants simply heard the words and had to memorize them

Comparison across various age groups in these experiments showed the following.
– In pre-school children memory was not aided by the cards; performance on the task was equally poor in both conditions.
– In adults, performance was equally good in both conditions. Adults did not need the cards because they had already internalized memory strategies.
– In schoolchildren, however, performance on the task was poor (on the pre-school level) when they were not using the cards and good (on the adult level) when they were.

	Performance on the task		
	Pre-school children	Schoolchildren	Adults
With cards	Poor	Good	Good
Without cards	Poor	Poor	Good

Table 7.1

This shows that school-age children can use cards as a tool for memory, and that the adult level of performance on this task is in their ZPD.

Interaction with a more knowledgeable other

More evidence comes from research studies showing that interaction with a "more knowledgeable other" leads to higher rates of cognitive development in children. See **Nedospasova (1985)** in "7.3.1 Role of peers and play".

7.1.3 Development of empathy and theory of mind

ESSENTIAL UNDERSTANDING

Empathy and theory of mind: the concepts

Theory of mind is broader than empathy. While the cognitive component of empathy is the general ability to take perspectives, theory of mind also includes such specific abilities as reading intentions and understanding false beliefs. At the same time, theory of mind is narrower than empathy because it does not include an emotional component. See "Empathy and theory of mind".

Theory of mind: animal studies

Animal studies help us get an insight into the development of theory of mind. Research shows that great apes (such as chimpanzees) have the ability to understand an actor's intentions and false beliefs.

- In a "rational imitation paradigm" that involved novel situations never before witnessed by an ape, Buttelmann et al (2007) were able to demonstrate that chimpanzees' ability to understand intentions was genuine and could not be reduced to problem-solving based on past experience. See **Buttelmann et al (2007)**.

- Similarly, modern research with the use of eye-tracking technology allowed researchers to establish that greater apes (chimpanzees, bonobos, orangutans) have the ability to understand false beliefs. See **Krupenye et al (2016)**.

Theory of mind in human children

Human children as young as 18 months can easily represent intentions of other people. Even when the novel act they witnessed is unsuccessful, they go straight to the correct sequence of actions rather than imitating the unsuccessful sequence. See **Meltzoff (1995)**.

Starting from 4 years old, human children also acquire the ability to understand false beliefs. This was demonstrated with the use of the **Sally-Anne task** specially designed for this purpose. It should be noted that autistic children lack this ability. See **Baron-Cohen, Leslie and Frith (1985)**.

As a concept, theory of mind is simultaneously broader and narrower than empathy. It is broader because it is not confined to understanding other people's emotional experiences. For example, understanding false beliefs is part of theory of mind, but not empathy. It is narrower because it does not include emotional components.

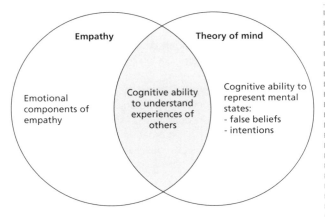

Figure 7.4 Empathy and theory of mind

Buttelmann *et al* (2007)—chimpanzees' ability to understand intentions

Essential understanding
✪ *Chimpanzees' theory of mind cannot be reduced to simple reproduction of sequences of actions observed in the past.*

Aim
To test theory of mind in the chimpanzee by separating it from simple ability to predict actions of others based on past experiences.

Participants
6 chimpanzees.

Method
Experiment (rational imitation paradigm).

Procedure
A chimpanzee was exposed to an actor performing unsuccessful attempts in a novel situation: a "rational imitation paradigm".

There was an apparatus that produced light and sound when turned on. Chimpanzees were amused by the machine. The experimenter first demonstrated how the apparatus was switched on, and then the chimpanzee was given a turn. However, the experimenter always used an unusual part of the body to switch on the apparatus, for example the head or a leg. There were two conditions.
- The unusual body part was used because the experimenter had no choice (for example he was holding a heavy bucket with both hands).
- There was no visible reason why the apparatus could not be switched on with a hand.

Results
When there was no rational explanation for why the human turned on the apparatus with his leg or his head, chimpanzees imitated this behaviour.

However, when the human's behaviour was restrained (for example, by carrying a bucket), the chimpanzees simply switched the apparatus on with their hand. They performed the same action, but in a more accessible way.

Conclusion
Chimpanzees, like humans, understand the goals and intentions behind the actions of others. They don't just memorize patterns of actions, they represent psychological states.

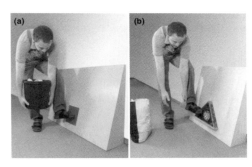

Figure 7.5 The experimenter turning on the light with his foot because his hands were full (a), then because he chose to (b)

Buttelmann *et al* (2007)

Krupenye *et al* (2016)—understanding false beliefs in great apes

Essential understanding

✪ *The use of modern technology (eye tracking) allows us to establish that great apes have the ability to understand false beliefs.*

Aim

To investigate the ability to understand false beliefs in great apes.

Participants

Three species of apes—chimpanzees, bonobos and orangutans.

Method

Experiment; repeated measures design. The dependent variable was measured using eye-tracking technology.

Procedure

Apes were shown a video with two human actors, one of them dressed in a King Kong suit. The setting included two tall haystacks and a door.

- King Kong hits the other man and quickly hides under one of the haystacks.
- The man disappears behind the door.
- The King Kong actor either stays in the original position (in the control condition) or hides under the other haystack (in the experimental condition).
- When the man returns, he is holding a long pole and he smacks the stack he thinks King Kong is under.

Researchers used eye-tracking technology to see where the apes were looking in anticipation of further actions.

Results

Apes spent more time looking at the stack they knew the man in the video believed King Kong to be under (even if that was not the stack King Kong was under actually).

Conclusion

Great apes possess the ability to understand false beliefs.

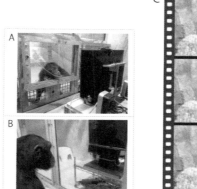

Figure 7.6 False-belief experiments with great apes

Meltzoff (1995)—representation of intentions in human children

Essential understanding

✪ *Human children as young as 18 months have the ability to represent the intentions of other people.*

Aim

To investigate the ability to represent the intentions of others in human children.

Participants

Forty 18-month-old children, equal number of boys and girls.

Method

Experiment; independent measures design.

Procedure

Children in the control group watched an adult perform completed acts. For example, the adult used a small rectangular block of wood to push a rectangular button in a wooden box. This action activated a buzzer.

In the experimental condition the adult's movements were exactly the same, but the action was unsuccessful. For example, the adult missed the button, and as a result the buzzer was not activated.

The dependent variable was the number of successfully accomplished imitation acts by the child.

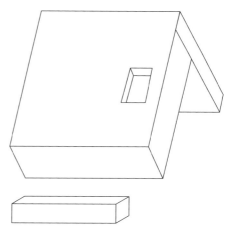

Figure 7.7 Equipment used in the experiment

Results

The number of successfully accomplished imitation acts did not differ in the two conditions. Children in the experimental group did not go through a period of trial-and-error but went straight for the correct action.

Conclusion

Researchers concluded that children were not just blindly imitating the actions of the adult, but representing the adult's mental states (intentions).

THE SALLY-ANNE TASK

This task is commonly used to establish if children possess understanding of false beliefs.

In this task the child is shown two dolls (Sally and Anne). What follows is a narrative accompanied by visuals. Sally has a basket and Anne has a box. Sally takes a marble, places it in her basket and leaves the room. While she is away, Anne moves the marble from the basket to the box. Sally returns, and the question is, "Where will she be looking for the marble?" If the child understands false beliefs, the answer will be "in the basket". If the child doesn't understand false beliefs, the answer will be "in the box".

Figure 7.8 Sally-Anne task

Baron-Cohen, Leslie and Frith (1985)

RESEARCH Baron-Cohen, Leslie and Frith (1985)—understanding false beliefs in human children

Essential understanding
⭐ *By the age of 4–5 years, human children normally have the ability to understand false beliefs, but this does not apply to children with autism.*

Aim
To investigate the ability of human children to understand false beliefs.

Participants
Clinically normal pre-school children (mean age 4.5 years), children with Down syndrome, and autistic children.

Method and procedure
The Sally-Anne task.

Results
– Most clinically normal children (86%) and most children with Down syndrome (85%) passed the task successfully.
– Most autistic children (80%) failed the task.

Conclusion
Human children normally acquire the ability to understand false beliefs around the age of 4 or 5 years.

Autistic children (at least at this age) do not possess the ability to represent false beliefs.

7.2 Developing an identity

7.2.1 Gender identity and social roles

- **Congenital adrenal hyperplasia (CAH)**—a genetic disorder causing one to have abnormally high levels of testosterone in the prenatal period
- **Gender constancy**—the idea that gender is fixed, constant in time and unchangeable (consists of gender labelling, gender stability and gender consistency)

- **Gender identity**—the perception of oneself as male, female or a third category
- **Gender roles**—societal expectations regarding the behaviour of an individual based on their biological sex
- **Gender socialization**—internalizing social norms of sex-appropriate behaviour

ESSENTIAL UNDERSTANDING

Gender, gender identity and gender roles: the concepts

Social identity is based on what groups a person identifies with ("I am a student", "I am a father"). See "**3.1.1 Social identity theory**" in "**Unit 3 Sociocultural approach to behaviour**". Social roles are sets of expectations regarding one's behaviour based on belonging to social groups. One might say that social identity is a set of internalized social roles.

Gender identity is part of social identity. Gender roles are sets of societal expectations regarding gender-appropriate behaviour. Gender identity is formed on the basis of internalized gender roles.

Gender identity refers to one's self-perception as male or female (or a third gender category).

Biological factors in the formation of gender identity

These include the following.
- Sex-determining hormones (such as testosterone), when injected prenatally, have been shown to produce long-term effects on gender-related behaviour in later life. See "**Sex-determining hormones**".
- Chromosomal variations (Turner's syndrome in females and Kleinfelter's syndrome in males) were shown to have similar effects. See "**Chromosomal variations**".

Cognitive factors in the formation of gender identity

These include the way children process gender-related information. Research in this area has focused on answering two questions.
- What is the main cognitive trigger of gender identity?
- What is the cognitive mechanism that is responsible for the formation of gender identity?

Two influential theories have suggested answers to these two questions: Kohlberg's cognitive developmental theory (Kohlberg 1966) and gender schema theory (Bem 1981).

In Kohlberg's developmental theory of gender, the trigger for the development of gender identity is gender constancy, and the mechanism of its development is cognitive dissonance. See "**Kohlberg's developmental theory of gender**".

Slaby and Frey (1975), in partial support of this theory, demonstrated that children with high scores on gender constancy prefer paying attention to same-sex adult models. See **Slaby and Frey (1975)**.

According to gender schema theory, the trigger for the development of gender identity is gender labelling, and the mechanism of its development is schematic processing. See **Bem (1981)**.

In support of this, Martin (1989) demonstrated that rigid information processing based on gender stereotyping is a consequence of simple gender labelling at a young age. See **Martin (1989)**.

Social factors in the formation of gender identity

Social influences in the development of gender can be divided into two categories:
- gender socialization by parents
- gender socialization by peers.

The idea of gender socialization by parents is based on social cognitive theory and the concept of vicarious reinforcement. See "**Gender socialization by parents**".

Gender socialization by peers occurs when gender-consistent behaviours are reinforced by other children. Draper and Cashdan (1988) showed that gender-related differences in behaviour are most pronounced when children play in sex-segregated groups. See "**Gender socialization by peers**".

SEX-DETERMINING HORMONES

Essential understanding

⭐ *Being exposed to sex-determining hormones such as testosterone in the prenatal period has been shown to have long-term effects on sex-typical behaviour in later life.*

Sex-determining hormones are produced in the prenatal period and have long-term effects on the hypothalamus, which in turn regulates the production of hormones in later life. Being exposed to such hormones in the prenatal period can have irreversible effects.

Some of the possible approaches to study include the following.

– Animal studies—for example, it was shown that injecting testosterone in developing female rats prenatally increases the incidence of male-typical behaviour in later life. These female rats engaged in higher levels of rough-and-tumble play and even demonstrated male-typical sexual behaviour (tried to mount other female rats) (Goy and McEwen 1980).
– Studying humans with rare genetic disorders that cause them to have high levels of testosterone in the prenatal period—for example congenital adrenal hyperplasia (CAH). Research shows that girls with CAH engage more frequently in male-typical behaviour (such as rough-and-tumble play, choosing boys as playmates) (Hines 2004).

CHROMOSOMAL VARIATIONS

Essential understanding

⭐ *Chromosomal variations also correlate with sex-atypical behaviour.*

Some people have atypical chromosomes deviating from the normal XY pattern for males and XX pattern for females, known as:

– Turner's syndrome: XO, females who lack the second X chromosome
– Kleinfelter's syndrome: XXY, males who have an extra X chromosome.

Research in this area is limited, but it does show that atypical chromosomes correlate with sex-atypical behaviour.

THEORY

KOHLBERG'S DEVELOPMENTAL THEORY OF GENDER

Essential understanding

⭐ *In Kohlberg's theory, the trigger for the development of gender identity is gender constancy, and the mechanism of its development is cognitive dissonance.*

According to Kohlberg (1966), the development of gender goes through the following stages.

Stage	Description	Age
Gender labelling	This is when children can identify themselves and other people as boys or girls, but they also believe that gender changes when physical appearance changes (for example, when a boy puts on a dress, he becomes a girl), and that gender can change in time.	2 years
Gender stability (over time)	This is when children recognize that gender is stable in time (girls will grow up to be mothers, and boys will become fathers), but they still see gender as something that can be changed by context.	4 years
Gender consistency (across various situations)	This is when gender is truly perceived as stable and constant regardless of the changes in physical appearance, passage of time or other factors. For example, a boy wearing a dress is still a boy.	5–7 years

Collectively this is known as **gender constancy**. Gender labelling, gender stability and gender consistency all contribute to the development of gender constancy.

Kohlberg's theory is as follows.

– **The trigger** for the development of true gender identity is understanding of gender constancy.
– **The mechanism** of development of gender identity is cognitive dissonance. Cognitive dissonance is the discomfort experienced when one's behaviour is inconsistent with one's beliefs. In order to avoid such discomfort people would normally try to change either their belief or their behaviour. (I am a boy, and boys do not play with dolls. So why am I playing with dolls? I should either change my belief and decide that I am a girl, or change my behaviour and stop playing with dolls. But I cannot change my belief because gender is constant. So I should stop playing with dolls.)

Slaby and Frey (1975)—support for Kohlberg's cognitive developmental theory of gender

Essential understanding

✪ *As gender constancy is achieved, children start demonstrating more selective attention to same-sex models. This suggests that gender constancy is the trigger of the development of gender identity.*

Aim

To investigate the role of gender constancy in the attention given to same-sex models.

Participants

Fifty-five children 2–5 years old.

Method

Correlational study; variables were measured through interviews and the measurement of eye fixation time.

Procedure

The level of gender constancy was assessed through an interview. Following this, children were shown a film in which a man and a woman engaged in parallel activities (they built a fire, played a musical instrument, drank juice). The man and the woman were on different sides of the screen.

The dependent variable was the amount of time the children's eyes were fixated on either of the sides of the screen.

Results

Children with higher levels of gender constancy showed more selective attention to same-sex role models.

For example, boys low on gender constancy looked at the male model about 48% of the time, while boys high on gender constancy looked at male models 61% of the time.

The opposite was true for girls.

Conclusion

Gender constancy is an important milestone in the development of gender identity because it triggers selective attention to same-sex models.

Results of the study also suggest that cognitive factors in the development of gender identity precede social factors: social learning of gender is not possible until the child selectively pays attention to same-sex models.

THEORY

GENDER SCHEMA THEORY—BEM (1981)

Essential understanding

✪ *According to gender schema theory, gender labelling is enough for the formation of gender identity to start, and the mechanism of its development is schematic processing.*

Gender schema theory does not question the idea that cognitive processes drive the development of gender, but it provides a different perspective on the key trigger as well as the mechanism of this process. It builds on the concept of schema. (For a general understanding of schema see "2.1.2 Schema theory" in "Unit 2 Cognitive approach to behaviour".) Gender schema theory suggests the following.

– Gender-typical stereotypes and behaviour are a consequence of normal information processing. Similar stereotypes are found in other aspects of a person's life.

– **The trigger** in the development of gender identity is the formation of gender labelling—the simple ability of children to label themselves and others as boys or girls.

– **The mechanism** of gender identity development is schematic processing. Once gender is labelled, it becomes a schema. As we know, schema influences information processing in all stages including encoding, so gender schema starts filtering all gender-related information that the child perceives.

RESEARCH **Martin (1989)—the influence of gender labelling on information processing**

Essential understanding

✪ *Younger children have more stringent gender stereotypes than older children. This shows that, contrary to Kohlberg's expectations, gender labelling alone is a powerful influence on information processing, and with age gender stereotypes are actually weakened rather than strengthened.*

Aim

To investigate the development of gender stereotyping with age.

Participants

Seventy-two children aged 4–10.

Method

Quasi-experiment (comparison of age groups).

Procedure

– Participants were given descriptions of eight target children (four boys and four girls). Some children were described as having a stereotyped interest (for example, "Tommy's best friend is a boy, and Tommy likes to play with airplanes"), and others were described as having a counter-stereotyped interest (for example, "Tommy's best friend is a girl, and Tommy likes to play with a toy kitchen set").

– Participants were then asked how likely it was that the child in the story would like to play with each of the following toys: car, train engine (masculine), sewing machine, doll (feminine).

Results

There was a difference in the way younger and older children predicted toy preferences.

- Younger children (3–6 years old) based their judgment solely on the target's sex (Tommy will like playing with a car because he is a boy [even though I was told that he likes to play with a toy kitchen set).
- Older children (6–10 years old) used information about the target child's interests (Tommy will like playing with a doll because I was told that he likes to play with feminine toys).

Conclusion

Rigid information processing based on gender stereotyping is a consequence of simple gender labelling at a young age. As the child develops, information processing becomes more complex.

GENDER SOCIALIZATION BY PARENTS

Essential understanding

✪ *Gender socialization by parents can take the form of direct tuition or vicarious learning.*

Theory

Gender socialization by parents can be described and explained by social cognitive theory (Bandura 1986). See "**Unit 3 Sociocultural approach to behaviour**". In line with his theory, Bandura claimed that gender socialization can occur through:

- direct tuition (when adults reinforce behaviour that is consistent with gender stereotypes)

- vicarious learning (when children observe others displaying gender-consistent behaviour and get reinforced for that).

Supporting research: Bobo doll studies

Bandura's classic Bobo doll research studies demonstrated that in aggressive behaviour (which is stereotypically masculine) children have a tendency to imitate same-sex models. This shows that children can learn sex-typical behaviour vicariously, especially when they can identify with the adult model. See "**3.1.2 Social cognitive theory**" in "**Unit 3 Sociocultural approach to behaviour**".

GENDER SOCIALIZATION BY PEERS

Essential understanding

✪ *It has been shown that gender-related differences in behaviour are most obvious when children play in sex-segregated groups. This suggests that there is a certain level of peer influence involved in gender socialization.*

Gender socialization by peers occurs when gender-consistent behaviours are reinforced, both directly and vicariously, by other children.

Draper and Cashdan (1988) showed, in their observational study among the !Kung bushmen of western Botswana, that when the number of available playmates is greater, children are more likely to form sex-segregated peer groups and, as a result, their behaviour becomes more gender typical. In this study children in foraging families showed less sex-related behavioural differences than children in farming families. This is because foraging families do not settle down for long, and the number of playmates available to their children is not large. Peer groups are not so sex-segregated, and hence gender differences are not so obvious.

7.2.2 Attachment

- **Attachment**—an emotional bond between an infant and a caregiver that manifests itself in being calm in the caregiver's presence and distressed when separated
- **Attachment styles**—individual variations in attachment behaviours
- **Contact comfort**—the physical and emotional comfort that the infant receives when in contact with the caregiver
- **Ethology**—the study of animal behaviour in natural environments

- **Imprinting**—a form of rapid learning, a biologically pre-programmed behavioural sequence in response to a specific environmental trigger
- **Secure base hypothesis**—the idea that infants use the attachment figure as a starting point for the exploration of the surrounding environment
- **Separation distress**—acute signs of anxiety and discomfort when the attachment figure leaves

ESSENTIAL UNDERSTANDING

Research questions

Attachment refers to a special form of emotional connection between individuals, most often used to describe relationships between children and their caregivers or between romantic partners.

Attachment is most clearly seen in **separation distress**, for example, the emotional reaction of a child being separated from its mother. Research has attempted to answer such questions as these.

- Is there a critical period for attachment?
- What is the mechanism of formation of attachment? Is it mainly a biological process?
- Are there any variations in attachment across individuals and cultures?
- Does attachment in childhood have any long-term effects on later life?

Biological basis of attachment (animal studies)

Harlow (1958) was the researcher who set out to find a suitable biological explanation for attachment behaviours. He used rhesus monkeys to investigate such phenomena as contact comfort and secure base.

In one of his experiments he showed that attachment is driven by contact comfort rather than satisfaction of basic needs. See Harlow (1958), "Experiment 1—contact comfort versus satisfaction of basic needs".

In another experiment Harlow supported the secure base hypothesis, the idea that the presence of a caring mother is necessary for the infant monkeys to feel secure and explore the environment. See **Harlow (1958)**, "Experiment 2—secure base hypothesis".

Harlow's research had many important implications for child care. However, it is being criticized on the grounds of ethics and generalizability to humans. See "**Evaluation of Harlow's research**".

Attachment in humans

John Bowlby was the first researcher to formulate a theory of attachment for human children. In this theory attachment includes both biological and cognitive components. Cognitive components of attachment are persistent and underlie the development of relationships later in life. See **John Bowlby—the theory of attachment for human children**.

Ainsworth (in a series of papers in 1970–78) further demonstrated that human children have individual differences in how attachment behaviours are manifested. These are known as attachment styles. Ainsworth described three attachment styles: secure, avoidant and ambivalent. See **Mary Ainsworth (1970–1978): attachment styles**

Van Ijzendoorn and Kroonenberg (1988) conducted a meta-analysis of cross-cultural research and showed that there are some variations in the prevalence of attachment styles. These variations were stronger within cultures than between cultures. See **van Ijzendoorn and Kroonenberg (1988)**.

RESEARCH · Harlow (1958), experiment 1—contact comfort versus satisfaction of basic needs

Essential understanding

✪ *Attachment is driven by contact comfort rather than simple satisfaction of basic needs.*

Aim

To investigate the role of contact comfort in attachment behaviours in infant rhesus monkeys.

Participants

8 infant rhesus monkeys.

Method

Experiment; independent measures design.

Procedure

An artificial surrogate monkey mother was built. There was a light bulb behind her making her warm, and a milk-dispensing mechanism was installed in the breast area.

There were two modifications of the artificial mother.
- The "cloth mother" was built from a block of wood and cotton cloth. The cloth made it possible for the infant monkey to cling to the mother, enabling "contact comfort".
- The "wire mother" was made of wire. It was identical to the cloth mother in everything except for providing comfort.

Infant rhesus monkeys were placed in a cage with both the cloth and the wire mother, so that they could choose which one of them to spend time with. There were two conditions (four monkeys in each).
- The cloth mother lactated; the wire mother did not.

- The wire mother lactated; the cloth mother did not.

The dependent variable was the amount of time spent with each of the mothers.

Results

Results showed that infant monkeys preferred to spend time with the cloth mother.

Even in the condition when the cloth mother did not provide any food, by the age of 20 days infant monkeys learned to use the wire mother only to get milk and spent the rest of the time with the cloth mother.

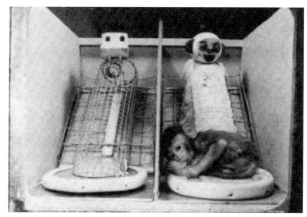

Figure 7.9 Wire and cloth surrogate mothers

Harlow (1958)

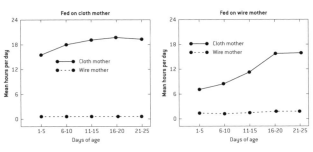

Figure 7.10 Time spent on the cloth and wire mother surrogates

Harlow (1958)

Conclusion

These results contradict the idea that attachment behaviour is secondary to satisfaction of basic needs. Since monkeys preferred the company of the cloth mother even when she did not satisfy their basic needs, attachment must be driven by something else—"contact comfort".

Harlow (1958), experiment 2—secure base hypothesis

Essential understanding

⭐ *Infants need a sense of security from their caregiver to be willing to explore the environment.*

Aim

In order to develop cognitively, children must interact with the environment. For this, they need to be brave enough to leave their mother's lap and explore the world. The secure base hypothesis is the idea that infants need a sense of security and comfort from their caregiver in order to be able to take risks and explore the environment.

Procedure

In this study infant rhesus monkeys were placed in a room containing multiple objects to play with. Interacting with such enriched environments is important for cognitive development. In three different conditions, the monkeys were alone, with a wire mother or with a cloth mother.

Results

Results showed that the cloth mother was used as a "secure base". When she was in the room, baby monkeys were actively exploring the environment and at the same time frequently rushing back to the mother to clutch her. Monkeys in the other two conditions were much more anxious and much less willing to explore the environment. They often froze and stayed motionless in the corner, screaming or crying.

EVALUATION OF HARLOW'S RESEARCH

Harlow made an important contribution to the study of attachment: he demonstrated that attachment cannot be reduced to simple anticipation of satisfaction of basic needs. Providing contact comfort and a secure base are important prerequisites of normal development.

At the same time, there are two major points of criticism.

- Applicability to humans—although rhesus monkeys and human babies are similar in many respects, generalizability of results can still be questioned.
- Ethical considerations—Harlow brought infant rhesus monkeys up in conditions that were expected to cause anxiety and delayed cognitive development.

THEORY

JOHN BOWLBY—THE THEORY OF ATTACHMENT FOR HUMAN CHILDREN

Essential understanding

⭐ *Attachment includes both biological and cognitive components. The cognitive components of attachment become the basis for developing relationships later in life.*

John Bowlby was the first psychologist who attempted to create a theory of attachment for human children. This theory was formulated in a series of papers from 1958 to 1960.

In this theory attachment includes two components.

- **The attachment behavioural system:** this refers to biologically pre-programmed instinctive sequences of behaviour in response to certain environmental triggers (this component was inspired by Lorenz's research with imprinting).
- **The internal working model:** this refers to the psychological aspects of attachment—beliefs about the self, the caregivers and the nature of one's relationships with the caregivers.

Bowlby thought that the internal working model is formed in early childhood and becomes the foundation for all subsequent relationships in adult life. For example, if a child is consistently neglected despite trying to get the parents' attention, he or she can acquire a deep belief, "I am unworthy". This fundamental belief will further influence other relationships.

Mary Ainsworth (1970–1978): attachment styles

Essential understanding

⭐ *Seeking contact comfort and establishing a "secure base" are common to all human infants, but there are individual differences in the way these behaviours are manifested. These differences may be described as attachment styles.*

Aim

To investigate individual differences in attachment behaviour in human children.

Participants

Children aged 12 to 18 months.

Method

Ainsworth developed an observational procedure for assessing attachment in infants: "The Strange Situation Paradigm".

Procedure

The mother and the infant are invited into a room where toys are available. There is a one-way mirror in the room through which researchers register the infant's behaviour. The mother and a confederate (a "stranger") then follow a scripted series of actions.

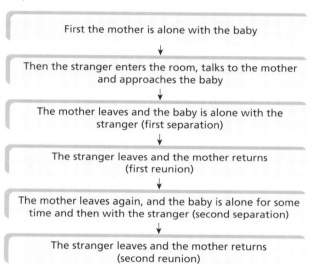

Figure 7.11 The Strange Situation Paradigm

Results

Common to all infants, and in support of Harlow's secure base hypothesis, infants were much more active in their exploration of the playroom when their mother was around.

At the same time, there were individual differences in children's behaviour that Ainsworth summarized as "attachment styles" of types A, B and C.

Type	Name	Frequency	Description
A	Insecure avoidant attachment	20% of infants	No signs of separation distress Indifferent to reunion No anxiety in the presence of the stranger
B	Secure attachment	70% of infants	Separation distress when the mother leaves Positive reaction to the reunion Avoids the stranger when alone, but acts friendly when the mother is near
C	Insecure ambivalent attachment	10% of infants	Intense separation anxiety Negative reaction to reunion: resists contact and even pushes the mother away Avoids the stranger at all times

Table 7.2

Conclusion

Attachment behaviours associated with contact comfort and "secure base" are common to human infants, but at the same time there exist individual differences in attachment behaviour patterns—attachment styles.

Van Ijzendoorn and Kroonenberg (1988)—cultural variations in attachment

Essential understanding

⭐ *Manifestations of attachment are influenced by social factors.*

Aim

To investigate how attachment styles vary cross-culturally.

Method and procedure

A meta-analysis of 32 studies using Ainsworth's "Strange Situation Paradigm" conducted in 8 countries.

Participants

18 studies from the USA; other studies from Germany, United Kingdom, Sweden, Japan, the Netherlands, China and Israel.

Results

The average across all US samples matched the distribution of attachment styles found in Ainsworth's research: A = 20%, B = 70%, C = 10%.

However, despite the average, there was considerable variation both between countries and between samples from the same country.

Interestingly, intracultural variation (that is, within a country) was even larger than cross-cultural variation (between countries).

Conclusion

Researchers explained that the variation could be caused by the socio-economic status of the family. This is supported by the observation that avoidant and ambivalent attachment styles were often registered in lower-class families, whereas children in middle-class, professional families mostly demonstrated secure attachment. We can conclude that manifestations of attachment are indeed influenced by sociocultural variables, more by social than cultural.

7.3 Influences on cognitive and social development

7.3.1 Role of peers and play

- **Inhibitory control**—the ability to suppress the first impulse when it can lead to a negative social reaction, for example, inhibiting the impulse to grab toys from other children because it can provoke conflict

- **Joint attention**—the ability to coordinate attention to objects with another partner
- **Perspective taking**—the ability to understand the viewpoint of another person; an important prerequisite of social skills

ESSENTIAL UNDERSTANDING

Development of play and peer interaction

Not all play includes peer interaction, and not all peer interaction is play, but there is considerable overlap between the two. To understand it, one needs to consider how play and peer interaction develop from birth to adolescence.

The development of play progresses through a series of stages starting from simple object manipulation and ending with highly elaborate play with rules. See "Development of play".

The influence of peers and play on cognitive development

Piaget assumed that cognitive development in peer interaction is driven by the process of perspective taking, so it will be enhanced in a group of equal peers who find each other relatable. Vygotsky believed that cognitive development is driven by interaction with "more knowledgeable others", be it adults or other peers. See "**The influence of peers and play on cognitive development**".

Damon and Killen (1982) found that discussion with peers promotes moral reasoning in children more effectively than discussion with adults. This supports Piaget's idea that comparing perspectives with relatable peers encourages children to develop more balanced reasoning. See **Damon and Killen (1982)**.

Nedospasova (1985) demonstrated that 5–7-year-old children overcome cognitive egocentrism more easily when they interact with an adult who is scaffolding the task for them. This supports Vygotsky's ideas on the role of more knowledgeable others and the zone of proximal development. See **Nedospasova (1985)**.

The influence of peers and play on social development

Interaction with peers and play in childhood also creates a foundation for the basic social skills, thus ensuring social adjustment in later life. See "**The influence of peers and play on social development**".

Hollos and Cowan (1973) found that children who grew up on isolated farms in Norway (and had little exposure to same-age peers) did not differ from a control group in how they solved logical tasks, but did not perform so well on social tasks involving taking into account another person's perspective. See **Hollos and Cowan (1973)**.

Roff (1963) used retrospective analysis of clinical records to show that military servicemen discharged from service had shown more signs of poor peer adjustment in childhood. This means that poor peer adjustment in childhood may have long-term effects on social behaviour in later life. See **Roff (1963)**.

Development of play

Age	Type of play	Description	Example
1–2	Object manipulation	The focus of the child's attention is the object itself and its properties (its shape, colour, tactile sensations it produces, and so on). The social function of the object or the meaning behind the object are ignored.	A spoon is just a shiny object with an interesting shape. Children are not interested in (or cannot understand) its function.
3–5	Pretend play	Objects are no longer the focus of attention, but social roles are. This enables children to understand the meaning behind objects.	Children can imitate a family dinner and use sticks instead of spoons. They are imitating the social scenario and the object itself is no longer important as long as it can be used as a symbol.
6–7	Play with rules	Neither object properties nor social roles are the focus of attention; the focus is on rules. Rules regulate complex sequences of social interactions and require complex cognitive structures.	Children can play games such as "Cops and Robbers" or simply act out a scene from a movie. They are assigned roles, and carefully following the requirements of the role is socially reinforced ("You are a sentry, you can't move!").

Table 7.3

THE INFLUENCE OF PEERS AND PLAY ON COGNITIVE DEVELOPMENT

Essential understanding
✪ *Both Piaget and Vygotsky acknowledged that cognitive development is driven by peer interaction, but their views differed on the kind of peers that are most important—any peers or more knowledgeable ones.*

Piaget (1932) believed that the component of peer interaction crucial for cognitive development is **perspective taking**.

– When perspectives on a particular problem differ, children can realize that their current beliefs may be incorrect. This is an uncomfortable realization.

– Children try to resolve the discrepancy. This becomes a force driving their cognitive development.

– Peers are more relatable than adults so their perspectives bear a larger influence. Perspectives of adults tend to be accepted without questioning, whereas in a group of peers no one assumes the leading role.

In contrast to that, **Vygotsky (1978)** believed that cognitive development of children is driven by hierarchical interactions in which one of the partners can take the leading position. Vygotsky coined the term "**more knowledgeable other**". This can be an adult or a child who has more expertise in something.

RESEARCH   Damon and Killen (1982)—moral reasoning and discussion with peers

Essential understanding
✪ *Constructive discussion with peers promotes cognitive development (supports Piaget's approach).*

Aim
To compare rates of development of moral reasoning in children engaging in discussions with peers and adults.

Participants
Children aged 6 to 9 who discussed ethical decision-making scenarios either in groups of three or with an adult.

Method
Experiment; independent measures design. The dependent variable was measured through a structured interview.

Procedure
Researchers viewed moral reasoning as a cognitive process and measured it through an interview in which the child was offered a moral dilemma and asked to solve it.

Damon and Killen's research compared moral reasoning in:
– children who discussed ethical dilemmas with peers
– children who discussed these dilemmas with adults.

Results
It was found that children who discussed the dilemmas with peers reached higher levels of moral reasoning faster.

Conclusion
Comparing perspectives among peers advances the rate of children's cognitive development. This supports Piaget's approach.

RESEARCH   Nedospasova (1985)—overcoming cognitive egocentrism through play with a more knowledgeable other

Essential understanding
✪ *Play with a more knowledgeable adult helps children overcome cognitive egocentrism.*

Aim
To investigate whether play can speed up overcoming cognitive egocentrism in children.

Participants
Children aged 5 to 7.

Method
Experiment; repeated measures design. The dependent variable (cognitive egocentrism) was measured with a variety of tasks including the three mountains task. See **Piaget and Inhelder (1956)**.

Procedure
The child who did not pass tests for cognitive egocentrism (such as the three mountains task) was presented with three dolls and told they were all brothers (in this example the child is a boy). He was then asked to identify with one of the dolls ("This is going to be you, your name is …"). He was asked how many brothers he had (two). After this one of the other dolls was selected and the child was asked how many brothers this doll had. A cognitively egocentric child would typically say one. After this the child was prompted with the dolls again until he gave the correct answer.

The procedure was repeated two more times:
– with graphical representations (circles) instead of dolls
– verbally (there were three brothers, their names were …) without any prompts.

Results
Children who participated in this procedure were much more likely to pass the three mountains task with little or no help from the experimenter.

Conclusion
Results of the study support Vygotsky's view that cognitive development in children is driven by interactions with more knowledgeable others, as well as the concept of zone of proximal development.

THE INFLUENCE OF PEERS AND PLAY ON SOCIAL DEVELOPMENT

Essential understanding
✪ *Peer interaction and play in childhood creates a foundation for the development of basic social skills and has long-term consequences in terms of a person's social adjustment.*

Perspective taking that is promoted in the process of peer interaction is important for cognitive as well as social development because it forms the basis of empathy and theory of mind. See "**Empathy and theory of mind**".

However, peer interaction and play also promote other skills that are important for social development, most notably

self-regulation while performing a social role. When play with rules emerges, it becomes important for children to follow the rules strictly while pretending to play a social role (for example, a doctor, a teacher). Other children reinforce this behaviour. This allows children to overcome their natural impulsivity for the sake of performing social functions.

The influence of peer interaction on social development is visible through the study of long-term effects of poor peer interaction in childhood.

RESEARCH   Hollos and Cowan (1973)—social development in children from isolated farms

Essential understanding
✪ *Interaction with peers is important for the development of social skills.*

Aim
To investigate social skills in children who grew up in isolated locations.

Participants
Children aged 7–9 who grew up on isolated farms in Norway and as a result had very few same-age peers to interact with were compared to children who grew up in a Norwegian town.

Method
Quasi-experimental comparison.

Procedure
Children from isolated farms were compared to a control group of children from less isolated locations.

A variety of tasks was used to measure both logical skills (for example, conservation tasks with water) and social skills (for example, one task was to retell a story accurately to a new person).

Results
The social skills of these children were not as developed as in the control group. However, there were no differences in terms of logical skills.

Conclusion
Growing up in isolated locations with little access to same-age peers has negative effects on the development of social skills, but not logical skills.

RESEARCH   Roff (1963)—peer adjustment in early childhood and anti-social conduct of the military

Essential understanding
✪ *Poor peer adjustment in early childhood may be predictive of misdemeanour in military servicemen.*

Aim
To investigate the possible childhood roots for receiving a dishonorable discharge from service in the military.

Participants
Military servicemen who had been referred to guidance clinics in childhood.

Method
Quasi-experimental comparison. The dependent variable was measured by retrospective analysis of military service records and clinical records.

Procedure
The researcher compared two groups of adults:

- socially disordered—servicemen who received a dishonourable discharge from service for antisocial conduct
- non-disordered—servicemen with exemplary military service records.

The clinical records in both groups were analysed for signs of poor peer adjustment in early childhood (such as inability to keep friends, being rated as asocial by a teacher).

Results
The percentage of servicemen who had experienced poor peer adjustment in childhood:
- 54% of servicemen discharged from service
- 24% of servicemen with exemplary records.

Conclusion
Although causation cannot be inferred in this study, it suggests a possible link between peer adjustment in early childhood and social behaviour in later life.

7.3.2 Childhood trauma and resilience

- **Critical period**—a specific time during which an organism has to experience certain stimuli in order for a certain psychological function to be developed
- **Deprivation**—continuous exposure to adverse circumstances

- **Resilience**—the ability to adapt to stressful situations and recover from the effects of adverse circumstances
- **Trauma**—an emotionally painful experience that has long-lasting effects on a person's development and well-being

ESSENTIAL UNDERSTANDING

Trauma and deprivation

According to the National Institute of Mental Health (NIMH), trauma is an emotionally painful experience which does not necessarily involve a physical injury and can result from being a witness to a distressing event (NIMH 2015).

The concepts of trauma and deprivation overlap considerably, especially when it comes to studying their effects.

Effects of deprivation in critical periods

Experiments with animals and case studies of human children who suffered deprivation seem to be the only acceptable methods to study the effects of deprivation in critical periods on development.

Case studies of deprivation in human children have shown that language deprivation in the critical period has an irreversible effect on language development. However, some cases are exceptions to that. The exceptions may be attributed to a variety of factors. See "Case studies of deprivation in human children".

Effects of trauma

When looking at trauma rather than deprivation, research has highlighted post-traumatic stress disorder (PTSD) as the most common consequence.

Fieldman and Vengrober (2011) showed that PTSD could be diagnosed in 38% of children living in close proximity to war zones in the Gaza strip. While this is much higher than the average, some children, while being exposed to the same experiences, did not develop PTSD. This suggests resilience. See **Fieldman and Vengrober (2011)**.

Resilience

Resilience is the ability to adapt to stressful situations and recover from the effects of adverse circumstances.

McFarlane (1983) demonstrated that the resilience of children depends to a large extent on the resilience of their parents. Severity of adversity did not affect resilience of children as much as the parents' response to it. See **McFarlane (1983)**.

Betancourt et al (2013) studied former child soldiers in Sierra Leone and found that many children were able to recover from even the most traumatic experiences. However, they also showed the crucial role of social support in overcoming trauma. See **Betancourt et al (2013)**.

TRAUMA AND DEPRIVATION

These concepts considerably overlap. While the concept of "trauma" is usually used to refer to a one-time event, deprivation refers to continuous exposure to adverse circumstances. Deprivation can take many forms including extreme poverty, malnutrition and language deprivation. The effects of trauma and deprivation on later development are similar, so trauma and deprivations are often studied in conjunction. Deprivation itself can also cause trauma.

EFFECTS OF DEPRIVATION ON HUMAN DEVELOPMENT: CRITICAL PERIODS

Essential understanding

✪ *Deprivation in critical periods is believed to damage the development of psychological functions irreversibly. Experiments with animals and case studies of human children who suffered deprivation are the two methods that are used to study these effects.*

Effects of deprivation on human development depend to a large extent on the timing of deprivation episodes. Specifically, it is believed that deprivation occurring in critical periods has an irreversible effect on cognitive and social development. It is thought that if a psychological function is not formed in the critical period (which is different for different functions), it will never be formed.

For ethical reasons, there are only two possible approaches to the study of effects of deprivation in critical periods on later development.

- Animal studies where deprivation is created intentionally. Such studies support the idea that deprivation in critical periods prevents psychological functions from being developed. However, such studies are criticized on the grounds of ethics and generalizability to humans.
- Case studies of children who underwent deprivation and were later discovered and studied by scientists.

Case studies of deprivation in human children

Essential understanding

✪ *Case studies of deprivation in human children have shown that language deprivation in the critical period irreversibly damages language abilities. Not all case studies demonstrate this consistently, but it is difficult to compare case studies with each other because they differ in a large number of factors.*

Case study	Researcher	Nature of deprivation	Effects on development
The case of Genie	Curtiss *et al* (1974)	From birth she was severely abused, neglected and isolated up to the age of 13 years and 7 months. She was locked alone in her room, tied to a chair and malnourished. She was not exposed to any interpersonal interaction.	After being discovered and given proper training, she developed some non-verbal communication skills but was never able to fully acquire a language. Her behaviour was highly antisocial and she did not show any signs of attachment. Her attention was directed at objects and sounds, but never at people.
The case of Anna	Davis (1947)	She was kept in a store room for 5.5 years, tied to her seat. She was neglected and suffered from malnutrition.	When discovered, she was placed in a foster home where she interacted with other inmates. By the age of 9 she started to conform to social norms and developed some speech (for example, she was able to understand instructions and follow them). Unfortunately, she died at age 10.
The case of Isabelle	Mason (1942)	Confined to a room with a deaf and mute mother, she spent 6.5 years in silence. However, she could still communicate with her mother through hand gestures.	When discovered and given training, she developed a rich vocabulary (up to 2,500 words) and the ability to produce complex grammatical structures.

Table 7.4

It is difficult to compare case studies because they differ in a whole range of factors. For example, case studies of Genie and Anna seem to suggest that there is a critical period for the development of language which, if missed, makes it impossible ever to acquire language abilities. The case of Isabelle seems to contradict that. However, in Isabelle's case, she could still engage in some form of communication with her mother. This could explain the different findings.

EFFECTS OF TRAUMA ON HUMAN DEVELOPMENT: PTSD

Research that focused on the effects of trauma (rather than deprivation) on later development has highlighted PTSD as the most common consequence. PTSD includes such symptoms as disturbing feelings and thoughts, acute emotional reactions to trauma-related triggers, spontaneous flooding of traumatic memories, excessive emotional arousal and anxiety.

Fieldman and Vengrober (2011)—PTSD in children living in the Gaza strip

Essential understanding

✪ *War-related experiences are traumatic to children, but parents' resilience and sensitivity contribute to the resilience of children.*

Aim

To examine PTSD symptoms in children exposed to war-related trauma.

Participants

Children aged 1.5–5 years living near the Gaza strip.

Method

Qualitative research (interviews).

Procedure

Children and their mothers were interviewed. Children's experiences and PTSD symptoms were rated by their mothers.

Results

- PTSD was diagnosed in 38% of the children in the study. This is much higher than in the general population of this age (less than 1%).
- However, some children, while being exposed to the same experiences, did not develop PTSD.
- When these resilient children were more closely investigated, it was found that:
  o their mothers had more social support
  o their mothers were more sensitive to their needs
  o such children actively sought maternal support (even during the interview itself).

Conclusion

War-related experiences are obviously traumatic for children; however, some children are resilient. Such children usually have more resilient parents (with a stronger social network of support). Their parents are also more sensitive to their needs and make themselves emotionally available.

RESEARCH   McFarlane (1983)—resilience in children who lost homes in Australian bushfires

Essential understanding
✪ *The resilience of children depends on the resilience of parents.*

Aim
To investigate predictors of PTSD symptoms in children who survived a natural disaster.

Participants
808 children in families who were affected by the devastating bushfires in Australia in 1983. Children themselves were not actually directly interviewed; data was gathered from teachers and parents.

Method
Interviews.

Procedure
Interviews took place 26 months after the fire. During the interviews both children and parents were scored for symptoms of PTSD.

Results
There was a positive correlation between PTSD symptoms in children and their parents.

PTSD symptoms 26 months after the fire were best predicted by such variables as separation from parents after the fire and continual maternal preoccupation with the disaster.

These factors were even more powerful predictors of PTSD symptoms than the degree of exposure to fire or the amount of losses suffered by the family.

Conclusion
When parents demonstrate resilience and model positive behaviour in times of stress, this becomes a factor of resilience in children.

RESEARCH   Betancourt *et al* (2013)—resilience in war-affected youth of Sierra Leone

Essential understanding
✪ *All children are resilient in some way.*

Aim
To investigate resilience among children who have been exposed to severely traumatizing experiences.

Participants
War-affected youths in Sierra Leone (aged 10–17 at baseline). Most of the participants were former child soldiers.

Method and procedure
Longitudinal study (six years); three interviews at different points of time.

Results
Researchers identified four groups of participants, grouped by how they developed symptoms of depression and anxiety over time.

1. Maintaining a low level of depression and anxiety throughout the study period (41%)
2. Improving over time (48%)
3. Stable reporting of severe difficulties (5%)
4. Worsening of symptoms (6%).

Interviews also helped researchers identify the major causes of continuing symptoms of anxiety and depression:
– loss of a caregiver
– family neglect
– community stigma (related to the child's past as a soldier).

Conclusion
Even after the most traumatic experiences it was possible for many children to recover from trauma, at least partially. However, lack of social support depletes resilience. Therefore it is important to give appropriate care and social support to children who have suffered traumatic experiences.

7.3.3 Effects of poverty on development

– **Family income**—the purely financial component of poverty
– **Family stress model**—the theoretical approach that sees parameters of parent-child interaction (such as communication styles) as the major pathway of poverty
– **Mediating variable**—a variable that enhances or reduces the influence of one variable (the predictor) on another (the outcome); if A affects B and B affects C, then B is the mediating variable between A and C
– **Outcome of poverty**—developmental consequence of living under conditions of poverty

– **Parental investment model**—the theoretical approach that sees material aspects of the home environment (such as availability of educational resources) as the major pathway of poverty
– **Pathway of poverty**—a mediating variable between family income and developmental outcomes of poverty
– **Poverty**—the state of having little or no means of basic support; it is a multifaceted phenomenon including a range of aspects

ESSENTIAL UNDERSTANDING

Outcomes and pathways of poverty

There is no doubt that poverty has a negative effect on development. A number of follow-up questions are of research interest. For example, are the effects of poverty reversible? Can the effect of family income be isolated from other associated variables? Is the timing of poverty episodes important? See "**Effects of poverty on development: research questions**".

Brooks-Gunn and Duncan (1997) made a distinction between outcomes of poverty and pathways of poverty. Outcomes of poverty are the eventual consequences of living in the state of poverty. Pathways of poverty are mediating variables, that is, variables that get affected by the state of poverty and that, in their turn, affect the development of children. See "**Outcomes of poverty**" and "**Pathways of poverty**".

There has been debate regarding which of the pathways of poverty are most significant in predicting the development of children. The two conflicting explanations are the family stress model and the parental investment model. The former stresses patterns of parent-child interaction while the latter stresses material goods and the presence of educational opportunities (Barajas, Philipsen and Brooks-Gunn 2007). See "**Mediators between poverty and delayed development: the family stress model versus the parental investment model**".

Methods and research

Two methods can be used to isolate the effects of family income from all other potentially confounding variables associated with poverty: statistical separation of effects and natural longitudinal experiments. See "**Isolating effects of family income from associated variables**".

Dickerson and Popli (2016), using statistical separation of effects in a large longitudinal study, found that family income (as an isolated variable) affects cognitive development both directly and indirectly through parental investment. See **Dickerson and Popli (2016)**.

Costello et al (2003) conducted a natural longitudinal experiment and demonstrated that natural fluctuation of family income causes fluctuations in social development: externalizing behaviours were affected but internalizing behaviours were not. See **Costello et al (2003)**.

EFFECTS OF POVERTY ON DEVELOPMENT: RESEARCH QUESTIONS

Essential understanding

⭐ *There is little doubt that poverty negatively affects cognitive and social development, but there are several follow-up questions that are of research interest.*

- Is it poverty (that is, family income) that affects development, or some other factor that goes hand in hand with poverty? Examples of factors associated with poverty are quality of parenting, parental education, substance abuse in the family and criminal activities in the neighbourhood.
- Are the effects of poverty on cognitive and social development reversible?
- Is the timing of poverty episodes significant?

OUTCOMES OF POVERTY

Brooks-Gunn and Duncan (1997) summarized research on the key outcomes of poverty:

- physical health—poverty leads to malnourishment, low birth weight, stunted growth
- cognitive ability as measured by standardized tests
- school achievement
- emotional and behavioural outcomes—externalizing behaviours such as aggression or fighting and internalizing behaviours such as depression or anxiety.

Note that "poverty" in this case means a combination of family income and all associated variables (such as parenting and parental education).

PATHWAYS OF POVERTY

Brooks-Gunn and Duncan (1997) also described the common mechanisms (pathways) through which poverty operates. Unlike outcomes, pathways are intermediate factors that are affected by poverty and that in turn affect development. The factors are:

- nutrition
- the home environment (opportunities for learning, the physical condition of the home, amount of time parents can afford to spend with the child)
- parental interactions with children (this emphasizes the qualitative side of parenting such as parenting styles, communication strategies, punishment practices)
- parental mental health (statistically, parents with a low socio-economic status have higher prevalence of mental health issues, which may affect children's behaviour as well)
- neighbourhood conditions (low-income families live in poor neighbourhoods with high levels of crime and unemployment, and poor schooling).

There is a debate regarding which of the pathways of poverty are the deciding factors. There are two notable sides in this debate (Barajas, Philipsen and Brooks-Gunn 2007).

The family stress theory claims that the leading pathways of poverty are the ones associated with within-family interpersonal interactions, such as parenting styles, communication strategies and the amount of time spent with children.

The investment model claims that the most important pathways are the ones associated with material goods: nutrition, educational opportunities, enriched environments, exposure to educational experiences.

ISOLATING EFFECTS OF FAMILY INCOME FROM ASSOCIATED VARIABLES

Essential understanding

✪ *To isolate the effects of family income from other components of poverty, two methods are widely used: statistical separation of effects and natural longitudinal experiments.*

Statistical separation of effects is the use of complex statistical methods to mathematically isolate the effect of one variable. This is achieved by analysing patterns of correlations between multiple variables. The idea can be illustrated with a Venn diagram.

Suppose you have measured three variables: A (family income), B (parental education) and C (cognitive development of the child), and you want to find out the "pure" effect of family income on cognitive development over and above the effect of parental education. If you just measure the correlation between A and C, this will be confounded by area 1. You need to subtract area 1 and estimate area 2. This is mathematically possible. Using statistical separation of effects, you can also use multiple variables at the same time.

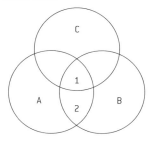

Figure 7.12 Venn diagram showing the statistical separation of effects

Natural longitudinal experiments are research studies that investigate how a naturally occurring fluctuation of family income affects the development of children. They are called natural because it is "the nature" that manipulates the independent variable. If poverty really affects development, we should observe some correspondence between fluctuations in family income and fluctuations in rates of children's development.

RESEARCH   Dickerson and Popli (2016)—the UK Millennium Cohort Study

Essential understanding

- *Poverty (as a complex of associated variables) has a negative effect on cognitive development.*
- *Family income (as an isolated variable) has both direct and indirect effects on cognitive development.*
- *The indirect effect of family income is through parental investment.*

Aim

To investigate correlations between multiple variables associated with poverty and cognitive development.

Participants

The researchers used data from the UK Millennium Cohort Study, a sample of 19,000 children born in the UK in 2000 or 2001.

Method

Longitudinal study. Interviews and standardized cognitive tests were used to collect data. Statistical separation of effects was used to analyse the collected data.

Procedure

The study was conducted in "sweeps": all participants were tested at the same points of time. Four such sweeps were used in the study: when participants were 9 months old, 3 years old, 5 years old and 7 years old. Information at each sweep was collected in face-to-face interviews with the parents. Standardized cognitive tests were also used at each sweep to assess cognitive development of the child.

Results

Before statistical separation of effects:

- children who experienced poverty had lower scores on standardized cognitive tests
- the timing of poverty episodes was important—the most recent episodes of poverty had the least impact, whereas being born into poverty had the largest impact on cognitive development.

After statistical separation of effects:

- family income had an effect on cognitive test scores over and above what could be explained by other variables associated with poverty (this shows the direct effect of family income on cognitive development)
- at the same time, a number of pathways were significant in predicting cognitive development (this shows the indirect effect of family income). These pathways were more in line with the parental investment model than

the family stress model, that is, providing educational opportunities and resources was shown to be more important than interpersonal interaction between parents and children.

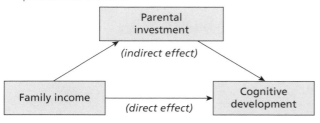

Figure 7.13 Direct and indirect effects of family income

Conclusion

- Poverty has a detrimental effect on the cognitive development of children. The earlier it occurs, the stronger the effect.
- Family income (isolated from other variables) affects cognitive development both directly and indirectly.
- The indirect effect is better explained by the parental investment model than the family stress model.

| RESEARCH | Costello *et al* (2003)—Great Smoky Mountains study |

Essential understanding

✪ *Family income affects externalizing behaviours of children in the family but not internalizing behaviours (over and above other family characteristics associated with poverty).*

Aim

To investigate the effects of the changing poverty status of the family on social development of children.

Participants

1,500 rural children aged 9–13 years. One quarter of the sample were Native American, the rest predominantly white American.

Method

Natural longitudinal experiment.

Procedure

Children were given annual psychiatric assessments over eight years. The naturally occurring variable was a casino that opened on the Indian reservation. This happened halfway through the study and it gave a natural boost to family incomes in every Native American family. The increase of income changed the poverty status of some of the Native American families. The family groups were:

- the ex-poor group (14%)—used to be poor but moved out of poverty
- the persistently poor group (53%)—used to be poor and remained poor
- the never poor group (32%).

Psychiatric symptoms were compared in these three groups of participants before and after the casino opening.

Results

Before the casino opened, the poor children (the first two groups) had more psychiatric symptoms than the never poor group.

After the casino opened, the psychiatric symptoms of the ex-poor children dropped to the level of never poor children.

However, this was only true for externalizing behaviours (such as aggression or conduct disorder). Internalizing behaviours (such as anxiety and depression) were not affected.

Levels of psychiatric symptoms among the persistently poor remained high.

Group	Incidence of externalizing behaviours	
	Before casino	**After casino**
Ex-poor (14%)	High	Low
Persistently poor (53%)	High	High
Never poor (32%)	Low	Low

Table 7.5

Conclusion

Since family characteristics (such as patterns of parent-child interaction or parental mental health) did not change during the course of the study, the observed reduction of externalizing symptoms may be attributed to the changing financial status. We may conclude that family income has an effect on social development of children over and above the other associated variables.

Topics

EXAM TIP

Research and ethics are two overarching themes in the IB psychology syllabus. This means that exam questions in paper 1 and paper 2 may refer to research methods or ethical considerations as they apply to a particular topic. Since psychology is an empirical discipline in which knowledge is based on research with living human and non-human subjects, knowledge of both research methodology and ethics is essential for you to understand each and every topic.

In addition, HL students will be formally assessed on research methods and ethics in paper 3. In this paper you will be given a stimulus material describing a research study. The study may be quantitative, qualitative or a mix of the two. You will be asked the following questions based on this stimulus material.

Question 1 (consists of three compulsory sub-questions)
1. Identify the research method used and outline two characteristics of the method. [3 marks]
2. Describe the sampling method used in the study. [3 marks]
3. Suggest an alternative or additional research method giving one reason for your choice. [3 marks]

Question 2 (consists of one of the following questions)
1. Describe the ethical considerations that were applied in the study and explain if further ethical considerations could be applied. [6 marks]
2. Describe the ethical considerations in reporting the results and explain additional ethical considerations that could be taken into account when applying the findings of the study. [6 marks]

Question 3 (consists of one of the following questions)
1. Discuss the possibility of generalizing/transferring the findings of the study. [9 marks]
2. Discuss how a researcher could ensure that the results of the study are credible. [9 marks]
3. Discuss how the researcher in the study could avoid bias. [9 marks]

(From the Diploma Programme *Psychology guide*)

The total number of marks for this paper is 24.

In this unit we will cover quantitative and qualitative methods of research in psychology as well as the overarching concepts of sampling, generalizability, credibility and bias. This knowledge can be used by all students to understand and critically evaluate research in all topics of the syllabus, and by HL students to answer question 1 and question 3 in paper 3.

8.1 Quantitative and qualitative research: Comparison

Parameter	Quantitative	Qualitative
Aim	Nomothetic approach: derive universally applicable rules. These rules may be applied to the behaviour of large groups of individuals.	Idiographic approach: in-depth understanding of a particular case or phenomenon. Obtained knowledge is not a universal law, but it is deeper (richer) in the sense that a particular case is understood more holistically.
Focus	Behavioural manifestations (operationalizations)	Human experiences, interpretations, meanings
Data	Numbers	Texts
Objectivity	More objective (the researcher is eliminated from the studied reality).	More subjective (the researcher is included in the studied reality). The researcher is an integral part of the procedure and a "tool of measurement".
Types	Experiment Quasi-experiment Correlational study	Observation Interview Focus group Case study

Table 8.1

8.2 Overarching concepts: Sampling, credibility, generalizability and bias

THE CONCEPTS

Four overarching concepts are used to describe a research study and make a judgment about its quality. The concepts are applicable to all research methods, but they can be approached very differently by qualitative and quantitative researchers. Sometimes different sets of terms may be used in each approach to refer to the same concept. For example, the idea of "credibility" may be referred to as "internal validity" in experimental research and "trustworthiness" in qualitative studies.

For this reason, it is important to clearly understand both the meaning of the four overarching concepts and the way they are manifested in experimental, correlational and qualitative research.

– A sample is the group of individuals taking part in the research study. **Sampling** is the process of recruiting these individuals for participation.

– **Credibility** is the extent to which results of the study can be trusted to reflect the reality. A study is credible when we have reasons to believe that its findings are true.

– **Bias** is the flipside of credibility. It characterizes various distortions introduced to the findings by the researcher, the research procedure, mistakes in the process of measurement, unnatural behaviour of participants, and so on.

– **Generalizability** is the extent to which the results of the study can be applied beyond the sample and the settings used in the study itself. The way qualitative and quantitative researchers approach generalizability is distinctly different.

Table 8.2 is an overview of the main concepts used to characterize sampling, generalizability, credibility and bias in experimental, correlational and qualitative research. The rest of this unit will be devoted to unpacking the ideas in this table.

EXAM TIP

The research study in the stimulus material in paper 3 may be quantitative, qualitative or a mix of the two. That is why you need to be able to identify the research method that was used and select terminology appropriate to that method. For example, while characterizing the "credibility" of a qualitative research study, it would be incorrect to use the term "internal validity" because that is only applicable in experimental research.

Overarching concepts	Quantitative research		Qualitative research
	Experimental studies	**Correlational studies**	
Sampling	Random sampling Stratified sampling Self-selected sampling Opportunity sampling	Same as experimental studies	Quota sampling Purposive sampling Theoretical sampling Snowball sampling Convenience sampling
Generalizability	External validity – Ecological validity – Population validity Construct validity	Population validity Construct validity	Sample-to-population generalization Case-to-case generalization Theoretical generalization
Credibility	Internal validity Ways to improve this: controlling confounding variables (eliminating or keeping constant in all conditions)	Credibility Ways to improve this: using reliable ways to measure the variables, avoiding biases in interpreting the results	Credibility/trustworthiness Ways to improve this: triangulation, establishing a rapport, iterative questioning, reflexivity, credibility checks, thick descriptions
Bias	Threats to internal validity: – selection – history – maturation – testing effect – instrumentation – regression to the mean – experimental mortality – experimenter bias – demand characteristics	On the level of measurement of variables: depends on the method of measurement On the level of interpretation of findings: – curvilinear relationships – the third variable problem – spurious correlations	Participant bias: – acquiescence – social desirability – dominant respondent – sensitivity Researcher bias: – confirmation bias – leading question bias – question order bias – sampling bias – biased reporting

Table 8.2 Overarching concepts

8.3 The experiment

CONSTRUCTS AND VARIABLES

Quantitative research operates with **variables**. A variable is any characteristic that is objectively registered and quantified. In relation to this, it is important to make the distinction between constructs and operationalizations.

– A **construct** is any theoretically defined variable, for example, violence, attraction, memory, anxiety.

– Constructs need to be **operationalized**. Operationalizing a construct means expressing it in terms

of observable behaviour. For example, anxiety can be operationalized as the amount of fidgeting in a chair while waiting for something important; the level of cortisol in the bloodstream; a self-report score on an anxiety questionnaire, and so on. A good operationalization will capture the essence of the construct and at the same time be clearly measurable.

VARIABLES IN THE EXPERIMENT

The simplest experiment includes one **independent variable (IV)** and one **dependent variable (DV)**, while the other potentially important variables are controlled.

The independent variable is the variable that is manipulated by the experimenter. The dependent variable changes as a result of this manipulation. We need to ensure that it is the change in the IV that causes the change in the DV, and for this reason we need to control the potential influences

of other variables. These other variables that can interfere in the relationship between the IV and the DV are called **confounding variables**.

For example, a researcher is conducting a simple experiment to see if word length affects short-term memory of word lists. Her hypothesis is that lists of shorter words will be easier to recall than lists of longer words. Her IV is word length and her dependent variable is memory recall. To test the hypothesis, she does the following.

Manipulate the IV	She splits her participants into two groups. One group is given a list consisting of one-syllable words (such as "rice"). Another group is given a list consisting of four-syllable words (such as "coincidence").
Measure the DV	After hearing the list of words, participants are required to recall it in the right order, and the researcher measures how many words they recalled correctly.
Control confounding variables	To ensure that any differences between the two groups can be attributed to the IV (and nothing else), researchers ensure that potential confounding variables are either eliminated or kept constant in both groups. – One confounding variable that may affect the results is participants' familiarity with the words. Researchers eliminate it by ensuring that all participants are perfectly familiar with all words: they exclude participants whose native language is not English and they use words commonly used in everyday language. – Another variable that may affect the results is background noise in the room. One cannot eliminate it entirely, but researchers make sure that both groups are tested in the same room and at the same time of the day. If noise is the same in both groups, it will affect them equally, which will not compromise the comparison.
Analyse the results	Compare the DV in the two groups. If the number of words correctly recalled in the long-word group is significantly smaller than the number of words correctly recalled in the short-word group, the experimental hypothesis will be supported.

Table 8.3

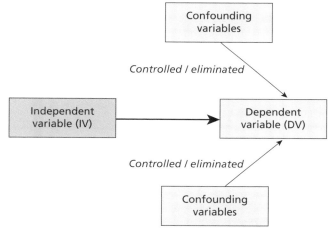

Figure 8.1 A simple experiment

SAMPLING IN QUANTITATIVE RESEARCH

The **target population** is the group of people to which the findings of the study are expected to be generalized.

The **sample** is the group of people that take part in the experiment. It is a sub-set of the target population.

We need to be sure that results of quantitative research can be generalized from the sample to the target population. For this to be possible, the sample must be **representative** of the target population. A sample is said to be representative if it reflects all of the essential characteristics of the target population.

SAMPLING TECHNIQUES IN QUANTITATIVE RESEARCH

Several sampling techniques can be used in quantitative research. The choice depends on the aim of the research, available resources and the nature of the target population.

Sampling technique	Explanation	Advantages	Disadvantages
Random sampling	Create a list of all members of the target population and randomly select a sub-set. This way every member of the target population has an equal chance of becoming part of the sample.	If the sample size is sufficient, researchers may be certain that even unexpected characteristics are fairly represented in the sample.	It is practically impossible to carry out truly random sampling, for example, the target population might be geographically dispersed.
Stratified sampling	First decide on the list of essential characteristics of the population that the sample has to reflect (such as age, occupation, language and so on). Then study the distribution of these characteristics in the target population (for example, age distribution). Then recruit participants randomly, but in a way that keeps the same proportions in the sample as has been observed in the target population.	Allows researchers to control representativeness of some key characteristics without relying on chance. Useful when the researcher is certain about which characteristics are essential and when the sample sizes are not large.	Requires more knowledge about characteristics of the target population; harder to implement.
Convenience (opportunity) sampling	Recruiting participants that are easily available, for example, undergraduate psychology students who participate in psychological research to earn credit as part of the course.	Useful when financial resources are limited. In some studies, there may be reasons to believe that people are not that different. For example, some basic properties of memory or sense perception may be common for most people and are independent of culture, education or other characteristics. Also useful when generalization of findings is not the primary purpose of the study (for example, in a pilot research study).	Generalization from opportunity samples is very limited because of the sampling bias. For example, psychology students are typically familiar with experimental procedures and sometimes can even guess the aim of the study, which does not apply to the wider population.
Self-selected sampling	Recruiting volunteers, for example, through newspaper advertisements. Anyone who wants to participate is included in the sample.	A quick and easy method to recruit participants while at the same time having wide coverage (for example, many different people read newspapers).	Representativeness and generalization are limited. A typical volunteer is more motivated than the average participant from a bigger population, and volunteers could also pursue monetary incentives for their participation.

Table 8.4

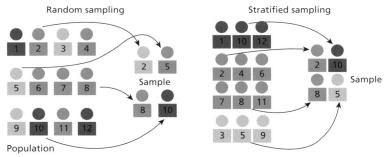

Figure 8.2 Random and stratified sampling

EXAM TIP

One of the sub-questions in question 1 in paper 3 asks: "Describe the sampling method used in the study". If you have identified the research study as quantitative (either an experiment or a correlational study), then you will need to determine which of the sampling strategies were used (random, stratified, convenience, self-selected) and describe how exactly the sampling strategy was implemented.

The choice of sampling strategy also links to the idea of generalization, so if the research study in the stimulus material is quantitative, you can also use this information in answering the question "Discuss the possibility of generalizing/transferring the findings of the study". However, note that the concept of generalizability is not limited to generalizing from the sample to the population (see Table 8.2 near the beginning of this unit). There are three aspects of generalizability in quantitative research: population validity, ecological validity, construct validity.

EXPERIMENTAL DESIGNS

There are three types of experimental design, depending on how the independent variable is manipulated:

- independent measures
- matched pairs
- repeated measures.

INDEPENDENT MEASURES DESIGN

In the independent measures design, the independent variable is manipulated by randomly allocating participants into different groups.

The rationale behind random group allocation is that all potential confounding variables cancel each other out.

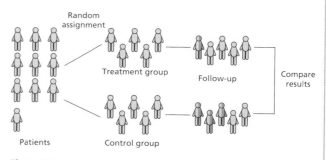

Figure 8.3 Independent measures design

MATCHED PAIRS DESIGN

Matched pairs design is similar to independent measures, but instead of completely random allocation, researchers use **matching** to form the groups.

Suppose, for example, that we need two groups of participants and it is especially important to us that they are equivalent in terms of age. We could randomly allocate them into groups and hope that random allocation will result in similar age distributions, but if the groups are not large, chances are that random allocation will create bias, and we don't want to take the chance of that happening.

First all participants of the study are assessed on the **matching variable** (we gather information on the participants' ages). Then all participants are ranked according to the matching variable and allocated randomly into groups pairwise as we move along the ranks. In the example, the researcher will take the two youngest participants and allocate them randomly into the groups, then take the next two youngest participants

and allocate them, and carry on in this way until participants of all ages have been allocated. This way the researcher may be sure that the two groups are equivalent in terms of age, while all other characteristics are kept random.

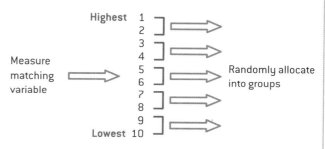

Figure 8.4 Matched pairs design

REPEATED MEASURES DESIGN

The same group of participants is exposed to two (or more) conditions and the conditions are compared. This way participants are compared to themselves, so these designs are also called "within-subject" designs.

An example would be a simple experiment that compares ability to recall lists of words when there is background music versus when there is no background music. In this study participants may first be given a list of words in silence. After they hear the list and recall it, another (but similar) list of words is given with background music. The number of words correctly recalled will then be compared in the music and no-music conditions.

An inherent limitation of the repeated measures design is the order effect. The **order effect** occurs when results of the second trial are affected by the fact of participation in the first trial. This may be due to either practice or fatigue.

To ensure that order effects are controlled, the researcher needs to use **counterbalancing**. In this technique the researcher randomly forms two groups of participants, and the order of trials in the group is reversed, for example,

"music" then "no music" in the first group, and "no music" then "music" in the second group. Note that comparison is still made between conditions, not between groups of participants.

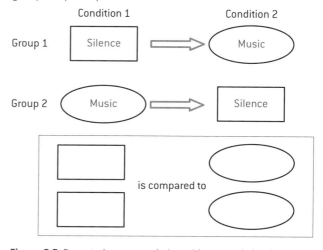

Figure 8.5 Repeated measures design with counterbalancing

Design	Advantages	Disadvantages	How to overcome the disadvantages
Independent measures	Can have multiple groups. Participants only take part in one condition, so there are no order effects. For the same reason it is more difficult for participants to figure out the true aim of the study.	Participant variability: since these are different people, it is likely that participants in the groups will not be completely equivalent at the start of the study (comparing apples and oranges).	When allocation into groups is random and groups are large enough, it is likely that pre-existing individual differences will cancel each other out and the groups on average will be equivalent.
Matched pairs	Useful when the researcher is particularly careful about certain confounding variables and wants to keep them constant in all groups. Useful when the sample size is not large and there is a chance that random allocation will end up producing groups that are not equivalent.	More difficult to implement because matching variables need to be measured first. Theory-driven: the researcher needs to know what variables are particularly likely to be confounding.	Keeping the experiment simple: matching is easier to implement when there is one matching variable and two groups.
Repeated measures	Participant variability is not a problem because participants are compared to themselves. This also means that sample sizes can be smaller (there is less "noise" in the data).	Order effects: fatigue or practice. Participants take part in more than one condition, which increases the chances that they will figure out the true aim of the study.	Counterbalancing, however, is difficult when there are many conditions (for example, counterbalancing of three conditions requires six groups of participants: ABC, ACB, BAC, BCA, CAB, CBA).

Table 8.5 Advantages and disadvantages of experimental designs

CREDIBILITY AND GENERALIZABILITY IN THE EXPERIMENT: TYPES OF VALIDITY

The quality of experiments is characterized by their construct, internal and external validity. Internal validity relates to credibility of the experiment, while external and construct validity characterize generalizability of results (see Table 8.2 near the start of this unit).

Construct validity is a characteristic of the quality of operationalizations. Operationalizations express constructs in terms of observable behaviour. For example, anger is a construct and a response to the question "How angry are you at the moment?" on a scale from 1 to 5 is its operationalization. Moving from an operationalization to a construct is always a bit of a leap. The construct validity of an experiment is high if this leap is justified and if the operationalization provides sufficient coverage of the construct. In this sense, construct validity relates to the overarching concept of generalizability—it characterizes generalizability of findings to the theory.

External validity is a characteristic of generalizability of findings to other people and other situations. There are two types of external validity.

– **Population validity** refers to the extent to which findings can be generalized from the sample to the target population. It depends on how representative the sample is.

– **Ecological validity** refers to the extent to which findings can be generalized from the experiment to other settings or situations. It depends on how artificial the experimental procedure is. In laboratory experiments participants often find themselves in situations that do not normally occur in their daily lives, and this can change their behaviour, making it less natural. The more closely the experimental procedure approximates real-life situations, the higher the ecological validity of the experiment.

Internal validity is a characteristic of the methodological quality of an experiment. In terms of the overarching concepts, it relates to the credibility of the research study. Internal validity is high when confounding variables have been controlled and we are quite certain that it was the change in the IV (not something else) that caused the change in the DV. In other words, internal validity links directly to bias—the less bias, the higher the internal validity of the experiment.

Usually there is an inverse relationship between internal validity and ecological validity.

BIAS IN THE EXPERIMENT: THREATS TO INTERNAL VALIDITY

Bias in experimental research comes in the form of confounding variables that can reduce internal validity. There are several common sources of threat to internal validity (based on Campbell 1969).

Threat to internal validity	Explanation	How it can be counteracted
Selection	For some reason groups are not entirely equivalent at the start of the experiment, and the way in which they differ affects the relationship between the IV and the DV (like comparing apples and oranges).	Random allocation into groups; sufficiently large group sizes
History	Outside events that happen to participants in the course of the experiment. It is especially a problem in lengthy experiments where the DV is measured sometime after the onset of the study.	Standardize experimental procedures as much as possible in all groups to avoid history effects created during the experiment itself.

Maturation	The natural changes that participants go through in the course of the experiment, such as fatigue or (if the procedure is extended in time) growth.	Having a control group. If we can assume that the rates of maturation are the same in both groups, the comparison will not be affected.
Testing effect	The first measurement of the DV may affect the second (and subsequent) measurements. Sometimes in independent measures designs the DV is measured twice. For example, if you assess the effectiveness of a training session to reduce anxiety, you could use an anxiety questionnaire both before and after the training. In repeated measures designs testing effect is a special case of order effects.	In independent measures designs there must be a control group, the same test and retest, but no experimental manipulation. In repeated measures designs, counterbalancing must be used.
Instrumentation	Occurs when the instrument measuring the DV changes slightly between measurements, compromising standardization of the measurement process. In psychology the "instrument of measurement" is often a human observer. For example, if observations are happening throughout the day, observers may grow tired and miss more important details by the end of the day.	Standardize measurement conditions as much as possible across all comparison groups and all observers.
Regression to the mean	This becomes a threat when the initial score on the DV is extreme (either very low or very high). For example, if you are assessing the effectiveness of a training session to reduce anxiety and your participants are a group of people whose initial anxiety score is very high, these participants will naturally become less anxious even if no session is conducted with them.	A control group with the same starting score on the DV, but no experimental manipulation.
Experimental mortality	Occurs when some participants drop out of the experiment. It only becomes a problem when the rate of dropping out is not the same in every experimental condition.	Whenever possible, design experimental conditions in such a way that participants do not feel discomfort causing them to withdraw from participation.
Demand characteristics	Occurs when participants understand the true aim of the experiment and alter their behaviour (intentionally or unintentionally) because of that. Demand characteristics are a bigger problem in repeated measures designs because participants take part in more than one condition.	Deception to conceal the true aim of the study (however, ethical considerations arise). Post-experimental questionnaires to find out to what extent participants were able to guess the true aim of the study.
Experimenter bias	Occurs when the researcher unintentionally influences participants' behaviour and the results of the study.	Using the **double-blind design** where neither the participants nor the experimenter knows who has been assigned to what condition.

Table 8.6 Threats to internal validity

EXAM TIP

If you identified the stimulus in paper 3 as an experiment, this is how you can approach answering some of the questions:

"Discuss the possibility of generalizing/transferring the findings of the study." Write about generalization to the theory (construct validity), to other settings (ecological validity) and to other people (population validity).

"Discuss how a researcher could ensure that the results of the study are credible." Write about internal validity and ways to avoid bias in experimental research.

Type	Explanation
True experiment	Allocation into experimental groups is done randomly. Researchers can assume that the IV is the only difference between the groups. This allows researchers to interpret results of the study as a cause–effect relationship (the IV influences the DV).
Quasi-experiment	Allocation into groups is done on the basis of pre-existing differences, for example, age, gender, cultural background, education, occupation. Researchers cannot be sure that the groups are equivalent in all other characteristics. As a result, because the IV is not manipulated by the researcher, cause–effect inferences cannot be made. In the way they are designed, quasi-experiments resemble experiments (because they involve a comparison of groups). However, from the point of view of the possible inferences, they are essentially correlational studies.
Laboratory experiment	Conducted in highly controlled, artificial conditions. Since confounding variables are better controlled this way, it increases internal validity but compromises ecological validity.
Field experiment	Conducted in real-life settings. The researcher manipulates the IV, but since participants are in their natural setting many confounding variables cannot be controlled. This increases ecological validity and decreases internal validity.

Natural experiment	Conducted in the participants' natural environments. In addition to that, the IV is not manipulated by the researcher but occurs naturally. For example, when television is introduced on a remote island for the first time, that is a naturally occurring variable. Another example is a smoking ban that was introduced in a city for a period of six months and then lifted. Just like with field experiments, the advantage of natural experiments is ecological validity and the disadvantage is internal validity due to a large number of confounding variables that are impossible to control. Another advantage of natural experiments is that they can be used when it is unethical to manipulate the IV.

Table 8.7 Special types of experiments

Type of experiment	Independent variable	Settings	Can we infer causation?
True laboratory experiment	Manipulated by the researcher	Laboratory	Yes
True field experiment	Manipulated by the researcher	Real-life	Yes (but there may be confounding variables)
Natural experiment	Manipulated by the nature	Real-life	Strictly speaking no
Quasi-experiment	Not manipulated; pre-existing difference	Laboratory or real-life	No

Table 8.8 Comparison of types of experiments

8.4 Correlational studies

WHAT IS A CORRELATION?

In correlational studies no variable is manipulated by the researcher, therefore cause–effect inferences cannot be made. Two or more variables are measured and the relationship between them is mathematically quantified.

A correlation is a measure of linear relationship between two variables. A correlation coefficient can vary from -1 to +1.
- A negative correlation means that there is an inverse relationship between two variables: the higher A, the lower B.
- A positive correlation means a direct relationship: the higher A, the higher B.

- A correlation close to zero means that there is no relationship between the two variables.

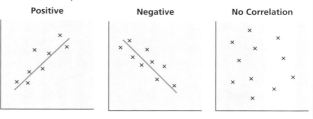

Figure 8.6 Correlations

EFFECT SIZE AND STATISTICAL SIGNIFICANCE

Just like with any other inferential statistical test, a correlation may be characterized by two parameters: effect size and statistical significance.

The **effect size** is the absolute value of the correlation coefficient (a number from 0 to 1). It shows how large the correlation is. Interpretation boundaries acceptable in social sciences are shown in the table below (based on Cohen 1988).

Correlation coefficient effect size (r)	Interpretation
Less than 0.10	Negligible
0.10–0.29	Small
0.30–0.49	Medium
0.50 and larger	Large

Table 8.9

Statistical significance shows the likelihood that a correlation of this size has been obtained by chance. If this likelihood is less than 5%, the correlation is accepted as statistically significant. There are conventional cut-off points used in interpreting statistical significance.

The probability that the result is due to random chance	Notation	Interpretation
More than 5%	p = n.s.	Result is non-significant
Less than 5%	p < .05	Result is statistically significant (reliably different from zero)
Less than 1%	p = < .01	Result is very significant
Less than 0.1%	p = < .001	Result is highly significant

Table 8.10

When interpreting correlations, one needs to take into account both the effect size and the level of statistical significance. If a correlation is statistically significant, it does not mean that it is large, because in large samples even small correlations can be significant (reliably different from zero). Researchers are looking for statistically significant correlations with large effect sizes.

Remember that cause–effect inferences cannot be made from correlational studies.

CREDIBILITY AND BIAS IN CORRELATIONAL RESEARCH

Bias in correlational research can occur on the level of variable measurement and interpretation of findings. The less bias there is in a correlational research study, the more credible it is. Credibility in correlational research is the same idea as internal validity in experimental research; however, the term "internal validity" is not used in correlational studies.

BIAS ON THE LEVEL OF VARIABLE MEASUREMENT

Depending on the method used to measure the variables, bias may be inherent in the measurement procedure. This bias is not specific to correlational research and will occur in any other research study using the same variable measured in the same way. For example, if observation is used to measure the variables, the researcher needs to be aware of all the biases inherent in observation. If questionnaires are used, biases inherent in questionnaires become an issue.

BIAS ON THE LEVEL OF INTERPRETATION OF FINDINGS

Source of bias in interpretation of findings	Explanation	How bias can be counteracted
Curvilinear relationships between variables	In calculating the correlation between two variables, we assume that the relationship between them is linear. Mathematically the formula of a correlation coefficient is a formula of a straight line. However, curvilinear relationships cannot be captured in a standard correlation coefficient.	If suspected, curvilinear relationships should be investigated graphically.
The third variable problem	There is always a possibility that a third variable exists that correlates both with A and B and explains the correlation between them. If you only measure A and B, you will observe a correlation between them, but it does not mean that they are related directly.	Consider potential "third variables" in advance and include them in the research study to explicitly investigate the links between A, B and these "third variables".
Spurious correlations	Spurious correlations are correlations obtained by chance. They become an issue if the research study includes multiple variables and computes multiple correlations between them. If you measure 100 correlations, there is a chance that a small number of them will be significant, even if in reality the variables are not related.	Results of multiple correlations should be interpreted with caution. Effect sizes need to be considered together with the level of statistical significance.

Table 8.11

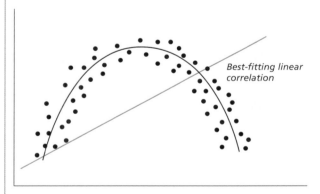

Best-fitting linear correlation

Figure 8.7 Curvilinear relationship

SAMPLING AND GENERALIZABILITY IN CORRELATIONAL STUDIES

Sampling strategies in correlational and experimental research are the same: random, stratified, opportunity, self-selected.

Generalizability depends on how representative the sample is of the target population. In its turn, representativeness of the sample depends on the sampling strategy. Random and stratified samples tend to be more representative than opportunity and self-selected samples. This aspect of generalizability is similar to the idea of population validity in experimental research.

Another aspect of generalizability is construct validity—the extent to which the way variables are measured (operationalized) captures the theoretical nature of the construct. This is also similar to experimental research (see Table 8.2 near the start of this unit).

8.5 Qualitative research

CREDIBILITY IN QUALITATIVE RESEARCH

Credibility in qualitative research is the equivalent of internal validity in the experiment; however, the term "internal validity" cannot be used. For qualitative research two terms are used interchangeably to express this idea: "credibility" (the generic term) and "trustworthiness".

In experimental research credibility (internal validity) is a measure of the extent to which the experiment tests what it is intended to test. Similarly, in qualitative research credibility (trustworthiness) is related to the question "To what extent do the findings of the study reflect reality as it is?"

Measure to increase credibility	Explanation

Triangulation	Combining and comparing different approaches to collecting and interpreting data:
	  – **method triangulation**—combining different methods
	  – **data triangulation**—using data from a variety of accessible sources
	  – **researcher triangulation**—combining and comparing observations of different researchers
	  – **theory triangulation**—using multiple perspectives or theories to interpret the data.

Establishing a rapport	Building a relationship of trust with the participant, emphasizing the necessity to be honest, the right to withdraw and the fact that there are no good or bad answers. All this prevents participants from altering their behaviour in the presence of the researcher.
Iterative questioning	Returning to the topic later in the process of interaction with the participant and rephrasing the question. This allows a deeper investigation of sensitive topics.

Reflexivity	Taking into account the possibility that the researcher's own biases may be affecting the results of the study. Reflexivity does not necessarily allow researchers to avoid bias, but it allows them to identify findings that may have been affected by bias. There are two types of reflexivity:
	  – **epistemological reflexivity**—taking into account strengths and limitations of the methods used to collect data
	  – **personal reflexivity**—taking into account personal beliefs and expectations of the researcher that might have resulted in bias.

Credibility checks	Checking accuracy of data by asking participants themselves to read transcripts of interviews or field notes of observations and confirm that the notes/transcripts reflect correctly what the participants said or did.
Thick descriptions (rich descriptions)	Describing the observed behaviour in sufficient detail so that it can be understood holistically and in context. Contextual details should be sufficient to make the description meaningful to an outsider who never observed this behaviour first-hand.

Table 8.12 Measures to ensure credibility in qualitative research

BIAS IN QUALITATIVE RESEARCH

Sources of bias in qualitative research can be associated both with the researcher and the participant. Hence there are two groups of biases: participant bias and researcher bias.

Bias	Explanation	Ways to overcome the bias
Acquiescence bias	A tendency to give positive answers whatever the question. It may occur due to the participant's natural agreeableness or because the participant feels uncomfortable disagreeing with something in the research situation.	Researchers should be careful not to ask leading questions. Questions should be open-ended and neutral. It should be clear that there are no "right" or "wrong" answers.
Social desirability bias	Participants' tendency to respond or behave in a way that they think will make them more liked or more accepted. Intentionally or unintentionally, participants may be trying to produce a certain impression instead of behaving naturally, and this is especially true for sensitive topics.	Questions should be phrased in a non-judgmental way. Good rapport should be established. Questions can be asked about a third person (for example, "what do your friends think about...?").
Dominant respondent bias	Occurs in a group interview setting when one of the participants influences the behaviour of the others. Other participants may be intimidated by such people or feel like they will be compared to the dominant respondent.	Researchers should be trained to keep dominant respondents in check and try to provide everyone with equal opportunities to speak.
Sensitivity bias	A tendency of participants to answer regular questions honestly but distort their responses to questions on sensitive topics.	Building a good rapport and creating trust. Reinforcing ethical considerations such as confidentiality. Increasing the sensitivity of the questions gradually.

Table 8.13 Types of participant bias in qualitative research

Bias	Explanation	Ways to overcome the bias
Confirmation bias	Occurs when the researcher has a prior belief and uses the research (intentionally or unintentionally) to confirm this belief. It may manifest itself in such things as selectivity of attention or tiny differences in non-verbal behaviour that may influence the participants.	Strictly speaking, this is unavoidable because in qualitative research the human observer is an integral part of the process. However, this bias can be recognized and taken into account through the process of reflexivity.
Leading questions bias	Occurs when the questions in an interview are worded in a way that encourage a certain answer. For example, "When did you last have angry thoughts about your classmates?"	Interviewers should be trained in asking open-ended, neutral questions.
Question order bias	Occurs when the response to one question influences the participant's responses to subsequent questions.	This bias cannot be avoided but can be minimized by asking general questions before specific ones, positive questions before negative ones and behaviour-related questions before attitude-related questions.
Biased reporting	Occurs when some findings of the study are not equally represented in the research report.	Reflexivity. Also independent researchers may be asked to review the results (researcher triangulation).

Table 8.14 Types of researcher bias in qualitative research

EXAM TIP

If you have identified the research study in the stimulus material in paper 3 as a qualitative research study, the material above will be helpful to answer the following paper 3 questions:

- Discuss how a researcher could ensure that the results of the study are credible.
- Discuss how the researcher in the study could avoid bias.

Not all biases are applicable to all qualitative research studies. For example, the leading question bias is an issue in an interview but not in an observation.

TYPES OF GENERALIZABILITY IN QUALITATIVE RESEARCH

There are three types of generalization that can be applied both to qualitative and quantitative research (Firestone 1993).

Type of generalization	Explanation	Equivalent in quantitative research
Sample-to-population generalization	Applying the results of the study to a wider population. It depends on how representative the sample is. The best way to ensure representativeness is to sample randomly. However, since the nature of sampling in qualitative research is non-probabilistic, this type of generalization in qualitative research is a weak point.	Population validity
Theoretical generalization	Generalizing results of particular observations to a broader theory. Theory plays a much greater role in qualitative research. We can generalize to a broader theory if **data saturation** has been achieved. Data saturation is a point when further data does not add anything new to the already formulated conclusions and interpretations.	A similar idea is construct validity because it refers to the "leap" from observable operationalizations to the unobservable construct.
Case-to-case generalization (transferability)	Applying the findings of a study to a different group of people or a different setting or context. In qualitative research case-to-case generalization is the responsibility of both the researcher and the reader of the research report. The researcher ensures that thick descriptions are provided so that the reader has sufficient information. The reader decides whether or not the new context is similar enough to the one described in the report for the findings to be applicable.	Ecological validity (generalizing from experimental settings to real-life settings)

Table 8.15

TYPES OF SAMPLING IN QUALITATIVE RESEARCH

Sampling in qualitative research is non-probabilistic. It does not aim to ensure representativeness in relation to a target population. Instead, it aims to ensure that participants recruited for the study have the characteristics that are of interest to the research question.

Sampling strategy	Explanation	Notes
Quota sampling	It is decided before the start of the research how many people to include in the sample and which characteristics they should have. This decision is driven by the research question. Various recruitment strategies are then used to meet the quota. It is not important how people are sampled. What is important is that people in the sample have the characteristics that are of interest to the researcher.	This approach is completely theory-driven because all characteristics of the sample are defined in advance based on the research question.
Purposive sampling	Similar to quota sampling, but the sample size and the proportions of participants within the sample are not defined in advance. It is a more "relaxed" approach to sampling driven by the research question. You recruit whoever has the characteristics that are of interest to you.	Slightly less theory-driven approach in that target characteristics of participants are defined in advance, but the composition of the sample is not.
Theoretical sampling	A special type of purposive sampling that stops when data saturation is reached. Data saturation is the point when no further information is obtained from new participants added to the sample.	Whether information is "new" or not is defined on the basis of the background theory.
Snowball sampling	A small number of participants is invited and asked to invite people they know who also have the characteristics that are of interest to the researcher. It can be used in combination with other sampling strategies.	Convenient with groups of people who are difficult to reach (for example, gang members).
Convenience sampling	Using the sample that is readily available.	The most cost-efficient method, but also the most superficial.

Table 8.16

8.6 Specific qualitative research methods: Overview

SPECIFIC QUALITATIVE RESEARCH METHODS

We will consider the following examples of qualitative research methods:
- observation
- interview
- focus group
- case study.

OBSERVATION

Common reasons to choose observation include the following.
- The focus of the research is on how people interact in a natural setting. Most other methods would require placing the participant in an artificially created environment.
- Meaningful knowledge in a research area cannot be easily articulated, so observing behaviour is preferable to asking participants for their interpretations.
- Observation allows the researcher to gain first-hand experiences with the phenomenon under study.

The main limitation of observation is the fact that the researcher is strongly involved in the generation of data through selective attention and interpretation. However, this is the case with most qualitative research methods. It makes reflexivity especially important.

TYPES OF OBSERVATION

- **Laboratory versus naturalistic**. Naturalistic observation is carried out in real-life settings that have not been arranged for the purposes of the study. Laboratory observation is carried out in specially designed environments. Participants are invited to the laboratory and most often they know that they are participating in psychological research.

	Pros	Cons
Naturalistic observation	Sometimes it is the only option, for example when it is unethical to encourage a particular behaviour in a laboratory (such as violence). Participants' behaviour is not influenced by the artificiality of the research procedure.	It may be time-consuming because the behaviour of interest only occurs at certain times.
Laboratory observation	It is possible to recreate situations that do not frequently emerge in real life. It is possible to isolate the behaviour of interest more efficiently.	Artificiality of the procedure may influence the behaviour of participants.

Table 8.17

- **Overt versus covert**. Overt observation occurs when participants are aware of the fact that they are being observed. In covert observation the researcher does not inform the members of the group about the reasons for their presence.

	Pros	Cons
Overt observation	Participants give informed consent, so ethical guidelines are followed.	Participants' expectations may influence their behaviour.
Covert observation	Participants do not suspect that they are being observed, so they behave naturally.	Often participants do not consent to being observed, which raises ethical issues.

Table 8.18

- **Participant versus non-participant**. In participant observation the observer becomes part of the observed group.

	Pros	Cons
Participant observation	Allows the researcher to experience the phenomenon "from within" and gain important insights.	There is a risk that the observer will become too involved with the group and lose objectivity.
Non-participant observation	More impartial.	Some details about the observed group can only be understood from the perspective of a group member.

Table 8.19

- **Structured versus unstructured**. In structured observation information is recorded systematically and in a standardized way, for example using a checklist of observed behaviours prepared in advance. In unstructured observation there is no checklist and observers simply register whatever behaviour they find noteworthy.

	Pros	Cons
Structured observation	The procedure is standardized so one can use multiple observers in the same research study.	May be inflexible: certain aspects of behaviour that were not included in the checklist will be missed.
Unstructured observation	More flexible: the researcher is not limited by prior theoretical expectations.	Less structured means less comparable across researchers and across participants.

Table 8.20

INTERVIEW

Common reasons to choose the interview include the following.

- It may be the only way to get an insight into participants' subjective experiences and interpretations. Since these phenomena are unobservable, sometimes the only option is to rely on participants' verbal reports.
- Interviews can be used to understand participants' opinions, attitudes and the meanings they attach to certain events.
- The only way to understand how participants respond to past events (for example, trauma) is also only through self-report—you cannot recreate those experiences.
- In-depth individual interviews are useful when the topic is too sensitive for people to discuss in a group setting.

Interview data comes in the form of an audio or video recording that is subsequently converted to an interview **transcript**.

Type	Explanation	Pros	Cons
Structured interviews	Such interviews include a fixed list of questions that need to be asked in a fixed order.	Especially useful when the research project involves several interviewers and it is essential to ensure that they all conduct the interview in a standardized way.	Some participants may have unique circumstances or opinions that cannot be accommodated in a structured interview.
Semi-structured interviews	Such interviews do not specify an order or a particular list of questions. The interview guide is somewhat like a checklist: the researcher knows that certain questions must be asked, but there is also flexibility to ask additional follow-up questions.	It fits the natural flow of conversation better. Better suited for smaller research projects. More effective in studying the unique experiences of each participant.	Less comparability across researchers and participants.
Unstructured interviews	Such interviews are participant-driven. Every next question is determined by the interviewee's answer to the previous one.	Very effective for investigating unique cases or cases where no theoretical expectations exist that would inform the wording of the questions.	The most "qualitative" of all three types. More time-consuming and results are more difficult to analyse and interpret.

Table 8.21 Types of interview

FOCUS GROUP

The focus group is a special type of semi-structured interview that is conducted simultaneously with a small group of people (usually 6 to 10). The unique feature of this method is that participants are encouraged to interact with each other, for example, to agree and disagree with each other on certain statements. This creates group dynamics that are observed and analysed by the researcher. The interviewer in this case also acts as a facilitator who keeps the interaction focused on the research questions.

Common reasons to choose the focus group include the following.
- Participants interact with each other rather than the researcher. This makes their behaviour more natural. Moreover, interaction between participants may reveal more aspects than would be revealed in a one-on-one conversation with the researcher.
- It is easier to respond to sensitive questions when you are in a group.
- Multiple perspectives are discussed which allows researchers to get a more holistic understanding of the topic.

Limitations of focus groups include the following.
- Dominant respondents can disrupt group dynamics. Their assertiveness may affect the behaviour of other participants and distort their responses.
- It is more difficult to preserve confidentiality in a group.
- Focus groups are especially demanding in terms of sampling and creating interview transcripts.

CASE STUDY

A case study is an in-depth investigation of an individual or a group. Case studies often involve a variety of other methods (such as interviews, observations, questionnaires) to deepen the understanding of an individual or a group of interest.

Even though case studies are essentially a combination of other methods, they are considered as a separate research method for the following reasons.
- The individual or the group that is the object of a case study is unique in some way. The purpose is to gain deep understanding of this particular individual or group.
- Since the researcher is interested in this particular case, sampling is not an issue.
- There is less focus on generalizability of results.
- The case is studied very thoroughly, using a combination of different methods, and often longitudinally.

Common reasons to choose the case study include the following.
- Case studies are useful to investigate phenomena that cannot be studied otherwise, for example, a case of unique brain damage or long-term deprivation.
- Case studies can contradict established theories and in this way urge scientists to develop new ones.

Limitations of case studies include the following.
- Researcher bias and participant bias are problems because the researcher interacts with the participant for prolonged periods of time, which may compromise impartiality (on the part of the researcher) and influence how natural the participant's behaviour is.
- Generalization of findings from a single case to other settings or a wider population is particularly problematic.
- In case studies it is especially difficult to protect the confidentiality of participants and their data.

Once you have clearly identified the method used in the research study in the stimulus material, think through the main limitations of this method and consider which of these limitations would be most relevant in the context of the described research study. Then select the method that best addresses this limitation.

Respect the original intention of the researcher and the original hypothesis or research question. For example, do not just say that qualitative research lacks sample-to-population generalizability therefore an experiment should have been conducted instead. If researchers chose to conduct a qualitative research study, they must have pursued different aims and sample-to-population generalizability might be unimportant to them.

Some possible examples of one method suggested in addition to (or instead of) another, along with one reason for this suggestion, are shown in the table below.

Original method	Suggested alternative/addition	The reason for this suggestion
Structured interview	Semi-structured interview	There are reasons to believe that the fixed questions in the fixed order forced some participants to respond unnaturally. As a result, some aspects of their experiences were missed.
Correlational study	Experiment	Correlational studies do not show causation, but causation in the context of the study is important. If one of the variables can be manipulated, then the study can be conducted as an experiment.
Overt non-participant observation	Covert participant observation	There are reasons to believe that the fact that participants knew they were being observed altered their behaviour, leading to participant bias.
Experiment, repeated measures design	Experiment, independent measures design	In a repeated measures design, participants take part in more than one condition that increases the chance that they will figure out the true aim of the study. This may lead to demand characteristics.

Table 8.22

8.7 Identifying the research method

For this question you need to clearly identify the method used in the study described in the stimulus material. The characteristics of the method that you choose to outline will depend on the specifics of the study. However, here are some tips on how you can approach this question.

- In your identification of the method, be specific. For example, instead of saying "experiment", identify the design. For observation, identify whether it is participant or non-participant, overt or covert. For interviews, identify whether it is structured, semi-structured or unstructured.
- For experiments, one of the characteristics may be what defines the study as an experiment. For example, the independent variable is manipulated, the dependent variable is measured and the confounding variables are controlled. Another characteristic of the method could be what defines the experimental design. For example, the independent variable is manipulated by allocating participants randomly into groups (for independent measures designs).
- For correlational studies, one characteristic is that variables are measured but not manipulated by the researcher, and hence cause–effect inferences cannot be made. Another characteristic may be the fact that variables in a correlational study can be measured using different methods, observations, questionnaires, brain scanning technology and so on. The fact that a study is correlational is defined by the way data is processed, but not by the method of gathering data.
- For qualitative studies the characteristics of the method that you identified could be the ones that help you to distinguish this method from other similar methods. For example, if the method is semi-structured interview, then what makes it different from other types of interview and other qualitative methods? Semi-structured interviews are different from other types of interview in that there is an interview guide that contains the list of topics that need to be covered, but the sequence of questions is not specified and there is some flexibility in how questions can be formulated. Semi-structured interviews (as well as all interviews) are different from other qualitative research methods in that there is a natural conversation between the researcher and the participant, rapport is created and questions are focused on the participant's subjective experiences and interpretations. A similar approach may be used for other qualitative methods too.

Ethics in psychological research

CODES OF ETHICS AND ETHICS COMMITTEES

The activities of psychologists are regulated by codes of ethics. Such codes have been developed by all major psychological professional associations, both internationally and within each country. Examples of well-known codes of ethics are those of the American Psychological Association (APA) and British Psychological Society (BPS).

Ethical decisions made before conducting a study often involve difficult trade-offs and require a careful cost-benefit analysis. For example, in many cases the credibility of results may be compromised if you do not use deception.

For this reason, professional associations of psychologists in all countries have ethics committees. These committees resolve ambiguous issues and approve research proposals. They can decide to approve a research study if the following two conditions are met.
- There is no way the study of a phenomenon can be conducted without relaxing an ethical standard.
- Potentially the study can reveal scientific information that will benefit a lot of people.

Ethical consideration	Explanation
Informed consent	Participation in the study must be voluntary and fully informed. This means that participants must be fully informed about the nature of the experimental task, the aims of the study, what they will be required to do and how their data will be used. Information provided to participants must be presented in an accessible way. If a participant is unable to provide informed consent (for example, a minor), consent should be obtained from parents or legal guardians. Participants must be given sufficient time to familiarize themselves with the consent form; they must feel free to ask questions and withdraw from participation. The form should include information about all aspects of the research process. It should also include contact details of the researchers.
Protection from harm	Throughout the study participants must be protected from all forms of physical and mental harm. This includes such aspects as protecting their self-esteem. It must also be ensured that participants do not suffer any negative consequences after participating in the study. In some cases special follow-up meetings must be arranged for this purpose. If vulnerable groups are used (children, elderly people and so on), researchers must ensure that special care is given to them and the procedure is not too challenging. Sometimes participant distress may be unexpected, in which case therapeutic help must be provided by the researchers after the study.
Anonymity and confidentiality	Data collected in the process of research, as well as the fact of participation in the study, must remain unknown to any third parties. Nobody should be able to establish the identity of participants from the published results or other disclosed information. This ethical norm has implications for how data is recorded and stored (for example, names in databases should be coded) and how results are reported. Participation in a research study is **confidential** if the researcher can connect the identity of a participant to the data obtained in the study, but the terms of the agreement prevent the researcher from sharing this information with anyone. Participation is **anonymous** if even the researcher cannot connect obtained information to a participant's identity, for example, an online survey where you do not provide your name.
Withdrawal from participation	Participants must feel free to withdraw from the study at any time they want without explaining their reasons. This must be made clear to them before the start of the study and reinforced again after the end of the experimental procedure. Participants can both withdraw from participation and withdraw their data—they can request for their data to be deleted from all records.
Deception	In many cases the true aim of the study cannot be revealed to participants as it may change their behaviour. This is why some degree of deception often has to be used. However, deception must be as minimal as possible and fully justified by the purposes of the study. The nature of deception must be revealed to participants after the study. Deception may take various forms, for example, the use of confederates, a false aim of the study and so on. Deception by omission involves withholding certain information or creating ambiguity about the study aims. It must be ensured that deception does not cause distress. If it is likely that participants will be distressed when deception is revealed, the study should be cancelled or special follow-up procedures should be in place.
Debriefing	After the study participants must be fully informed about its nature, its true aims, and how the data will be stored and used. Participants must be allowed a chance to ask any questions they may have, and these questions must be openly answered. If necessary, a follow-up meeting should be arranged to monitor participants' well-being. They must be given an opportunity to withdraw their data. Participants must be told if they were deceived and the reasons for the deception must be explained.

Table 9.1 Ethical considerations in conducting the study

ETHICAL CONSIDERATIONS IN REPORTING AND APPLYING THE FINDINGS

Ethical considerations in reporting and applying results of a study include:

- reporting the individual results to participants
- publishing the findings
- applying the findings.

REPORTING THE INDIVIDUAL RESULTS TO PARTICIPANTS

Primary and incidental findings

All findings in a research study may be divided into primary and incidental. **Primary findings** are those discovered as part of the main aim of the research. **Incidental findings** are those discovered unintentionally.

Risks and benefits

The risks and benefits of disclosing findings to participants should be carefully considered. There is an important difference between findings that simply may be of interest to participants and findings that could potentially affect their well-being. For example, suppose the study involved the use of brain scanning and researchers discovered a vague dark area in the scan—an incidental finding. On the one hand, informing the participant about this can help the person make informed medical decisions and possibly prevent the development of a disease. On the other hand, this may cause participants to seek further diagnosis, which could lead to more costs, anxiety and more incidental findings. This could be a false result; after all, researchers were not looking for any abnormalities in the brain.

Including information in informed consent

For primary findings, researchers should include information in the consent process on how results will be communicated to participants.

For incidental findings, researchers should develop a plan for handling these and clearly communicate this plan to participants during the consent process. It is good ethical practice to communicate to participants how incidental findings will be handled, even if the plan is not to disclose this information. Participants should know these plans and be able to withdraw from the study if they do not feel comfortable about them.

Unanticipated incidental findings

If plans regarding the disclosure of incidental information were not communicated to participants and if they did not agree to such plans on the consent form (for example, because the incidental findings were completely unanticipated), decisions regarding disclosing incidental findings to participants must be approved by the ethics committee.

In making decisions in these cases the following guidelines will be considered by the ethics committee:

- make decisions that maximize benefits and minimize harms
- respect a participant's will to know or not to know results of the study
- take into account the extent to which the testing procedure is reliable.

Examples of an unreliable testing procedure are a depression inventory that is still in development and has not been properly standardized, a brain scan that is performed by a non-clinician, an experimental measurement procedure that is used for the first time. If results are communicated to participants in such cases, they must be referred to a follow-up diagnostic procedure using a standard well-accepted method.

PUBLISHING THE FINDINGS

- **Confidentiality**. The identity of participants must be protected and there should be no way to identify them from the published results. This is especially sensitive in case studies of unique individuals (for example, an unusual brain damage).
- **Data fabrication**. Publication of research results must be true to what was actually obtained in the study and presented in an unbiased way. If an error is found in already published results, measures should be taken to correct it.
- **Sharing research data for verification**. It is the responsibility of researchers to securely store primary data obtained in their research. Rules of good science dictate that any research study should be transparent for replication: procedures should be described in detail so that they are easily replicable by an independent researcher. Even without actual replication it should be possible to cross-check a researcher's analysis and conclusions based on the same data set. Any request from an independent researcher to share raw data should be satisfied, provided both parties use the data ethically, responsibly and within the limits of agreed-upon purposes.
- **Social implications of reporting scientific results**. Researchers must keep in mind how their conclusions are formulated in publications and be mindful about potential effects these conclusions may have on the scientific community and society in general. This is especially pertinent when results are published in popular journals that target a wider audience including non-scientists. Blunt conclusions like "intelligence is inherited" do not reflect the full complexity of the situation but can be taken at face value by non-scientists. If they become popular, such beliefs are resistant to change. They may affect public policies, for example, in the field of education.

APPLYING THE FINDINGS

When findings of psychological research are published, they can become the basis for treatment, prevention, intervention and other programmes that can potentially affect lives. For example, imagine it has been conclusively established that human intelligence is fully inherited and cannot be influenced by environmental factors. Such knowledge would dramatically change our approach to education. So before making such claims, we must be sure that they are well substantiated.

For this reason, the following must be considered in applying results of a research study (that is, designing a practical programme based on it).

- The extent of **generalizability** of the study to other contexts and other populations. If there is doubt that results of a study are applicable to other groups or contexts, the study cannot be used as a basis for an intervention programme without further preliminary research. For this reason, authors of research papers must be explicit in their description of the sample and the target population, the sampling strategy, the research procedure and other details that enable informed judgments about generalizability.

- Limitations of the study in terms of **credibility**. Since such limitations directly affect the conclusions and the extent to which findings can be applied in real-life scenarios, these limitations must be explicitly recognized. It is not ethical for researchers to hide weaknesses inherent in the research from the readers. Neither is it ethical to publish results selectively. This creates publication bias, and intervention programmes will be based on distorted information.

- Findings should be **replicated** by independent researchers to ensure credibility. It is impossible to avoid all potential biases in one standalone research study, so replication is the only way to make sure that research conclusions are valid. With this in mind, researchers must provide all possible opportunities for such replication. Procedures must be described in sufficient detail in published papers to ensure that the study is clear and replicable. Primary data should be stored and provided on request to independent researchers on mutual agreement.